T0390140

School Spaces for Student Wellbeing and Learning

Hilary Hughes · Jill Franz ·
Jill Willis
Editors

School Spaces for Student Wellbeing and Learning

Insights from Research and Practice

 Springer

Editors
Hilary Hughes
Queensland University of Technology
Kelvin Grove, Brisbane, QLD, Australia

Jill Franz
Queensland University of Technology
Kelvin Grove, Brisbane, QLD, Australia

Jill Willis
Queensland University of Technology
Kelvin Grove, Brisbane, QLD, Australia

ISBN 978-981-13-6091-6   ISBN 978-981-13-6092-3   (eBook)
https://doi.org/10.1007/978-981-13-6092-3

Library of Congress Control Number: 2018967741

This Springer imprint is published by the registered company Springer Nature Singapore Pte Ltd.
The registered company address is: 152 Beach Road, #21-01/04 Gateway East, Singapore 189721, Singapore

Foreword

If we may, we will begin with a reflection on processes of school design in our own setting. The purpose is to illustrate the importance of the underlying assumptions of this book.

The relationship between design and practice has a contested history, with suggestions that design alone can change behaviour locked in conflict with those that it has little or no impact. Neither argument has developed a sophisticated model of the relationship between them. There has been recognition of the complex nature of the influences that are brought to bear on design and on the nature of the knowledge that is needed for design to 'work':

> The struggles to agree upon what counts as design knowledge and its cultural identity can therefore be perceived as affecting and being affected by a complex system involving economy, production, social significance, consumption, use of objects, and so on (Carvalho, Dong, & Maton 2009, p. 484).

What counts as acceptable design knowledge changes over time, sometimes very rapidly. In England between 2003 and 2010, there was considerable government interest and investment in designs that aimed to provide inspiring learning environments and exceptional community assets over an extended period. The intention was to ensure that 'all young people are being taught in buildings that can enhance their learning and provide the facilities that they and their teachers need to reach their full potential'. The design process was to involve 'proper consultation with the staff and pupils of the school and the wider community' (DfES, 2002, p. 63) in order that 'authorities and schools will be able to make visionary changes and enable teaching and learning to be transformed' (DfES, 2003, p. 7).

The initiative involved the decentralisation of funds to local education partnerships that were required to build and improve secondary school buildings as well co-ordinate and oversee the educational transformation and community regeneration that was envisaged:

> The aim is not just to replace crumbling schools with new ones, but to transform the way we learn. This represents a break with the old way of doing things and should change the whole idea of 'school', from a physical place where children are simply taught to one where a community of individuals can share learning experiences and activities (CABE, 2006, p. 1).

Aspirations for the outcomes of the programme known as Building Schools for the Future (BSF) were couched in terms of collaboration between schools, the development of new forms of infrastructure, new models of school organisation, an enhanced teaching force, new patterns of distributed leadership, personalised approaches to teaching and learning involving significant and novel use of ICT and new forms of central governance. These new schools were spoken of as 'new cathedrals of learning' that were to be designed through high levels of consultation with key interest groups including parents and children. The design process was to involve 'proper consultation with the staff and pupils of the school and the wider community' (DfES, 2002, p. 63) in order that 'authorities and schools will be able to make visionary changes and enable teaching and learning to be transformed' (DfES, 2003, p. 7).

The term 'personalisation' was a common feature of many policy documents and although it was linked to a myriad of meanings, it generally became associated with shifts in modes of control over learning with students taking more responsibility for the selection, sequencing and pacing of their work in school. The personalised approach was to be made feasible through access to new technologies and the availability of a mixed economy of open and flexible spaces. The argument promoted in favour of this significant investment was couched in terms of transformation of learning and teaching along with enhanced participation and community involvement and engagement. Sustainability was a major consideration especially with respect to energy usage.

Considerable emphasis was also placed on the need for new approaches to school leadership:

> Our determination is to ensure that every Head is able to do more than run a stable school. Transformation requires leadership which: can frame a clear vision that engages the school community; can motivate and inspire; pursues change in a consistent and disciplined way; and understands and leads the professional business of teaching. To achieve their full potential, teachers need to work in a school that is creative, enabling and flexible. And the biggest influence is the Head. ... Heads must be free to remodel school staffing, the organisation of the school day, school week and school year and be imaginative in the use of school space – opening up opportunities for learning in the community, engaging with business and developing vocational studies (DfES, 2002, p. 26).

However, as Kraftl (2012) points out, there is some doubt as to whether this radical vision of restructuring was realised in the realities of practice in schools and communities:

> BSF connected with the promise of three further discourses: school (children), community and architectural practice. It anticipated that new school buildings would instil transformative change – modernising English schooling, combating social exclusion and leaving an

architectural 'legacy'. However, it is argued that BSF constituted an allegorical utopia: whilst suggesting a 'radical' vision for schooling and society, its ultimate effect was to preserve a conventional (neo-liberal) model of schooling (Kraftl, 2012, p. 847).

More recently, the subject of design quality in schools has come to the fore with government pronouncements on the wastage of money on architectural fees and what has been referred to as over-indulgent design within the BSF programme. The architectural profession has responded that they had been asked to produce higher quality environments particularly in terms of the acoustic environment, the quality of daylighting and higher quality ventilation, the provision of ICT and the reduction in energy costs. Some buildings may prove extremely good value for money in terms of their impact on the educational achievements of their pupils; others may not.

The policy environment in which the schools we studied were located was one in which capital investment was made in order to secure radical change in the practices of schooling. Teaching, learning, management and community participation and engagement were to be transformed as new schools were designed and built to meet the envisaged needs of the twenty-first century. More recently, policy on the role of design in rebuilding the schools estate in England has been through another major change as attempts are made to achieve good value and efficiency in times of austerity. In 2010, the Building Schools for the Future programme was scrapped. The Priority School Building Programme (PSBP) was established in 2011 and intended to reduce school building costs by approximately a third in comparison with those incurred during BSF. Project time has also been reduced from 24–36 months to 12 months in order to drive efficiency. This involves limiting consultation with school communities and multiple stakeholders to an initial 6-week period. So-called Control Options were produced in order to demonstrate how a very limited number of Baseline Designs should be applied in practice:

> Good quality education does not necessarily need sparkling, architect-designed buildings… Throughout its life [BSF] has been characterised by massive overspends, tragic delays, botched construction projects and needless bureaucracy (Gove, as cited in Kraftl, 2012, p. 866).

Some time ago, Earthman (2004) concluded that while inadequate school buildings cause health problems and lower student morale, and contribute to poor student performance, he was not convinced that school buildings need necessarily be any more than adequate, although the notion of adequacy fails to find a satisfactory definition. A recent review conducted by OECD (2013) sought to identify how 'investments in the physical learning environment'—that is 'the physical spaces (including formal and informal spaces) in which learners, teachers, content, equipment and technologies interact'—can translate into improved cognitive and non-cognitive outcomes (p. 1). In order to do this, they explored the ways in which spatiality, connectivity and temporality mediate pedagogical and other relationships that can improve student learning. The emphasis here on mediation is important. It suggests a very different mechanism is at play than one of determination. They recognised that empirical evidence was far from extensive and agreed with Woolner, Hall, Higgins, McCaughey, and Wall (2007) that:

> The research indicates that there is an overall lack of empirical evidence about the impact of individual elements of the physical environment which might inform school design at a practice level to support student achievement (Woolner et al., 2007, p. 47).

More recently however, Barrett, Zhang, Davies, and Barrett (2015) have suggested that differences in the physical characteristics of primary school classrooms explain 16% of the variation in learning progress. They claim that this is the first time that clear evidence of the effect on users of the overall design of the physical learning space has been isolated in real life situations. Their findings point to a classroom rather a whole-school design effect:

> Surprisingly, whole-school factors (e.g. size, navigation routes, specialist facilities, play facilities) do not seem to be anywhere near as important as the design of the individual classrooms. This point is reinforced by clear evidence that it is quite typical to have a mix of more and less effective classrooms in the same school. The message is that, first and foremost, each classroom has to be well designed. (Barrett et al., 2015, p. 3).

A more comprehensive view argued by Sailer and Penn (2010, p. 12) is that:

> Humans shape their buildings through design practice (social agency affecting spatial structure); humans shape their organisations through management practice (social agency affecting social structure); then buildings shape organisations (spatial agency affecting social structure); both organisations as well as buildings constrain agents in their behaviours (social structures and spatial structure-agency affecting social agency).

This complex dialectical view of the relationships between buildings, human action including management, social organisations and social structures informs the way schools and their designers, constructors and occupiers should be studied.

This is where this book *Designing learning spaces for student wellbeing* makes an important contribution. It sets out to include the perspective of wellbeing in the theory and practice of learning space design. In so doing, the authors bring new ways of theorising the relationship between design, human action and wellbeing into play. There is considerable emphasis on conceptualising school spaces as places of bodily engagement. The authors draw on aspects of recent developments in social geography, sociocultural theory and sociomaterial theory. Some of the arguments will provoke responses and disagreements. In our minds that is all to the good. This is a field that needed a 'shake' both in terms of its gaze and theorisation. This book provides valuable challenges to multiple policy and practitioner fields.

Oxford, UK   Harry Daniels
                                                                                             Hau Ming Tse
                                                                                     Department of Education
                                                                                       University of Oxford

References

Barrett, P., Zhang, Y., Davies, F., & Barrett, L. (2015). *Clever classrooms: Summary report of the HEAD Project (holistic evidence and design)*. Salford: University of Salford. Retrieved from https://www.cleverclassroomsdesign.co.uk/reports-guidance.

Carvalho, L., Dong, A., & Maton, K. (2009). Legitimating design: A sociology of knowledge account of the field. *Design Studies, 30*(5), 483–502.

Commission for Architecture and the Built Environment (CABE). (2006). *Assessing secondary school design quality. Research Report*. London: CABE. Retrieved from: https://www.thenbs.com/PublicationIndex/documents/details?Pub=CABE&DocID=281242.

Department for Education and Skills (DfES). (2002). *Time for standards: Reforming the school workforce*. Ref: DfES/0751/2002. London: DfES.

Department for Education and Skills (DfES). (2003). *Classrooms of the future: Innovative designs for schools*. London: DfES.

Earthman, G. I. (2004). *Prioritization of 31 criteria for school building adequacy*. Baltimore, MD: American Civil Liberties Union Foundation of Maryland. Retrieved from: http://www.aclu-md.org/facilities_report.pdf.

Kraftl, P. (2012). Utopian promise or burdensome responsibility? A critical analysis of the UK Government's Building Schools for the Future Policy. *Antipode, 44*(3), 847–870.

OECD. (2013). *Innovative learning environments*. Paris: OECD. Retrieved from http://www.oecd.org/education/ceri/innovativelearningenvironmentspublication.htm.

Sailer, K., & Penn, A. (2010). Towards an architectural theory of space and organisations: Cognitive, affective and conative relations in workplaces. In *2nd Workshop on Architecture and Social Architecture*, EIASM, Brussels, May 2010. Retrieved from: http://discovery.ucl.ac.uk/1342930.

Woolner, P., Hall, E., Higgins, S., McCaughey, C., & Wall, K. (2007). A sound foundation? What we know about the impact of environments on learning and the implications for building schools for the future. *Oxford Review of Education, 33*, (1), 47–70. https://doi.org/10.1080/03054980601094693.

Preface

> *Steven stood on the deck of the old school building.*
> *The breeze rustled through the nearby trees, and brought*
> *snatches of sounds from the playground. The researcher had*
> *asked Steven to identify a space where he could think and*
> *learn. He took a deep breath, opened his arms and gave an*
> *eloquent sigh. The music room was where he could play his*
> *cello to the trees. No words were needed.*

This book attempts to put words to Steven's experience, and inform a vision that school spaces support wellbeing and learning. Schools are everyday places for many children. Students learn in school spaces like outdoor decks, playgrounds and corridors as well as formal classrooms. Yet not all school spaces are comfortable or conducive for learning. Noise and movement created by many people can fill or even overwhelm the senses. Spaces can create a sense of social inclusion or isolation.

This book is an expansive exploration of wellbeing as an integral dimension of students' experience of learning spaces at school. By grounding the discussion in the varied perspectives of researchers, scholarly educators and students, we aim to advance thinking and practice of learning space design across a wide range of school settings from early years to secondary school.

The authors present a variety of methods, evidence, theoretical models, creative ideas and illustrative case studies—with a view to supporting the creation of inclusive learning environments where students feel safe, supported and inspired to learn (Fraillon, 2004; Masters, 2012). So in this book, readers can view learning spaces, design and wellbeing through various theoretical lenses including spatiality, liminality, sociomateriality, imagination and student voice. Featured methods include large-scale quantitative survey, qualitative case study, participatory action research, ethnography and sociomaterial analysis and visual data analysis. The research findings inform innovative designing through participatory, values-based approaches.

The concern that inspired us to develop this book is that the wellbeing and associated needs of learners are generally overlooked in design research and practice. Therefore, we sought to raise awareness of relationships between learning space and learner wellbeing, shifting the emphasis from technical aspects of learning space design and assessing the potential impacts of the physical school built environment on learning. We also intentionally widened the focus from formal classrooms to encompass informal learning spaces such as playgrounds whose importance to students often goes unrecognised (Luz, 2008). In addition, the book addresses the lack of studies that consider the potential and use of physical school spaces to support innovative pedagogy (Cleveland & Fisher, 2014).

While the editors and several authors represent the growing body of learning space research at Queensland University of Technology, this book has provided a rewarding opportunity for interdisciplinary collaboration with colleagues in Australia and Great Britain. The contributors range from internationally recognised researchers to recent doctoral graduates and scholarly practitioners (as indicated by the authors' biographies). The authors also share the first-hand perspectives of students and teachers whose voices are often silent in learning space design policy and practice (Newton, 2009; Newton & Fisher, 2009).

The following overview of chapters highlights complexity of designing school spaces that intentionally foster student wellbeing and learning.

Overview of Chapters

The book's chapters are arranged thematically in four parts which relate to: conceptual understandings of learning spaces and wellbeing; students' lived experience and needs of learning spaces; realisation of learning space design theory in practice; and a new conceptually based model for learning space design that fosters *wellbeing as flourishing*. As a connecting thread, the chapters include a declaration of the authors' understanding of wellbeing related to learning space design; and conclude with a short indication of implications for practice arising from their research or commentary.

Part I: Conceptual Understandings of School Spaces, Learning and Wellbeing

Part I sets the book's conceptual context. *Jill Franz* (Chapter 'Towards a Spatiality of Wellbeing') reviews current research on the relationship between school spaces and student wellbeing and proposes *spatiality of wellbeing* as a basis to addressing the fragmented and underexplored focus on the physical school environment (natural and built). *Lisa Kervin, Barbara Comber and Aspa Baroutsis* (Chapter 'Sociomaterial Dimensions of Early Literacy Learning Spaces: Moving Through Classrooms with Teacher and Children') draw on sociocultural theory and ethnographic findings to demonstrate the connectedness of students' learning and wellbeing in classroom environments. Disrupting taken-for-granted definitions, *Lyndal*

O'Gorman (Chapter 'Promoting Children's Wellbeing and Values Learning in Risky Learning Spaces') proposes that risky social and emotional learning spaces offer children opportunities to explore issues such as social justice and sustainability. *Kerry Mallan's* (Chapter 'School Design and Wellbeing: Spatial and Literary Meeting Points') spatiality-informed analysis of several texts reveals how young people's literature gives imaginative form to the spatial practices of school, and how design and affect impact children's wellbeing and experience of school life.

Part II: Student Experience of School Spaces for Wellbeing and Learning

Part II presents research findings that reveal the diversity of school students' experience and needs of learning spaces. *Kylie Andrews and Jill Willis* (Chapter 'Imaginings and Representations of High School Learning Spaces: Year 6 Student Experiences') highlight how physical, emotional and social wellbeing factors colour Year 6 students' expectations of their future high school spaces, and indicate students' need for control, consultation, critique and compromise in the design and use of learning spaces. A qualitative case study by *Hilary Hughes, Jill Franz, Jill Willis, Derek Bland and Annie Rolfe* (Chapter 'High School Spaces and Student Transitioning: Designing for Student Wellbeing') explores Year 7 students' experience of transitioning to high school and presents a set of suggestions to inform the design of high school facilities that support student wellbeing. Seeking to inform the design of school libraries as learning spaces, *Derek Bland, Hilary Hughes and Jill Willis* (Chapter 'Students Reimagining School Libraries as Spaces of Learning and Wellbeing') invited school students to talk about and draw their imagined ideal library spaces, and then identified spatial characteristics that enhance students' learning opportunities sense of wellbeing. *Beth Saggers and Jill Ashburner's* (Chapter 'Creating Learning Spaces that Promote Wellbeing, Participation and Engagement: Implications for Students on the Autism Spectrum') extensive literature review demonstrates the importance of creating learning spaces that promote participation, engagement and wellbeing for all students, especially those on the autism spectrum with sensitivities to environmental stimuli. Based on their evaluation of the UK Open Futures programme, *Pamela Woolner and Lucy Tiplady* (Chapter 'Enhancing Wellbeing Through Broadening the Primary Curriculum in the UK with Open Futures') argue for altering school space to enable curriculum broadening and enhance student wellbeing.

Part III: Participatory Designing of School Spaces for Wellbeing and Learning

Part III offers four case studies that illustrate the application of theory to practice when designing learning spaces that foster student wellbeing. *Hilary Hughes and Raylee Elliott Burns* (Chapter 'Fostering Educator Participation in Learning Space Designing: Insights from a Master of Education Unit of Study') outline a postgraduate unit of study that models participatory values-based designing with a view to developing teachers' capacity as learning space designers. *Hilary Hughes and Christopher Nastrom-Smith* (Chapter 'Participatory Principles in Practice: Designing Learning Spaces that Promote Wellbeing for Young Adolescents

During the Transition to Secondary School') report on the designing of a junior secondary school precinct that fostered the wellbeing of Middle Years students, through a participatory process that welcomed *student voice* and benefited from collaboration between school community members and architects. *Adeline Kucks and Hilary Hughes* (Chapter 'Creating a Sensory Garden for Early Years Learners: Participatory Designing for Student Wellbeing') describe a project with early years students to create a sensory garden that supports play-based pedagogy and creates opportunities for learners to engage with the natural environment. Highlighting the potential of the learning environment as 'third teacher', *Vanessa Miller* (Chapter 'Creating the Third Teacher Through Participatory Learning Environment Design: Reggio Emilia Principles Support Student Wellbeing') draws upon Reggio Emilia principles and findings of her participatory action research to present an evidence based model for teachers and students to co-create spaces conducive to contemporary learning.

Part IV: Reconceptualisation of School Spaces for Wellbeing and Learning

Part IV introduces a new way of thinking about and undertaking learning space design. *Jill Franz* (Chapter 'Designing 'Space' for Student Wellbeing as Flourishing') proposes a *Salutogenic design framework for wellbeing as flourishing*. Drawing together the various wellbeing elements explored throughout the book, the framework offers a theoretically based holistic design approach that responds to the values, interests and aspirations of students, and supports the opportunity that education affords in enhancing their capability to live fulfilling lives. Jill argues that a capabilities approach to *wellbeing as flourishing* most vividly reveals the potential of design to open up possibility and facilitate transformative change in students. At its heart, the salutogenic framework recognises students' embedded and embodied relationship with the physical environment and the need for it to be personally comprehensible, manageable and meaningful.

Looking Forwards

For schools seeking to create spaces that are conducive to contemporary learning and wellbeing, the book offers a selection of transferable student-centred design approaches that are participatory and values based. It also opens the way for further research in this field that explores a wider range of school contexts and expands awareness of the wellbeing dimension of learning space design. We are delighted that the many voices in this collection will inform a range of professionals who are interested in school design. Together the contributions in this book illustrate that designing is an ongoing process of compelling concern for students, teachers, writers, parents, librarians, therapists, leaders, gardeners and artists as well as builders, planners and architects. Every school has designers who can take action to enhance school spaces to be places of wellbeing and learning.

Kelvin Grove, Brisbane, Australia

Hilary Hughes
Jill Franz
Jill Willis

References

Cleveland, B., & Fisher, K. (2014). The evaluation of physical learning environments: A critical review of literature. *Learning Environment Research, 17*(1), 1–28.

Fraillon, J. (2004). *Measuring student well-being in the context of Australian schooling: Discussion paper.* Victoria: ACER/MCEETYA.

Luz, A. (2008). The [design of] educational space: A process-centred built pedagogy. In A. Clarke, M. Evatt, P. Hogarth, J. Lloveras, & L. Pons, (Eds.), *Proceedings of E&PDE 2008: International Conference on Engineering and Product Design Education* (pp. 339–344). Universitat Politecnica de Catalunya, Barcelona, Spain, 4–5 September, 2008.

Masters, G. (2012). *National school improvement tool.* Australian Council for Educational Research (ACER). http://research.acer.edu.au/cgi/viewcontent.cgi?article=1019&context=tll_misc.

Newton, C. (2009). Disciplinary dilemmas: Learning spaces as discussion between designers and educators. *Critical and Creative Thinking: The Australian Journal of Philosophy in Education, 17*(2), 7–27.

Newton, C., & Fisher, K. (2009). *Take 8, learning spaces: The transformation of educational spaces for the 21st century.* Canberra: Australian Institute of Architects.

Acknowledgements

Sincere thanks to the many colleagues, friends and family members who have encouraged and supported the development of this work, in particular:

Office of Education Research, QUT; Nick Meclchior and Sanjievkumar Mathiyazhagan, Springer; David Hughes.

Special thanks to all the authors for your thoughtful and timely contributions to the book, it has been a great pleasure to work collegially with all of you.

We warmly acknowledge the high quality constructive feedback offered to authors by the following peer reviewers:

Dr. Cherie Allan, Kylie Andrews, Dr. Aspa Baroutsis, Dr. Janet Buchan, Prof. Suzanne Carrington, Dr. Alison Clark, Prof. Julie Davis, Dr. Raylee Elliott Burns, Prof. Kenn Fisher, Prof. Val Klenowski, Dr. Carly Lassig, Emeritus Professor Kerry Mallan, Dr. Melinda Miller, Dr. Vanessa Miller, Dr. Craig Murison, Dr. Ceridwen Owen, Assoc. Prof. Beth Saggers, Dr. Mary M. Sommerville, Dr. Maryanne Theobald, Dr. Pamela Woolner.

Also thanks to Denise Frost (QUT Library) for copyediting and referencing support.

We especially appreciate the insights that many people (adults and young people) have shared as participants in the research projects featured in this book.

Hilary Hughes
Jill Franz
Jill Willis

Contents

Editors, Illustrator and Contributors

About the Editors

Hilary Hughes is Adjunct Associate Professor in the Faculty of Education, Queensland University of Technology, Australia where from 2005 to 2018, she taught several units in the Master of Education including Designing Spaces for Learning. Her research interests include learning space design, information literacy and informed learning and international student experience. She has been Chief Investigator for two Australian Research Council (ARC) Linkage projects and has completed several other funded projects. In her research, she draws on extensive previous experience as reference librarian and information literacy educator. Her qualifications include Ph.D. (QUT, Australia), M.A. in Librarianship (Sheffield University, UK) and B.A. Combined Honours in Spanish and Romance Linguistics (Birmingham University, UK). In 2010, she was Fulbright Scholar-in-Residence at University of Colorado Denver, USA. e-mail: h.hughes@qut.edu.au

Jill Franz is a Professor in the School of Design, Creative Industries Faculty, Queensland University of Technology (QUT). Her qualifications in architecture, interior design, education and teaching have contributed to extensive experience as a design practitioner as well as design educator and researcher. In addition to teaching and supervising doctoral and other research students, she is involved in a range of research projects to do with the environment and its potential to enhance health, wellbeing and social justice. She is currently a chief investigator with Hilary Hughes on a federally funded ARC Linkage project: *Innovative procurement theories to optimise education per cost of school*. e-mail: j.franz@qut.edu.au

Jill Willis is an assessment researcher and senior lecturer in the Faculty of Education at Queensland University of Technology. She is committed to supporting teachers and school systems to rethink how they promote student agency and equity through their everyday assessment and pedagogy practices. Learning space designs and collaborative leadership are explored as innovative structures that can support collective agency. She also researches how self-assessment feedback loops inform personal and system change. Her qualifications include Ph.D. (QUT, Australia), M. Ed. in Educational Leadership (JCU), Graduate Diploma in Education (BCAE) and B.A. (UQ). e-mail: jill.willis@qut.edu.au

Illustrator

Derek Bland has been involved in education and social justice since 1980. He joined Queensland University of Technology (QUT), Brisbane, Australia, in 1991 to establish a special entry and student support initiative to assist people from socio-economically disadvantaged backgrounds. Completing his Ph.D. in 2006, he taught and researched inclusive education and ways in which imagination can engage marginalised people with formal education. He retired in December 2016 to focus on creative art but is continuing his research and engagement with QUT as a visiting fellow and is the editor of a recently published book, *Imagination for Inclusion: Diverse contexts of Educational Practice* (Routledge). e-mail: derekbland@leakythoughts.com

Contributors

Kylie Andrews teaches in primary, secondary and tertiary contexts and her qualifications include B.A., DipEd, M.Ed. (Research). She has worked as a sessional academic and research assistant at QUT in Brisbane, Australia. Her Masters research explored Year 6 students' imaginings of their future high school learning spaces. This research recognises that learning spaces have the potential to increase engagement and aid wellbeing. She is concerned that middle years students remain engaged in their learning and transition smoothly between primary and secondary school. e-mail: kylie.andrews@qut.edu.au

Jill Ashburner has an extensive career in the disability sector spanning 40 years, including a number of senior occupational therapy positions. Her doctoral study explored sensory processing and classroom behavioural, emotional and educational outcomes of children with ASD. As Manager Research and Development at Autism Queensland since 2007, her research has focused on sensory processing, education of students with ASD, professional development of clinicians working in the ASD field, school bullying, written expression and telehealth. She is currently leading Autism CRC projects on written expression, structured teaching, an evaluation of a post-school transition program and goal-setting for adults and adolescents with ASD. e-mail: jill.ashburner@autismqld.com.au

Aspa Baroutsis is a Postdoctoral Research Fellow at Griffith Institute of Education Research, Griffith University, Australia. She researches in the areas of sociology, educational policy and social justice with a particular interest in spatial justice. Her research interests include mediatisation, media constructions and representations of identity, children and young people's voice and teachers' work. e-mail: a.baroutsis@griffith.edu.au

Barbara Comber is a Research Professor in the School of Education at the University of South Australia and Adjunct Professor in the Faculty of Education at Queensland University of Technology. Her research interests include teachers' work, critical literacy, place-conscious pedagogy and social justice. Her research examines the kinds of teaching that make a difference to young people's literacy learning trajectories and what gets in the way. Her recent books *Literacy, Place and Pedagogies of Possibility* (Comber, 2016) and *Literacy, Leading and Learning: Beyond Pedagogies of Poverty* (Hayes, Hattam Comber, Kerkham, Lupton & Thomson, 2017) explore these issues. e-mail: barbara.comber@unisa.edu.au

Harry Daniels is Professor of Education at the University of Oxford. He has directed research more than 40 projects funded by The Economic and Social Research Council (ESRC), various UK central and local government sources, The Lottery, The Nuffield Foundation and the EU. His current research includes *Design matters? The effects of new schools on students', teachers' and parents' actions and perceptions*. This is funded by the Arts and Humanities Research Council (AHRC) (2012–2016). This project investigates the ways in which a design shapes a practice and a practice shapes a design. As such it is concerned with the formation of context in particular settings and the relevance of particular forms of evidence to particular settings. He has an extensive publications record that includes a series of internationally acclaimed books on sociocultural psychology. His qualifications include B. Sc. (Liverpool), M.A. (Oxford), Ph.D. (London), Diploma in Psychology and Special Needs (London) and PGCE (Leicester). e-mail: harry.daniels@education.ox.ac.uk

Raylee Elliott Burns is a researcher and education consultant with experience in program design and implementation, teaching and mentoring in the Master of Education (Teacher-Librarianship) at Queensland University of Technology. Her doctoral research developed as a work-in-progress informing the design and implementation of the QUT MEd unit of study *Designing spaces for learning*. Her thesis and continuing interests are outlined in Chapter 9 of *The Translational Design of Schools* (2016, Fisher, Ed. pp. 195–213). Her work embraces the 'small stories' and the underpinning values of educators and learners whose lives and work occupy the spaces of schools. Their 'voices of experience' offer multidimensional potential for participation in designing and redesigning spaces for learning and teaching in consensus with accredited designers. e-mail: rayleebob@bigpond.com

Lisa Kervin is an Associate Professor in Language and Literacy in the Faculty of Social Sciences at the University of Wollongong where she is an active member of the Early Start Research Institute. current research interests are focused on young children and how they engage with literate practices and she is currently involved in research projects funded by the Australian Research Council focused on young children and writing, digital play and transition. She has researched her own teaching and has collaborative research partnerships with teachers and students in tertiary and primary classrooms and prior-to-school settings. e-mail: lkervin@uow.edu.au

Adeline Kucks is a primary school teacher in the Northern Gold Coast region of Queensland, Australia who has been teaching since 2004. Her qualifications include M.Ed. (Early Years), B.Ed. (Primary) and ATCL. She has been working in the 'transition to school' space for the last 6 years and has a passion for seeing young learners start school successfully and receive an outstanding early education. Her work over the last 12 months has seen her develop an inclusive transition program that works with children who have difficulty or disability begin school successfully. The outdoor learning environment has played a significant part in the transition program at her school. e-mail: akuck3@eq.edu.au

Kerry Mallan is Emeritus Professor at Queensland University of Technology, Australia. Her main area of research is in children's texts and cultures. She has published extensively on literature for young people, bringing theoretical readings with respect to gender, sexuality, spatiality and posthumanism. Her most recent sole authored books are *Secrets, Lies and Children's Literature* (2011) and *Gender Dilemmas in Children's Fiction* (2009). She also co-authored *New World Orders in Contemporary Children's Literature: Utopian Transformations* with Clare Bradford, John Stephens and Robyn McCallum (2008). e-mail: k.mallan@qut.edu.au

Vanessa Miller is an experienced primary teacher, counsellor and behaviour specialist who is currently working as the Head of Primary in a Christian school in New South Wales, Australia. She has a particular interest in learning environment design and learner-responsive pedagogy, inspired by two study visits to the municipal schools of Reggio Emilia (Italy). She completed an Education Doctorate at QUT in 2017 about the nature and potential of a participatory designing process to create learning environments conducive to contemporary learning approaches. e-mail: vanessamiller8@gmail.com

Christopher Nastrom-Smith is Director of Junior Secondary and a member of the Senior Leadership Team at Cannon Hill Anglican College, in Brisbane, Australia, where his role focuses on the academic and pastoral welfare of Years 7–9 students. His qualifications include M.Ed. (LeadMgt), B.Ed., DipBus, AMICDA and MACEL. His past research has explored how curriculum development, learning spaces and teacher pedagogy can be customised to enhance the transitional experiences of students as they move from primary school into lower secondary school. Chris completed his Masters of Education (Leadership and Management) at QUT in 2015 and part of his coursework complemented the design of Cannon Hill Anglican College's Junior Secondary Precinct. e-mail: cnastrom-smith@chac.qld.edu.au

Lyndal O'Gorman is a Senior Lecturer in the School of Early Childhood and Inclusive Education at Queensland University of Technology. Prior to this, she taught in Education Queensland primary schools in Brisbane and Far North Queensland.

Her qualifications include Diploma of Teaching (Early Childhood), Bachelor of Education and Ph.D. Her current teaching and research endeavours at QUT include the topics of early childhood and primary arts education, education for sustainability, play pedagogies, interdisciplinary learning and teaching and early childhood leadership. Lyndal is building a substantial track record of research investigating the intersection of the arts and education for sustainability. She was co-leader of the 4th Transnational Dialogues in Early Childhood Education for Sustainability, in Victoria, British Columbia, in September 2017. e-mail: lm.ogorman@qut.edu.au

Annie Rolfe is a sessional academic team member in the School of Design, Creative Industries Faculty, Queensland University of Technology (QUT) where she is involved in a range of projects that explore health and wellbeing in designing. Annie draws on her experience in interior design practice and her previous career in nursing to designing a range of interiors including health facilities. Annie's teaching focuses on theories of wellbeing and spatial justice in Design Psychology and Design in Society. Her current (2018) M.Phil. research evaluates alternative approaches to school design and procurement and their impacts on educational outcomes. This study is associated with the Australian Research Council Linkage project: *Innovative procurement theories to optimise education per cost of school.* e-mail: a2.rolfe@qut.edu.au

Beth Saggers is an Associate Professor in the School of Early Childhood and Inclusive Education at Queensland University of Technology (QUT). She currently lectures in Autism Spectrum Disorders (ASD), catering for diversity, inclusive practices, and behaviour support. She has over 30 years of experience working with students on the autism spectrum across a range of age groups and educational settings. She is an active research participant in the national Autism Cooperative Research Centre (Autism CRC). Her research interests include developing supportive learning environments for students with autism, the perspectives of key stakeholders, and supporting challenging and complex student needs. e-mail: b.saggers@qut.edu.au

Lucy Tiplady has worked as an academic researcher since 2005 and is a Research Associate within the Research Centre for Learning and Teaching (CfLaT), Newcastle University, UK. She has gained B.A. (Hons) English Studies (University of Nottingham, UK) and Graduate Diploma in Psychology—Distinction (Newcastle University, UK). She has worked on a diverse range of projects and evaluations within Education and has developed subject specialisms in the areas of practitioner enquiry and visual and participatory research methods. Working collaboratively with schools and the wider education community has led to her interest in how research methods can be used as tools for enquiry to aid practitioner and student learning. She has worked with colleagues within CfLaT in exploring the use of visual tools to mediate and enhance interviews and in collaborative and co-produced research with a range of stakeholders. e-mail: lucy.tiplady@newcastle.ac.uk

Hau Ming Tse is a Research Fellow in the Department of Education, University of Oxford. She is also Associate Lecturer in the School of Architecture at Oxford Brookes University. A qualified architect, she was educated at the University of Bath, the University of Cambridge and the Architectural Association, London. After graduating, she worked for 9 years at David Chipperfield Architects, where she was an Associate Director. Her research explores the relationship between space, perception and the environment, and her work focuses on productive points of interaction and innovation between theory and practice in learning environments. Current field research examines the complex relationship between design and practice in some of the most challenging primary and secondary schools in the UK. e-mail: hauming.tse@education.ox.ac.uk

Pamela Woolner is CfLaT Co-Director and Senior Lecturer in Education, Newcastle University. Her has a growing international reputation in understanding learning environments, with research that includes investigations of underlying issues for learning space design and research into the use and development of space in British schools. Her work includes a seminal review, *The impact of school environments*, a book about school space aimed at users (the *Design of learning spaces*) and an interdisciplinary edited collection, *School design together*, exploring participatory design. e-mail: pamela.woolner@newcastle.ac.uk

What If …

Derek Bland, 2017

Part I
Conceptual Understandings of School Spaces, Learning and Wellbeing

Towards a Spatiality of Wellbeing

Jill Franz

Abstract Despite increasing attention to designing learning environments that are conducive to contemporary pedagogy, there is limited understanding about how physical spaces influence student learning in holistic and existential ways. In addition, while research shows an association between student wellbeing and learning, the interrelationship between these concepts and the spatial and material implications are underexplored. Consequently, this chapter seeks to expand current thinking about learning spaces to support conceptually informed school design. As a way forward, it brings together a capability approach to education with an existential understanding of wellbeing to propose *spatiality of wellbeing* as an overarching construct that points to the potential of the physical school environment to have an enduring and profound influence on student wellbeing and learning.

Introduction

In educational research, there is growing resistance to a prevailing compartmentalised approach to operationalising wellbeing in schools with several researchers calling for it to be more relational and embedded. While there is emerging support for this latter approach, little has been done to explore its spatial and material implications in the context of school learning environments. This chapter is an initial response to this situation.

The chapter is in three main parts. The first examines the relationship between wellbeing and schooling and how it is conceived discursively as well as described operationally in education literature. It is at the school level where various conceptions of wellbeing intersect and where the relational nature of wellbeing, particularly its nature as embodied and embedded, is most apparent. Unlike the relationship between learning and the physical school environment, which has been explored extensively as summarised in the second part of the chapter, there is no research that

J. Franz (✉)
Queensland University of Technology, Brisbane, Australia
e-mail: j.franz@qut.edu.au

© Springer Nature Singapore Pte Ltd. 2019
H. Hughes et al. (eds.), *School Spaces for Student Wellbeing and Learning*,
https://doi.org/10.1007/978-981-13-6092-3_1

coherently considers how a relational understanding of learning *and* wellbeing connects with the actual material space of the school. This is addressed in the third part of the chapter. Here, a *capability approach* to education is considered along with an *existential understanding of wellbeing* and our embodied relationship with the physical world to inform a *spatiality of wellbeing*. As explained, when the concept of spatiality is framed in this way, the potential of the physical school environment to facilitate and support student capability and wellbeing in a holistic and profound way is revealed.

Wellbeing and Schooling

In this first part of the chapter, I critique current educational discourse and associated conceptions of wellbeing that are representative of the *conceived space* of wellbeing and schooling. As conveyed in Fig. 1, in the school context, this space holds in tension two conceptions of wellbeing: wellbeing as compartmentalised and detached; and wellbeing as embodied and embedded. Examining these conceptions at the micro level of the school reveals the various ways in which wellbeing is operationalised through the process of schooling. This establishes the conceptual foundation for the subsequent parts of the chapter and the development of a *spatiality of wellbeing* construct. Each of the conceptions is discussed below.

Wellbeing as Compartmentalised and Detached

Current educational discourse to do with wellbeing generally reflects a dominant neo-liberal agenda. From a neo-liberal point of view, knowledge, skills and attributes, including wellbeing attributes such as resilience and self-efficacy, are regarded in terms of their ultimate potential to enhance economic competitiveness and subsequently, national economic performance (Spratt, 2017, p. 27). Here, wellbeing is regarded as what Atkinson (2013) would term a *determinant* or a *significant process factor* (p. 139). There are various educational policies and initiatives internationally that reflect this primary ideology. In Australia, a notable example is the *Melbourne Declaration on Educational Goals for Young Australians (MCEETYA)* which explicitly associates wellbeing with 'the nation's ongoing economic prosperity and social cohesion' (p. 4) and identifies the vital role played by schools in 'ensuring' this occurs. In addition, wellbeing can be used to operationalise policy (Ereaut & Whiting, 2008) as revealed in an international study by Blackmore, Bateman, Loughlin, O'Mara, and Aranda (2011) where wellbeing is conceptualised as one of several (learning) attainment indicators.

Emphasising the role of wellbeing in policy and pedagogy, Spratt (2017) brings together the work of Ereaut and Whiting (2008) on children's wellbeing with her own work to identify the compartmentalised and sometimes overlapping discursive areas

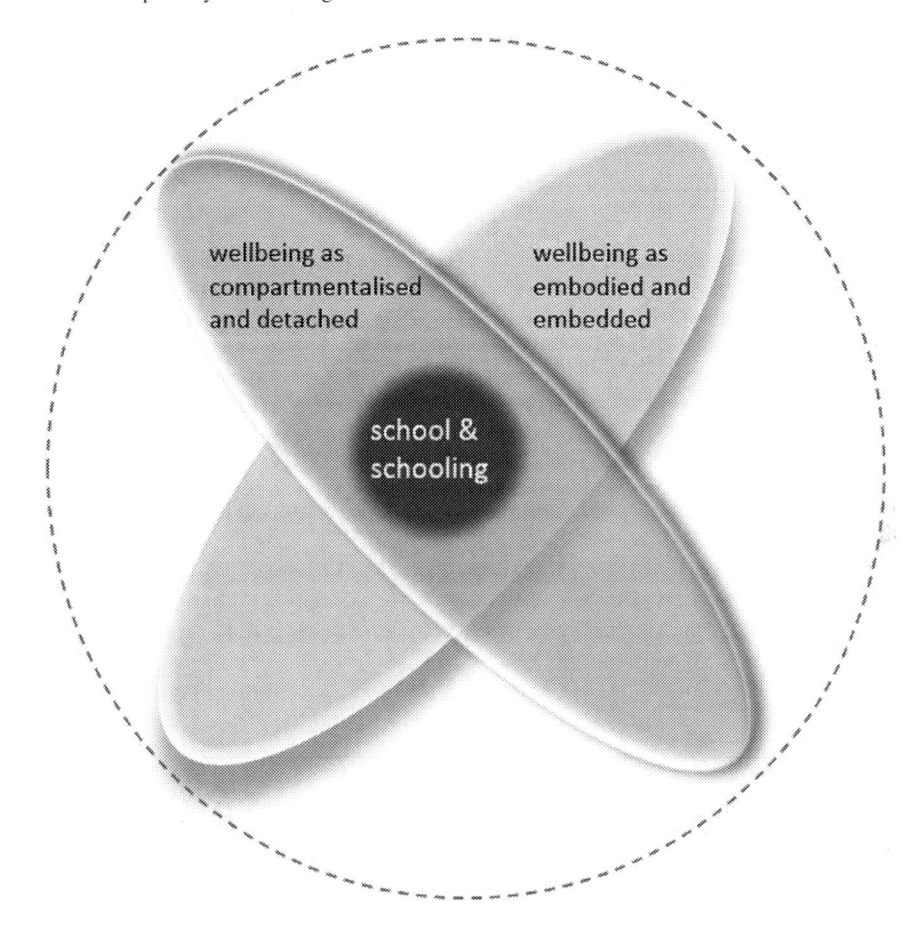

Fig. 1 Space of wellbeing and schooling

of: physical health promotion; social and emotional literacy; sustainability; care; and flourishing. First, with regard to *physical health promotion*, there are signs that policy is helping to shift some of the focus of responsibility from the individual and internal structural aspects to external structural aspects and the provision of school social and physical environments that are safe, comfortable and health promoting (Spratt, 2017; Watson, Emery, Bayliss, Boushel, & McInnes, 2012). This also aligns with a growing focus on supporting mental health. In addition, there is the emerging interest in the role of furniture and the spatial configuration of learning spaces to minimise the health impacts of sitting and to encourage incidental exercise. Moves to open up access to mainstream schooling for children with disabilities and special needs have also demanded greater attention to the physical environment and its sensory, spatial (and empowering) qualities. However, on the whole, where there is attention to the indoor and outdoor physical school environment, it is generally considered with regard to injury prevention and protection from environmental hazards, such as poor ventilation, sun exposure and play equipment. In this regard, attention to the physical environment for physical wellbeing remains compartmentalised, highly selective and minimal.

The compartmentalisation of wellbeing is further evident when it is categorised as emotional wellbeing, psychological wellbeing, social wellbeing and so on Watson et al. (2012, pp. 1, 2). This is especially apparent in education through the emergence of discourse to do with *social and emotional literacy*. In her review of this discourse, Spratt (2017) highlights the role of social and emotional competencies in preparing students to operate effectively in the world, and within the school context; and of the way in which they support other school goals such as improved behaviour. The substantial interest in social and emotional literacy has prompted numerous ways in which it is operationalised. Serious concerns have been expressed by several scholars, including Ecclestone and Hayes (2009), who question its propensity to foster a therapy culture and, for students, an increasing sense of vulnerability (Spratt, 2017, p. 45). In addition, Watson et al. (2012) and Spratt (2017) highlight the tendency for many to regard emotional wellbeing as a universal set of individualised skills.

Discourse on social and emotional literacy also overlaps, in part, with the discourse on *sustainability*, most notably in emerging research validating the positive effects on children attitudinally, socially and emotionally of outdoor learning and hands-on experience with nature. Thus, Spratt proposes that 'human wellbeing is deeply entangled with the way in which we care for the environment' (2017, p. 55), calling attention to school curricula and pedagogical practices that are 'sustainability' focussed. However, the review of literature suggests that the potential for the physical school environment to support these initiatives and wellbeing as a whole, and in a fundamentally transformative way, remains largely unrealised.

Unlike in the previous discursive themes, where wellbeing is treated as incorporating discrete components, the discourse on *care* may appear on the surface to offer the possibility of a more holistic appreciation of wellbeing, therein addressing concerns such as highlighted by Ereaut and Whiting (2008) and Atkinson (2013) that wellbeing cannot be explained by its constituent parts alone. In addition, the discourse on care also invites focus and scrutiny on the relationship between the child and others, including the rights of children to be involved in matters that impact them, as proclaimed by the United Nations Convention on the Rights of the Child (2009). Associated considerations include power and agency, and the nature of care when there are underlying conflicting ideologies. In terms of the latter, the work of Fielding (2012) on school as a *person-centred learning community*, as opposed to the school as an *organisation*, is particularly insightful. For Fielding, the school as an organisation is exemplified at a very impersonal level through a pragmatic concern for meeting specific academic targets and benchmarks, or at a more high performance level where concern for students and their personal development is regarded as a means of enhancing school performance. So while a school may appear to adopt a welfare liberal position by promoting a caring ethos, it can in fact be using this instrumentally to address school organisational goals, the performance against which is externally and/or quantifiably measured. Such situations highlight a concern regarding 'the potentially coercive nature of "care"' (Hendricks as cited in Spratt 2017, p. 63).

Acknowledging a more holistic appreciation of wellbeing within the context of prevailing neo-liberal ideology (Spratt, 2017, p. 64) regards schools as *person-centred learning communities*. Here, while external requirements and benchmarks are taken seriously, the primary aim is to address these by focussing on individual personal development and human *flourishing* within a democratic learning community. In this respect, Spratt's thinking is very much influenced by the contemporary work of Nussbaum (2006, 2011), Drez and Sen (1995), and Sen (2009), and the notion that education plays an intrinsic role in developing the *capability* for students, as students and later as adults, to lead a life of value to themselves and society. Thus, *wellbeing as flourishing* is conceived in this sense as an outcome, with the purpose of schooling being to 'enhance the freedoms that children have to achieve wellbeing, as flourishing, both in the present and in the future' (Spratt, 2017, p. 123). Note that this is not primarily a hedonic concern for happiness but rather what Kristjánsson (2017) would describe as a neo-Aristotelian concern for eudaimonic wellbeing; a concern that draws attention to human capability and optimal functioning. In schooling, Spratt (2017) regards Nussbaum's capability of *senses, imagination and thought* as significant in helping to develop potential. However, she also argues the need for schooling to consider that although children may have capability, they generally rely on adults to create or help create the conditions necessary to foster the capability (p. 53). As revealed further on, this presents opportunities for exploring more fully the relationship of children and the physical/material environment, and the latter's sensorial and aesthetic agency.

In most cases, the approaches to wellbeing just described reflect a particular understanding of wellbeing in relationship to health. The research reviewed suggests wide ranging educational endorsement of the World Health Organization (WHO, 1946) understanding that: 'Health is a state of complete physical, mental and social wellbeing and not merely the absence of disease or infirmity'. While this conflation of health and wellbeing helps to move the understanding of health from a clinical deficit position (Fraillon, 2004), it also perpetuates a components approach to wellbeing (Atkinson, Fuller, & Painter, 2012; Atkinson, 2013) reflecting and reinforcing a neo-liberal reliance on performance indicators and measures. As illustrated, wellbeing can be viewed either as the outcome of policy-making or as part of the process of policy-making; as an outcome of learning or as a determinant of learning. In addition, Atkinson (2013) suggests that the dominant framing of wellbeing informed by neo-liberal ideology casts wellbeing as predominantly individualised, with the components of wellbeing viewed as commodities that can be acquired or achieved (p. 139) and that as internalised, are to be self-managed (p. 140). What remains of fundamental concern for Atkinson (2013), however, is that perpetuating use of wellbeing as a synonym of health restricts an expansive understanding of wellbeing beyond physical and psychological dimensions to one that is relational in a more embodied and embedded sense.

Wellbeing as Embodied and Embedded

In the educational research area, there are signs of growing resistance to fine grain articulation of wellbeing and its associated compartmentalisation. For example, Watson et al. (2012) instead propose a broader conceptualisation of wellbeing as 'subjectively experienced, contextual and embedded, and relational' (p. 224). This understanding emerges from their problematisation of *wellbeing, being well* and children as *beings* and *becomings* (p. 38) and their challenging of the Cartesian mind–body dualism (p. 31). As they explain, the work represents '…a relational and embedded view of wellbeing that acknowledges the phenomenological body in experiencing and reporting wellbeing; but it is also a deeply social view of the human body that acknowledges the importance of others in the project of human flourishing' (p. 223).

While the likes of Watson et al. (2012) and Stevens (2010) argue for an embodied and embedded view of wellbeing, little has been done in education (or elsewhere) to explore the consequences of this spatially, despite the claim that:

> Framing wellbeing as relational and situated makes explicit that wellbeing can have no form, expression or enhancement without attention to the spatial dynamics of such effects (Atkinson, 2013, p. 142).

In this sense, wellbeing is understood by Atkinson 'to be emergent through situated and relational effects that are dependent on the mobilisation of resources within different social and spatial contexts…' (p. 142). While this reflects an embodied role of emotions, it is in a dynamic not static sense. Further in terms of its situated and relational nature, wellbeing is regarded as:

> Complex assemblages of relations not only between people, but also between people and places, material objects and less material constituents of places including atmosphere, histories and values (Panelli and Tipa, 2009). Wellbeing is thus conceptualised as in constant production and reproduction (Atkinson, 2013, p. 142).

Despite Atkinson recognising the spatiality of wellbeing as described, it remains at a highly conceptual level, and as such is operationally problematic. The final part of this chapter suggests a way in which this may be addressed. Before doing so, however, the interconnection of wellbeing and learning warrants investigation of the current situation in education and the prevailing forces informing the spatiality of learning and the design of learning spaces.

Space, Spatiality and Learning

In the educational literature reviewed, space and spatiality are often used interchangeably or in a conflated sense. This is the case even when authors are careful to make distinctions between the two concepts and is compounded when space and learning are brought together as *learning space, a learning space* or, in the collective sense of *learning spaces.* With respect to *learning spaces,* the term is relatively new emerging in line with the notion of a contemporary society and neo-liberal government agenda heavily invested politically and economically in preparing a workforce for the twenty-first century (Ministerial Council on Education Employment Training and Youth Affairs, 2008; Productivity Commission, 2016). In Australia and many other countries, this has had widespread impact at a macro policy level as well as at the more local level of school curricula, pedagogy and resourcing (including built infrastructure), from early childhood education through to secondary school and beyond to post compulsory vocational and tertiary education.

Despite general acceptance of this conceptual shift and its implications for the conceptualisation of learning spaces, research continues to reflect varying paradigmatic emphases not only in terms of the conceptualisation of learning spaces but also of their relationship with learning outcomes. An overview of the literature tends to suggest a dichotomous relationship between research to do with physical learning spaces and that adopting a socially framed perspective. What I propose, however, is that research in general tends to sit on a spatiality (relational) spectrum, reflecting in various ways a dialectic rather than dualistic understanding of the relationship between people and their environment, albeit one where either social or physical/material aspects are emphasised. For instance, there appears to be a tendency for policy-directed research to be situated more towards the social end of the spectrum, and research with a particular interest in the physical nature of learning environments at the material end. Meanwhile, research involving the everyday experience of teaching and learning in the school context is positioned in a very fluid way around the middle of the spectrum. In this latter respect, there is an implicit belief that 'space is neither absolute, relative [n]or relational in itself, but it can become one or all simultaneously depending on circumstances. [And for teachers] The problem of the proper conceptualisation of space is resolved through human practice with respect to it' (Harvey as cited in Harvey, 2004, p. 5).

For Mulcahy, Cleveland and Aberton (2015) and Mulcahy (2016), adopting a relational (sociomaterial) approach to conceptualising *learning space* aligns with the understanding of it as 'a product of interrelations and materially embedded practices, connected in space and time to wider flows of ideas, technologies and discourses in society' (McGregor as cited in Mulcahy et al., 2015, p. 591). Unfortunately, in drawing attention to the sociocultural context of schooling, their work overtly dismisses the notion of absolute (real) space, and in this respect inadvertently downplays the significance of the physical environment (built and natural). While there appears to be an attempt to conceive of *sociomaterial* (written as one word) in a mutually inclusive sense, the discourse still privileges the social over the (physical) material.

An early study that focusses on the school as architectural space, but in an integrative way by drawing on spatial, educational and ecological design theory, is that by Gislason (2007). For Gislason, a building, such as a school building, is 'more than a merely physical structure, as it is also packed with visual and spatial messages about how to feel and act in a certain location' (p. 6). As he elaborates, 'there is not a strict correspondence, though, between environment and behaviour' (p. 6). Thus, the relationship we have with and in buildings is phenomenologically as well as socially implicated. Therefore, 'We must be both situated and orientated, if we are to dwell meaningfully...' (Gislason, 2007, p. 8).

In a similar vein, although with a greater focus on the relationship between spatial patterning and social outcomes, is a body of work described as *space syntax*. The concept was first articulated by Hillier and Hanson (1984) in their book *The Social Logic of Space* where they argue for investigating the *space of space* in order to then understand the space of social phenomena (Hillier, 2008, p. 224). Thus:

> Space not only behaves lawfully when manipulated, but also these laws are the means by which it has agency in human affairs (Hillier, 2007)—not agency in the old sense of spatial determinism, but in the sense that spatial configurations provide the conditions for the emergence of different kinds of complexity in human affairs (Hillier, 2008, p. 228).

As Hillier notes, space syntax has affinity with the work of Gilles Deleuze, a key twentieth-century philosopher, in placing emphasis on the material within space. Such affinity is acknowledged in the work of Dovey and Fisher (2014) to do with school learning spaces, specifically the use of assemblage theory to analyse the relationship between spatial configuration and pedagogy. Of central interest for Dovey and Fisher is the relationship of emerging learning space typologies to issues of power, control and discipline. In undertaking their study involving middle schools, their focus was on the adaptability of various spaces to different practices, and spatial interconnection or *assemblage*. In line with Deleuze and Guattari (1987), an assemblage is conceptualised as 'a whole that is formed from the interconnectivity and flows between constituent parts—a sociological cluster of interconnections between parts wherein the identities and functions of both parts and whole emerge from the flows between them' (Dovey & Fisher, 2014, pp. 49, 50).

Bringing together the concept of place with the Deleuzian philosophical notion of assemblage, Duhn (2012) describes how '"place" holds the potential to expand and challenge understandings of how the self relates to the world, both human and more-than-human' (p. 99). Particularly useful here is the notion of *place-as-assemblage* (Deleuze & Guattari, 1988) owing its agentic capacity to the vitality of its materiality [Bennett as cited in Duhn (2012, p. 99)]. Place-as-assemblage with its consideration of the agency of matter provides conceptual territory for Duhn's preliminary exploration of pedagogy in the early years' education in relation to an *ethics of flourishing* (p. 102). She argues that thinking of place as an assemblage makes place visible as a social, material and discursive field whereby:

> A pedagogy of places assembles and folds into places of pedagogy.... Pedagogies of places negotiate flows and create spaces where matter, desire, human and more-than-human come together to modulate the self in relation to the world (p. 104).

For Ellis and Goodyear (2016) '…connections between place and learning can be subtle and powerful. To understand them, one needs to understand complex, shifting assemblages involving human beings and things: material, digital and hybrid' (p. 150).

In this second part of the chapter, I have highlighted how, in contrast to wellbeing, the spatial implications of learning have received significant attention in policy and academic discourse. Of particular interest is the way in which emerging initiatives to do with space, spatiality and learning as just discussed resonate, albeit to varying levels, with a relational understanding of wellbeing as embodied and embedded. Unfortunately however, the research fails to address the need, as Boddington and Boys (2011, p. xix) argue, for a perspective that considers how the relational view of spatial consciousness connects with actual material spaces, and with individuals and groups in terms of their embodied perceptions and *lived* experiences. Such a perspective, I argue, is possible through a *spatiality of wellbeing* that recognises the integral relationship of learning and wellbeing and its existential connection with the actual material space of the school.

Towards a Spatiality of Wellbeing

In introducing this chapter, I drew attention to how the discursive space of education and schooling is dominated largely by neo-liberal ideology and a view of wellbeing that, while acknowledging it as relational (involving various interconnecting individual, environmental and temporal factors), is fragmented and chiefly driven at the policy level by broader economic and social government agendas. This contrasts with welfare liberal ideology and discourse regarding wellbeing as contextual and situated and which, in the context of education, sees wellbeing as more connected with and embedded in learning and the ultimate personal, political and educational goal of human flourishing.

The notion of human flourishing as wellbeing, in the sense of living a life of value, has experienced a resurgence in areas such as the humanities through increasing interest in wellbeing and wellness. However, it is really only through the work of the economist Sen (1985, 1999, 2009) and his collaborator Nussbaum (1993, 1997, 2006, 2011), and their focus on capabilities, that the educational relevance of flourishing as wellbeing has become more apparent. In this respect, there is work such as Walker (2005), as well as more recent work including Wilson-Strydom and Walker (2015) in higher education and Spratt (2017) to do with school education that provides rich theoretical ground for exploring the interrelationship of wellbeing, learning and capability, and subsequently its implications for reconceptualising the physical school environment in a way that highlights its agentic potential.

Wellbeing, Learning and Capability

According to Sen (1999), flourishing as wellbeing is the *capability to choose* a life a person has reason to value; that is, that comprises what is understood by the person as valuable *functionings*, which can be many things such as being adequately nourished or practicing as a doctor. In this sense then, *functionings* are 'the various things a person may value doing or being' (Sen as cited in Walker, 2005, p. 104). However, as posed by Walker (2005), while a person may value these things, do they have the freedom to achieve these things? (p. 104). Herein, freedom plays a multifaceted role: it is what is required to develop capabilities (such as through the opportunity to be educated) and also what is involved when one has a *capabilities set* that allows for choice (the exercise of agency) of what is considered the most valued. Unlike Nussbaum, Sen does not stipulate what is to be valued arguing that it is the freedom to make decisions that is of fundamental importance and that such decisions can only be made collectively in the context of the time and situation. In relation to education, Nussbaum, in contrast to Sen, adopts a virtue-based approach. Nussbaum argues that it is the role of education to help cultivate the capability for effective democratic citizenship and that such cultivation relies on students developing certain *functionings*. In this regard, she highlights as significant critical thinking, imaginative understanding and world citizenship based on the awareness of being a human being 'bound to all other human beings by ties of recognition and concern' (Nussbaum, 2006, p. 389). More recently in higher education discourse, and in line with Nussbaum, educators Merridy Wilson-Strydom and Melanie Walker argue that the conceptualisation of flourishing should be extended to include a moral imperative. For them, 'to flourish and act in a moral way would be to live, act and reason with others' according to human values such as equity, diversity, empowerment, participation and sustainability. It is 'being a certain kind of person and behaving in certain ways that makes a human being a good human being' (Wilson-Strydom & Walker, 2015, p. 311).

Examination of a capabilities approach to understanding wellbeing as flourishing (and acting in a moral way) invariably leads to the conclusion that education has a significant and fundamental role to play, not only at the higher education level as argued by Walker (2005) and Wilson-Strydom and Walker (2015) but also at the pre-tertiary level of schooling. In this respect, formal education from early childhood through to the tertiary level itself is a basic capability that can have a profound impact on the development of other capabilities, functionings and opportunities for continuing development in school and beyond. This begs the question, though, as to what are the *valuable* capabilities that enable and allow students as diverse beings 'to flourish in education and through education to flourish in the future?' (Wilson-Strydom & Walker, 2015, p. 310).

First of all, it is important to clarify that a capabilities approach does not replace or devalue the development of knowledge or skills normally associated with schooling such as acquiring basic numeracy or literacy skills. Rather, as highlighted by Walker (2005), these are regarded in terms of their potential for a student to develop more complex abilities, in the process opening up a range of career possibilities. In this sense, then, literacy can be both a functioning as well as a capability. An additional example is a current focus in education on team work which can enable the development of a range of skills and predispositions, including a sense of fairness. According to Walker (2005), 'learning fairness in working and playing with others makes it possible to develop more complex capabilities of deliberation, respect and empathy, all of which expands the opportunities open to a young person to choose a life he or she has reason to value' (pp. 107, 108). And, in terms of informing and enhancing a more socially democratic model of schooling as endorsed by Spratt (2017, p. 122), Walker (2005) argues that in 'doing and making social justice, agency and autonomy are both desired functionings and valuable capabilities' (p. 108), and as such demand attention in and through schooling.

Developing desired functionings and capabilities, however, relies on being able to participate in and engage with schooling; that is, on factors that facilitate the conversion of an opportunity such as education into a functioning such as learning (Spratt, 2017, p. 123). For Spratt (2017), amongst the factors that will affect participation and engagement is a student's current state of wellbeing, demanding that:

> …teachers adopt caring pedagogical approaches that account for affective aspects of learning and value the dignity of individuals within the community of the classroom, in order that all children can engage with the learning (p. 126).

Consequently, in line with both Nussbaum (2006) and Macmurray (2012), Spratt (2017) regards the creative arts and affective sense experience, and narrative imagining they afford, as crucial to the development of meaningful engagement, critical thinking, empathy and ultimately democratic citizenship. As stated in Macmurray (2012), education of the emotions and 'its attendant emphasis on spontaneity, imagination and creativity' is one of the factors 'central to the nexus between formal schooling and our capacity to live good lives together' (p. 663).

Given this recognition of the value of the body, senses and emotions in learning for flourishing, it is somewhat surprising that none of the contemporary work reviewed, including the seminal work just discussed, considers the physical environment of the school, particularly its materiality, as a significant condition or conversion factor. This I propose may be due to the tendency to regard the collective notion of wellbeing at an abstract level rather than as a functioning *experience* involving the person in their own individualised dialectic relationship with the environment, physical as well as social. Also absent is any substantial discussion of wellbeing in existential terms or, in future oriented terms, as potential and possibility. In this regard, a phenomenological appreciation of wellbeing that attends to individual experience in embodied and embedded ways offers promise. As revealed in the following section, it opens up multiple existential possibilities that help articulate the *spatiality of wellbeing*.

Wellbeing as Existential Possibility

In the context of this chapter, *existential* is used with reference to:

> …the experience of existence; our human condition. It engages our human concerns relating to life, ageing and death, being and becoming, embodiment and identity, choice and meaningfulness, belonging and needs, sense of time and space, freedom and oppression, and so on (Finlay, 2011, p. 19).

An existential theory of wellbeing as proposed by Todres and Galvin (2010) envisages a juxtaposition of existential dwelling (offering connectedness and peace) and existential mobility (and qualities of flow and possibility), and in later work (Galvin & Todres, 2011), their integration as existential dwelling/mobility. In this respect, 'well-being is about access to one's existential possibilities in time and space, with one's body and with others' (Todres & Galvin, 2010, p. 3). As conveyed in Fig. 2, these possibilities can emphasise different aspects of this interrelationship, including: spatial, temporal, intersubjective, embodied, mood related aspects and personal identity. In addition, these existential possibilities can be affected in various ways depending on the dialectic dimensions of relatedness, which are described as *mobility* (a creative restlessness that moves us forward—becoming) and *dwelling* (a grounding in the present moment that affords peacefulness—being). Informed by this work (Todres & Galvin, 2010; Galvin & Todres, 2011), in terms of spatial dwelling in the context of schooling and school life one could ask: what is there in the physical school environment that offers a sense of 'being at home' and associated feelings of stillness and peace?

While the previous description of wellbeing as existential possibility reminds us that it is embedded through experience, being an inherently relational structure the conceptualisation can also accommodate current categorisation of wellbeing as social wellbeing, physical wellbeing, and so on, but in a holistic way. For instance, mental wellbeing (Khawaja, Ibrahim, & Schweitzer, 2017) is often associated with the presence of a positive *mood* and state of relaxation and personal relatedness, which Todres and Galvin (2010) might conceptualise respectively as *mooded dwelling* and *personal identity dwelling*. Similarly, seeking out new challenges encouraged by the capacities of problem solving, critical thinking and creativity (Kuhn, Black, Keselman, & Kaplan, 2000) suggests adventure and *spatial mobility*. In addition, the conceptualisation of wellbeing as existential possibility addresses the concerns regarding current definitions that conflate it with health. Existentially, for Todres and Galvin (2010), wellbeing in relation to health is 'a positive possibility that is independent of health and illness, but is a resource for both. In other words, well-being can be found within illness and well-being is more than health' (p. 5).

While the discussion thus far argues that wellbeing as existential possibility responds to the need for a more holistic and cohesive appreciation of wellbeing as a phenomenon, from an architectural perspective its relevance and application rely on a deeper appreciation of what Johnson (2015) calls 'the embodied meaning of architecture' (p. 48), informed by emerging cross-disciplinary research in neuroscience and architecture.

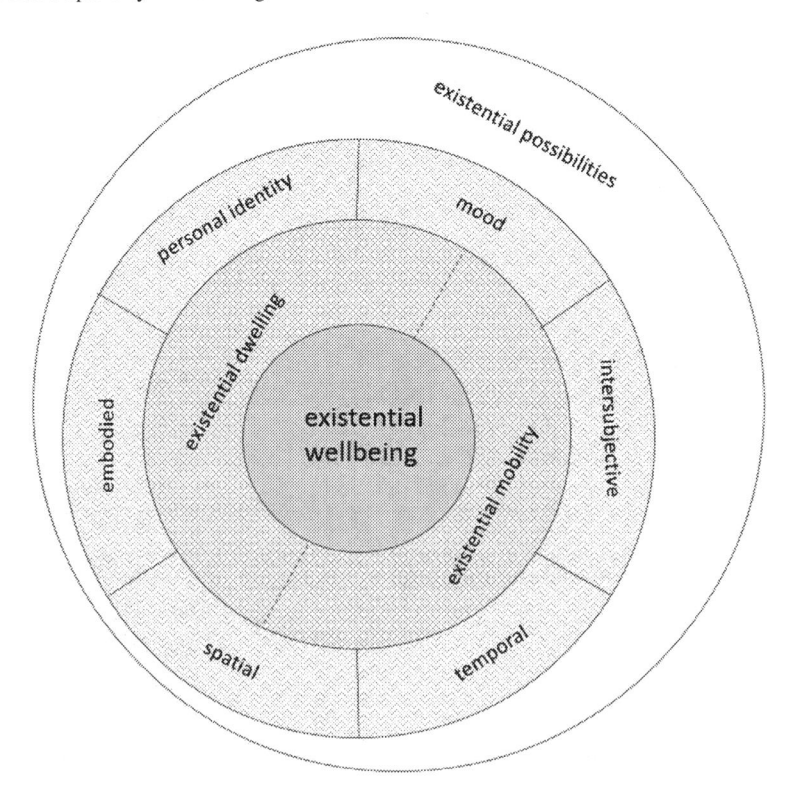

Fig. 2 Wellbeing as existential possibility. Based on Todres and Galvin (2010)

Embodied Meaning of Architecture

For Johnson (2015), architecture stands at the intersection of supporting our basic survival needs as well as 'a deep desire for meaning as part of our attempts to grow and flourish' (p. 33). It should be within our expectations of buildings 'to inspire and excite us, to promote mental states that lead us to discover, understand and create, to heal and find our way, to summon the better angels of our nature' (Albright, 2015, p. 198). Fundamental to this notion is the materiality and arrangement of spaces and physical structures and their relationship to our bodies and their multisensory capacity to engage the world emotionally through *affect* (Mallgrave, 2015, p. 19). As increasingly supported in emerging research in neuroscience, the role of emotions is significant in conditioning our responses in a precognitive or pre-reflective way, as: 'Emotions are embodied within our perceptions, and it is only later that we reflect upon our "feelings" toward some event' (Mallgrave, 2015, p. 19). Further, Mallgrave describes how it is the ambience or atmosphere of a space that, through its qualities, people first encounter, and they do this initially in a pre-reflective way, largely through their peripheral vision. Even when awareness and thought are involved, these too involve the sensorimotor areas related to movement and corporeal awareness, and it is in this respect that our responses to physical, social and cultural environments are embodied (p. 20).

A focus on wellbeing, then, naturally draws attention to the human body and its sensorimotor characteristics. Our biology forces us to acknowledge a fundamental connection to our physical as well as social world, whereby:

> In the everyday world our bodies spontaneously express our moods; others directly pick them up and respond to them. Merleau-Ponty calls this phenomenon 'intercorporeality' (Pérez-Gómez, 2015, p. 228).

In this respect, wellbeing as existential possibility permits, indeed demands greater attention by designers and educators to spatiality in the atmospheric sense. When this is considered in relation to the Deleuzian notion of *assemblage* and *flow-of-affects*, we see a conceptualisation of wellbeing as a situated yet dynamic assemblage of relations involving a range of elements that comprise our environment, including ephemeral conditions such as atmosphere. A phenomenological understanding complements this situated and relational notion of wellbeing. While it recognises that our social *situatedness* is a foundational element of the phenomenon of *intercorporeality*, it also draws attention to the body, and its sensory and aesthetic capabilities and our embodied relationship to the world, particularly the spatial and material world.

Conclusion

Spatiality is generally regarded as 'the relationship between different kinds of space and place, including the network space of relations and objects' (McGregor, 2004, p. 347). While recognising wellbeing as spatial in the relational sense, this chapter proposes that such understanding, on its own, is insufficient for appreciating the potential of the physical environment to have an enduring and profound influence on student wellbeing. As argued in this chapter, the potential only becomes apparent by adopting a capabilities approach to wellbeing as flourishing. When this is considered in terms of existential possibility, learning and wellbeing are integrally connected through embodied engagement. Being initially affective in a pre-reflective way, this demands specific attention to the spatial, material and atmospheric qualities of the physical school environment and their role in enhancing student learning, capability and wellbeing.

In conclusion, the *spatiality of wellbeing* developed in this chapter starts to close the gap between learning, wellbeing and the physical school environment providing the basis for:

- Philosophically as well as theoretically contextualising current and emerging research on student wellbeing;
- Inspiring and guiding future research in terms of the spatiality of wellbeing;
- Prompting educators as well as designers to capitalise further on the creative and empowering potential of design, its process as well as its outcome; and

- Challenging approaches to school design that tend to focus exclusively on material, structural and functional *performance* neglecting the elements and qualities of environments that are experientially and existentially significant to wellbeing in an everyday teaching and learning sense.

References

Albright, T. D. (2015). Neuroscience for architecture. In S. Robinson & J. Pallasmaa (Eds.), *Mind in architecture* (pp. 197–217). Cambridge, MA: MIT Press.

Atkinson, S., Fuller, S., & Painter, J. (2012). Wellbeing and place. In S. Atkinson, S. Fuller, & J. Painter (Eds.), *Wellbeing and place* (pp. 1–14). Farnham: Ashgate.

Atkinson, S. (2013). Beyond components of wellbeing: The effects of relational and situated assemblage. *Topoi, 32*(2), 137–144. https://link.springer.com/article/10.1007/s11245-013-9164-0.

Blackmore, J., Bateman, D., Loughlin, J., O'Mara, J., & Aranda, G. (2011). *Research into the connection between built learning spaces and student outcomes: Literature review. Paper No. 22.* Melbourne: Department of Education and Early Childhood. https://www.education.vic.gov.au/Documents/about/programs/infrastructure/blackmorelearningspaces.pdf.

Boddington, A., & Boys, J. (Eds.). (2011). *Re-shaping learning: A critical reader*. Rotterdam: Sense Publishers.

Deleuze, G., & Guattari, F. (1987). *A thousand plateaus: Capitalism and schizophrenia, Vol. 2* (B. Massumi, Trans.). Minneapolis, MN: University of Minnesota Press.

Deleuze, G., & Guattari, F. (1988). *Bergonism* (H. Tomlinson, & R. Galeta, Trans.). Minneapolis, MN: University of Minnesota Press.

Dovey, K., & Fisher, K. (2014). Designing for adaptation: The school as socio-spatial assemblage. *The Journal of Architecture, 19*(1), 43–63. https://doi.org/10.1080/13602365.2014.882376.

Drez, J., & Sen, A. (1995). *India: Economic development and social opportunity*. New Delhi: Oxford University Press.

Duhn, I. (2012). Places for pedagogies, pedagogies for places. *Contemporary Issues in Early Childhood, 13*(2), 99–107.

Ecclestone, K., & Hayes, D. (2009). *The dangerous rise of therapeutic education*. London: Routledge.

Ellis, R. A., & Goodyear, P. (2016). Models of learning space: Integrating research on space, place and learning in higher education. *Review of Education, 4*(2), 149–191. https://onlinelibrary.wiley.com/doi/abs/10.1002/rev3.3056.

Ereaut, G., & Whiting, R. (2008). *What do we mean by 'wellbeing'? And why might it matter? Research Report DCSF-RW073*. UK: Department for Children, Schools and Families.

Fielding, M. (2012). Education as if people matter: John Macmurray, community and the struggle for democracy. *Oxford Review of Education, 38*(6), 375–392.

Finlay, L. (2011). *Phenomenology for therapists*. Chichester: Wiley-Blackwell.

Fraillon, J. (2004). *Measuring student well-being in the context of Australian schooling: Discussion paper*. Melbourne, Vic: ACER/MCEETYA.

Galvin, K., & Todres, L. (2011). Kinds of well-being: A conceptual framework that provides direction for caring. *International Journal of Qualitative Studies on Health and Well-being, 6*(4), 10362. https://doi.org/10.3402/qhw.v6i4.10362.

Gislason, N. (2007). Placing education: The school as architectural space. *Paideusis, 16*(3), 5–14.

Harvey, D. (2004). Space as a key word. Paper for Marx and Philosophy Conference, 29 May 2004, Institute of Education, London. http://institut-kunst.ch/wp-content/uploads/2014/10/harvey2004.pdf.

Hillier, B. (2007). Studying cities to learn about minds. In C. Holscher, R. Conroy-Dalton and A. Turner (Eds.), *Space Syntax and Spatial Cognition* (pp. 11–31). SFB/TR8, Bremen: Universitata Bremen.

Hillier, B. (2008). Space and spatiality: What the built environment needs from social theory. *Building Research & Information, 36*(3), 216–230. https://doi.org/10.1080/09613210801928073.

Hillier, B., & Hanson, J. (1984). *The social logic of space.* Cambridge: Cambridge University Press.

Johnson, M. (2015). The embodied meaning of architecture. In S. Robinson & J. Pallasmaa (Eds.), *Mind in architecture* (pp. 33–50). Cambridge, MA: MIT Press.

Khawaja, N. G., Ibrahim, O., & Schweitzer, R. D. (2017). Mental wellbeing of students from refugee and migrant backgrounds: The mediating role of resilience. *School Mental Health, 9,* 284–293. https://doi-org.ezp01.library.qut.edu.au/10.1007/s12310-017-9215-6.

Kristjánsson, K. (2017). Recent work on flourishing as the aim of education: A critical review. *British Journal of Educational Studies, 65*(1), 87–107. https://doi.org/10.1080/00071005.2016. 1182115.

Kuhn, D., Black, J., Keselman, A., & Kaplan, D. (2000). The development of cognitive skills to support inquiry learning. *Cognition and Instruction, 18*(4), 495–523. https://doi.org/10.1207/ s1532690xci1804_3.

Macmurray, J. (2012). Learning to be human. *Oxford Review of Education, 38*(6), 661–674. https:// doi.org/10.1080/03054985.2012.745958.

Mallgrave, H. F. (2015). "Know thyself": Or what designers can learn from the contemporary biological sciences. In S. Robinson & J. Pallasmaa (Eds.), *Mind in architecture* (pp. 9–31). Cambridge, MA: MIT Press.

McGregor, J. (2004). Spatiality and the place of the material in schools. *Pedagogy, Culture and Society, 12*(3), 347–372.

Ministerial Council on Education, Employment, Training and Youth Affairs. (MCEETYA). (2008). *Melbourne declaration on educational goals for young Australians.* http://www. curriculum.edu.au/verve/_resources/National_Declaration_on_the_Educational_Goals_for_ Young_Australians.pdf.

Mulcahy, D., Cleveland, B., & Aberton, H. (2015). Learning spaces and pedagogic change: Envisioned, enacted and experienced. *Pedagogy, Culture & Society, 23*(4), 575–595. https://doi.org/ 10.1080/14681366.2015.1055128.

Mulcahy, D. (2016). Policy matters: De/re/territorialising spaces of learning in Victorian government schools. *Journal of Education Policy, 31*(1), 81–97. https://doi.org/10.1080/02680939.2015. 1099077.

Nussbaum, M. (1993). Non-relative virtues: An Aristotelian approach. In M. Nussbaum & A. Sen (Eds.), *The quality of life* (pp. 242–269). Oxford: Oxford University Press.

Nussbaum, M. (1997). *Cultivating humanity: A classical defence of reform in liberal education.* Cambridge, MA: Harvard University Press.

Nussbaum, M. (2006). Education and democratic citizenship: Capabilities and quality education. *Journal of Human Development, 7*(3), 385–395. https://doi.org/10.1080/14649880600815974.

Nussbaum, M. (2011). *Creating capabilities: The human development approach.* Cambridge, MA: Harvard University Press.

Panelli, R. & Tipa, G. (2009). Beyond foodscapes: Considering geographies of Indigenous wellbeing. *Health & Place, 15*(2), 455–465.

Pérez-Gómez, A. (2015). Mood and meaning in architecture. In S. Robinson & J. Pallasmaa (Eds.), *Mind in architecture* (pp. 219–235). Cambridge, MA: MIT Press.

Productivity Commission. (2016). *National education evidence base. Report No. 80.* Canberra: Australian Government.

Sen, A. (1985). Well-being, agency and freedom: The Dewey Lectures 1984. *The Journal of Philosophy, 82,* 169–221.

Sen, A. (1999). *Development as freedom.* Oxford: Oxford University Press.

Sen, A. (2009). *The idea of justice.* Cambridge, MA: Harvard University Press.

Spratt, J. (2017). *Wellbeing, equity and education: A critical analysis of policy discourses of wellbeing in schools*. Cham: Springer.

Stevens, P. (2010). Embedment in the environment: A new paradigm for well-being? *Perspectives in Public Health, 130*(6), 265–269.

Todres, L., & Galvin, K. (2010). "Dwelling-mobility": An existential theory of well-being. *International Journal of Qualitative Studies on Health and Well-Being, 5*(3), 5444. http://www.tandfonline.com/doi/pdf/10.3402/qhw.v5i3.5444.

United Nations. (2009). *Convention on the rights of the child*. Geneva: United Nations. http://www2.ohchr.org/english/bodies/crc/docs/AdvanceVersions/CRC-C-GC-12.pdf.

Walker, M. (2005). Amartya Sen's capability approach and education. *Educational Action Research, 13*(1), 103–110.

Watson, D., Emery, C., Bayliss, P., Boushel, M., & McInnes, K. (2012). *Children's social and emotional wellbeing in schools*. Bristol: Policy Press.

World Health Organization (WHO). (1946). *Constitution of the World Health Organization as adopted by the International Health Conference, New York, 19–22 June, 1946; Signed on the 22 July 1946*. New York, NY: World Health Organization (WHO).

Wilson-Strydom, M., & Walker, M. (2015). A capabilities-friendly conceptualisation of flourishing in and through education. *Journal of Moral Education, 44*(3), 310–324. https://doi.org/10.1080/03057240.2015.1043878.

Sociomaterial Dimensions of Early Literacy Learning Spaces: Moving Through Classrooms with Teacher and Children

Lisa Kervin, Barbara Comber and Aspa Baroutsis

Abstract Classroom spaces are complex social worlds where people interact in multifaceted ways with spaces and materials. Classrooms are carefully designed agents for socialisation; however, the complexity and richness of learning experiences are partly determined by the teacher. This chapter draws from sociocultural perspectives to consider processes of thinking and learning as distributed and mediated across people and resources within the learning space. We argue that learning and wellbeing cannot be separated as students activate their social and emotional literacies when navigating the classroom environment. Drawing on data drawn from an ethnographic study of classrooms located in a community of high poverty, we critique how teachers describe their classroom spaces and selection of resources to facilitate their teaching of writing. We illustrate how geographies of place, movement and resources, interact with, and expand the social dimensions of classroom spaces.

Introduction

Classrooms are taken for granted as sites of learning; yet school built environments are often interpreted and reinterpreted in ways which are contingent upon context and the availability of financial resources (Blackmore, Bateman, O'Mara, Loughlin, & Aranda, 2011). Current education reforms in Australia tend to focus on increasing teacher accountability and transparency so as to improve literacy standards. In an education climate focused on results, the social and material dimensions of schooling and of different school communities are often overlooked. In this context, it is perhaps less surprising that in 2017, 24% of Australian children reported feeling like outsiders in their schools and 28% feeling like they do not belong (OECD, 2017, p. 345). This

L. Kervin (✉)
University of Wollongong, Wollongong, NSW, Australia
e-mail: lkervin@uow.edu.au

B. Comber
University of South Australia, Adelaide, SA, Australia

A. Baroutsis
Griffith University, Nathan, QLD, Australia

© Springer Nature Singapore Pte Ltd. 2019
H. Hughes et al. (eds.), *School Spaces for Student Wellbeing and Learning*,
https://doi.org/10.1007/978-981-13-6092-3_2

represents an increase of approximately 16% from 2003, emphasising the importance of a focus on the sociomaterial dimensions of schooling.

Classroom spaces are complex social worlds where people interact in multifaceted ways with spaces and materials. This highlights the complexity and dynamism of learning spaces and the experiences enacted within, which are in part determined by the teachers' and schools' philosophies of education in interplay with the lives of children. As such, classrooms are spaces where events unfold and ultimately shape the social and academic experiences of the learner (Warf & Arias, 2009).

This chapter investigates the social and material dimensions of learning spaces; that is, we undertake a sociomaterial analysis and argue that the geographies of place, movement and resources, interact with, and expand classroom spaces. Therefore, the classroom becomes the object of our study, an active element of belonging and learning. The chapter starts by outlining our theoretical understandings of wellbeing, space and literacy. Here, we take Leander's (2004) argument that space organises individuals, hence we look to the ways that teachers and students interact, or appropriate, classroom spaces to facilitate teaching and learning (Gee, 2008). We acknowledge that learning and wellbeing are intertwined (OECD, 2017); that is, children activate social and emotional literacies as they navigate the classroom environment. Next, we discuss our research methods, outlining our data sets and illustrate how a sociomaterial analysis allows us to explore the social, material, spatial and pedagogical relationships in a writing classroom. Specifically, we look to how materials, ideas, practices and pedagogies are brought together in ways that are always active and interrelated to investigate everyday teaching and learning practices. We then discuss our findings, drawing on a video analysis of a teacher's tour of his classroom, children's perceptions of writing as expressed in their drawing and talking, and researcher observations. Combined, these data form the basis of our discussion demonstrating a classroom in action. We conclude by summarising the importance of the social, material, spatial and pedagogical dimensions of learning.

Theoretical Understandings of Space, Wellbeing and Literacy

Critical scholars of architecture and urban planning argue that buildings, cities, malls and all built environments need to be understood not as empty containers that just anyone can inhabit for any purpose at any time (Lefebvre, 1991; Soja, 2010). Rather, such structures, including schools, playgrounds, universities and so on are designed and constructed in particular places to house specific populations and to enable and constrain activities therein (Foucault, 1979). Hence, the spatial politics of purpose-built institutions always require negotiation and interrogation in terms of the occupants for whom they were designed.

Intertwined with the elements of the spatial dimension of classrooms is children's sense of wellbeing. While *wellbeing* is a ubiquitous term that has variable interpretations (Anderson & Graham, 2016; Gillett-Swan & Sargeant, 2015; McLeod & Wright, 2015), it is frequently identified as a significant concept in education systems (McLeod & Wright, 2015; OECD, 2017). While we acknowledge that both the teachers' and the children's wellbeing are important, this chapter focuses only on children's wellbeing. In Australia, the Melbourne Declaration (MCEETYA, 2008) states that, 'Schools play a vital role in promoting the intellectual, physical, social, emotional, moral, spiritual and aesthetic development and wellbeing of young Australians' (p. 4). Drawing on this statement and our understandings of *wellbeing* (McLeod, 2015), we seek to refine wellbeing in terms of two specific concepts that are derived from these broader understandings. We draw on the notions of *belonging* and *affect*. We argue that as children in the early school years work towards developing their writing and learning identities, their sense of belonging during writing and their affective experiences are linked to wellbeing. We consider the notion of *place-belongingness* (Antonsich, 2010), where children are able to feel positive about their learning experiences. For example, this could include experiences of safety related to their material environment or experiences of success in relation to their pedagogical environment. Therefore, as we explore belonging we also intertwine affect. Here, we draw on understandings of children's emotions being embodied and performed in relation to others in social and pedagogical spaces (Kuby, 2014).

Wellbeing is not something that can be designed once and for all, even in optimal classroom spaces; rather, it needs to be co-constructed in situ, between the teacher, the children, the placement of furniture, bodies, technologies, tools and so on. If particular children become regularly associated with spaces of trouble, extra surveillance or restricted access, their sense of belonging may be challenged. For example, they may come to associate writing time with either pleasure or fear or time with friends. The sociospatial practice of writing is what comes to count (Dyson, 2016). On the other hand, children may negotiate safe and creative spaces in early years school settings where their imaginations and stories thrive (Dyson, 2016; Marsh, 2016).

In literacy education studies, the sociospatial nature of the classroom became a key focus of attention following Leander and Sheehy's (2004) edited collection, *Spatializing literacy research and practice*. Classrooms are not voids simply to be designed and filled with the requisite numbers of teachers, students, tools, technologies, texts and so on. Instead, spaces are always under construction and always under negotiation. We look to the classroom as an example of a *material culture* through which the types of experiences it comprises, resources it offers and the physical space itself are acknowledged and examined. This then reveals the interrelationships between the time, scale, space, resources, people and interactions that contribute to the classroom experience. Understanding the dynamic nature of social spaces and what is being negotiated and accomplished through the interactions of different people with the everyday stuff therein and beyond the walls is crucial. Teachers' and children's sense of wellbeing and belonging is contingent on the extent to which they can productively and positively deal with being 'thrown together' (Massey, 2005). How different people enact social and learner identities within classrooms is worked through, over time. This suggests that positionings have complex spatial histories.

As the classroom is a social space, a negotiated space, (Comber, 2016; Dyson, 2016), young children need to learn to navigate this unfamiliar territory and they need to learn to *read classroom life* as a dynamic phenomenon. For example, the child seated near the teacher's desk comes to realise that s/he is often the subject of teacher attention, sometimes to be helped, sometimes to be scolded (Baroutsis, Kervin, Woods, & Comber, 2017). In the process, learning identities are constructed (Marsh, 2016). In early years of school, a major dimension of that learning identity is one's capability with reading and writing. As literacy researchers have observed, early literacy instruction can be seen as subjecting the child to the discipline of schooling such as practicing the bodily habitus associated with handwriting letters in the proper ways. Early writing in the spaces of classrooms is often a highly public act, given that writing is visible to peers and teacher (Dixon, 2010; Luke, 1992). Luke (1992) has described this inculcation as training in 'the body literate' (p. 107). Classrooms are typically regulated environs, where children learn to confine their bodies in space and time, where children learn the discipline of early literacy simultaneously with the discipline of early schooling (Dixon, 2010).

Site and Participants

This chapter draws on data collected as part of a federally funded Australian two-school ethnography where teachers, researchers and children have worked together to provide a fresh understanding of how the teaching of writing is enacted across schools at this time. Here, we focus on data from one composite class of 6- to 8-year-old children and their teacher from one of the participating schools.

The school is situated in an urban suburb of a large seaside city of New South Wales, Australia in a community of high poverty, with families from diverse cultural and linguistic backgrounds. This suburb was formerly a hub for heavy industry that provided employment for the local population. The school is a coeducational government funded school with a student population of approximately 180. This figure represents a 19% drop in enrolment since 2008. Currently, 12 teachers and four non-teaching staff work with children across kindergarten to Year 6 (Australian Curriculum, Assessment and Reporting Authority, 2016). The participants represented in this chapter include one teacher and 25 students in a Grade 1/2 composite class. The teacher was in his third year of teaching and the children were in their second or third year of schooling. Together, the teacher and students embraced a wide range of literacy learning opportunities in their classroom.

Education institutions uphold and reproduce educational arrangements and knowledge traditions which shape educational practice. Understanding the school context is important to contextualise processes teachers and students enact in classrooms. Proximity to and engagement with particular practices and bodies influence a sense of belonging for children as these established processes orientate bodies in specific directions, affecting who has access to and experiences a sense of belonging within educational sites. While others have shown how belonging relates to race, class, gender and ethnicity (Ahmed, 2012; Kustatscher, 2017), the scope of this chapter is limited to the ways in which children are constituted as learner writers and how they are positioned in relation to the classroom space, materials and time. Our intent is to explore the interplay between *the teacher* and *the children* in terms of the pedagogy of writing as a sociomaterial accomplishment.

Methods

The chapter draws from three data sets produced in one classroom extracted from a larger data set from multiple classrooms in two schools. First, we examine how the teacher describes his classroom spaces and selects resources to facilitate the teaching of writing through the analysis of the teacher's video tour of the classroom. He filmed and annotated key decisions he made about the organisation of spaces and the inclusion of resources. Second, we draw on the children's perspectives of their experiences of their classroom spaces during the processes of learning to write. This is observed through children drawing and talking about their writing experiences during a survey that was administered during an individual interview with a researcher. These data were analysed using a descriptive content analysis where the theoretical framework informed coding categories. Finally, we share key observations taken from 70 min of classroom writing time. In all, analysis of these data provides examples for discussion in this chapter as we identify various perspectives around the sociospatial dimensions of the classroom.

Our study focuses on the sociomaterial aspects of the classroom and the ways the teacher and children represent social, material and pedagogical dimensions of classrooms. We interpret the classroom as a site of material culture (Miller, 1987) through which the types of experiences it comprises, the resources it offers and the physical environment itself can be examined. This view of 'material culture' acknowledges the interrelationships between the time, space, resources, people and interactions. A sociomaterial approach allows for the careful examination of interplay between the physical, temporal and spatial elements that contribute to young children's experiences within this classroom context.

Engaging with experiences within the classroom is a complex process for both the teacher and children, and is affected by a range of assemblages (Fenwick, 2014). The term *assemblage* describes how things and people are gathered together in classrooms in complex and fluid ways that are both locally relevant but also influential in more extended social configurations such as the school, the community, and education. The sociomaterial approach perceives pedagogy as a collection of uncertain and heterogeneous relational practices which are not the exclusive concern of the individual teacher, rather a collective responsibility. Those responsible are the many players, webs and non-coherences embedded within the pedagogical act. This approach offers our research a 'method by which to recognise and trace the multifarious struggles, negotiations and accommodations whose effects constitute the things in education' (Fenwick & Landri, 2012, p. 2). In addition, our approach incorporates children's bodily experiences in and with the sociomateriality of classroom life as intrinsically related to their sense of wellbeing.

Our research acknowledges that literacy is culturally specific (Heath, 1983) because it is not only 'situated within material culture… it is in itself a material, cultural practice' (Rowsell & Pahl, 2011, p. 178). Literacy practices are learned within classrooms, which we consider as dynamic cultural systems. Classrooms structure and promote roles, activities and tools through which literacy practices are enabled. In this chapter, we focus on the intricacies of classroom writing as we examine the assemblage of materials, ideas, practices and pedagogies that are always active and interrelated. Our objective is to 'understand how things come together, and manage to hold together' (Fenwick & Edwards, 2011, p. 2) to produce knowledge about writing pedagogy, through careful examination of the *situatedness* (Fenwick, 2014) of learning processes and their many interrelations. Importantly, we are interested in the ways in which literacy and learning literacy always involve sociomaterial relationships; relationships in early years classrooms that can profoundly affect young children's sense of belonging and competence at school.

Perspectives of Writing

In outlining and analysing our findings, we focus on the writing classroom space as the third teacher. Particularly, we foreground the sociomaterial dimensions of this space, that is, the human collaborations and material interactions that occur within the classroom and the potential affective consequences on children. We provide three accounts of the classroom space, each adding a subsequent layer of understanding. The teacher's account outlines how the classroom is imagined (Appadurai, 1996), identifying the carefully constructed spaces, and the artefacts that are created in anticipation of children learning to write. The children's accounts represent instances of how the prepared space was taken up; the junctures and disjunctures between the imagined and the actual. Finally, the researchers' perspectives, drawn from classroom observations, generate a discussion about the classroom in action. That is, we identify the lived and negotiated spaces, both imagined and experienced, material and discursive, that operate to ensure children's wellbeing through the fostering of a sense of belonging.

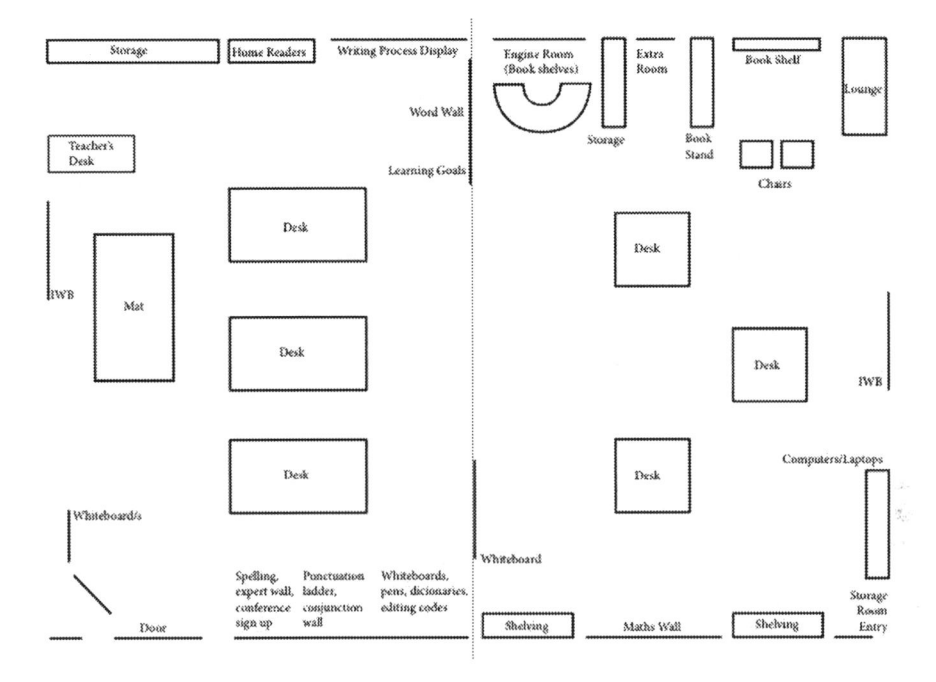

Fig. 1 Floor plan of the classroom space

The Classroom Space

This classroom space is a large double classroom, occupied by the teacher and 25 students in the Grade 1/2 composite class. The teacher identified spaces in his classroom designated for different curriculum areas and learning opportunities. Children's writing and artworks are displayed on the walls and on lines suspended across the room.

The classroom floor plan (see Fig. 1) shows that on the western end of the classroom (top, left hand side of Fig. 1), there is a floor area in front of a whiteboard and an Interactive Whiteboard (IWB) for the purposes of whole class teaching. The teacher's desk is in the corner of this space, housing the computer that operates the IWB. Set back from this space are table groupings where the children work during writing times. At the other end of the room, he has a reading corner (complete with a range of children's literature, cushions, low chairs and bean bags) where the children gather for story time. To the side of this space are other tables where the children complete their numeracy studies. Between these spaces is an *engine table*; this is a blue semicircular table, slightly removed from the other table groups, which provides an intimate space for the teacher to engage small groups of children in explicit teaching of writing skills and strategies.

Designing Classroom Spaces: A Teacher's Perspective

We now consider the imagined classroom from the teacher's perspective. Drawing on a video tour of the teacher's classroom, we were able to identify the teacher's intent that goes into the design of classroom spaces. Children engage with materials as resources within their environment, and as they become more proficient with literate practices, they talk, handle materials and participate in activities in ways that are expected of them by teachers and school (Rogers, 2003). Teachers make pedagogical decisions as they implement routines and interactions with the intention of facilitating student learning. Leander (2004) describes this as '…a set of discursive and material practices and resources that actively engages in the production of power relations and ideology' (p. 127).

In the video tour of his classroom, the teacher highlights specific spaces, resources, and practices for the children during writing time. He named specific spaces and resources, and identified practices he expected his students to engage with. In his one minute and twelve second video accompanied by a 130-word commentary annotating the visual dimension of the tour, he drew our attention to:

- The *writing wall,* which contained spelling words for the week, the developmental groups the children were organised into and a visual representation of the writing process. The spelling words were printed in a list format and served as a visual reminder to the children about specific words for study. The identification of developmental groups for the children acted as an organisational structure for that period of time as both the teacher and children could identify who was working with whom and their planned focus. These groups were fluid and were updated every week by the teacher, informed by his observations and assessment of the children during writing time. The visual representation of the writing process was covered with self-adhesive strips and individual names so the children could each position their name with the part of the writing process they were up to (that is, planning, drafting, revising and publishing). The teacher indicated in his commentary that this helped him know where the children 'were at'.
- The *word wall* contained a laminated sheet for each letter of the alphabet. Words were written onto these sheets using a whiteboard marker. The children could remove individual sheets during writing time. Children were expected to use and return these so all the class could use the resource.
- Individual *learning goals* were handwritten by the teacher and hung onto the wall. It was the teacher's intention that each child would remove their learning goal prior to writing and have this on their desk during writing time as a reminder of their specific focus.
- The *punctuation area* displayed punctuation marks the children were expected to know and use. Alongside it was a ladder that provided a hierarchy of the punctuation marks and children's names were arranged alongside this to show individual competence with the punctuation form.
- The *writing centre* ran across the wall near the entrance to the classroom. It provided writing samples that were rated (one star to five star, with five star being the

best). Some samples were from children and others were from curriculum support documents, these were intended to provide models of what was expected during writing time. The teacher identified specific workshops for guided instruction and allocated names of children to these. There was a sign-up sheet for children if they wanted to talk with the teacher.

- *Experts* in the areas of planning, spelling, paragraphs, editing, feedback and conferencing were identified with a photograph and named as available to support their peers during independent writing time.

As the teacher spoke about each named area, he offered targeted video footage of that area within the classroom space. Evident in the video footage were arrows on the floor which marked the teacher's anticipated movement of children through these resources.

The teacher planned specific areas and resources for distinct purposes in his classroom. The physical layout of the room specified areas for specific practices. For example, there were areas to work as a whole class, in small groups and independently. He demonstrated his understanding that writing is a systematic process through his design of the classroom space. The design enabled the children to physically move in ways to enable the children to engage with carefully selected resources. As an example, the teacher demonstrated his expectation about how processes should be enacted within his classroom design through marking arrows on the floor.

As the teacher described his classroom, he used educational discourse to describe spaces, resources and expectations for the children. The teacher's descriptions were informed by curriculum guidelines and his exposure to professional development experiences. For example, the school encouraged the use of Hattie's *Visible Learning* strategies. It gave us a sense of his pedagogical imagination as he foresees spaces and furniture variously occupied by individuals, pairs, groups and the whole class with different tasks in mind. The classroom space as a literacy landscape has been given a great deal of attention and forethought by this early career teacher as he planned ahead for the ways in which he could support young learners to produce texts. Notably and not surprisingly his focus is on the child as a pedagogical subject in this case, 'the developing writer'. In the process, his priorities became academic and managerial as he tries to anticipate different needs and resources that different children will need.

The teacher created personalised resources within the classroom. While these have come from published ideas (for example, writing process model, or the punctuation ladder), he recreated these and personalised them with the children's names, all of which are able to be moved around to represent fluidity in process. Children's written and artistic work samples were displayed widely across the classroom. In most cases, these are whole class sets of products. There were no published posters or display-type resources in the room. There was a wide range of published children's literature. There were many writing samples the teacher has jointly constructed with the children. These constructed writing spaces, materials and organisation of customised resources aim to teach the children how to be developing writers who set individual goals and are self-regulating.

Using Classroom Spaces: Children's Perspectives

Following the teacher's perspectives on his Grade 1/2 composite class, we now explore the children's experiences of their writing spaces in the same classroom (see Fig. 1). Here, we are able to see how the teacher's imagined classroom took form through the children's actual experiences. The children in this class (n = 20) responded to open-ended survey questions about their writing including how, when, where, with what and with whom they were writing in their classroom. This was followed by an invitation to draw a picture of themselves writing, during which we adopted a *draw and talk* (Coates & Coates, 2006; Hopperstad, 2010) approach which enabled the children to explain their drawings (n = 19). As noted here, one child declined to provide a drawing but responded to the survey questions. Through these modes of data collection, we were able to note the social, material and pedagogical dimensions of belonging that supported the children's wellbeing.

In comparison to the teacher's perspectives about the materials and spaces used for writing, the children also referred to word and writing walls; however, this was less prominent in the children's perspectives. Like their teacher, the children spoke about the usefulness of word and writing walls in their classroom. While none of the children included these walls in their drawings, they did talk about them in their commentary or responses to questions. For example, some children (20%) referred to the word walls suggesting that they found it helpful when writing to have their teacher 'put words on the word wall'. Many more children (40%) referred to the writing walls, particularly the writing processes of planning and drafting, with fewer references to publishing and no references to revising.

The other aspects of the teacher's video tour that were less frequently addressed by the children's drawing and talking include learning goals, the writing centre, the punctuation area and the wall of experts. Only two children (10%) mentioned learning goals as being helpful when writing. While one child (5%) made a reference to the star system in the writing centre, suggesting good writing 'is when you get three stars all over'. Similarly, punctuation was only referred to by two children (10%) and no specific references were made to the punctuation area identified by the teacher. These children associated punctuation with good writing; however, they tended to identify specific punctuation such as full stops or commas. Finally, two children (10%) also spoke about the conferencing time when they are given help with the editing of their writing. However, this last point, the notion of the *expert*, can be seen in the broader context of children working collaboratively with their peers and teachers.

Similar to our findings in the larger study (see Kervin, Comber, & Woods, 2017), a prominent aspect of the perspectives of children from this class included a focus on the social dimensions of their classroom spaces, that is, their relationships with others. This focused on their collaborations with other children and their teachers. The children's commentary on their interactions during the writing process is seen through detailed drawings of their classrooms. In particular, their drawings emphasised the social space through the arrangement of the tables and chairs in their classroom that facilitated collaboration. The emphasis on social spaces was seen in the children's

Fig. 2 Child's drawing depicting facial expressions

responses and drawings with 55% of children making reference to their table config-urations in their talk and 89% in their drawings. The children's drawings frequently included faces and facial expressions. Most of the drawings (74%) included a face and in all of these instances, the faces were drawn with smiles (see Fig. 2).

The children's drawings of their writing spaces focused on particular materials that represented writing. Figure 3 shows the dominant depiction of writing that included representations of tables and chairs (89%). When tables were drawn in the children's pictures, just under a third of the drawings (59%) grouped the tables together and indicated collaborations with other children, similar to the drawing in Fig. 3. In this picture, we see three characters working on their own independent piece of writing, but located in a shared table grouping. The author has depicted himself with a smile, while the other two participants are faceless. This finding from this particular class, when compared to the findings of the larger study (see Baroutsis et al., 2017) shows a larger incidence of depictions of children interacting with other children during writing.

In addition to the collaborations with their peers, although these were far less frequent, there were also depictions of children working with adults (see Fig. 4). The semicircle table captured in this illustration is the engine table. The teacher and a child are located either side of the table. The teacher is smiling, whereas the student is not.

Fig. 3 Child's drawing of desks in the classroom, including the blue engine table

Fig. 4 Child's drawing depicting writing around the blue engine table on the right

Discussion of a Writing Classroom in Action

In drawing this chapter to a close, we will now add to the previous two perspectives using our classroom observations. We discuss an episode of writing in this classroom (see Fig. 1) when all the research team were present, thereby enabling us to draw on additional perspectives and comparisons of the imagined and actual classroom spaces. In so doing, we are also able to draw together our understandings of the material, social, and pedagogical dimensions in relation to children's wellbeing.

Our descriptions in this section are from a 70-min writing episode that was introduced using the picture book, *Flood* by Jackie French and Bruce Whatley (2011). The lesson was delivered by the male classroom teacher (T1) who provided the video tour and assisted by a female school leader (T2) who was invited into his classroom specifically for our visit. T1, with the assistance of T2, models the construction of a planning document that the children will need to create and use to write a letter about a flood. We draw on the field notes and observations combined with elements of the previous data sets to identify some of the material, social, and pedagogical dimensions of the classroom space.

Preparing for Writing

This first excerpt outlines the classroom space and the human and non-human materials where the teacher prepares the children for writing. As with previous indications in the video tour, the elements of this lesson are purposefully planned and specifically executed. Here, we are introduced to new spaces in the classroom, the white board and the carpet area that have not been covered by the teacher's video tour or the children's drawings.

10:12 am We enter the space; children are sitting on the floor in front of the white board. Children seem to have positioned themselves in rows on the floor. Those in the front are sitting (some with knees pulled up in front of them) looking at T1 and the book. This pattern continues across most of the floor.

T1 has a handwritten list on yellow card clipped to the whiteboard. T2 is sitting on a chair behind the children.

10:27 am Children all seem focused. Some fidgeting on the floor.

10:39 am There is a real calmness in the classroom. The children are sitting on the floor, most are looking at what T1 is doing. There are some children a little more reclined than others, but attention remains with T1. T2 reaches out and touches a child on the back to remind them to focus.

10:41 am T1 invites the children to stand up, shake it out and find somewhere new to sit. T2 directs two children to remain with her.

10:51 am Children are fidgeting and moving—most legs are pulled up or children are reclined, some yawns.

In these excerpts from our observations, we predominantly see a teacher-focused lesson with explicit and visible teaching (Bernstein, 1975). Even without prompting from the teachers, the children position their bodies in rows on the carpet, demonstrating the self-regulating effect of surveillance (Foucault, 1979). The children's bodies are oriented towards the teacher and the whiteboard that he is working on. As Ingold (2012) suggests, we think *from* rather than *about* the body. As such, the view from the children's eyes places the teacher, who is standing, in an elevated position and the children need to tilt their heads backwards to make eye contact. The children are seated on the carpet, and interacting with that surface of the floor as parts of their body come into contact with the carpet. The carpet frees the children from the constraints of the desks and chairs that they often associated with writing in their drawings. The carpet provides a fluid space for movement. Some children have nestled themselves against the wall, some are fidgeting and others are partially reclined, while others started interacting with their peers. Later in the lesson, picking up on the fidgeting, the teacher provides an opportunity for the children to 'shake it out' demonstrating an understanding that they have been sitting and focused on the same thing for a very long time.

While we as the researchers observed eager yet patient children, in some of these situations, the children were reprimanded for a loss of focus which may have been due to the elongated lesson where the children were moderately passive within the frame of the lesson. Interestingly, school is considered a place where children learn socialisation skills as a means of promoting place-belongingness. However, in this example, children quickly learned that these social interactions are only permissible in certain situations and in this lesson the interaction between the children was frowned upon. Regardless, the children's behaviour was viewed as a choice that demonstrated not their lack of desire to learn, rather, they were uncomfortable sitting for a long time on the carpet. The reprimand by a teacher seemed to indicate that the upright position is the only body placement that is pedagogically sound and promotes learning. Here, fluidity and movement that is encouraged by sitting on the carpet is not permitted and children were constrained through the rearrangement of their seating positions (Nespor, 1997). That is, a number of children were told to move from their location on the carpet and asked to sit at the back of the room in close proximity to the second teacher. As a practice, this isolation of children from their peers through 'spatial detachment' is likely to develop feelings of non-belonging to the social group (Nespor, 1997, p. 188).

Planning and Modelling Writing

The second excerpt elaborates on elements of the social, material, spatial and pedagogical dimensions of the lesson. Here, the teacher has designed the lesson so that the children are able to experience success and belonging.

10:04 am T1 has a handwritten list on yellow card clipped to the whiteboard. This features an overview of the learning intentions for the writing lesson. He stands in front of the children and discusses his expectations for the children during writing time. He states that 'This is what you need to do to be successful.'

10:42 am T1 asks the children what part of the writing process they have just finished. He says he expects everyone should be able to answer this. T1 invites T2 to be his 'composing partner'. T2 asks T1 about the purpose of the text. T2 moves to the front of the room and stands next to the whiteboard. T1 orally demonstrates how he will compose the text to this mother. He uses the pictures, points to these and composes his text. T2 prompts him to think about how he might be feeling. T1 states, 'When you're composing, your learning partner should... share ideas, give feedback.'

10:54 am T1 models the page setup such as margin and title for the children. He revisits the learning intention with the children. They chorally read it out.

10:56 am Child asks, 'When are we going to start writing?' T1 states, 'Not today, but maybe after lunch.'

The children are provided with the knowledge and materials to successfully undertake their writing tasks. This is done specifically through the two teachers modelling the writing process. First, the teacher outlines the learning intentions that are listed on a large yellow card and stuck to the whiteboard, thereby bringing the visual and material modes of literacy to the classroom (Kress, 1997). Second, through this modelling of the writing task, the teachers clearly identify the expectations for learning and the standard at which this is to be completed. The teachers also provide a demonstration of what 'composing partners' are likely to do with the intention to provide children with a clear understanding of the roles they should adopt to help each other learn. This modelling provides the children with exemplars for communication and collaboration through the role modelling by the teachers. Additionally, the teachers' 'acting-out' identifies the required behaviour that they anticipate will improve both children's social learning and their writing (McLeod, 2015). However, in the next section, we see tensions come into play between the expertly planned and modelled lesson, and the children's experience of writing as temporal aspects. We acknowledge that these aspects are often inherent in institutional practices, often outside the control of individual teacher.

Encouraging and Supporting Writing

This final excerpt from our field notes and observations affirms the teacher's practices associated with encouraging and supporting the children during learning. These practices are likely to develop positive emotions in relation to writing.

10:23 am T1 is continuing to read the text. He breaks every so often and checks children's understanding of words.

10:39 am A child offers an extended response to the image T1 has put up on the board. T1 encourages the response and thanks the child for his insight.

12:24 pm A child tells T1 they're not happy with their work. He assures him it's ok and to keep going.

12:35 pm A child asks T1 for another [planning] sheet. T1 asks, 'Another one or a new one?' Child confirms it's another one. T1 says, 'Good boy,' and passes him another sheet. T1 adds, '[Name], you are killing it! Well done mate!'

Here, as with the children's drawings, we note that children can 'live out emotions through their body language, play, and art' (Kuby, 2014, p. 1286). The socially driven interactions between the teacher and the children, outlined in our observations, demonstrate how the teacher in this class encouraged children when they were writing. Fostering inclusive social interactions and relationships enables children to develop positive emotional responses, often expressed through the embodied experience. This was evident in the children's drawings. However, not all experiences of writing were positive. In Fig. 4, we observe the child's neutral or possibly negative facial expression as a reaction to being isolated from the other children when working on the engine table. Consequently, we see that both positive and negative experiences of writing affect belonging and the social and emotional wellbeing of children, as well as their productivity as they learn to write.

Conclusions

In this chapter, we have argued that classroom spaces are not neutral or static; rather they are negotiated constantly. We have shown how this teacher organises his ideal environment for children to learn to write and the materials needed to cater for the tasks he designs. He anticipates the students' needs and children variously engage with those offerings and participate in a range of ways. Some children do appear to feel like they belong. Some readily earn stars and become experts and helpers. Other children fly under the radar, deliberately or not, we can only speculate here. Other children earn the extra attention of the second teacher in the room or find themselves regular attendees at the engine table. Day by day and minute by minute, the children and their teacher negotiate classroom spaces in social and pedagogical ways to do the *work* of school. The notion of *assemblage* draws our attention to the complex and fluid ways things and people are gathered together in classrooms, each learning to *read* what is going on. In this complex process, children are also learning to relate to each other and their teacher(s), to learn the expectations associated with being together on the carpet, to listening with stillness and near silence for extended periods. This involves significant discipline as they regulate their bodies in close proximity to peers and also try to attend to what is salient as their teacher(s) speak or read or draw. The sheer complexity of the early writing classroom indicates how much young learners need to manage when they begin school and how much teachers need to do to be ready for them.

Sociomaterial Dimensions of Early Literacy Learning Spaces …

References

ACARA. (2016). *National assessment program literacy and numeracy: Achievement in reading, writing, language conventions and numeracy: National report for 2016*. Sydney: ACARA.

Ahmed, S. (2012). Whiteness and the general will: Diversity work as willful work. *Philosophia, 2*(1), 1–20.

Anderson, D. L., & Graham, A. P. (2016). Improving student wellbeing: Having a say at school. *School Effectiveness and School Improvement, 27*(3), 348–366 (2016). https://doi.org/10.1080/09243453.2015.1084336.

Antonsich, M. (2010). Searching for belonging: An analytical framework. *Geography Compass, 4*(6), 644–659 (2010). https://doi.org/10.1111/j.1749-8198.2009.00317.x.

Appadurai, A. (1996). *Modernity at large: Cultural dimensions of globalization* (Vol. 1). Minneapolis: University of Minnesota Press.

Baroutsis, A., Kervin, L., Woods, A., Comber, B. (2017). Understanding children's perspectives of classroom writing practices through drawings. *Contemporary Issues in Early Childhood*. https://doi.org/10.1177/1463949117741743.

Bernstein, B. (1975). *Class, codes and control: Towards a theory of educational transmission* (Vol. 3). London: Routledge & Kegan Paul.

Blackmore, J., Bateman, D., O'Mara, J., Loughlin, J., & Aranda, G. (2011). *Research into the connection between built learning spaces and student outcomes: Literature review: Paper no. 22*. East Melbourne, VIC: Department of Education and Early Childhood Development. Retrieved May 22, 2018, from http://dro.deakin.edu.au/view/DU:30036968.

Coates, E., & Coates, A. (2006). Young children talking and drawing. *International Journal of Early Years Education, 14*(3), 221–241.

Comber, B. (2016). *Literacy, place, and pedagogies of possibility*. New York: Routledge.

Dixon, K. (2010). *Literacy, power, and the schooled body: Learning in time and space*. London: Routledge.

Dyson, A. H. (Ed.). (2016). *Child cultures, schooling and literacy: Global perspectives on children composing their lives*. New York & London: Routledge.

Gee, J. P. (2008). A sociocultural perspective on opportunity to learn. In P. A. Moss, D. C. Pullin, J. P. Gee, E. H. Haertel, & L. J. Young (Eds.), *Assessment, equity, and opportunity to learn* (pp. 76–108). Cambridge, NY: Cambridge University Press.

Fenwick, T. (2014). Sociomateriality in medical practice and learning: Attuning to what matters. *Medical Education, 48*(1), 44–52.

Fenwick, T., & Edwards, R. (2011). Introduction: Reclaiming and renewing actor network theory for educational research. *Educational Philosophy and Theory, 43*(1), 1–14 (2011). https://doi.org.10.1111.j.1469-5812.2010.00667.x.

Fenwick, T., & Landri, P. (2012). Materialities, textures and pedagogies: Socio-material assemblages in education. *Pedagogy, Culture & Society, 20*, 1–7 (2012). https://doi.org/10.1080/14681366.2012.649421.

French, J., & Whatley, B. (2011). *Flood*. Sydney: Scholastic Australia.

Foucault, M. (1979). *Discipline and punish: The birth of the prison* (A. Sheridan, Trans.). London: Peregrine.

Gillett-Swan, J. K., & Sargeant, J. (2015). Wellbeing as a process of accrual: Beyond subjectivity and beyond the moment. *Social Indicators Research, 121*(1), 135–148 (2015). https://doi.org/10.1007/s11205-014-0634-6.

Heath, S. B. (1983). *Ways with words: Language, life, and work in communities and classrooms*. New York: Cambridge University Press.

Hopperstad, M. H. (2010). Studying meaning in children's drawings. *Journal of Early Childhood Literacy, 10*(4), 430–452 (2010). https://doi.org/10.1177/1468798410383251.

Ingold, T. (2012). Toward an ecology of materials. *Annual Review of Anthropology, 41*, 427–442. https://doi.org/10.1146/annurev-anthro-081309-145920.

Kervin, L., Comber, B., Woods, A. (2017). Toward a sociomaterial understanding of writing experiences incorporating digital technology in an Early Childhood classroom. *Literacy Research: Theory, Method, and Practice, 66*(1) 183–197 (2017). https://doi.org/10.1177/2381336917718522.

Kress, G. (1997). *Before writing: Rethinking the paths to literacy.* London: Routledge.

Kuby, C. R. (2014). Understanding emotions as situated, embodied, and fissured: Thinking with theory to create an analytical tool. *International Journal of Qualitative Studies in Education, 27*(10), 1285–1311 (2014). https://doi.org/10.1080/09518398.2013.834390.

Kustatscher, M. (2017). The emotional geographies of belonging: Children's intersectional identities in primary school. *Children's Geographies, 15*(1). 65–79 (2017). https://doi.org/10.1080/14733285.2016.1252829.

Leander, K. M. (2004). Reading the spatial histories of positioning in a classroom literacy event. Spatializing literacy research and practice. In K. Leander & M. Sheehy (Eds.), *Spatializing literacy research and practice* (pp. 115–142). New York: Peter Lang.

Leander, K., & Sheehy, M. (Eds.). (2004). *Spatializing literacy research.* New York: Peter Lang.

Lefebvre, H. (1991). *The production of space* (D. Nicholson-Smith, Trans.). Oxford: Blackwell.

Luke, A. (1992). The body literate: Discourse and inscription in early literacy training. *Linguistics and Education, 4,* 107–129.

Marsh, J. (2016). Cases featuring child agency: Gareth and Ta'von. In A. H. Dyson (Ed.), *Child cultures, schooling and literacy: Global perspectives on children composing their lives* (pp. 17–27). New York: Routledge.

Massey, D. (2005). *For space.* London: Sage.

McLeod, J. (2015). Happiness, wellbeing and self-esteem: Public feelings and educational projects. In K. Wright & J. McLeod (Eds.), *Rethinking youth wellbeing: Critical perspectives* (pp. 179–195). Singapore: Springer. https://doi.org/10.1007/978-981-287-188-6_11.

McLeod, J., & Wright, K. (2015). Inventing youth wellbeing. In K. Wright & J. McLeod (Eds.), *Rethinking youth wellbeing: Critical perspectives* (pp. 1–10). Singapore: Springer. https://doi.org/10.1007/978-981-287-188-6_1.

Ministerial Council on Education, Employment, Training and Youth Affairs (MCEETYA). (2008). *Melbourne Declaration on the Educational Goals for Young People.* Melbourne: Ministerial Council on Education, Employment, Training and Youth Affairs. Retrieved May 22, 2018, from http://www.curriculum.edu.au/verve/_resources/National_Declaration_on_the_Educational_Goals_for_Young_Australians.pdf.

Miller, D. (1987). *Material culture and mass consumption.* Oxford: Blackwell.

Nespor, J. (1997). *Tangled up in school: Politics, space, bodies, and signs in the educational process.* New York: Routledge.

OECD. (2017). *PISA 2015 Results (Volume III): Students' well-being.* Paris: OECD Publishing. Retrieved May 24, 2018, from http://dx.doi.org/10.1787/9789264273856-en.

Rogers, R. (2003). *A critical discourse analysis of family literacy practices: power in and out of print.* New York: Routledge.

Rowsell, J., & Pahl, K. (2011). The material and the situated: What multimodality and new literacy studies do for literacy research. In D. Lapp & D. Fisher (Eds.), *Handbook of research on teaching the English language arts* (pp. 175–181). New York, NY: Routledge.

Soja, E. (2010). *Seeking spatial justice.* Minneapolis: University of Minnesota Press.

Warf, B., & Arias, S. (Eds.). (2009). *The spatial turn: Interdisciplinary perspectives.* London: Routledge.

Promoting Children's Wellbeing and Values Learning in Risky Learning Spaces

Lyndal O'Gorman

Abstract In this chapter, the author disrupts taken-for-granted definitions of learning spaces as she considers spaces that might support children's wellbeing and values learning. She discusses learning spaces as thinking spaces, planning spaces, physical spaces and spaces for children's active citizenship and values learning. Such spaces, whether highly designed or not, offer opportunities for supporting children's wellbeing through risk-taking. Much has been written about the value of learning spaces that support physical risk-taking. In this chapter, the author proposes 'emotional obstacle courses' that support children's social and emotional risk-taking. Risky social and emotional learning spaces offer children opportunities to explore issues such as social justice and sustainability. While such spaces might be risky for educators and children, they may support children's learning to become change agents in a complex world. If educators aim to support the wellbeing of children and societies, then such risks are worth taking.

Introduction

It is important to think carefully about the design of learning spaces if we are going to support children's wellbeing and encourage their learning. However, there are different ways of considering what wellbeing is, and what learning spaces are. In this chapter, I consider examples of planned and unplanned learning spaces that encourage risk-taking on the part of children and educators. Risky spaces hold much potential for deep values learning and active citizenship, enabling them to become agents of change. However, there are tensions to be considered when educators seek to balance physically and emotionally risky learning encounters with concerns about children's wellbeing.

L. O'Gorman (✉)
Queensland University of Technology, Brisbane, QLD 4000, Australia
e-mail: lm.ogorman@qut.edu.au

© Springer Nature Singapore Pte Ltd. 2019
H. Hughes et al. (eds.), *School Spaces for Student Wellbeing and Learning*,
https://doi.org/10.1007/978-981-13-6092-3_3

Defining Wellbeing—Two Schools of Thought

Much has been written about wellbeing—what it is and how it can be supported in learning contexts and elsewhere. In 2001 Ryan and Deci conducted a much-cited review of research relating to the history of theories pertaining to wellbeing, distinguishing two related schools of thought regarding this topic. This represents an important distinction not identified in the psychological literature of the 1960s and 1970s (Heintzelman, 2018). One category labelled *hedonic* wellbeing reflects the perspective 'that well-being consists of pleasure or happiness' (Ryan & Deci, 2001 p. 143). The hedonistic view of wellbeing is applied broadly by modern psychologists, in the sense that it considers pleasure and happiness of the mind, as well as the body. The second category, *eudaimonism*, suggests that wellbeing is about more than happiness, and includes the pursuit of that which is worth doing in life, activities reflecting 'virtue, excellence, the best within us, and the full development of our potentials' (Huta & Waterman, 2014, p. 1427). While these two categories of wellbeing have been discussed at length in the philosophical and psychological literature over several decades, recent commentators such as Heintzelman (2018) report ongoing discussion about whether distinctions between hedonic and eudaimonic wellbeing are necessary. For the purposes of this chapter, I find the distinction to be worthwhile.

Distinguishing between hedonism and eudaimonism is important because there are clear implications in both categories for the approaches that educators might take to the design of learning spaces that support children's wellbeing. Learning spaces that are designed to maximise children's wellbeing in terms of pleasure and happiness might look and feel quite different to learning spaces that are designed to maximise children's wellbeing in relation to the full development of their potential and the pursuit of virtue. Authors over a number of decades (see for example Waterman, 1993; Huta & Ryan, 2010) have expanded the discussion of hedonic versus eudaimonic wellbeing by exploring how eudaimonic wellbeing might be promoted when people's life activities align with their deeply held values. Thus, in relation to the latter position on wellbeing, learning space design ought to be carefully considered in light of how educators might provide opportunities for learners to explore their deeply held values and how they might do 'what is worth doing' on the basis of those values.

Learning Spaces that Support Wellbeing

Learning spaces are much more than arrangements of classroom walls, desks and chairs even though these components might be the first things we think about in the context of designing learning spaces. Taking a broader view of learning spaces in this chapter, I hold that learning spaces can be thinking spaces, planning spaces and spaces for children to learn how to be active citizens in the world; and these can be physical and non-physical learning spaces. Moreover, these spaces can be risky learning spaces, as I will explore later in this chapter. Non-physical learning spaces are just as important—and just as risky—as physical learning spaces. Getting these spaces right is also critical for supporting children's wellbeing, whether we view wellbeing as the achievement of pleasure and happiness, or whether we also seek to support learners to act on their deeply held values.

There is limited worth in carefully planning functional and attractive physical learning spaces, either formal educational spaces or public spaces, if those spaces limit children's opportunities for deep and broad thinking and imagination, for planning their learning in collaboration with their peers and their teacher, and for learning how they can make a difference in the world, both in formal learning contexts and beyond. This sits well with a broad definition of *curriculum*, aligned with that of Connelly and Clandinin (1988) who suggested in their seminal work that *curriculum* means more than a formal learning framework but rather a path followed by the learner; in its broadest sense it represents a person's life experience. This idea of a learning path that children follow is also fundamental to the theories of early childhood philosophers such as Montessori (Emerson & Siraj-Blatchford, 2018). More recently, Rosiek and Clandinin (2015) highlight the complexities and nuances of how the term has moved in the literature beyond the sense of a mandated curriculum to encompass the planned, enacted, assessed, learned, lived, hidden, null and experienced curriculum. Thus, Connelly and Clandinin's early view of curriculum as life experience finds common ground with the eudaimonic category of wellbeing in which enactment of values and finding purpose in life is fundamentally important.

There is much literature about how schools and early childhood centres might support children's wellbeing (for example, IUHPE, 2009; OECD, 2017). Perhaps wellbeing is a precursor to deep engagement with the task of learning. If children are physically safe and well they are more likely to be able to learn effectively (Becker, McClelland, Loprinzi, & Trost, 2014). However, consideration of health and wellbeing must extend beyond aspects related only to the physical (Dyment, Bell, & Green, 2017). We also need to consider children's emotional, mental, social, cultural and spiritual wellbeing and how learning spaces promote values learning and enactment. It is very challenging to think about the types of spaces that can support all of these different aspects of wellbeing and how we might go about designing or indeed *un*designing, such environments.

Non-traditional Learning Environments

We should include in thinking about learning spaces, those environments that are different from traditional classrooms. Non-traditional learning spaces such as the outdoors, museums and galleries are also well positioned to support children's learning and wellbeing.

Outdoor learning environments provide a different type of learning space that provide many benefits for children's wellbeing and values learning. Early childhood education has included a strong focus on outdoor learning environments as foundational for supporting young children's health and wellbeing across physical, social, mental and spiritual dimensions (Dyment et al., 2017; Little, Elliott, & Wyver, 2017). The label *kindergarten* was originally coined by Froebel to describe the natural unfolding of children's development as like a garden. Perhaps continued use of the term to describe early childhood settings in Australia and the US now also serves to illustrate the traditional endorsement of gardens and the outdoors as important learning contexts for children. The national Australian Curriculum for older children also supports the importance of outdoor learning, endorsing natural environments for their capacities to support children's skills, understandings and values with respect to sustainable relationships with nature (ACARA, n.d.).

In certain parts of the world there is a growing movement that is challenging ideas about traditional learning spaces and promoting full-time learning in outdoor environments. Forest schools and outdoor or bush kindergartens are a flourishing phenomenon (Elliott & Chancellor, 2014; Waite, Bølling, & Bentsen, 2016). This movement, having started in northern Europe and extending to countries such as Australia and Japan (O'Gorman, Elliott, Inoue, Ji, Elliot, & Green, 2017) has partially come in response to concerns that modern children are not spending sufficient time in nature or the outdoors. The argument is that this results in a loss of connection with the natural world, reduced physical activity and fewer opportunities for risk-taking. Urbanisation of populations, large houses and small allotments provide fewer opportunities for children to play outside and thus potentially decrease wellbeing (Little et al., 2017). US commentator Louv (2005) coined the term *nature deficit disorder* to virtually pathologise this problem when he discussed the impact of children in Western contexts spending less time in nature. I acknowledge that my commentary in this chapter also emanates from a Western world view. However, I would encourage readers and other commentators to consider that generalisations about children's limited contact with the natural world may not apply in many international contexts.

The outdoors is not the only type of non-traditional learning space. Informal learning spaces that hold the potential to support children's wellbeing also include sites such as museums and galleries. Piscitelli and Penfold (2015) describe the potential of art galleries and museums as places for young children's experiential and active learning. As such, these contexts represent a different kind of learning space. Such spaces can be designed such that collections are curated to enhance public access, with programmes specifically planned, through collaborative partnerships between educational and cultural institutions, to support children's genuine arts and culture education (Piscitelli, 2012). Such experiences might potentially support children's multisensory aesthetic development, social interaction, collaboration, diverse learning styles, empowerment and self-expression These are key components of a learning space conducive to broader, eudaimonic conceptualizations of wellbeing that are inclusive of values enactment.

Risk Supports Wellbeing

It is an interesting paradox that risk-taking opportunities support children's wellbeing. Risk involves events and behaviours and consequences with uncertain outcomes (Aven & Renn, 2009). Adult and institutional concern about risk in children's play has had a detrimental effect on the provision of outdoor play spaces according to commentators such as Little (2017), as societies have become increasingly wary of potential injuries and the possibilities of litigation.

Outdoor learning environments are generally seen as riskier spaces than traditional indoors classrooms, with falls from playground equipment found to be the most common cause of injury at school in a Victorian study (Clapperton, Cassell, & Wallace, 2003). There is much in the literature about the value of children's risk-taking, with most commentary referring to physical risk-taking. And yet, risky play provides many benefits including children having to deal with complex emotions, frustration, change and unexpected outcomes—benefits that extend beyond the obvious physical benefits resulting from running, climbing and balancing (Little, 2017; Sandseter, 2009). Successful negotiation of risky territory thus also potentially supports children's social and emotional wellbeing (Little, 2017) when they are supported by a teacher or more experienced other.

The UN has outlined a number of children's rights, including the right to play and the right for children to express ideas about matters that are important to them (Office of the United Nations High Commissioner for Human Rights, 2017). Children also have a right to experience environments that support their development and quality of life. Wyver et al. (2010) argue that an over-emphasis on risk management on the part of parents and educators impinges on children's rights to learning spaces that support such growth. I suggest that the children's rights discourse might be extended to the argument that children's wellbeing (growth, development and quality of life) is inextricably linked to children's right to take risks within their play.

Outdoor learning environments that support risk-taking may include components that are both planned and unplanned. Planned aspects can include climbing equipment and play structures, while unplanned components could include trees and slopes, along with loose parts such as rocks, sticks and stones (Gibson, Cornell, & Gill, 2017). Risky spaces might also include private, secluded spaces where children can play beyond the scrutiny of adults or teachers (Little, 2017).

When children learn in spaces that are not predesigned by adults, they may have increased opportunities to take risks. Outdoor learning environments early childhood settings aim to encourage children to take risks and manage uncertainties. The Australian birth to five curriculum, *Belonging, being and becoming: The early years learning framework* (DEEWR, 2009) includes the aim that children become confident and involved learners (Outcome 4). The document advocates for play that enhances children's sense of autonomy, interdependence, agency and social and emotional wellbeing. As young children negotiate change, unexpected circumstances and failure, which are aspects they are more likely to encounter in unplanned learning contexts, their wellbeing is ultimately enhanced (DEEWR, 2009). These principles are common to early childhood curricula beyond Australia's borders. For example, the Swedish preschool curriculum advocates a balance between providing a secure environment while encouraging children to negotiate challenges in their play, both in planned and natural environments (Skolverket, 2010). Turning again to the idea of eudaimonic wellbeing, these benefits of challenging and risky play are foundational for self-actualization and values enactment. This requires teachers to make pedagogical choices that enable children to take risks, while actively supporting them through the process of risk-taking and negotiating challenging circumstances. In this chapter, I argue that such circumstances may be both physical and emotional.

Risky play will inevitably result in physical injuries such as cuts and bruises (Sandseter & Sando, 2016). These may not always be considered as negative outcomes, but rather 'part of normal development for children of all abilities' (RoSPA, n.d.). Despite the stated benefits of risky play outlined in this section, an increase in concern for children's safety on the part of governments and parents has led to a reduction in children's freedom to play. If opportunities for children to take risks are reduced, opportunities for children to exercise their right to play are also reduced. Wyver et al. (2010) describe the phenomenon of 'surplus safety' (p. 263) in Australia, the UK and USA and express concern about the consequences of this loss of freedom on children's long-term wellbeing, particularly when there is increased concern about the health impacts of permanently 'safe' environments; impacts that include increased susceptibility to obesity and type II diabetes (Wyver et al., 2010). So, flexible outdoor learning spaces support children's wellbeing by providing opportunities for active learning, physical challenge and risk-taking.

Learning Spaces that Support Social and Emotional Risk-Taking

Flexible learning spaces, whether indoors or outdoors, provide opportunities for children to take social and emotional risks as well as physical risks. Designing learning environments that provide opportunities for children to take physical risks is one thing, but how can educators design learning environments than encourage children to take social and emotional risks? Social risk-taking is essential for negotiating friendships, dealing with moral conflicts, identity development and values learning that encourages social cohesion and the ability to reflect on others' points of view (Lunn Brownlee, Johansson, Walker, & Scholes, 2017)—fundamental requirements for wellbeing that incorporates self-actualization and values enactment. Early childhood is a critical period for developing these social skills.

Children need to learn in environments that provide them with time and space to develop these skills in a supportive context that allows them to take risks in their social play encounters, in the playground, the forest or the classroom. Such environments may feature a combination of play-based and teacher-directed learning encounters, as outlined in the *Early years learning framework* (DEEWR, 2009). In this chapter,

I endorse the position taken by authors such as McArdle and McWilliam (2005), Siraj-Blatchford (2009) and Thomas, Warren and deVries (2011) who challenge the often expressed binary between play and intentional teaching approaches in early childhood discourse. Learning spaces that support collaboration and play are critical for social skill development. Schools and early childhood sites can be complex environments that challenge young children's social and emotional capacities on many levels (Denham & Brown, 2010). Social play encounters inevitably provide children with risky situations that challenge their social and emotional wellbeing on a daily basis. Educators typically focus much of their efforts towards guiding young children though risky emotional spaces. Such spaces may be created when children's values conflict those of their peers and teachers. However, such conflicts can be viewed as a necessary prerequisite for conversations about ethics and for provoking positive change in terms of big issues of justice, rights, responsibility and care (Hagglund & Johansson, 2014).

However, is it possible that educators could further support children's social and emotional risk-taking and values learning by initiating ideas and topics that may challenge children emotionally? In the same way that teachers might intentionally plan an obstacle course to challenge children's motor skills and physical risk-taking, learning spaces could be planned to include 'emotional obstacle courses' that introduce children to confronting global issues such as environmental degradation and social injustice. The appearance of plastic rubbish in a children's playground on a windy day may, for example, lead to a teacher-initiated discussion about global impacts of plastic pollution, extending children's learning beyond the here and now. Hagglund and Johansson (2014) in their discussion of the importance of values conflicts in early childhood education, suggest that it may be necessary to *not* conceal 'the dark side of life' (p. 46) from children.

Perhaps concern about emotional risk has meant that educators generally avoid topics and teachable moments that hold the potential to disturb children's emotional equilibrium. It could be that the phenomenon of 'surplus safety' also applies to emotional risk-taking. This is, in part, because of the strong influence of *developmentally appropriate practice* (DAP) and authors such as Sobel (1996) who present the idea of cognitive readiness regarding when children should be introduced to big issue concerns such as human impacts on natural environments. However, authors such as Ryan and Grieshaber (2004) suggest that teachers' knowledge of child development may not be sufficient in a global, postmodern society. Social justice issues such as child labour and dislocation may be considered by some to be more 'appropriate' for children in upper primary or secondary school. Phillips (2010) challenges this view, arguing that storytelling, for example, can be used to provoke critical awareness of others' positions and thus engage young children as active citizens in response to issues of social justice.

Children enter classrooms with a range of backgrounds and experiences, with access to technologies that have transformed the way people communicate and learn. Perhaps children are more aware of global challenges than they have ever been. I suggest that educators should not pretend that global problems do not exist but rather engage with big issues and encourage children's agency by encouraging them to develop the emotional and agentic tools to respond positively to circumstances that are difficult. Teachers can assist children who are faced with a challenge such as how to navigate playground equipment or to resolve social conflicts. Children may also need the support of a teacher as they navigate emotionally risky situations, whether emergent or teacher-initiated. While it may be true that when children are stressed their disposition for learning is affected negatively, their self esteem lowered and they may become anxious (Chawla, Keena, Pevec, & Stanley, 2014), educators have a responsibility to help children to engage in emotionally risky situations without ignoring the existence of those situations.

When planes flew into the World Trade Centre on 11 September 2001, I was teaching a class of Year One children. I made a decision that day, as thousands of teachers across the world would have done, to talk about the tragedy as soon as I gathered my class together. It was a difficult incident to unpack to 25 5-year old, but the events of that day could not be ignored. And that lesson could not have been carefully planned. The learning space that day was uniquely spontaneous—an unplanned thinking space for contemplating big ideas that those young children had not been required to consider previously—an emotional obstacle course that none of us knew would be arranged for us.

The work of educators is to create thinking spaces and to implement teaching strategies that encourage children's empowerment so that they can grapple with complex ideas and emergent problems. Chawla and Cushing (2007) present a number of practical applications of the concept of 'action competence' (p. 447) within environmental education, where children are actively involved in identifying and addressing environmental problems through political action. Examples of strategies that might encourage action competence include experiencing nature, democratic decision-making, discussing environmental issues and setting goals for success, within the bounds of what is age appropriate for children. Vygotsky's (1978) *zone of proximal development* (ZPD) is the difference between what a learner can do without help and what the learner cannot do. When educators operate within the ZPD, they create space for children to learn to be participants in an increasingly complex world, and their active citizenship builds their sense of wellbeing, mitigating feelings of fear and helplessness and anxiety as outlined by Chawla et al. (2014). I argue that there are times when educators may need to plan learning spaces carefully so that children have opportunities for values enactment in the shape of active citizenship and agentic decision-making (Lunn Brownlee et al., 2017) in response to big issues. This might mean that a skilled educator acts as a careful observer, active listener, clear communicator and co-learner while also carefully introducing ideas that hold the potential to challenge children's emotional capacities. Thus, children might begin to develop the tools to deal with conflict and complexity; to lay the foundations for action competence so that they learn to be empowered agents of change in complex local and global environments.

(Un)Designing Learning Spaces for Children's Wellbeing

If risk is good for children's wellbeing, and physical, emotional and social risk-taking involves unexpected outcomes, then learning environments that support the unexpected might sometimes involve reduced planning on the part of educators. Even outdoor play and learning environments for children, such as school playgrounds, can be dominated by planned spaces such as sports grounds (Dyment et al., 2017). Letting go of the need to always design detailed planning spaces involves a degree of risk on the educators' part. While careful planning can be beneficial, deep learning might also occur in spaces that are not planned in detail.

Perhaps the learning spaces that will best promote children's wellbeing include both designed and undesigned spaces. Considering again Connelly and Clandinin's (1988) broad view of curriculum as a life experience, or a path to follow, can be helpful here. Life is essentially both planned and unplanned; paths can be both predictable and unpredictable. Inclusion of space for profound life experiences such as deep and broad thinking, collaboration, discussion of values and participation in the world, requires decluttering of the formal, planned programme of learning, and, I suggest, reduced emphasis on formal planning and timetabling of children's lives in formal learning contexts. Such spaces may be designed learning spaces, as well as undesigned learning spaces. Undesigned spaces, in particular, are risky spaces because educators are required to let go of their sense of control and to share responsibility with children to design, daily, their own physical, mental, emotional and spiritual learning spaces; their own paths and life experiences. In this sense, teachers move away from their programme planning role to instead become the creator of an environment that is the *third teacher*; an environment that is both stimulating and supportive of children's wellbeing (Edwards & Gandini, 2015). Undesigned learning spaces also present opportunities for risk-taking, both physical and emotional, initiated by both educators and children.

Careful planning of physical learning spaces and of curricula gives educators a sense of security and control, such that they are meeting the needs of the system through their plans. Planning is not all bad, and commentators such as Ryan and Northey-Berg (2014) have explored the 'contested terrain' (p. 204) of play and intentional teaching in early childhood contexts—but planning needs to include flexibility. Flexible learning environments that build on emergent curricula, as described by authors such as Arthur, Beecher, Death, Dockett and Farmer (2014) hold benefits for children's wellbeing. This is because when children are involved in designing their own learning environments they gain a sense of independence, responsibility and agency. As mentioned previously, the UN has determined that it is a fundamental right of children to have a say in matters that are important to them. This means that children should have a right to contribute to the design of their learning spaces—both physical and non-physical. Enabling this right will assist children's physical, social, emotional and spiritual wellbeing and will help prepare them to be active world citizens who can confidently enact their values beyond the classroom.

Learning Spaces for Children's Emotional
Risk-Taking—Agency, Active Citizenship and Sustainability

Sometimes learning spaces might be designed, while at other times they may not. If educators are going to (un)design learning spaces to help children to pursue 'virtue, excellence, the best within us, and the full development of our potentials' (Huta & Waterman, 2014, p. 1427), we need to support them to develop agency, creativity, active citizenship and risk-taking so that they can act on the basis of their deepest values. Here I adopt Lunn Brownlee et al. (2017) definition of active citizenship as 'children experiencing and internalising moral and democratic values, and developing their own opinions and moral responsibility' (p. 3). The world is a dynamic and diverse place. The planet is facing many challenges—environmental, social and political. When educators are designing learning spaces (to a greater or lesser degree), those spaces need to encourage agency, creativity and risk-taking to support children's moral values and responsibilities, which perhaps represents their *moral wellbeing*, in all domains—physical, emotional, social, spiritual. I will now illustrate an example of such a risky space.

Research with children can be a risky space. I am currently undertaking a research project that involves children accessing images of pollution, human consumption and the ways in which nature is affected negatively by human practices (O'Gorman, 2017). The project brings into sharp focus the ways in which the Arts (in this case, digital imagery) can help children to understand complex themes about environmental destruction, human overconsumption, social injustice—ideas that sit under the collective umbrella of sustainability. Arts education and education for sustainability have much in common. They both share potential for critical thinking, imagination, problem solving and transformation (O'Gorman, 2015). Both hold the potential for ethical and moral risk for educators who provide planned and unplanned opportunities for children to respond to complex and confronting ideas and images (O'Gorman, 2017). Sobel (1996), in his book *Beyond ecophobia: Reclaiming the heart in nature education* warns against what he calls *ecophobia*—a fear of ecological problems and the natural world. He argues that if we prematurely ask children to deal with problems beyond their understanding and control, then educators risk distancing them rather than connecting them to nature. Other commentators such as Little et al. (2017) present a different view, describing the benefits of dynamic and spontaneous learning opportunities that can occur when children might find a dead baby bird that has fallen out of a nest in a high tree. Such encounters, according to Little et al., offer possibilities for questions about the perspectives of other species and the moralities of life and death in nature. Such conversations are emotionally risky, but it is an educator's job to navigate such challenging terrain. In response to Sobel's caution against presenting children with problems beyond their understanding and control, should we not work towards increasing children's understanding and enhancing their sense of control, and in so doing help them to establish and articulate their deepest core values? While Davis and Elliott (2014, p. 2) argue that early education that creates either 'worriers' or 'warriors' is inherently wrong, they advocate for approaches that emphasise a critical, participatory orientation towards big issues within environmental education and education for sustainability more broadly.

When educators engage with children in risky learning spaces, they open the door for children to express their views about big issues, and to respond by learning to become agents of change. Learning spaces that support agency are thinking and talking spaces, spaces for ideas to be challenged and for emotions to be felt and expressed. Increased recognition is being given to the importance of encouraging young children's agency and advocacy for social, political and environmental issues (Davis & Elliott, 2014). Risk-taking provides opportunities for questioning, challenge-setting, collaboration, acceptance of failure and celebration of success. Learning spaces should encourage children to work together and to learn from each other. Social learning in school and early childhood learning contexts underpins values relating to active citizenship and social justice. These ideas connect with the notion of cultural wellbeing, which is about belonging and connectedness to people, natural places and cultures (Emery, Miller, West, & Nailon, 2015). If we want children to learn about big issues such as environmental degradation and social injustices and to become active participants in response to those issues, we need to consider carefully the types of learning spaces that will provide opportunities for children to learn about privilege, sharing, equal opportunity, and sustainability.

The well established sociologies of childhood tell us that children are considered as capable and competent members of society (Dahlberg, Moss, & Pence, 2013), and that they are able to address challenges and complexities from which adults may have protected them previously. If we take this view seriously, then this may require educators to challenge our taken-for-granted assumptions about young children, risk-taking, and the learning spaces that we may design for them.

I argue here that educators should not avoid engaging with children about big issues, but rather should consider how they might help children to develop the tools of active citizenship that will enable them to participate positively, with action. But this is risky business for educators. As noted by Hagglund and Johansson (2014), when young children are viewed as having certain rights, and are considered as agents of change for sustainability, it is likely that 'certain questions and dilemmas' (p. 40) may emerge. Such questions and dilemmas might include grappling with how to manage children's engagement with potentially disturbing ideas. One of the key ethical issues encountered in my research involves presenting children with images that are potentially distressing to them. The serendipitous discovery of the dead baby bird, and the subsequent rich conversation, is a different learning encounter, a differently designed learning space, than one in which a teacher might show children pictures of baby birds killed by plastic pollution on that windy day when plastic bags fly into the playground. If we follow through with Hagglund and Johansson's view, then children have the right to see evidence of how humans impact negatively on the natural environment, so that those children can contribute to solutions to these complex problems. Learning encounters that foster the values of democracy, active citizenship and participation in early childhood can be carried forward through the lifespan (Green, 2014).

There are tensions between acknowledging children's capacity for agency and active citizenship and the associated risks of acting on this. Thinking about these issues may provoke us and make us uncomfortable, leaving us with more questions about the planned and unplanned risks of our work with children. Perhaps agency and active citizenship must be prompted by a degree of discomfort. Learning spaces that negotiate uncomfortable ideas rather than avoid them are seriously risky spaces for young children and their teachers, because children's wellbeing should always be at the forefront of our considerations. However, we might be comforted by the longer term view of eudaimonic wellbeing that acknowledges the enactment of values rather than the experience of short term pleasure and happiness.

- Designing learning environments that enable children's exposure to uncomfortable ideas thus risking their emotional wellbeing would be unethical if educators did not, at the same time, encourage children to develop the tools to deal with complex issues. Learning spaces that support the flourishing of children's agency and collaborative problem solving capacities are keys to maintaining children's wellbeing in these risky spaces. Learning spaces can be planned or unplanned to open up possibilities for children to develop creative responses to big issues in collaboration with others. The (un)design of these thinking spaces, planning spaces and spaces for learning to be active participants, world citizens, and solvers of complex problems should balance risk with supporting children's wellbeing. Risky spaces indeed.

Conclusions

In this chapter I have argued that learning spaces that support children's wellbeing are necessarily risky spaces—for children and educators. Learning spaces that challenge children physically, socially and emotionally might be unplanned and unpredictable. However, such spaces provide opportunities for children to gain, through both play and intentional teaching, tools that will help them to become action takers and creative problem solvers. My aim in writing this chapter is to contribute to challenging conversations about the capacities of children for active citizenship, values enactment and agency. While I support the view that children are capable and competent, I endorse Davis and Elliott's (2014) argument that we should not require them to take responsibility for solving the big issues that face the world. Rather, educators have a crucial responsibility to provide children with thinking spaces and planning spaces that prepare them to be active and agentic world citizens. While we might acknowledge children's capacity for creativity and active citizenship, there are associated risks and challenges of designing (or undesigning) learning spaces that respond to this. As educators negotiate this balancing act there may be value in reconsidering the links between wellbeing and pressing global imperatives. In the words of Ryan and Deci (2001, p. 161)

Perhaps the concern of greatest importance, not only for psychological theorists, but also for humanity, is the study of the relations between personal well-being and the broader issues of the collective wellness of humanity and the wellness of the planet. It is clear that, as individuals pursue aims they find satisfying or pleasurable, they may create conditions that make more formidable the attainment of well-being by others. An important issue, therefore, concerns the extent to which factors that foster individual well-being can be aligned or made congruent with factors that facilitate wellness at collective or global levels.

I argue that if educators aim to create learning spaces that support the wellbeing of children and societies, then the risks outlined in this chapter are worth taking—not just for children who inhabit the learning spaces we work in now—but for all children who share the planet, now and into the future.

Implications for Designing Spaces for Wellbeing

- Learning spaces must support children's wellbeing by providing them with opportunities for deep and broad thinking and imagination, for planning their learning in collaboration with their peers and their teacher and for learning how they can make a difference in the world. What might such learning spaces look like?
- In this chapter I have argued that risk supports wellbeing and that children have the right to take risks in supportive learning spaces. Educators ought to consider how to support children's risk-taking; physical, social and emotional. Planning for emotional risk-taking is a complex business, and educators need to consider how best to do this. By supporting children's exploration of ideas and topics that may challenge them emotionally, educators might lay the foundations for children to develop their potential as agents of change.
- Perhaps the learning spaces that will best promote children's wellbeing are those that included both designed and *un*designed spaces. Inclusion of space for profound life experiences such as deep and broad thinking, collaboration, discussion of values and participation in the world, may require decluttering of the formal, planned programme of learning, and reduced emphasis on formal planning and timetabling of children's lives in formal learning contexts. Such spaces consider the environment, both stimulating and supportive, as children's third teacher.
- In this chapter I take the view that wellbeing involves 'doing what is worth doing'. Therefore, children's values learning, and their wellbeing might be enhanced by involving them in challenging conversations about global issues. If teachers view children as capable and agentic, then conversations about big issues and how even very young children can address those issues, are essential.
- If educators aim to create learning spaces that support the wellbeing of children and societies, they need to consider not just children who inhabit current and local learning spaces, but all children who share the planet, now and into the future.

References

Arthur, L., Beecher, B., Death, E., Dockett, S., & Farmer, S. (2014). *Programming and planning in early childhood settings* (6th edn.). South Melbourne, Vic: Cengage.

Australian Curriculum Assessment and Reporting Authority (ACARA). (n.d.). Outdoor learning. Retrieved June 2, 2018, from https://www.australiancurriculum.edu.au/resources/curriculum-connections/portfolios/outdoor-learning/.

Aven, T., & Renn, O. (2009). On risk defined as an event where the outcome is uncertain. *Risk Research, 12*(1), 1–11.

Becker, D., McClelland, M., Loprinzi, P., & Trost, S. (2014). Physical activity, self-regulation, and early academic achievement in preschool children. *Early Education and Development, 25,* 56–70.

Chawla, L., & Cushing, D. (2007). Education for strategic environmental behaviour. *Environmental Education Research, 13*(4), 437–452. https://doi.org/10.1080/13504620701581539.

Chawla, L., Keena, K., Pevec, I., & Stanley, E. (2014). Green schoolyards as havens from stress and resources for resilience in childhood and adolescence. *Health and Place, 28,* 1–13. https://doi.org/10.1016/j.healthplace.2014.03.001.

Clapperton, A., Cassell, E., & Wallace, A. (2003, Summer). Injury to children aged 5–15 years at school. *Hazard, 53,* 1–16.

Connelly, F., & Clandinin, D. (1988). *Teachers as curriculum planners: Narratives of experience.* New York: Teachers College Press.

Dahlberg, G., Moss, P., & Pence, A. (2013). *Beyond quality in early childhood education and care: Languages of evaluation.* Oxon, UK: Routledge.

Davis, J., & Elliott, S. (2014). Introduction. In J. Davis & S. Elliott (Eds.), *Research in early childhood education for sustainability: International perspectives and provocations* (pp. 1–17). Oxon, UK: Routledge.

Denham, S., & Brown, C. (2010). "Plays nice with others": Social–emotional learning and academic success. *Early Education and Development, 21*(5), 652–680.

Department of Education Employment and Workplace Relations (DEEWR). (2009). *Belonging, being & becoming: The early years learning framework for Australia.* Canberra, A.C.T: Department of Education, Employment and Workplace Relations for the Council of Australian Governments. Retrieved June 2, 2018, from https://docs.education.gov.au/documents/belonging-being-becoming-early-years-learning-framework-australia.

Dyment, J., Bell, A., & Green, M. (2017). Green outdoor environments: Settings for promoting children's health and well-being. In H. Little, S. Elliott, & S. Wyver (Eds.), *Outdoor learning environments: Spaces for exploration, discovery and risk-taking in the early years* (pp. 38–58). Crows Nest, NSW: Allen & Unwin.

Edwards, C., & Gandini, L. (2015). Teacher research in Reggio Emilia, Italy: Essence of a dynamic, evolving role. *Voices of Practitioners: Teacher Research in Early Childhood Education, 10*(1), 89–103.

Elliott, S., & Chancellor, B. (2014). From forest preschool to Bush Kinder: An inspirational approach to preschool provision in Australia. *Australasian Journal of Early Childhood, 39*(4), 45–53.

Emerson, S., & Siraj-Blatchford, J. (2018). The legacy of Maria Montessori. In D. Boyd, N. Hirst, & J. Siraj-Blatchford (Eds.), *Understanding sustainability in early childhood education* (pp. 139–158). London, UK: Routledge.

Emery, S., Miller, K., West, V., & Nailon, D. (2015). Supporting children's cultural wellbeing through arts based education. *The Social Educator, 33*(3), 42–53.

Gibson, J., Cornell, M., & Gill, T. (2017). A systematic review of research into the impact of loose parts play on children's cognitive, social and emotional development. *School Mental Health, 9,* 295–309. https://doi.org/10.1007/s12310-017-9220-9.

Green, M. (2014). Transformational design literacies: Children as active place-makers. *Children's Geographies, 12*(2), 189–204.

Hagglund, S., & Johansson, E. (2014). Belonging, value conflicts and children's rights in learning for sustainability in early childhood. In J. Davis & S. Elliott (Eds.), *Research in early childhood education for sustainability: International perspectives and provocations* (pp. 38–48). Oxon, UK: Routledge.

Heintzelman, S. (2018). Eudaimonia in the contemporary science of subjective well-being: Psychological well-being, self-determination, and meaning in life. In E. Diener, S. Oishi, & L. Tay (Eds.), *Handbook of well-being*. Salt Lake City, UT: DEF Publishers.

Huta, V., & Ryan, R. (2010). Pursuing pleasure or virtue: The differential and overlapping well-being benefits of hedonic and eudaimonic motives. *Journal of Happiness Studies, 11*(6), 735–762.

Huta, V., & Waterman, A. (2014). Eudaimonia and its distinction from hedonia: Developing a classification and terminology for understanding conceptual and operational definitions. *Journal of Happiness Studies, 15,* 1425–1456.

International Union for Health Promotion and Education (IUHPE). (2009). *Achieving health promoting schools: Guidelines for promoting health in schools*. Cedex, France: IUHPE.

Little, H. (2017). Risk-taking in outdoor play: Challenges and possibilities. In H. Little, S. Elliott, & S. Wyver (Eds.), *Outdoor learning environments: Spaces for exploration, discovery and risk-taking in the early years*. Crows Nest, NSW: Allen & Unwin.

Little, H., Elliott, S., & Wyver, S. (2017). Why do outdoor play and learning matter? In H. Little, S. Elliott, & S. Wyver (Eds.), *Outdoor learning environments: Spaces for exploration, discovery and risk-taking in the early years*. Crows Nest, NSW: Allen & Unwin.

Louv, R. (2005). *Last child in the woods: Saving our children from nature-deficit disorder*. Chapel Hill, NC: Algonquin Books.

Lunn Brownlee, J., Johansson, E., Walker, S., & Scholes, L. (2017). *Teaching for active citizenship: Moral values and personal epistemology in early years classrooms*. Oxon, UK: Routledge.

McArdle, F., & McWilliam, E. (2005). From balance to blasphemy: Shifting metaphors for researching early childhood education. *International Journal of Qualitative Studies in Education, 18*(3), 323–336.

OECD. (2017). *Starting strong 2017: Key OECD indicators on early childhood education and care*. Paris: OECD Publishing. https://doi.org/10.1787/9789264276116-en.

Office of the United Nations High Commissioner for Human Rights. (2017). *Convention on the rights of the child*. Retrieved June 2, 2018, from http://www.ohchr.org/EN/ProfessionalInterest/Pages/CRC.aspx.

O'Gorman, L. (2015). Early learning for sustainability through the arts. In J. Davis (Ed.), *Young children and the environment: Early education for sustainability* (2nd ed., pp. 209–224). Port Melbourne, Vic: Cambridge University Press.

O'Gorman, L. (2017). Sustainability, the Arts and big numbers: The challenge of researching children's responses to Chris Jordan's images. *International Journal of Early Childhood*. https://doi.org/10.1007/s13158-017-0199-z.

O'Gorman, L., Elliott, S., Inoue, M., Ji, O., Elliot, E., & Green, C. (2017, September). International perspectives on early childhood education for sustainability in the Asia-Pacific. Poster session presented at the World Environmental Education Congress. Vancouver, CAN.

Phillips, L. (2010). Social justice storytelling and young children's active citizenship. *Discourse: Studies in the Cultural Politics of Education, 31*(3), 363–376. https://doi.org/10.1080/01596301003786993.

Piscitelli, B. (2012). Young children, the arts and learning: Outside of school, at home and in the community. In S. Wright (Ed.), *Children, meaning-making and the arts* (2nd ed., pp. 158–176). Frenchs Forest, NSW: Pearson.

Piscitelli, B., & Penfold, L. (2015). Child-centered practice in museums: Experiential learning through creative play at the Ipswich Art Gallery. *Curator, 58*(3), 263–280.

Rosiek, J., & Clandinin, D. (2015). Curriculum and teacher development. In D. Wyse, L. Hayward, & J. Pandya (Eds.), *The SAGE handbook of curriculum, pedagogy and assessment* (pp. 293–308). Los Angeles, CA: Sage.

The Royal Society for the Prevention of Accidents (RoSPA). (n.d.) *Play safety*. Retrieved June 2, 2018, from https://www.rospa.com/play-safety/.

Ryan, R., & Deci, E. (2001). On happiness and human potentials: A review of research on hedonic and eudaimonic well-being. *Annual Review of Psychology, 52*, 141–166.

Ryan, S., & Northey-Berg, K. (2014). Professional preparation for a pedagogy of play. In L. Brooker, M. Blaise, & S. Edwards (Eds.), *SAGE handbook of play and learning in early childhood* (pp. 204–215). London, UK: Sage.

Ryan, S., & Grieshaber, S. (2004). It's more than child development: Critical theories, research, and teaching young children. *YC Young Children, 59*(6), 44–52.

Sandseter, E. (2009). Characteristics of risky play. *Journal of Adventure Education and Outdoor Learning, 9*(1), 3–21.

Sandseter, E., & Sando, O. (2016). "We don't allow children to climb trees": How a focus on safety affects Norwegian children's play in early-childhood education and care settings. *American Journal of Play, 8*(2), 178–200.

Siraj-Blatchford, I. (2009). Quality teaching in early years. In A. Anning, J. Cullen, & M. Fleer (Eds.), *Early childhood education: Society & culture* (pp. 147–157). London: Sage.

Skolverket. (2010). *Curriculum for the preschool Lpfö 98*. Retrieved June 2, 2018, from http://www.ibe.unesco.org/curricula/sweden/sw_ppfw_2010_eng.pdf.

Sobel, D. (1996). *Beyond ecophobia: Reclaiming the heart in nature education*. Great Barrington, MA: Orion Society.

Thomas, L., Warren, E., & deVries, E. (2011). Play-based learning and intentional teaching in early childhood contexts. *Australasian Journal of Early Childhood, 36*(4), 69–75.

Vygotsky, L. (1978). *Mind in society: The development of higher psychological processes*. Cambridge, MA: Harvard University Press.

Waite, S., Bølling, M., & Bentsen, P. (2016). Comparing apples and pears?: A conceptual framework for understanding forms of outdoor learning through comparison of English Forest Schools and Danish udeskole. *Environmental Education Research, 22*(6), 868–892. https://doi.org/10.1080/13504622.2015.1075193.

Waterman, A. (1993). Two conceptions of happiness: Contrasts of personal expressiveness (eudaimonia) and hedonic enjoyment. *Journal of Personal Social Psychology, 64*, 678–691.

Wyver, S., Tranter, P., Naughton, G., Little, H., Sandseter, E., & Bundy, A. (2010). Ten ways to restrict children's freedom to play: The problem of surplus safety. *Contemporary Issues in Early Childhood, 11*(3), 263–277. https://doi.org/10.2304/ciec.2010.11.3.263.

School Design and Wellbeing: Spatial and Literary Meeting Points

Kerry Mallan

Abstract In many works of fiction for young people, school settings often play a significant part in staging the interactions between characters, child and adult alike. Schools and children's literature share common characteristics: both are created by adults for children; both serve a socialising and pedagogical function; and both are highly responsive to cultural and technological change. As children's literature's implied audience is the child reader who is experiencing school in all its variant aspects, it is then important to consider how fiction represents the idea of the school as both space and place, and the insights (and lessons) it offers in terms of transformative possibilities either through constructions of fantastic or realistic school settings, or implied through negative examples. Drawing on the influential studies of spatiality by Henri Lefebvre and Michel de Certeau, and interdisciplinary research, this chapter considers the extent to which a selection of contemporary texts for young people gives an imaginative form to the spatial practices of school that research documents. By drawing together two modes of knowing—the 'real' and the imaginary—this chapter shows how each plays an important part in understanding how design and affect impact on children's wellbeing and their experience of school life.

Introduction

In the tradition of fiction, as well as in popular culture, children and school are inextricably linked. 'School' is a topic about which children and adults talk, read and write, and many child characters become memorable for the part they play in stories about school. Tom Brown, Harry Potter, Madeleine, Matilda, and countless other characters demonstrate the nexus between young people and school in fiction from the eighteenth century to today. Adults too, figure in these fictions fulfilling various disciplinary, supportive, instructive, and ancillary roles (such as school cleaners,

K. Mallan (✉)
Queensland University of Technology, Brisbane, Australia
e-mail: k.mallan@qut.edu.au

© Springer Nature Singapore Pte Ltd. 2019
H. Hughes et al. (eds.), *School Spaces for Student Wellbeing and Learning*,
https://doi.org/10.1007/978-981-13-6092-3_4

canteen workers, and so on). Often the student-teacher relationship is antagonistic (Harry Potter and Severus Snape); sometimes the relationship is one of mutual affection (Matilda and Miss Honey). While children grow up and leave behind the imaginary places of fiction, school as a physical and remembered site remains, as research by Miller and Shifflet (2016, p. 21) attests: 'recollections of school are stored for years and may have long-term implications'. Schools also ensure that memory of their past is commemorated through symbol and language—school name, emblems, mottos and anthems—as well as through their architecture, design and iconography. It is through such symbolic and narrative investment that school as a 'place' becomes a collection of spaces, and social practices within these spaces become a mode of daily existence comprising movements, understandings and social and power relations (Mallan, 2001). For Lefebvre (1991) and de Certeau (1984) spatial practices delineate everyday acts, often taken for granted, that serve to define and characterise a space.

Schools, and their fictional representations, express their hierarchical structure, disciplinary control, and function through spaces that delineate zones of activity (sport, teaching, play), spaces that restrict entry (teachers' staffroom, sick room, toilets), and spaces that are out of bounds. School spaces (classroom, playground, staff room, foyer, hallways, laboratories, sports fields, toilets) are constructed according to time, use and purpose. These spaces are highly visible, and typically ensure that the patterns and flows of behaviour and movement in the institutional space are clearly known, made known, and observable. The increased presence of technology in schools makes tracking and surveillance more effective for both those inside and outside the school grounds; it also ensures a different kind of spatial pedagogy. All these features are taken up in this chapter.

By conceptualising school space in terms of complex interacting social and power relations, space inevitably becomes contested as 'both individuals and social groups are constantly engaged in efforts to territorialise, to claim spaces, to include some and exclude others from particular areas' (Massey, 1998, p. 126). While individual teachers and students inflect space with their own embodied presence, how interior and exterior spaces are temporally organised, designed and used gives insight into the dynamics of school life, and the meaning and affect it has for those who inhabit it. Integral to the dynamics is how the ambience of the learning environment affects student wellbeing across personal, cognitive, social, moral and academic domains (Clement, 2010).

In *Space and Place: The Perspective of Experience,* Yi-Fu Tuan suggests: 'Feelings and intimate experiences are inchoate and unmanageable to most people, but writers and artists have found ways of giving them form' (1977, p. 202). Henri Lefebvre in *The Production of Space* gives a similar acknowledgment by contrasting official *representations of space*, which carry the sanction of government authority, with *spaces of representation* generated through image and metaphor in the work of artists and writers.[1] For Lefebvre, the 'spaces of representation' with their symbolic and emotionally-infused elements are more apt to embody the 'clandestine or underground side of social life' (1991, p. 33), and, as we shall see, they also capture the secret or subversive side of school life. Thus for Lefebvre there is a dynamic at play between the socially mandated representations of space and the metaphorical, imagistic and emotionally charged lived spaces that we read about in fiction. Such a dynamic is central to this chapter.

My intention is to show how a selection of children's literature gives an imaginative form to the spatial practices of school life that research documents. By drawing together the two modes of knowing—the 'real' and the imaginary—I hope to show that each plays an important part in understanding how design and affect impact on children's wellbeing and their experience of school life. In developing this connection, the discussion draws on examples from research, personal experience and children's literature to consider: the interior spatial design of classrooms and how this shapes the interactions between teachers and students; the exterior spaces that transcend school buildings; and technological spaces that control the flow and movement inside and outside classrooms/schools as well as enable smart connected learning. Examples from children's literature include early children's literature as well as contemporary examples from an international selection.

The chapter covers a wide time span but the purpose is not to give a comprehensive account. Rather, it is to offer selective instances. To frame the discussion, the following section provides a brief overview of how school spaces and children's literature have tracked together during key social and educational changes particularly, in the UK and Australia, and the part that architectural design and pedagogy have played and continue to play in shaping the school environment and the spatial practices that emerge.

A Spatial and Literary History of School Design: UK and Australia

The spatial history of school design in Australia reflects the Australian geographical, social, and cultural environment. It is also derived from the spatial histories and educational reforms from Britain and to a lesser extent, the United States (Healy & Darian-Smith, 2015). During the Victorian era, schools in England gradually moved away from a tradition of domestic instruction that dated back to Rousseau's *Émile, or On Education* (1762), with its experiential approach to childhood and education, to an increasingly institutionalised form. Elizabeth Gargano notes that the rapid institutionalisation of education and the shrinking of domestic instruction gave rise to the question of 'who had the right to define and shape the experience of childhood, and

---

[1] 'Lefebvre's parallel syntax emphasises the parallel and complementary functions of his terms' (Gargano, 2008, p. 165).

where that process of definition would take place' (2008, p. 1). Alongside the competing agendas over the changing spatial terrain of childhood, novelists added their own stories 'depicting the space of school as a divisive, segmented, and conflicted site' (Gargano, p. 1). Gargano notes that at the beginning of the nineteenth century, England did not have a national system of schools, education was not compulsory and there was no standardised curriculum. However, by the end of the century all three elements were in place, albeit with separate spheres of instruction for boys and girls. The differentiated curriculum saw the teaching of domestic arts for girls and military drills for boys and showed how biology determined the course of a child's education, and future service to home and country.

Accompanying these dramatic shifts was a diverse array of school narratives, for both mainstream and child readers, that either gave glowing accounts of school life such as Evelyn Sharp's *The Making of a Schoolgirl* (1897) or showed school as a conflicted space, as memorably portrayed in *Tom Brown's Schooldays* (1857) by Thomas Hughes, which emphasised the public school's role in character building above all else. Stories such as these were to retain a significant influence on school stories for many years to come. For example, Galway (2012) argues that J.K. Rowling's use of traditional elements of the nineteenth-century school story, especially Hughes' novel, is clearly evident in the Harry Potter books. A significant figure in both the Harry Potter series and *Tom Brown's Schooldays* is the bully (Malfoy and Flashman respectively): a character who causes his victims to suffer his taunts and mistreatments in silence. However, both texts show how the institutional space (Rugby and Hogwarts) can also foster positive values (bravery, loyalty, honesty) and afford a developing sense of personal wellbeing for its protagonists, through the course of their maturation and acculturation into school life.

Australia followed a similar trajectory as Britain, moving from a home-based model of instruction to a more institutionalised one. However, early purpose-built school buildings were like houses ('school houses'): 'often built at the scale and in the style of a house', comprising one or two rooms with little adornment (Willis, 2014, p. 140). As Julie Willis explains, these early school houses were in place before the advent of universal compulsory primary schooling at the end of the nineteenth century. However, as the states began to provide funding for school education, the construction of larger and more imposing school buildings, especially in urban areas, expanded into the twentieth century as changing social expectations towards education prompted an increase in enrolment.

Australia did not have a national curriculum until 2014, and its states have always been responsible for their school design.[2] Willis documents significant features of the early twentieth-century schools which tended to include a hall space running down

---

[2]While states still develop their own standardised designs for school buildings, a significant change occurred in 2009 when the *Nation Building—Economic Stimulus Plan* committed substantial funds to modernise Australian school facilities through the Building the Education Revolution program.

Fig. 1 Marburg State School, Ipswich (Queensland, Australia) built circa 1920s (Picture Ipswich)

the centre of the building, with individual classrooms opening on to it, and toilets and cloakrooms placed near the entrances. The style of architecture also reflected the climatic conditions of the state. For example, Victoria employed the red-brick Federation style of architecture, whereas Queensland commonly had elevated timber buildings on elongated stumps which created a usable and shaded place underneath the buildings, and often featured encircling verandahs, louvres, and lightweight timber construction to allow ventilation (see Fig. 1). The state-based approach to design, therefore took account of geographical location (urban, rural, remote), varied climate, size of school population, and differing student needs (primary, secondary, special, technical). Furthermore, as with England, the designs of state schools differed from those adopted by private or Catholic schools.

Early children's books not only reflected the school space as home or institution, but also clearly designated these spaces as gendered, classed and white, resulting in marginalisation and emotional stress for many students. The discursive representation of school space in these early stories rarely featured Indigenous or migrant children. This absence continued well into the middle of the twentieth century. Stories targeting boy readers combined school and adventure, or focused on the micro-politics of boarding schools with boy protagonists engaged variously in: retrieving stolen precious items, outwitting cruel teachers, being bullied by other students, and gaining eventual recognition for heroic and manly behaviour [see for example: *The Boys of*

Springdale, or, The Strength of Patience by Richardson (1875); *The Black Star: A School Story for Boys* by Walpole (1925)]. While girls' school stories also featured girls moving out of the school to engage in minor adventures [*Sheila the Prefect* by Pyke (1923)], there was a significant number that used the genre as a vehicle for moral education and the value of self-sacrifice and humility [*A Very Naughty Girl* by Meade (1901); *Nellie Doran: A Story of Australian Home and School Life* by Agatha (1914)].[3] These imaginative representations of school life illustrate the varied, affective nature of spatial practices. While students generally conduct themselves in ways that conform to the mandated spatial behaviours expected of them, they also enact contrasting practices that covertly express their defiance to rules that are specific to the spatial realm of the school. This dynamic interplay between spatial modalities aligns with Lefebvre's thinking that official representations of space can coexist with spaces of representation, that is, those practices that are marginalised and covert (such as rule breaking) and operate outside of official norms (1991). For male protagonists, these non-normative activities often assisted them in achieving a sense of belonging with their peers. By contrast, the rebellious spirit of female characters often resulted in their being chastened and learning the error of their ways.

As this brief selection implies, school stories largely used the school as a trope and a focal point that brings the various characters together, but it was also the point of departure as often the narrative moved into the extra-school spaces of the bush, coastline or surrounding urban or rural locales for the major plot events. Nevertheless, school buildings and the classrooms they accommodated were a pervasive influence in shaping the lives of the characters and their interactions with one another. Stories that relied less on the extra-curricular adventures of their protagonists and more on the internal dynamics of the classrooms and boarding schools provide insights into how changing educational practices were reflected in and through architectural design. The following sections take up these evolving spatial histories and discourses with consideration as to how the school environment impacts student wellbeing.

School Environment and Wellbeing: Disciplinary and Heterotopic Spaces

The large enrolments in schools and in many cases the inadequate size of classrooms to accommodate large numbers of students became a feature of education in both England and Australia beginning at the end of the nineteenth century and through to the mid-twentieth century—and beyond in some places. How to discipline students became a prime concern, especially when the teacher was outnumbered by students. The monitor system was a means by which students and adult teacher assistants could watch other students and assist in the maintenance of classroom discipline

---

[3]These early Australian titles and more are available in full text from *AustLit: Children's Literature Digital Resources* https://www-austlit-edu-au.ezp01.library.qut.edu.au/austlit/page/5960611.

Fig. 2 Monitors stand on watch over students, circa 1910 (Ruth Hollick Collection, State Library of Victoria)

(see Fig. 2). This close surveillance of students while they worked is a significant feature of the disciplinary regime of most classrooms.

In *Discipline and Punish* (1977), Michel Foucault considers enclosure and partitioning as two aspects of disciplinary space. Classrooms from their early beginnings and up to the 1960s were (and continue to be for the most part) rectilinear, enclosed spaces that are self-contained (or partitioned off by folding doors as in Fig. 2), and defined by certain everyday routines, drills and movements. Gargano explains that 'the linear and orderly arrangement of desks, ordained by both teacher and architect, reflects a contemporary spatial practice, reinforcing the schoolroom's orderly and regulated domain' (2008, p. 24). Just as importantly, spatial practices are also about regulating student behaviour through 'collective movements, rote recitations, and enforced silence' (Gargano, p. 25). The spatial practices reflect the hierarchy of authority and differential power relations in classrooms and demonstrate the strong partnership between traditional classroom design and prevailing pedagogy.

Foucault also considers 'coercion in teaching' as an embedded feature of classroom space, which he argues was brought about 'with the introduction of a standardized education' (1977, p. 184). However, students are not always docile bodies and, as alluded to above, numerous fictions invite us to consider students' resistance to adult strictures and control in both covert and overt ways. This point of coercion and resistance is given mild expression in the picture book, *What Was the War Like, Grandma?* (Tonkin, 1995) which recalls through the reminiscences of the eponymous Grandma an Australian childhood during World War II:

(a)   **(b)**

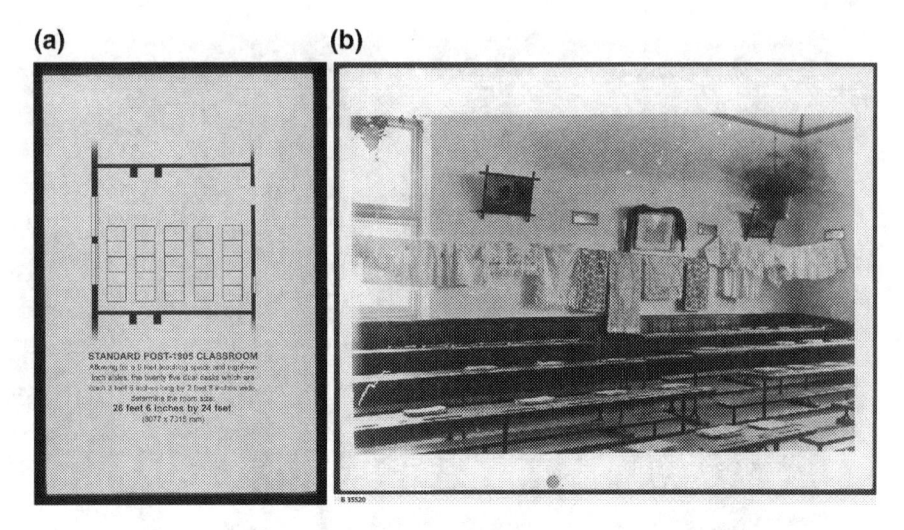

Fig. 3 **a** Standard Post-1905 classroom (State Library of Victoria) b **Restricted classroom space circa 1920s** (State Library of South Australia)

> Most teachers were women or old men as the young men had enlisted. We had seventy pupils in our class. The desks were crammed so closely together that our new teacher wouldn't squeeze between them. When we were naughty all he could do was throw chalk and dusters at us, but mostly we tried to be good because of the war (unpaged).

As this excerpt illustrates, both teacher and students were held hostage by the spatial limits of the overcrowded classroom. *What Was the War Like, Grandma?* vividly captures the standard post-1905 classroom in Australia. Figure 3a illustrates the standard classroom dimensions, and Fig. 3b is a photographic record of typical arrangement and style of classroom desks and seats (forms) from the beginning of the twentieth century to mid-1950s which were designed to maximise control over space with little room for movement, and no flexibility.

The 1960s and 1970s marked a turning point in the philosophical approach of curriculum, school design, and organisational structure in Australia and other parts of the world. Influenced by vocal critics such as Freire (1970), Illich (1971), and the earlier educational philosopher Maria Montessori, these changes argued for a more progressive education which harked back to earlier approaches that embraced child-centredness, freedom, self-discovery and a breaking down of entrenched hierarchies and power inequalities (McLeod, 2014). While these philosophies of progressive and radical education were not taken up universally, they nevertheless provided the impetus for change in many schools across the world. There continue to be examples of 'classrooms without walls' which offer an alternative, and community schools despite the increasing demands of accountability, standardised curriculums, and benchmarking.

In her research on how progressive thinking has shaped alternative school design and spatial setting, Julie McLeod notes that a key underpinning was the promise to 'liberate students from the confines of the classroom and the constraints of institutionalisedlearning' (2014, p. 174). To achieve this purpose, schools (often in collaboration with local communities and architects) variously occupied community buildings, and designed innovative open-planned and purpose-built classrooms that afforded flexibility and utility. These new learning spaces reflected an aesthetic and an impression that was 'not-like school' (pp. 174–5). McLeod draws on Foucault's idea of heterotopia to explain how these not-like schools exist within and alongside more traditional schools.

Unlike utopias, heterotopias are real places 'designed into the very institution of society', yet they are 'utterly different from all the emplacements that they reflect or refer to' (Foucault, 1998, p. 178). Heterotopias contain an ordering which marks them out as different and as an example of 'an alternative way of doing things' (Hetherington, 1997, p. viii). For Foucault, the idea of a heterotopia was as an escape—'an escape from the norms and structures that imprison human subjects and their desires to flourish in their heterogeneity and difference' (Mallan, 2009, p. 179). In the following examples drawn from a nature kindergarten in Norway and children's literature we can see how this kind of escape or departure from the more restrictive enclosures and routines that mark the normal spatial practices in schools is realised. They also support Clement's findings (2010) regarding the value of motivation and engagement in learning as key contributors to student wellbeing.

Nature Schools

Nature school is a generic term for alternative schools, normally kindergartens or preschools that use the natural environment as the 'classroom'. Sometimes referred to as 'forest schools' or 'outdoor schools' in Europe, or 'bush schools' in Australia, these spaces embrace a philosophy of using the natural environment as a place of learning, play and interaction, which can be traced back to the influence of Rousseau's eighteenth century educational treatise *Émile*. Rousseau's philosophy rested on the belief that children should be free to develop at their own rate and learn by discovery. His work has its critics, but it has seemed to be the inspiration for radical experiments in child rearing that seek a transformation of human society through an education that is 'as close to nature as it is possible to attain in the world as we now find it' (Parry, 2006, p. 249). One example of a nature kindergarten that I have visited is

Langøy Friluftsbarnehage in north-west Norway.[4] This is a private kindergarten that caters for children aged 1–6 years.[5]

Outdoor play has a long tradition in kindergartens and preschools in many countries. However, Norwegian preschools tend to spend at least 70% of the day outdoors during summer semester, and about 31% during the winter semester (Lysklett & Berger, 2016). At Langøy Friluftsbarnehage, children and staff spend most of the day outdoors regardless of the weather and temperature. Langøy Friluftsbarnehage comprises a relatively small, multi-level building that is designed to follow the contour of the small ridge on which it sits. When one steps inside the building there are familiar features which signify its use by young children—child-size toilets, a cloak rack, but there are no formal classroom spaces that one often sees in kindergartens. There is a small gymnasium with minimal equipment, a science room which has some tables and chairs and cases of specimens and books. The gym and the science rooms are integrated spaces inside the building and are used only when the weather is extremely cold or the children's clothes have become soaked by rain. The flow of movement within the internal space is unrestricted and there are no designated signs which demarcate a 'teachers only' area.

Outside the main building there is a barbeque cabin with built-in power (Fig. 4). There is a fire pit in the centre of the space and heating cables under the floor. The teacher explained during our visit that the children will come in and warm themselves on extremely cold days but would then go outside within 15 min to continue with their play.

The kindergarten also has a farm that is home to sheep, chickens and ducks and it is the children's responsibility to ensure that the animals are given food and water every day, as well as keep the animal cottage clean. During the lambing season, children witness the birth and sometimes the death of lambs that are too weak to survive. They also supplement the feeding of the new-born lambs with bottles of milk.

In addition to an open-air barbeque garden and a big tumble space with an assortment of outdoor play items, there is the children's construction site which contains 500 lafta wooden boards of different sizes and designed for easy assemblage (Fig. 5).

The kindergarten has its own seaside house and three boats (including a pirate ship), a transparent canoe and kayaks.[6] To get to the lake the children walk down a steep gravel slope (Fig. 6). While I stumbled on the slippery slope and over the wet rocks, the children (aged two to three years) were confident and sure-footed

---

[4]My visit was part of a research project, Nature in Children's Literature (NaChiLit) conducted through the Western Norway University of Applied Science (https://www.hvl.no/en/research/group/nachilit/).

[5]Norway has approximately equal numbers of private (53%) and public (47%) preschools (Lysklett & Berger, 2016, p. 96).

[6]All kindergarten employees have updated life-saving certificates, and the children must wear their own life-jackets when near the water.

Fig. 4 The red wood barbeque cabin (Author)

as they played bringing water in buckets, making shell and rock constructions, and taking turns in paddling the canoe with a staff member who helped guide the canoe with a long rope. The children spend time on the boats fishing and dissect the fish to understand the anatomy before taking the fish home where it becomes part of the family meal. Negotiating rough terrain and having opportunities to meet physical challenges are all part of the 'risky play' that the teachers view as important for children's development. Research has shown that compared with standardised playgrounds, children find the natural environment a more exciting place to play and explore, and one that offers more intense and varied physical activities (Lysklett & Berger, 2016). Importantly, the approach at Langøy Friluftsbarnehage supports the emotional, psychological and social wellbeing of the children by promoting confidence, a sense of autonomy, resilience and good relationships among the school community.

Working in a nature preschool requires a different kind of pedagogy and teacher-student interaction than one normally finds with traditional preschool settings. Lysklett and Berger's research into outdoor activities in Norwegian nature preschools reveal the following findings:

- staff highlight the flexibility (of time and activity) and freedom that they and the children have when they are away from buildings for the majority of the day;
- children come to respect 'invisible fences, borders and waiting areas' when they are in the woods or down by the lake;
- trust and responsibility between children and staff are fundamental to the organisation of the daily activities (2016, pp. 102–3).

Fig. 5 Children's construction site (Author)

The nature kindergarten is not without its own rules and routines to ensure the safety of the children. However, the organisation of the day is less bound by the more measured time-space flows and demands of conventional school life. The children have a lot of input into what they will do in the day (for example, go to the lake or to the woods), but they also are guided into specific learning activities that have a conservation focus as well as informally incorporating early literacy, numeracy, environmental science and socialisation. When the children are exploring the woods or visiting a nature playground several kilometres from the kindergarten they take their food in their backpacks and sometimes sleep in the woods on sheets brought by the teachers. These long hours outdoors are not dictated by time schedules for lunch or sleep at the centre, which are more adhered to in the daily routine of traditional

Fig. 6 Gravel path down to the lake (Author)

kindergartens: 'nature preschools are organised so that children spend more time in natural settings' (Lysklett & Berger, 2016, p. 106).

Nature schools for young children share in some respects the open classrooms spaces movement that emerged in the 1960s and 1970s in the UK, Australia and USA. Ginger (1974, p. 40) wrote at that time that openness was 'more than creating space' but also about how that space was used, whether it involved experimenting with the placement of walls and the built environment. Central to the open classroom philosophy is teacher openness to children's interests, freedom and choice (McLeod, 2014). The notion of open learning, the environment as a space of exploration and community involvement in school programs are some of the topics that are taken up in contemporary children's literature: for example, *Going Bush* (2007) by Nadia Wheatley and Ken Searle is a book made in collaboration with students from nine schools who recount their experiences of learning about the natural environment and the traditional owners of the land during their excursion to the Wolli Creek Valley (Sydney). Although the children are encouraged to explore, use their senses and record their impressions there is nevertheless a structure which shapes the time and movement throughout the day long excursion.

Science Fair Day (Plourde, 2008) conveys a different kind of open-learning activity, where a class of excited and inventive children causes pandemonium when given free rein to make their own science inventions. In this (fictional) picture book, the classroom is depicted as a spatial domain of disorder and confusion, which is at odds with the more familiar notion of it as an organised and regulated space. All three examples—the nature school, *Going Bush,* and *Science Fair Day* are examples of heterotopic spaces which exist alongside more traditional classrooms, and each in its own way creates an alternative to the dominant pedagogical and spatial order.

A feature of the open schools discussed in this section highlights the positive impact this approach has on children in terms of their social and emotional wellbeing, their interactions with the human and nonhuman environment, and their curiosity and passion. In the final section I turn to consider how advanced technologies are changing the instructional design of classroom learning as well as their role in terms of control of movement inside and outside the school environment.

Smart Schools and Technological Spaces

Digital and new media technologies have become an influential and embedded aspect of the lives of children and adults in post-industrial societies. Technology is both vilified and praised in terms of its impact on the health and wellbeing of young and old. While the flying piece of chalk or duster once used to control classrooms, as noted in *What Was the War Like, Grandma?,* has not been replaced (thankfully) by a computer projectile, computers, tablets and other devices are now part of the technological spaces of classrooms for learning, record keeping, web browsing and so on. In this section, I begin by recounting how the city of Songdo in South Korea has planned an education system that uses 'intelligent networking capabilities to weave together people, services, community assets, and information into a single pervasive solution' (Selinger & Kim, 2015, p. 161). My discussion draws on the example of Songdo Chadwick International School for K–12 by Selinger and Kim who illustrate how a so-called 'smart city' can transform education and learning through a ubiquitous ICT infrastructure that serves as a platform for a 'highly connected learning environment' (2015, p. 163). The school is based on the Chadwick School, which was first opened in California over four decades ago by Margaret Lee Chadwick. The Chadwick philosophy of liberalism, creativity and an inquiry-based curriculum is in sharp contrast to Korea's more traditional 'cramming' system of education and teacher-directed study.

Transforming teaching and learning requires transforming the way physical and technological space is used. As Selinger and Kim note, 'every space can promote learning'. They elaborate: 'There are learning opportunities, materials, displays, and technology throughout the building in passageways, cafeterias, offices, and other public spaces in addition to instructional space' (p. 164). Chadwick International School accommodates three phases of schooling—Elementary, Middle and High.

All classrooms are physically connected 'supporting the concept of collaboration through the entire campus' (p. 164), with so-termed 'collaboratories' (an open space for collaborating and sharing ICTs) on every floor to encourage learning outside regular classrooms. In addition there are TelePresence (virtual reality technology) rooms and video-conferencing facilities in classrooms. The overall school design and precinct takes account of security and transportation flow with separate areas for student drop-off and visitor access.

The pervasive video access across Songdo city enables students at Chadwick International School to link to the community, businesses, industries, and universities. Selinger and Kim argue that this blurring of school walls means that teachers need to change how they see their role shifting from 'dispensers of knowledge to become orchestrators of the learning environment' (p. 165). To support teachers in this new role, the school prepares teachers to consider themselves as learners just like their students, offering a directory of online courses and tutorials relevant to their field, and by preparing them to deliver 'just-in-time learning' when a situation arises which requires the application of a new skill or concept. Some of the features of Songdo Chadwick International School are evident in other places such as the 'Connected Classrooms Programs' in Australia, UK, and the USA.

At this point there is no available evidence on how successful Songdo Chadwick International School has been in realising its desired outcomes. However, research on South Korean school life in general shows that key elements impact student wellbeing and school life satisfaction: social relations with friends, teachers, and parents, and the teacher-student relationship (Kim & Kim, 2013). These findings are similar to other research findings on student wellbeing (Clement, 2010).

Digital technology and digital culture is an increasing presence in fiction for young people which offers readers a window onto worlds that are both familiar and strange. Many of the narratives are cautionary tales warning of the dangers of social media, cyberbullying, stolen identity and so on (Mallan, 2008). While many of these activities have their source in the school environment, the online activities (and damage) are often done out of school, blurring the boundaries between school spaces and non-school spaces. For the final example from children's fiction, I draw on Cory Doctorow's *Little Brother* (2008) as it represents a different but nevertheless realistic interpretation of technological spaces that are now familiar to many students.

George Orwell's dystopian novel *Nineteen Eighty-Four* (1949) was one of the first to write of a society where citizens lived under constant surveillance through the figure of 'Big Brother'. *Little Brother* takes its cue from Orwell's story. Surveillance is, however, not simply directed at adults as young people are also the object of the electronic gaze, and their everyday online activities are recorded and stored by new information technologies. In reference to the increased use of technological surveillance and disciplinary powers held by many school authorities, Michelle Fine and colleagues (2003) comment that there is a clear message that many young people who transgress school rules and security systems are 'untrustworthy, suspicious, and potential criminals' (p. 144). This observation mirrors the way students who transgress security systems are treated in *Little Brother*. *Little Brother* responds to the increased security measures adopted in schools in many parts of the West (especially in the US) since the terrorist attacks of 9/11.

The story events in *Little Brother* take place largely outside of school, but the first couple of chapters detail how Marcus and his friend navigate the surveillance technologies the school has in place. Unlike the more egalitarian approach cited in Songdo Chadwick International School where teachers and students are both learners, *Little Brother* explicitly reinforces the idea that young people are more tech-savvy than adults, especially teachers. It is this superior knowledge that enables Marcus and other students to subvert the security devices that school has in place on school issued laptops and other devices. When Marcus decides to cut school to go downtown he has to negotiate the school's surveillance system—the gait-recognition cameras have replaced the face-recognition cameras, which were ruled unconstitutional. As Marcus explains

> Gait-recognition software takes pictures of your motion, tries to isolate you in the pics as a silhouette, and then tries to match the silhouette to a database to see if it knows who you are. It's a biometric identifier, like fingerprints or retina-scans (Doctorow, 2008, p. 10).

This instance of information sharing through the text is a different kind of 'network education' to what Songdo envisages, but it is one that Doctorow sees as important for young people to know so that they can be more in control and aware of the forces that impact on their lives. In successfully circumventing the school's surveillance mechanisms, Marcus' day takes an unexpected turn when terrorists blow up the Bay Bridge, causing major death and destruction, and turning San Francisco into chaos: an event that resonates with the attack on the World Trade Center, the resulting chaos in New York City, and subsequent hypersecurity. Like his fictional counterparts discussed earlier, Marcus is a rule breaker, who becomes a hero because of his actions to overcome evil and powerful forces. In the process he learns more about himself and gains an awareness of how his personal safety and wellbeing are dependent on a number of factors that are largely outside of his control. *Little Brother* highlights most cogently Foucault's (1977 argument that individuals will resist the imposition of controls and other regulatory practices that attempt to shape oneself as a certain kind of subject.

Conclusion

Songdo Chadwick International School and *Little Brother* are fitting examples with which to conclude this chapter as they represent a point in the trajectory of school design that highlights increased freedom to negotiate student learning, along with an increased potential to restrict students' spatial practices. The two examples serve as a reminder of how these two contrasting states—freedom and restriction—have always characterised schooling and the significant part schools play in shaping students' psychological, cognitive and emotional wellbeing.

The selective examples of children's literature discussed above highlight the complexity of school spaces adding a further dimension to historical and empirical accounts. de Certeau says that stories 'are spatial trajectories' (1984, p. 115) and, as we have seen in this chapter, children's literature maps trajectories between punitive and idealised school spaces. Fiction does not simply hold up a mirror of society, but enables us to think about the past, the present, and as Wells (1933) memorably put it, 'the shape of things to come'.

References

Agatha, M. (1914). *Nellie Doran: A story of Australian home and school life*. Sydney: E. J. Dwyer.

AustLit: The Australian Literature Resource. (n.d.). *Children's literature digital resources: An Australian children's literature project*. Retrieved from https://www-austlit-edu-au.ezp01.library.qut.edu.au/austlit/page/5960611.

Building the Education Revolution (BER) Program. (2009). Retrieved from https://web.archive.org/web/20130621091808/http://deewr.gov.au/building-education-revolution.

Clement, N. (2010). Student wellbeing at school: The actualization of values in education. In T. Lovat, R. Toomey, & N. Clement (Eds.), *International research handbook on values education and student wellbeing* (pp. 37–62). Dordrecht: Springer. https://doi.org/10.1007/978-90-481-8675-4_3.

de Certeau, M. (1984). *The practice of everyday life* (trans: Rendall, S.). Berkeley: University of California Press.

Doctorow, C. (2008). *Little brother*. London: Harper/Voyager.

Fine, M., Freudenberg, N., Payne, Y., Perkins, T., Smith, K., & Wanzar, K. (2003). "Anything can happen with police around": Urban youth evaluate strategies of surveillance in public places. *Journal of Social Issues, 59*(1), 141–158 (2003). https://doi.org/10.1111/1540-4560.t01-1-00009.

Foucault, M. (1998). Different spaces. In P. Rabinow (Ed.), *Michel Foucault, aesthetics, method and epistemology, the essential works of Michel Foucault, 1954–1984* (Vol. 2, pp. 175–185). Harmondsworth: Penguin.

Foucault, M. (1977). *Discipline and punish: The birth of the prison* (trans: Sheridan, A.). London: Allen Lane, Penguin.

Freire, P. (1970). *Pedagogy of the oppressed* (trans: Ramos, M.) Harmondsworth: Penguin.

Galway, E. A. (2012). Reminders of rugby in the halls of Hogwarts: The insidious influence of the school story genre on the works of J. K. Rowling. *Children's Literature Association Quarterly, 37*(1), 66–85 (2012). https://doi.org/10.1353/chq.2012.0011.

Gargano, E. (2008). *Reading Victorian schoolrooms: Childhood and education in nineteenth-century fiction*. New York: Routledge.

Ginger, R. (1974). Overview—open education in Victoria. *The Educational Magazine, 31*(1), 40–41.

Healy, S., & Darian-Smith, K. (2015). Educational spaces and the 'whole' child: A spatial history of school design, pedagogy and the modern Australian nation. *History Compass, 13*(6), 275–287 (2015). https://doi.org/10.1111/hic3.12237.

Hetherington, S. (1997). *The Badlands of modernity: Heterotopia and social ordering*. New York: Routledge.

Hughes, T. (1857). *Tom Brown's schooldays*. Oxford: OUP.

Illich, I. (1971). *Deschooling society*. Harmondsworth: Penguin.

Kim, D. H, & Kim, J. H. (2013). Social relations and school life satisfaction in South Korea. *Social Indicators Research, 112*, 105–127. https://doi.org/10.1007/s11205-012-0042-8.

Lefebvre, H. (1991). *The production of space* (trans: Nicholson-Smith, D.). Cambridge, MA: Blackwell.

Lysklett, O. B., & Berger, H. W. (2017). What are the characteristics of nature preschools in Norway, and how do they organize their daily activities? *Journal of Adventure Education and Outdoor Learning, 17*(2), 95–107. https://dx.doi.org/10.1080/14729679.2016.1218782.

McLeod, J. (2014). Experimenting with education: spaces of freedom and alternative schooling in the 1970s. *History of Education Review, 43*(2), 172–189 (2014). https://doi.org/10.1108/HER-03-2014-0019.

Mallan, K. (2001) No place like …: Home and school as contested spaces in *Little Soldier* and *Idiot Pride*. *Papers: Explorations into Children's Literature, 11*(2), 7–15.

Mallan, K. (2008). Space, power and knowledge: The regulatory fictions of online communities. *International Research in Children's Literature, 1*(1), 66–81. https://doi.org/10.3366/E1755619808000112.

Mallan, K. (2009). *Gender dilemmas in children's fiction*. Houndmills, UK: Palgrave Macmillan.

Massey, D. (1998). The spatial construction of youth cultures. In T. Skelton & G. Valentine (Eds.), *Cool places: Geographies of youth cultures* (pp. 121–129). London: Routledge.

Meade, L. T. (1901). *A very naughty girl*. London: Chambers.

Miller, K., & Shifflet, R. (2016). How memories of school inform preservice teachers' feared and desired selves as teachers. *Teaching and Teacher Education 53*, 20–29. https://doi-org.ezp01.library.qut.edu.au/10.1016/j.tate.2015.10.002.

Nature in Children's Literature (NaChiLit). https://www.hvl.no/en/research/group/nachilit/.

Orwell, G. (1949). *Nineteen eighty-four*. London: Penguin.

Parry, G. (2006). Émile: Learning to Be Men, Women, and Citizens. In P. Riley (Author), *The Cambridge companion to rousseau* (pp. 247–271). Cambridge: Cambridge University Press. https://doi.org/10.1017/CCOL9780521572651.009.

Plourde, L., & Wickstrom, T. (2008). *Science fair day*. New York: Dutton Children's Books.

Pyke, L. M. (1923). *Sheila the prefect*. London: Ward, Lock.

Richardson, R. (1875). *The boys of Springdale, or, the strength of patience*. Edinburgh: Oliphant.

Rousseau, J. -J. (1762) *Émile, ou de l'éducation*. English edition: Rousseau, J-J. (1979). *Émile, or on education* (trans: Bloom, A.). Harmondsworth: Penguin.

Selinger, M., & Kim, T. (2015). Smart city needs smart people: Songdo and smart + connected learning. In D. Araya (Ed.), *Smart cities as democratic ecologies* (pp. 159–172). Houndmills, UK: Palgrave Macmillan. https://doi.org/10.1057/9781137377203_11.

Sharp, E. (1897). *The making of a schoolgirl*. Oxford: OUP.

Tonkin, R. (1995). *What was the war like, Grandma?: Emmy remembers World War II*. Port, Melbourne: Heinemann Australia.

Tuan, Y.-F. (1977). *Space and place: The perspective of experience*. Minneapolis: University of Minnesota Press.

Walpole, A. H. (1925). *The black star: A school story for boys*. Sydney: Cornstalk.
Wells, H. G. (1933). *The shape of things to come*. London: Hutchinson.
Wheatley, N., & Searle, K. (2007). *Going bush*. Crow's Nest, NSW: Allen & Unwin.
Willis, J. (2014). From home to civic: designing the Australian school. *History of Education Review* 43(2), 138–151 (2014). https://doi.org/10.1108/HER-02-2014-0009.

Is This the Best We Can Do?

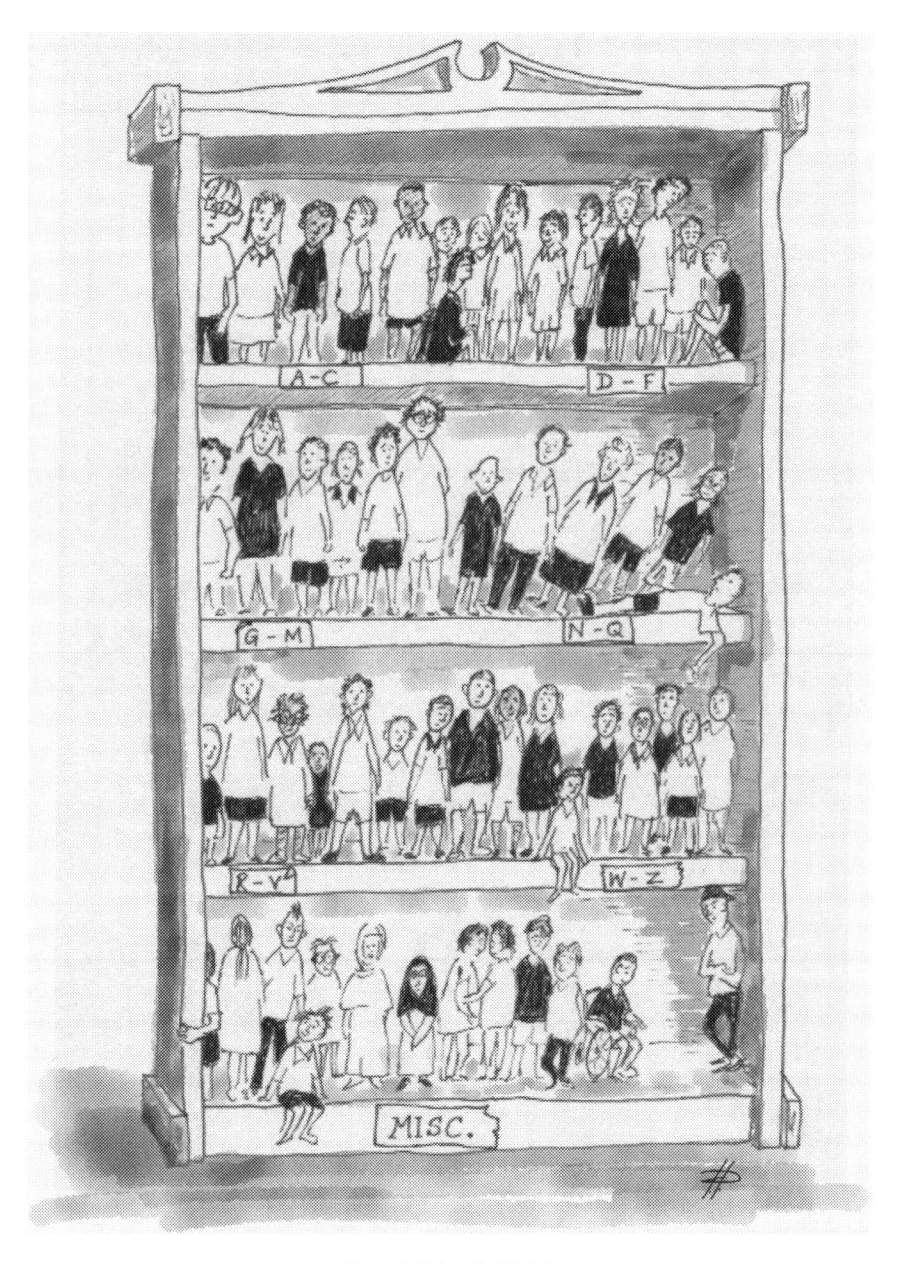

Derek Bland, 2017

Imaginings and Representations of High School Learning Spaces: Year 6 Student Experiences

Kylie Andrews and Jill Willis

Abstract As they transition from primary to high school, students' imaginings of their future learning spaces are informed and creative. This chapter explores the visual representations of high school learning spaces as imagined by some Year 6 students in their final year of primary school in Queensland, Australia. Their images and interview responses reveal five key spatial attributes concerning high school learning spaces. Connections to nature, open spaces that were sustaining and promoted thinking, spaces that enabled them to be active and make choices were clear preferences evident in student responses. These responses highlight how physical, emotional and social wellbeing factors were integral to their ideal spaces for learning. The chapter also considers the implications for students, educators and designers regarding issues of control, consultation, critique and compromise in thinking about the design and use of learning spaces.

Introduction

Starting high school is one of the big transitions in the life of a learner. For Luca (Fig. 1) the learning door was about to open as he finished his final year of primary school, and his imagined picture was one of vague and hopeful optimism. In his explanation about his image, the red walls and purple ceilings were associated with a belief that high school would be stimulating and adventurous. However, the individual desks in rows pointed to his anticipation that learning would be individualised, formal and indoors. Luca's image was collected as part of a Master of Research project (Andrews, 2016). In this qualitative case study, 22 students aged around 12 years were invited to imagine their future high school and to represent both their expected

---

[1] Phrases Provided by Students in Their Annotations or Interview Responses.

K. Andrews · J. Willis (✉)
Queensland University of Technology, Brisbane, Australia
e-mail: jill.willis@qut.edu.au

K. Andrews
e-mail: kylie.andrews@qut.edu.au

H. Hughes et al. (eds.), *School Spaces for Student Wellbeing and Learning*,
https://doi.org/10.1007/978-981-13-6092-3_5

Fig. 1 Luca's water colour drawing, representing his imaginings of a high school learning space. 'The door opening to a new learning space and how different it is from primary school to high school'. (Luca)

and ideal learning spaces in drawings and words. By sharing their experiences and opinions in this way, they provided first-hand insights about the learning spaces they felt suited and hindered their learning experiences.

This chapter presents select findings of students' imagined visual representations of future high school spaces that provide evidence about students' lived awareness of the spatial impact on learning and relationships. As the study's findings highlight, middle years students are imaginative, creative and critical consumers of learning spaces who have articulate thoughts to share concerning the impact of spaces on their wellbeing. In particular, their imaginings show a preference for natural, open, sustaining, active and autonomous spaces that foster their learning and wellbeing. The findings also illustrate how student wellbeing is socially constructed and integrates social, emotional, academic and spatial dimensions (Lefebvre, 1991). In sharing the Year 6 students' imaginings of their future spaces, this chapter aims to inform and inspire the design of high school learning spaces that positively impact the wellbeing of students as they transition to high school. The changing school structure in Queensland, outlined in the next section, provided an ideal context for the case study.

Policy Context—Year 7 Moving to High School in Queensland

In 2015, Year 7 became the first year of high school for students in Queensland, where previously it had been the final year of primary school. This reform was due to the Queensland Government's *Flying Start* policy (Queensland Government, 2011) as a response to an identified need to better support young adolescents as they transition to high school. Six principles of Junior Secondary were identified: enhancing student wellbeing, establishing a distinct junior secondary identity, emphasising quality teaching, parent and community involvement, leadership and local decision-making (Queensland Government, 2011). Across the state of Queensland every high school planned and created learning spaces to welcome Year 7 students.

The time of transitioning from Primary to Secondary school has been defined as a period of change that can be 'both challenging and exciting, in which children and families adjust to new roles, identities and expectations, new interactions and new relationships' (Hanewald, 2013, p. 62). New teachers, new friends, new opportunities, a greater range of classes and classrooms, and new freedoms have to be negotiated by students. The period of transition can often be problematic for middle years learners, who can experience emotional concerns related to socialisation, academic expectations and physically negotiating a larger campus. These concerns can lead to declining engagement and academic underachievement (Carrington, 2006; Hanewald, 2013). Adding to the challenge of transition, Year 6 and 7 students are in early adolescence, a period of personal development when issues of identity and independence dominate their experiences (Tyler, 2004). Peers become more important as a reference point than family, and the young person experiences physiological, neurological and psychological changes that impact on their appearance and behaviour (Pendergast & Bahr, 2010). The multiple changes being experienced by young people have implications for the way that adolescents live their lives as students, their social and cognitive development and their engagement with schooling through social spaces. These clusters of concerns are also recognisable in the literature about student wellbeing.

Spatial Wellbeing as an Integrated Concept

Wellbeing is variously defined. An Australian Treasury report (Gorecki & Kelly, 2012, p. 31) defines wellbeing generally as 'a person's substantive freedom to lead a life they have reason to value'. However, there is no accepted way of representing or measuring wellbeing for children in the academic literature (Organisation for Economic Co-operation and Development (OECD), 2009, p. 24). Most often wellbeing for students is defined by a collection of social and cultural components that provide a supportive ecology, although there is a growing trend of wellbeing increasingly 'reduced' to the concept of personal resilience, emotional wellbeing and the absence of mental ill health (Atkinson, Fuller & Painter, 2012, p. 6). The *Australian Child Wellbeing Project* (ACWP) defined wellbeing as 'comprising a broad range of objective circumstances that young people experience, social relationships that they engage in, and their perceptions of these circumstances and relationships' (Redmond, et al., 2016. p. 1). The report identified that while most middle years students identified that they are 'doing well' groups that were recognised as disadvantaged, who had additional pressures arising from poverty and fewer social networks for support, and who experienced academic difficulties, had greater indicators of reduced wellbeing (Redmond et al., 2016). Schools are places where wellbeing can be fostered, and the perceptions of young people about their experiences are important indicators of how we can enhance their wellbeing.

Where learning environments are associated with wellbeing, it is not usually the physical environments that are being referred to but rather what psycho-social environment can be established through teaching to achieve desired social and academic outcomes. The *Melbourne declaration on educational goals for young Australians* (Ministerial Council on Education, Employment, Training and Youth Affairs (MCEETYA, 2008) identifies that 'student motivation and engagement in these [middle] years is critical and can be influenced by tailoring approaches to teaching, with learning activities and *learning environments* that specifically consider the needs of middle years students' (p. 12). Adolescent Success, formerly the Middle Years of Schooling Association (MYSA, 2012), also recommend *places* for middle years students that include democratic classrooms, a shared vision, small learning environments, positive and safe environments and a sense of community and care. The World Health Organisation (WHO), (2003, p. 1) identifies interactions that a school's environment can enhance social and emotional wellbeing, and learning when it:

- is warm, friendly and rewards learning;
- promotes cooperation rather than competition;
- facilitates supportive, open communications;
- views the provision of creative opportunities as important;
- prevents physical punishment, bullying, harassment and violence, by encouraging the development of procedures and policies that do not support physical punishment and that promote non-violent interaction on the playground, in class and among staff and students; and
- promotes the rights of boys and girls through equal opportunities and democratic procedures.

To understand the interrelationship of physical spaces and wellbeing as a more integrated concept, Lefebvre's spatial triad was used in this study as a theoretical framework to review the literature and student data.

Lefebvre's Triad of Physical, Mental and Social Space Related to Learning Spaces

The holistic and dynamic experience of spaces has been theorised in Lefebvre's Spatial Triad (1991) as three distinctive, yet interrelated physical, mental and social spaces that we produce, reproduce and inhabit. Lefebvre referred to the physical aspect of space as *spatial practice* (1991, p. 38) which is the perceived view of material spaces. In a school context, this view would include physical spaces such as classrooms, playgrounds, walkways and toilets. The second aspect involves imagining, as it is the conceived view of space such as architectural plans and maps which Lefebvre refers to as *representations of space* (1991, p. 39). Lefebvre believed that those who conceive the spaces invest the design with their views of the world, and therefore reproduce power relationships. The third aspect of the triad is the lived experience where social relations take place; representational spaces (1991, p. 39). In a school, this may describe where groups of students relax at lunchtime or live by rules about what is socially acceptable in the spaces. The three aspects of the triad offer a balanced model that embraces the social construction of spatiality (Watkins, 2005) and challenges the notion that school spaces are immobile and 'container-like' (Leander, Phillips & Taylor, 2010, p. 331). The interplay between these spatial dimensions shows how physical space impacts on wellbeing.

There is a well-established body of knowledge around the physical design or *spatial practices* in schools from which implications for students' well being can be drawn (Blackmore, Bateman, Loughlin, O'Mara & Aranda, 2011; Cleveland & Fisher, 2014; Horne Martin, 2006). For example, middle years students who are facing rapid physiological change require space to move around without feeling clumsy, impacting physical and psychological wellbeing (Pendergast & Bahr, 2010). For optimal learning, the physical spaces need to minimise distraction, provide students' independence, allow for flexibility and cater for peer mentoring, active learning and collaboration (Blackmore et al., 2011; Woolner, 2010). In a review of the literature focusing on school environments, Woolner (2010) identified noise, air quality, temperature, space, lighting, and maintenance as all impacting the physical, psychological and social experience of students. Horne Martin's (2006) review adds colour, room organisation, function and density as factors impacting student learning and performance.

Learning spaces, shape social relations and practices of instruction and interaction as representational spaces. Interactions between teachers and students, and students with their peers can be more collaborative in flexible and agile spaces (Mulcahy, Cleveland & Aberton, 2015). There is evidence of improvement in student/teacher relationships and interactions, evidence of increased levels of student interpersonal competencies, engagement and teamwork in redesigned learning spaces (Blackmore et al., 2011). The researchers also noted affective outcomes, such as sense of belonging, inclusion, self-esteem and self-confidence. The design of learning spaces has the potential to open up opportunities for meaningful learning or can stultify learning through limiting the flexibility of social interactions. This has implications for student wellbeing and academic outcomes (Walker, Brooks & Baepler, 2011) and is of particular importance to the young adolescent's socio-cultural wellbeing (Nicholson, 2005).

As students are rarely involved in conceiving school designs (McGregor, 2004), this study sought student *representations of space*. A sense of community, ownership and improving wellbeing emerge when students are allowed to participate and their ideas are heard regarding their learning spaces (Horne Martin, 2006, p. 100). Lefebvre gives examples of designers, architects and social engineers as those who conceive and therefore contain the power of decision-making in the *representations of space* (1991, p. 38). However, even young children have negotiated with architects, and proved themselves as competent, creative and pragmatic, and provided views and ideas that the adult designers had not considered (Clark, 2010). In the research conducted by Johnson (2008) and Comber, Nixon, Ashmore, Loo & Cook (2006) students' conceived views of space informed the physical and social development of new learning spaces. Ghaziani contends that children's voice is 'perhaps the most important and needs to be heard' when considering school design (2008, p. 235). This contention contrasts with Morrow's summation that young people's participation appears to be 'virtually non-existent' (2011, p. 69), despite being both reasonable and insightful. Students are major stakeholders within schools, and their views and perspectives can improve a school (Rudduck & Flutter, 2004), yet students regularly continue to be excluded from the design process of their learning spaces (Cleveland & Fisher, 2014). This study sought to provide an opportunity for one group of middle years learners to voice their perspectives, as it investigated Year 6 perceptions about their primary school spaces and imaginings about their high school learning spaces, to explore what is important to students as they transition to high school.

Research Design

The qualitative case study involved 22 students from one class of Year 6 children in a large Brisbane state school. The students were acknowledged as 'experts in their own lives' (Clark, 2010, p. 188) who would be able to provide a Year 6 perspective of their lived primary school experience and their pre-transition imaginings of high school learning spaces. The research question was: *How do Year 6 students imagine their future high school spaces?* Visual and interview data were gathered in two stages. First, to introduce the concept of learning spaces, the participants photographed their preferred learning space in their primary school and wrote a brief annotation explaining their choice. Second, the students created an image of their imagined high school spaces. Students could use provided collage material, water colour pencils or their iPads to create their visual images. The majority of students opted to use the water colour pencils, the second largest group used the collage material and one student represented his imaginings through an iPad image. Imagination is considered an important way to access critical and creative thinking, and is useful in problem-solving and creating sociological change (Bland, Carrington & Brady, 2009; Egan, 2008). Rich insights and new understandings are provided when students imagine their ideal school or their future learning spaces (Bland, Hughes & Willis, 2013; Burke & Grosvenor, 2003). After completing their image, the students wrote or dictated an annotation, which was important as it provided another opportunity for their perspective to be articulated. Finally, the students responded to semi-structured interview questions based on their imagined representations of high school spaces. Interview questions included:

- Tell me about your picture.
- Is there anything else you want me to notice about your picture?
- If you could change or add anything what would it be?
- What makes this a learning space for you?

The students' visual, spoken and written responses develop an understanding of how Year 6 students imagine their future learning spaces.

Data were analysed through detailed inductive analysis and interpretation. An open coding inductive approach was used to analyse the semi-structured interviews and annotations (Denzin, 2002). Transcripts of the students' responses were colour coded according to their emerging ideas, summarised and collated with cross-referencing to the other Year 6 responses. The dominant themes of the Year 6 students' imaginings revealed prior knowledge of high school spaces plus their hopes, anxieties and expectations about what these spaces might be like and how the spaces might impact their academic and social wellbeing. Significant codes included connections with nature, perceptions of freedom, environmental factors (light, air quality, sound and temperature), the social aspect of space and emotional impact of space (comfort, relaxation, happiness). The students' visual representations were analysed in two ways. Bland's typology of imagination (2009) was used when analysing the students' created images. This deductive process separated the images into four categories of imagination: fantasy, creative, critical and empathic. The images were also interpreted according to the three most visually prominent features of each image to create a matrix of common features. Some of the codes included the provision for physical activity (soccer goal posts, pools, ovals, playground equipment), nature (trees, sun, flowers, mountains), spaciousness, and learning outdoors. The third analytic step was to collate the codes from both visual and verbal data sets into themes, from which five spatial attributes of high school learning spaces were noted to be of particular importance to the Year 6 students. These attributes were then analysed from a theoretical perspective and aligned with Lefebvre's (2009) Spatial Triad.

The full Master of Education thesis, which was conducted with ethical clearance from Queensland University of Technology, is published online (Andrews, 2016). The main findings of spatial attributes of high school learning spaces and their implications are summarised below.

Five Spatial Attributes of High School Learning Spaces

The five spatial attributes and their relationships with the physical, social and mental aspects of Lefebvre's Spatial Triad are shown below (Fig. 2).

The students' visual and verbal responses indicated that they imagined future high school physical spaces that reflected five dominant preferences. They imagined spaces that would allow them to be *actively* engaged in their learning while giving them space to be *autonomous*, that is responsible for their own learning. They imagined *sustaining* spaces with positive environmental factors, such as quietness

Fig. 2 Five types of spaces
imagined by students

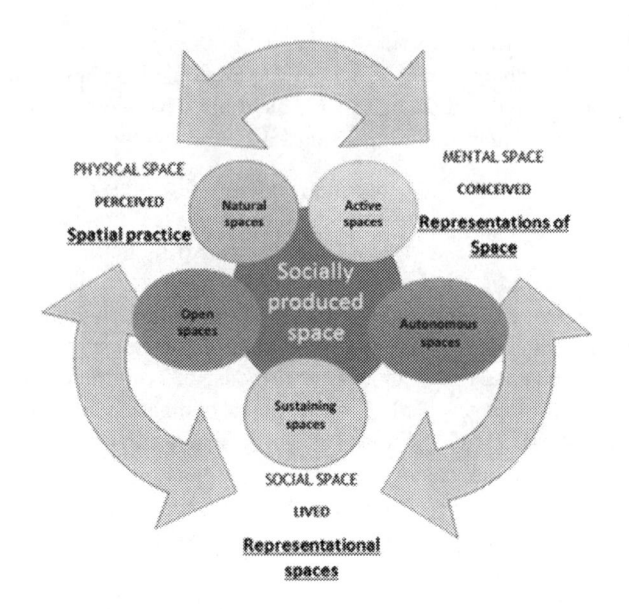

and fresh air that would allow them to focus on their learning, while also providing opportunities to learn with friends. Quite often these spaces were *open spaces*,
linked to elements of *nature*, whether being located outdoors, or connected through
windows. Selections of students' illustrations of imagined spaces are represented in
this chapter to explain these themes. The images often reflected quite a few of the
themes.

Natural Spaces—'Near the Nature'[1]

The most strongly supported finding of this research was the importance that Year 6
students placed on learning in natural spaces. All but 3 of the 22 students included
some form of natural connection in their representations of high school, through
either a specific annotation or visualisation of a natural feature such as the sun, sky,
grass and trees. Hope (Fig. 3) imagined sitting in her high school classroom with a
full view of a natural setting through the glass wall. Other students imagined learning
outside connected with nature, suggesting slightly romanticised views of enjoying
cooler temperatures, breezes, shade, quietness and feeling peaceful. The possibilities
of sunburn, discomfort, insect bites, wind and rain did not feature in their imaginings.
Despite these realities that might dissuade adults and children from wanting to learn
outdoors, other studies with young people have shown that direct access to nature
is clearly important to students (Bland et al., 2013; Burke & Grosvenor, 2003). It
is important that this desire to be with or near nature is taken seriously by school
decision makers as Taylor and Kuo (2006) have identified that green or natural spaces

Fig. 3 Hope's image of a classroom with a glass wall to look out over trees. 'This space relaxes me. Combination of colour and nature' (Hope, interview)

are important for children's healthy development, wellbeing and attention capacity. Views of nature and easy contact with nature are important for student learning. When the Year 6 students imagined natural high school spaces they combined cognitive benefits (attention), mood benefits (relaxation) and aesthetic qualities with learning while being connected with nature. While the finding was not new, the emphasis the students placed on the natural environment was significant and unexpected.

Open Spaces—'Not Crammed'

Open spaces were favoured by the majority of students and this theme often over-lapped with the preference for connections to nature. The findings reflect previous recommendations to ensure spacious learning spaces that allow students to spread out (Barrett & Zhung, 2009; Clark & Uzzell, 2006). Students gave reasons for these spatial choices, referring to comfort, environmental factors, room to stretch out, views of nature, greater concentration and opportunities to be with friends. The students' choices reflected a conscious decision to move away from the 'container'-like spaces of a typical classroom (McGregor, 2004, p.15) into open and larger spaces. Zed (Fig. 4) imagined a spacious, open outdoor space that provided the benefits of learning in an uncrowded space and making him feel relaxed. Other students created spaces that were uncrowded and this suggests that the desire for low-density spaces was common to the Year 6 participants. Their thinking may have been influenced by the density issues experienced in their primary classroom with 31 students fitted into an average-sized classroom. Ten students specifically mentioned their need for space in their interview responses and they visually depicted open, 'not crammed' or 'less squishy' images for high school spaces. Previous research into density has shown that it is a tangible factor affecting student outcomes within learning spaces (Blackmore et al., 2011) and is associated with negative psychological and cognitive

Fig. 4 Zed's image of an
open and spacious high
school learning space. 'An
outdoor scene. Big, open
space, lot of room, lots of
trees, not crowded, learning
by myself. Not an oval. This
space makes me relaxed,
grass and trees' (Zed,
annotation)

Fig. 5 Joe's image focused
on the trees integrated with
the buildings. 'You are not
crammed inside the
classroom, it's so quiet when
you're outdoors you can hear
birds and that.' (Joe,
interview)

experiences (Horne Martin, 2006). The students' preference to learn in open and
uncrowded spaces reinforced these previous findings (Fig. 5).

Sustaining Spaces—'Helps Me Think'

Joe's image highlights the importance of providing healthy high school learning
spaces that sustain their senses. In particular, quietness and quality of air emerged
as significant issues directly linked to learning as many students said they helped
them think or focus. Horne Martin (2006, p. 98) cites literature supporting the need
for good ventilation for students' health and their ability to concentrate. The Year 6
students seemed to associate 'fresh air' with a number of environmental and cognitive
factors: temperature, smell, nature and providing better conditions for concentration.
Lethargy and inattention have been linked to warm and stuffy classrooms (Burke &
Grosvenor, 2003; Horne Martin, 2006; Warner & Myers, 2009). The large proportion

Fig. 6 Edie's collage. 'I like school. I want my school to be open, so like nature's everywhere. I want it to be exciting and motivating. There is a slide and a bench to sit on to socialise.' (Edie, annotation). 'Make it a healthy and active environment' Edie, interview)

of participants who specifically mentioned fresh air believed that they were more likely to breathe and feel fresh air in outdoor spaces rather than in their classroom. Quietness was another dominant theme. Imagining a quiet space was important for 10 of the 22 students as they considered how they learnt best and what spatial conditions might support their learning in high school.

The varied responses indicate the personal nature of learning and act as a reminder that students' learning preferences should be identified and accommodated by educators. While some students may thrive in a busy, talkative room, others may become frustrated and confused. Flexible and agile spaces that enable collaborative as well as individual learning spaces are emerging as school environment design responses that may meet these preferences for sustaining, quiet spaces (Blackmore et al., 2011) (Fig. 6).

Active Spaces—'Something to Do'

As Edie highlighted in her collage and annotation, it is important to provide playful and active spaces for incoming Year 7 students to a high school context. Active spaces are important to students in their learning spaces (Bland, Hughes & Willis, 2013; Ghaziani, 2008) although the importance of play is mostly associated with early childhood spaces (Blackmore et al., 2011; Clark, 2010; Dudek, 2005). In the students' high school imaginings, gender differences appeared in the expression of playfulness. Boys were more likely to represent sporting facilities and spaces. This reflects previous research in gender and space that reports outdoor spaces are 'still largely monopolised by boys, particularly for sport activities' (Blackmore et al., 2011, p. 23). A number of girls imagined playful settings including playground components, and described their desire for 'fun' spaces providing opportunities to 'do something'. Overall, there was no gender difference in the Year 6 students' desire

to learn in active and engaging spaces, but there was some evidence that the girls' imaginings represented more creative ideas concerning activity, for example, a disco, slide and swings (Bland, 2009) while the boys represented more competitive physical activity. This finding suggests a possible focus for further research attention as the desire for activity and engagement of their bodies has implications for middle years' pedagogy.

Autonomous Spaces—'New Experiences, Endless Possibilities, New Environment'

Middle years students grow in their desire for independence and autonomy (Carrington, 2006) and as Lee's image indicates, there is a desire for freedom and fresh new experiences. The students generally imagined spaces away from close teacher supervision while learning in the classroom at high school. This finding aligns with other research showing that informal spaces are associated with more liberty for children (Thomas, 2010) (Fig. 7).

When students were asked who shared the space with them they all mentioned friends. Teachers were only mentioned after a follow-up question regarding whether they imagined a teacher present. Sharing autonomous spaces with peers rather than teachers was a recurring theme in this study. The importance of peers is well documented in middle years literature (Carrington, 2006, Groundswater-Smith, Mitchell & Mockler, 2007; Pendergast & Bahr, 2010) and recognised through research in youth and learning spaces (Hopkins, 2011). Year 6 students placed importance on high school spaces where they work independently, supported by technology, with the teacher on the periphery. The minor role given to teachers in this study seems to invert the normal power structure of a classroom from a teacher-centred focus to student-centred emphasis. The peripheral role of the teacher is not a theme apparent in the learning spaces literature yet it was notable in the students' interview responses. Students seemed ready to take ownership of their wellbeing in their transition to high school, as shown through their imagination of their future selves as autonomous learners. They held an overwhelmingly positive view of transition to high school with only two students identifying some concerns about moving to high school in interviews. There is potential for learning spaces to support this autonomy.

Four Implications: Control, Consultation, Critique and Compromise

Year 6 students imagined their future high school spaces in both realistic and wishful ways that indicated *where* they would prefer to learn as well as *how* they would like to learn. Thus, they generally imagined natural, open, sustaining, active and autonomous spaces. While these five themes were dominant across the responses, students imagined physical, mental and social spaces, the three elements of Lefebvre's triad, in different ways. For example, while some imagined themselves at high school engaging quite actively outdoors, running around, others saw themselves sitting quietly under the shade of a tree reading a book. In these spaces, their images evoked embodied spaces (Cook & Hemming, 2011). For example, they depicted students leaning up against a tree, spreading out their legs and getting comfortable. Learning spaces are socially produced and reproduced by the people who inhabit them, reinforcing the understanding of space as a socially produced concept. The importance of ongoing consultation with students in the social production of space has clear links to student wellbeing ideals of democratic collaboration and feeling safe, engaged and valued. To assist educators, professional designers and for those interested in promoting spatial wellbeing in middle years practices four principles of engaging students as stakeholders in designing spaces for learning are proposed.

1. Control

It appears that just as adults like to have some control over our spatial choices, middle years students also desire to have some control over where and how they learn. One student was explicit in her interview explaining her desire for control over her own desk space (Fig. 8), while others wanted control over being able to talk to friends and interact while they were learning. Students indicated in their interview responses that they appreciated having some control, or at least some input, over where they might learn best and with that came a sense of freedom. Lefebvre (1991) recognised that it is through spatial choices that power is produced and that designers or conceivers of space often hold spatial power. The students in this study were able to identify their spatial choices indicating that student involvement in spatial decisions can occur beyond consultation in the original building plans, as input into the subsequent use of space and pedagogical approach is also empowering.

Implications for educators include using a learner-centred pedagogical approach that provides opportunities for greater learner independence and peer collaboration

Fig. 8 Sue's image

within flexible learning spaces (Willis, 2014). The use of portable technology devices also allows for meaningful learning opportunities with flexibility in terms of where such devices can be used. Teachers could also consider using a variety of open and natural spaces that invite a sense of student autonomy during class time. Classroom layout could also be thoughtfully considered and arranged in negotiation with students.

2. Consultation

Lefebvre's (1991) notion of social representational spaces highlights the importance of considering the 'inhabitants and users' (p. 39) of spaces and developing an understanding of how the conceived and perceived spaces are produced. In every iteration of the data collection process, the Year 6 students readily engaged in the process of consultation. Students' views could beneficially inform spatial, pedagogical and curriculum choices to support their transition to high school.

For professional designers, the findings demonstrate the benefit of consulting students as key stakeholders within a school, and of attending to student voices throughout the learning space design process (Rudduck & Flutter, 2004). For example, this case study draws designers' attention to the importance that Year 6 students attach to outdoor, natural areas and the potential contribution to their wellbeing of views of nature and easy access to natural environments. The social implications of creating and enjoying interactions within learning spaces necessarily involves the provision of spaces that encourage communicating and learning between students and teachers (Arndt, 2012). Students in this study articulated their concern for quieter spaces to help them think clearly, whilst also wanting opportunities to collaborate and learn with their peers. These desires warrant pedagogical and acoustic design attention from education decision makers as students negotiate the social spaces of high school. Students can be creative, pragmatic and effective problem solvers regarding their schooling spaces. Taking the opportunity to negotiate with all school

Fig. 9 Ella's image. 'I picked the city because learning at night is cooler and a calmer environment. Learning through the day is hot. Night—having colour and light is a good way to learn—in nature and open space… Amazing if a school could let students learn outside because it is more engaging and you're more likely to pick up things.' (Ella, annotation)

stakeholders about the natural and built spaces of schools would enable designers to achieve best design practice.

3. Critique

The study shows that Year 6 students are able to critique their current learning spaces in constructive and creative ways. Their imaginings of high school spaces often reflected a critique of 'stuffy' classrooms that made them drowsy and noise levels that impacted on their ability to concentrate. Critique was also evident in Ella's imagined learning space (Fig. 9), being at the city in the cool of the night—she wondered why school had to be during the heat of the day. Practical implications can be drawn from the poetic creativity of her image such as administrative changes in school times to suit adolescent circadian rhythms as well as cooler temperatures on summer nights (Wolfson & Carskadon, 1998). Student imagination is not bound by logistics, yet produces ideas worthy of serious adult attention and discussion.

Some of the more fantastic collage images of playgrounds and interactive spaces suggested a desire to be fully engaged in learning spaces through emotional, social, cognitive and physical attachments. Munns (2007) describes engagement as taking students into their learning and building attachments. Year 6 students mentioned fun, beauty, activity and inspiration as desired aspects of their future spaces. The students' critique suggests that educators, school administrators and designers could support student transition to high school by providing playful spaces. This design approach would contribute to the advantages of getting young adolescents fit, curious and moving with play equipment designed for them (Sturm, Tieben, Deen, Bekker & Schouten, 2011).

4. Compromise

Not all of the student ideas can be realised. In the process of negotiating some control for the students over their learning spaces, through consultation and critique, students and teachers need to work out compromises between what is wanted and what is possible. Students are creative, hopeful and passionate, but they are not unreasonable (Burke & Grosvenor, 2015). Valuing and hearing their views, even when their ideas do not result in change is an important process and one that will be appreciated by young adolescents and beneficial to the adult decision makers in their lives (Rudduck & Flutter, 2004).

Year 6 students may have imagined their future high school learning spaces in specific ways but there was no guarantee, or indeed likelihood that they would experience the freedom or connectedness they desired. The Year 6 students conceived spaces that revealed combinations of realistic and wishful elements that used all types of imagination from critical, creative and fantasy (Bland, 2009) and interacted with all of the spatial relations within the spatial triad (Lefebvre, 1991). Their conceived spaces reflect Lefebvre's recognition that purely material or idealistic spaces need to acknowledge the complexities of lived experiences, which in this case was the way that children anticipated they could symbolise and use spaces. Soja (1996, p. 6) refers to this as 'real-and-imagined' space. While students quite often represented high schools as containers with static spatial structures like rooms, desks, windows and even slides, in their images there was always engagement with the living energy of nature through trees, wind and snow, and with others through fun, diversity and collaboration, or a desire for reflection and focus. It is through the relationships and the interactions that are both social and symbolic that spaces continue to be lived and produced. Many of the students were imagining spaces that would lead to positive emotions and energy, and these symbolic and embodied connections can be realised through encouraging more learner-centred pedagogies, active spaces and through negotiated compromise.

Conclusion

This study confirms key findings which are similar to those of previous research. However, notable differences emerged regarding the extent of student focus on nature and their desire to work in open and informal spaces with fresh air. The Year 6 students' prioritising of natural, outdoor spaces enhanced by environmental factors such as fresh air has added to an understanding of the importance of the natural world, and non-built spaces within schools for students. Year 6 students also imagined active and engaging spaces that would provide social opportunities to be with peers and to learn in more autonomous ways and spaces. Students spoke confidently of their preferences for learning. What students understood 'learning' to mean within their depiction of learning spaces is a potential focus for future similar research. While the student responses in this qualitative case study cannot be considered representative of all students, they provide a valuable understanding of the ways that Year 6 students imagine their future high school spaces. These insights have the potential to inform the design of spaces that better support student transition to high school. The research design provides a foundation for further much-needed research that will enhance student middle years students' wellbeing at a critical juncture of their schooling.

Summary of Implications for Designing Spaces for Wellbeing

- Design spaces that connect with nature, either through windows or informal outdoor learning spaces.
- Provide open spaces that allow for formal, informal and autonomous learning experiences and relationship building.
- Consider the environmental factors of air quality, noise and density in the design process.
- Encourage participatory involvement to explore what spaces encourage a sense of wellbeing in students.
- Consider ways in which students can have opportunities for consultation, critique and mechanisms for reaching compromises that give students a measure of greater control in spatial decisions.

References

Andrews, K. (2016). *High school learning spaces: Investigating Year 6 students' imaginings and representations*. (Unpublished Masters dissertation). Queensland University of Technology, Brisbane. https://eprints.qut.edu.au/101159.

Arndt, P. (2012). Design of learning spaces: Emotional and cognitive effects of learning environments in relation to child development. *Mind, Brain and Education, 6*(1), 41–48. https://doi.org/10.111/j.1751-228X.2011.01136.x.

Atkinson, S., Fuller, S., & Painter, J. (2012). *Wellbeing and place*. Surrey: Ashgate.

Barrett, P. S., & Zhang, Y. (2009). *Optimal learning spaces: Design implications for primary schools. SCRI Report 2*. Salford: SCRI. http://usir.salford.ac.uk/18471/.

Blackmore, J., Bateman, D., Loughlin, J., O'Mara, J., & Aranda, G. (2011). *Research into the connection between built learning spaces and student outcomes*. Melbourne: State of Victoria (Department of Education and Early Child Development). http://www.education.vic.gov.au/Documents/about/programs/infrastructure/blackmorelearningspaces.pdf.

Bland, D. (2009). Re-imagining school through young people's drawings. In *1st International Visual Methods Conference, 15–17 September 2009*, Clothworkers Centenary Concert Hall, University of Leeds. (Unpublished).

Bland, D., Carrington, S., & Brady, K. (2009). Young people, imagination and re-engagement in the middle years. *Improving schools, 12*(3), 237–2.

Bland, D., Hughes, H., & Willis, J. (2013) *Reimagining Learning Spaces: A research report for the Queensland Council for Social Science Innovation*. Brisbane: Queensland University of Technoloy. https://eprints.qut.edu.au/63000/.

Burke, C., & Grosvenor, I. (2003). *The school I'd like: Children and young people's reflections on an education for the 21st century*. Abingdon, Oxon: Routledge Falmer.

Burke, C., & Grosvenor, I. (2015). *The school I'd like: Revisited: Children's and young people's reflections on an education for the 21st century*. Abingdon, Oxon: Routledge.

Carrington, V. (2006). *Rethinking middle years: Early adolescents, schooling and digital culture*. Crows Nest, NSW: Allen & Unwin.

Clark, A. (2010). *Transforming children's spaces: Children's and adults' participation in designing learning environments*. London: Routledge.

Clark, C., & Uzzell, D. (2006). The socio-environmental affordances of adolescents' environments. In C. Spencer & M. Blades (Eds.), *Children and their Environments* (pp. 176–196). Cambridge: Cambridge University Press.

Cleveland, B., & Fisher, K. (2014). The evaluation of physical learning environments: A critical review of the literature. *Learning Environments Research, 17*(1), 1–28. https://doi.org/10.1007/s10084-013-91949-3.

Comber, B., Nixon, H., Ashmore, L., Loo, S., & Cook, J. (2006). Urban renewal from the inside out: Spatial and critical literacies in a low socioeconomic school community. *Mind, Culture and Activity, 13*(3), 228–246. https://doi.org/10.1207/s15327884mca1303_5.

Cook, V. A., & Hemming, P. J. (2011). Education spaces: Embodied dimensions and dynamics. *Social and Cultural Geography, 12*(1), 1–8. https://doi.org/10.1080/14649365.2011.542483.

Denzin, N. (2002). The interpretive process. In A. M. Huberman & M. B. Miles (Eds.), *The qualitative researcher's companion* (pp. 349–366). Thousand Oaks: Sage.

Dudek, M. (2005). *Children's spaces*. Oxford: Architectural Press.

Egan, K. (2008). *The future of education: Reimagining our schools from the ground up*. New Haven: Yale University Press.

Ghaziani, R. (2008). Children's voices: Raised issues for school design. *CoDesign, 4*(4), 225–236. https://doi.org/10.1080/15710880802536403.

Gorecki, S., & Kelly, J. (2012). Treasury's wellbeing framework. *Economic Round-up*, 3, 27. https://treasury.gov.au/publication/economic-roundup-issue-3-2012-2/economic-roundup-issue-3-2012/treasurys-wellbeing-framework/.

Groundswater-Smith, S., Mitchell, J., & Mockler, N. (2007). *Learning in the middle years: More than a transition*. South Melbourne: Thomson.

Hanewald, R. (2013). Transition between primary and secondary school: Why it is important and how it can be supported. *Australian Journal of Teacher Education. 38*(1). http://dx.doi.org/10.14331/ajte.2013v38n1.

Hopkins, P. (2011). Young people's spaces. In P. Foley & S. Leverett (Eds.), *Children and young people's spaces: Developing practice* (pp. 25–39). New York: Palgrave Macmillan.

Horne Martin, S. (2006). The classroom environment and children's performance—is there a relationship? In C. Spencer & M. Blades (Eds.), *Children and their environments: Learning, using and designing spaces* (pp. 91–107). Cambridge: Cambridge University Press.

Johnson, K. (2008). Teaching children to use visual research methods. In P. Thomson (Ed.), *Doing visual research with children and young people*. Abingdon: Routledge.

Leander, K. M., Phillips, N. C., & Taylor, K. H. (2010). The changing social spaces of learning: Mapping new mobilities. *Review of Research in Education, 34*(1), 329–394. https://doi.org/10.3102/0091732X09358129.

Lefebvre, H. (1991). *The production of space*. Malden, MA: Blackwell Publishing.

McGregor, J. (2004). Space, power and the classroom. *Forum. 46*(1), 13–18. http://eric.ed.gov/?id=EJ738537.

Middle Years of Schooling Association (MYSA). (2012). *Middle Schooling: People, practices and places*. MYSA position paper. http://www.adolescentsuccess.org.au/wp-content/uploads/2012/10/MYSA-Position-Paper.pdf.

Ministerial Council on Education, Employment, Training and Youth Affairs (MCEETYA). (2008). *Melbourne declaration on educational goals for young Australians*. Canberra: Ministerial Council on Education, Employment, Training and Youth Affairs. http://www.curriculum.edu.au/verve/_resources/National_Declaration_on_the_Educational_Goals_for_Young_Australians.pdf.

Morrow, V. (2011). Researching children and young people's perspectives on place and belonging. In P. Foley & S. Leverett (Eds.), *Children and young people's spaces: Developing practice* (pp. 59–72). Basingstoke: Palgrave MacMillan.

Mulcahy, D., Cleveland, B., & Aberton, H. (2015). Learning spaces and pedagogic change: Envisioned, enacted and experienced. *Pedagogy, Culture & Society, 23*(4), 575–595. https://doi.org/10.1080/14681366.2015.1055128.

Munns, G. (2007). A sense of wonder: Pedagogies to engage students who live in poverty. *International Journal of Inclusive Education, 11*(3), 301–315. https://doi.org/10.1080/13603110701237571.

Nicholson, E. (2005). The school building as third teacher. In M. Dudek (Ed.), *Children's spaces* (pp. 44–65). Oxford: Architectural Press.

Organisation for Economic Co-operation and Development (OECD). (2009). *Doing better for children*. http://www.oecd.org/els/family/doingbetterforchildren.htm.

Pendergast, D., & Bahr, N. (Eds.). (2010). *Teaching middle years: Rethinking curriculum, pedagogy and assessment* (2nd ed.). Crows Nest, NSW: Allen & Unwin.

Queensland Government. Department of Education. (2011). *A flying start for Queensland children: Why year 7 will be part of high school from 2015*. http://deta.qld.gov.au/initiatives/flyingstart/pdfs/why-high-school.pdf.

Redmond, G., Skattebol, J., Saunders, P., Lietz, P., Zizzo, G., O'Grady, E., ... Roberts, K. (2016). *Are the kids alright? Young Australians in their middle years: Final summary report of the Australian Child Wellbeing Project*. http://research.acer.edu.au/well_being/6.

Rudduck, J. & Flutter, J. (2004). *How to improve your school: Giving pupils a voice*. London: Continuum.

Soja, E. W. (1996). *Thirdspace: Journeys to Los Angeles and other real-and-imagined places*. Oxford: Blackwell.

Sturm, J., Tieben, R., Deen, M., Bekker, T., & Schouten, B. (2011). PlayFit: Designing playful activity interventions for teenagers. In *DiGRA '11. Proceedings of the 2011 DiGRA international conference: Think design play*. http://www.digra.org/digital-library/publications/playfit-designing-playful-activity-interventions-for-teenagers/.

Taylor, A., & Kuo, F. (2006). Is contact with nature important for healthy child development? State of the evidence. In C. Spencer & M. Blades (Eds.), *Children and their environments: Learning, using and designing spaces* (pp. 124–140). Cambridge: Cambridge University Press. https://doi.org/10.1017/cb09780511521232.009.

Thomas, H. (2010). Learning spaces, learning environments and the dis 'placement' of learning. *British Journal of Educational Technology, 41*(3), 502–511. https://doi.org/10.1111/j.1467-8535.2009.00974.x.

Tyler, R. (2004). Improving pedagogy in the middle years. *Professional Voice., 3*(2), 17–22.

Wolfson, A., & Carskadon, M. (1998). Sleep schedules and daytime functioning in adolescents. *Child Development, 69*(4), 875–887. https://doi.org/10.1111/j.1467-8624.1998.tb06149.x.

World Health Organization. (2003). *Creating an environment for emotional and social well-being: An important responsibility of a health-promoting and child-friendly school. WHO Information Series on School Health, Document 10*. Geneva: WHO. http://www.who.int/school_youth_health/media/en/sch_childfriendly_03_v2.pdf.

Walker, J.D., Brooks, D.C., & Baepler, P. (2011). Pedagogy and space: Empirical research on new learning environments. *Educause Review Online*. www.educause.edu.au/ero/article/pedagogy-and-space.

Warner, S. A., & Myers, K. L. (2009). The creative classroom: The role of space and place toward facilitating creativity. *Technology Teacher, 69*(4), 28–34. https://www.researchgate.net/profile/Scott_Warner2/publication/234560419_.

Watkins, C. (2005). Representations of space, spatial practices and spaces of representation: An application of Lefebvre's spatial triad. *Culture and Organization, 11*(3), 209–220. https://doi.org/10.1080/14759550500203318.

Willis, J. (2014). Making space to learn: Leading collaborative classroom design. *Journal of Educational Leadership, Policy and Practice, 29*(1), 3–16. http://eprints.qut.edu.au/75060.

Woolner, P. (2010). *The design of learning spaces*. New York: Continuum.

High School Spaces and Student Transitioning: Designing for Student Wellbeing

Hilary Hughes, Jill Franz, Jill Willis, Derek Bland and Annie Rolfe

Abstract Transition to high school can be challenging for students who encounter a complex new learning environment and unfamiliar physical spaces. Little research examines relationships between physical school spaces and wellbeing at this critical stage when students are at risk of disengagement from learning. This qualitative case study explored Year 7 students' wellbeing experience and needs when transitioning to high school in Queensland, Australia. Findings indicate that Year 7 students: prefer their home area where they feel supported; need fresh air and outdoor spaces to run and play; gravitate towards informal spaces such as handball courts and gardens; use the library for relaxation and quiet time alone; and feel intimidated and unsafe among older students in interstitial spaces such as pathways and stairwells. The study's findings support a set of suggestions for designing school spaces that enhance the wellbeing of Year 7 students.

Introduction

Transitioning from primary to high school can be an exciting but also daunting experience for young people as they negotiate a complex new learning environment and a maze of unfamiliar physical spaces. According to the *Melbourne declaration on educational goals for young Australians* 'effective transitions between primary

H. Hughes (✉) · J. Franz · J. Willis · D. Bland · A. Rolfe
Queensland University of Technology, Brisbane, Australia
e-mail: h.hughes@qut.edu.au

J. Franz
e-mail: j.franz@qut.edu.au

J. Willis
e-mail: jill.willis@qut.edu.au

D. Bland
e-mail: derekbland@leakythoughts.com

A. Rolfe
e-mail: a2.rolfe@qut.edu.au

© Springer Nature Singapore Pte Ltd. 2019
H. Hughes et al. (eds.), *School Spaces for Student Wellbeing and Learning*,
https://doi.org/10.1007/978-981-13-6092-3_6

and secondary schools are an important aspect of ensuring student engagement' (MCEETYA, 2008). However, there is little research about how high school spaces contribute to—or limit—the wellbeing of transitioning students. Therefore, this qualitative case study explores the first-hand experience of Year 7 students enrolled at three schools in Queensland, Australia. This chapter provides a snapshot of the study's innovative methodology and key findings. The full report is available online (Hughes, Franz, Willis, Bland & Rolfe, 2016).

This research took place at a time of major reform in the Queensland school system. The recently implemented *Flying Start* policy (DET, 2018) caused the relocation of Year 7 from primary to secondary school. This reform has significant spatial implications for Queensland high schools with the need to accommodate the additional Year 7 cohort (generally aged 12–13). Beyond the physical challenges of Year 7 transition, is the need for schools to support the wellbeing of students who are generally younger and less mature than previous new high schoolers. Recommendations from *Flying Start* pilot programs indicate four priorities: transition events, specialist junior secondary teachers, understanding the needs of adolescent learners and regular feedback. However, the impacts of high school learning spaces on transitioning students' wellbeing received limited attention. Below we outline the understanding of wellbeing that underpins this research.

Understanding of Spaces and Wellbeing

In this study, *high school spaces* comprise any physical spaces used by students within their high school including: classrooms, libraries, labs, sports halls; recreation and lunch areas; outdoor playgrounds and sports fields; and in-between (interstitial) spaces such as walkways and stairwells.

The study builds upon an ecological understanding of wellbeing that integrates social, cultural, health and educational elements of a young person's development. Informed by existing literature (Fraillon, 2004; AIHW, 2012; Burke, 2014; Simmons, Graham & Thomas, 2015; Watson, Emery, & Bayliss, 2012) we developed a spatial wellbeing framework with six interrelated aspects:

- Physical wellbeing: physical safety and states of being energetic, vital, healthy
- Cognitive wellbeing: solving problems, planning, learning, being creative
- Social wellbeing: relationships especially with school friends; sense of belonging; freedom from bullying
- Emotional wellbeing: Being happy, confident
- Psychological wellbeing: Feeling good about oneself (self-esteem); able to do things you want to do (self-efficacy); having a sense of self (identity)
- Existential wellbeing: Feeling 'at home'; that you fit in; aesthetic appreciation

The following section outlines the literature that informed this study, beginning with the relationships between school environment and student wellbeing. The potential of the physical school environment to support transitioning students' wellbeing has received little research attention, despite an evident link between student wellbeing, learning experience and educational outcomes. Describing this link as 'unequivocal' Fraillon claims: 'Improved outcomes in all aspects of student wellbeing are positively associated with improved outcomes in all other aspects of schooling' (2004, p. 12). The link operates in two interrelated ways: one where wellbeing impacts learning (Fraillon, 2004); the other involves the 'absolute effect' (Desjardins, 2008) where what happens in school, both formal and informal, is understood to impact student wellbeing in the present and the future (O'Toole, 2008).

There is growing awareness of the relationship between learning and the school environment (Blackmore, Batemann, Loughlin, O'Mara, & Aranda, 2011; Brooks, 2011; Cardellino, Leiringer, & Clements-Croome, 2009; Gislason, 2009; Harrison & Hutton, 2012; Rudd, Reed, & Smith, 2008; Tanner, 2009; Woolner, 2015). However, the relationship with student wellbeing is less well understood. Soutter (2011) found that students separate wellbeing from their educational experiences. In contrast, an Australian study (Simmons et al., 2015) revealed that students connect a wide range of factors to wellbeing, such as learning approach, the school environment (physical and socio-emotional), relationships and opportunities. These students indicated that the look and feel of the physical environment had a social and emotional influence on them. While learning they wished to have fun, which they associated with visual and physical access to nature, and spaces that allow creativity.

The influence of school environments on learning outcomes is challenging to measure (Blackmore et al., 2011; Byers, Imms, & Hartnell-Young, 2014). Evaluation of the physical school environment tends to emphasise operational and building sustainability (Sanoff, 2001; Wheeler & Malekzadeh, 2015). As Cleveland and Fisher (2014, p. 7) state 'there are few published evaluations of contemporary educational facilities that take into account the effectiveness of their design as pedagogical settings'. Moreover, research tends to ignore the many informal spaces (such as lunch areas) that students experience on a daily basis at school. Interstitial (or in-between) spaces, such as corridors and behind a shed are often significant to students but unrecognised by adults (Luz, 2008). Further research is also needed on relationships between student wellbeing and school environment to extend current understandings such as those of Marley et al. (2015) that link psychological needs (for example, enjoyment and feeling safe) and specific environmental attributes (for example, building circulation, connection to community and spaces for creativity, physical activity and play).

It is particularly critical to investigate environment-related challenges of *transitioning* students and associated impacts on their wellbeing. In their transition to high school, young people experience various challenges in adjusting to a new physical, educational and social environment—with generally less support than they gained at primary school (Mackenzie, McMaugh, & O'Sullivan, 2012; Brewin & Stratham, 2011). Negative transition experiences can have a profound effect on a young person's wellbeing through a sense of anonymity, alienation from peers, increased anxiety and decreased self-esteem (Brewin & Statham, 2011; Simmons, 1987). Their achievement may decline, with literacy and numeracy plateauing or even regressing (Barber & Olsen, 2004; Pendergast et al., 2005). Many students, particularly low achievers and those from low-income families, begin disengaging from education, culminating in early school leaving (Lamb, Walstab, Teese, Vickers, & Rumberger, 2004).

These challenges are compounded by the tendency to disregard students and their perspectives about learning space design (Newton & Fisher, 2009). This is a significant oversight, since transitioning offers an opportunity for students to reimagine school spaces that meet their expectations and needs (Bland, Hughes & Willis, 2013). In addition, there is a conceptual gap about the existential dimension and physical significance of the school environment (built and natural) as place. This is problematic as 'wellbeing, however defined, can have no form, expression or enhancement without consideration of place' (Atkinson, Fuller & Painter, 2012, p. 3).

Research Approach: Qualitative Case Study

In response to the identified research gaps, this study addressed the research question: *What is the relationship between student transition to Year 7, high school spaces and student wellbeing?* As a qualitative collective case study (Simons, 2009) it explored the 'complexity and uniqueness' of the phenomenon of Year 7 students' transitioning experience. Set in the real-life context of secondary schooling and the *Flying Start* reform (DET, 2018), the study focused on Year 7 students at three Queensland high schools, as key stakeholders in the design of their learning environments.

The research team used a variety of data collection methods based around our six-dimensional understanding of wellbeing. For the year 7 students, we simplified these as a set of 'wellbeing playing cards' that represented aspects of wellbeing and limited wellbeing (Fig. 1). The blanks were wildcards that students could use to convey other feelings. The reverse sides identified negative feelings, for example: *Areas where I can NOT hangout with my friends.*

During the 2 days at each school, we carried out the following data collection activities:

- **Student-led tours**: Participants showed and talked about their more and less preferred spaces at school, and particular 'wellbeing aspects' they associated with each space. Researchers took photographs of these spaces with students holding relevant wellbeing cards.
- **Mapping activity**: Participants placed wellbeing cards on enlarged maps of their school to identify where they experience aspects of wellbeing or limited wellbeing. They discussed their choices with each other and researchers, providing a 'whole campus' view of their experience.
- **Notions of wellbeing discussion**: Participants used segmented *notions of wellbeing* diagram (Fig. 2) to explain their understanding of *wellbeing* related to transition and high school spaces.
- **Drawing activity**: In small groups, participants drew and discussed their ideal school that supports transition and wellbeing. Figure 3 shows a sample drawing with a short summary statement of the students' explanation.

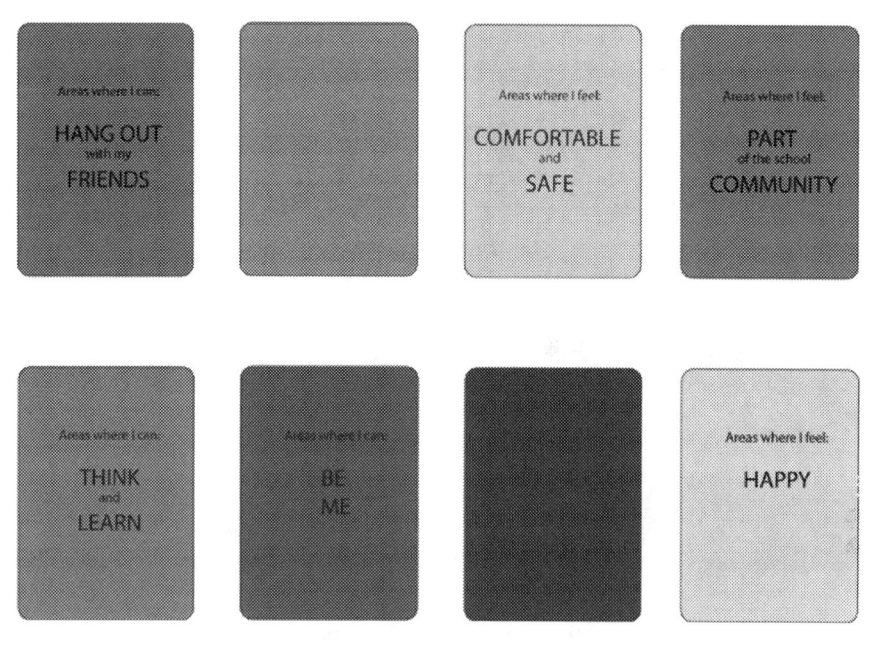

Fig. 1 Wellbeing cards used by students during data collection

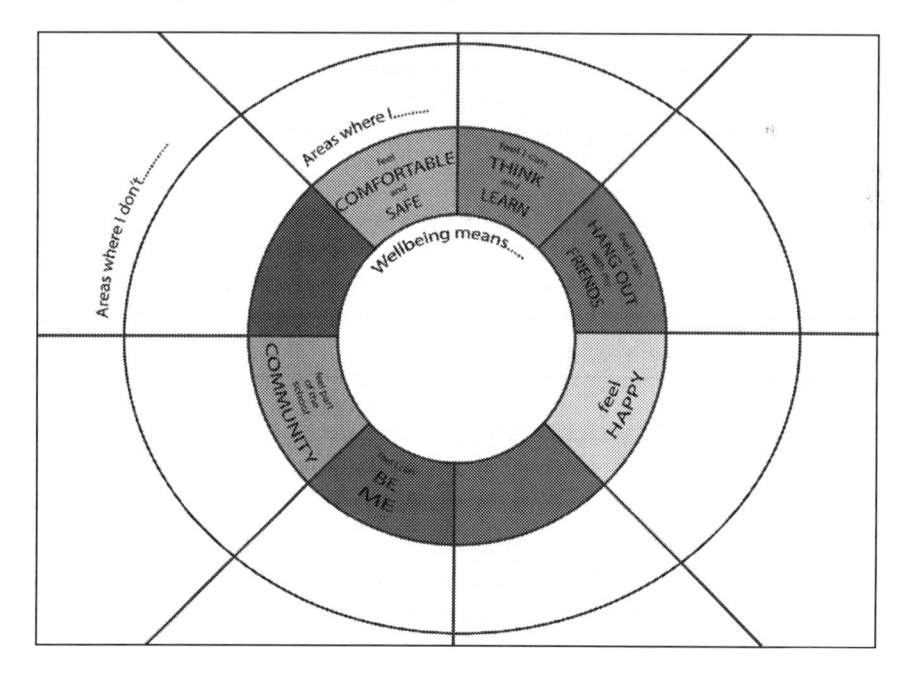

Fig. 2 Segmented diagram: Notions of wellbeing

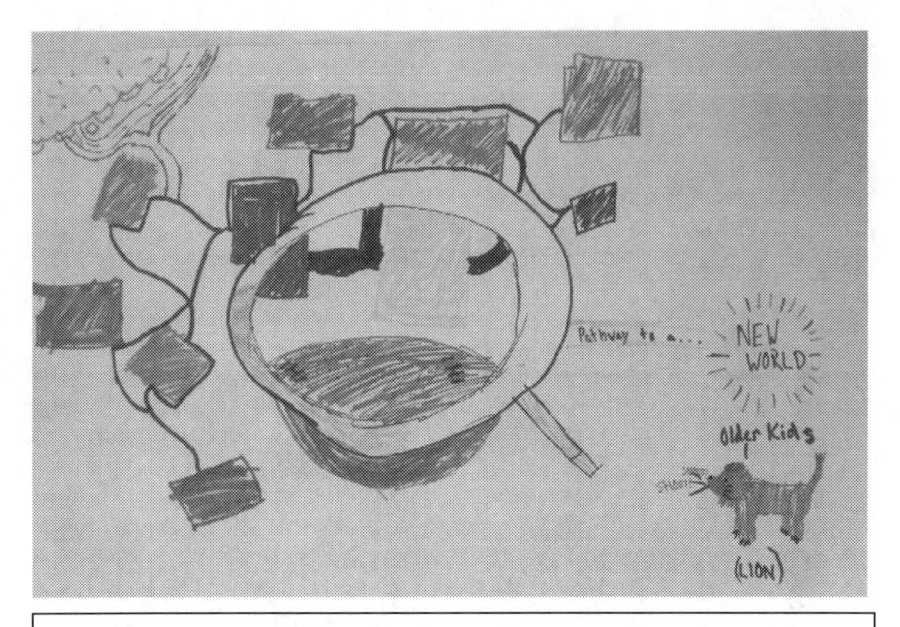

This drawing shows a pathway linking the school to a "new world".
The Year 7 area is under a magnifying glass, to represent "discovering
yourself" at high school. The lion represents intimidating older students.

Fig. 3 Drawing of an ideal school (Student Group 1 School B)

Data collection yielded an array of verbal and visual data. The student discussions
were professionally transcribed. The researchers analysed this data thematically by
coding and categorising emergent concepts in accordance with established qualitative practice (Miles, Huberman & Saldana, 2014). For the student drawings, we
used a visual data analysis approach developed by the researchers (Bland, 2012;
Franz, 2010). We examined each drawing and verbal explanation to identify visually
prominent features, which we categorised according to the six aspects of wellbeing
represented by the playing cards. For example, we assigned the lion in Fig. 3 to the
category *not comfortable and safe* and the interconnecting paths to *can be me* and
can think and learn.

Case Study Findings

Three case study schools in Brisbane, Queensland were identified in consultation
with Department of Education and Training (DET). As shown in Table 1 below, the
schools were varied in nature. The 33 student participants were selected by their
school.

Table 1 Overview of the 3 case study schools

Participants	School A	School B	School C
	13 Year 7 students	10 Year 7 students	10 Year 7 students
Total student enrolment (2016)	• Years 7–12 • 1750 students • 375 Year 7 students, 13 classes • Average socio-economic status	• Years 7–12 • 1100 students • – • Higher socio-economic status	• Prep—Year 12 • 2400 students • 400 Year 7 students, 14 classes • Higher socio-economic status
School	Opened in 1950s—relocated to this site within last 10 years. Purpose-built Year 7 building at far end of site opened 2015	Opened in 1970s, located in a residential area. Purpose-built Year 7 building on edge of campus opened 2015	Amalgamation of a high school and primary school. Year 7 students located in older block in middle of campus
Curriculum	Wide academic and vocational curriculum	Strong academic and sporting program	Wide academic options, strong performing arts
References	ACARA (2016), DET (2015), school web sites		

Case Study: School A

School A was clean, well maintained and less than 10 years old. It had an almost industrial appearance. The campus occupied an area of almost 1 km with buildings on both sides of a wide concrete pathway. Separate classroom blocks and outdoor spaces were assigned to each year level with demarcation lines on the walkways.

The purpose-designed Year 7 building was on one end of the campus, at considerable distance from the main entrance, administration office, library and tuckshop. It was added in 2015 to create a physical and social base for Year 7 students where they can develop a sense of belonging and safety. The adjacent Year 7 oval was a large grassed area with a stone 'yarning circle'. Behind the building were the Year 7 leaders' garden and a fenced patio with seating.

Year 7 student perspectives

The following photos (Fig. 4) were taken by Year 7 students during the school tour. The coloured cards indicate *wellbeing* aspects they associated with particular spaces.

The students most often associated wellbeing with designated Year 7 spaces such as their lunch area, the Year 7 leaders' garden and the stone circle. They often identified more than one aspect of wellbeing with a particular space. So for example, they associated the Year 7 seating area with *learning, hanging out with friends, feeling part of the community, free to be me, happy* and *safe*. In the words of one of the students:

Fig. 4 Spaces of wellbeing for School A students

> I like hanging out with my friends and being a little bit crazy… like being free from being really serious.

Students had differing preferences. For example, some liked the sports hall where they could be active with friends, while others sought peaceful and quiet spaces in the library. Colourfulness, spaciousness and visual stimulation were also important to some students who felt unhappy in dull, crowded rooms:

> We don't like that [building], all of us…There's no colour. It's just grey…. It's just very enclosed and very dark and there's not really that much colour.

The photos in Fig. 5 represent spaces around School A where Year 7 students experience limited wellbeing.

The three main spaces of limited wellbeing were classrooms, corridors and the play area near the car park. Students associated these spaces with *not feeling comfortable and safe*. Especially during lesson breaks, crowded walkways were daunting

Fig. 5 Spaces of limited wellbeing for School A students

when students of all year levels are jostling in various directions. Older, larger students were intimidating, especially in corridors and around the tuckshop:

> If you walk past sometimes they'll like look at you and then they'll say stuff to you like 'go back to your area'… It sort of like makes you nervous so you're trying to like hurry up and get out of their area.

Some Year 7 students were uncomfortable having to negotiate the 'kissing alley', a passageway where older students gathered with their boy/girlfriends.

The students wished for safer play areas that were away from traffic and offer greater shade:

> There should be a fence near that car park…Because like your handball goes down there and then you go to go get it and then teachers yell at you.

The location of the Year 7 building at the extreme end of the campus was both an advantage and a disadvantage. It provided Year 7 students a relatively safe haven to learn and socialise with peers, to settle into the high school environment without being totally immersed in it.

However, the separation of the Year 7 building from specialist classrooms and the sports hall was also problematic due to the long distances the school's youngest (and often smallest) students had to walk carrying heavy bags, inevitably arriving late for some classes. Some felt quite lost and intimidated when required to go outside the normal Year 7 confines where encounters with older students and 'strange' teachers could be intimidating. Other students reported that the enforced boundaries between their Year 7 space and the other years' spaces lessened their sense of belonging to the whole school community. One described feeling cut off from 'pretty much all the other places, apart from the grade seven area and the sports hall'.

The students' suggestions for enhancing their school spaces related to greater physical appeal, comfort and safety, such as: artwork around the school; shade over outdoor eating and play spaces; and a fence between the play area and car park.

Case Study 2: School B

School B was tightly packed on the side of a hill, with sports fields at the bottom. The school grounds were green and well tended, with established trees and garden beds. A creek wrapped around three sides of the campus which adjoins bushland and residential streets.

The new purpose-designed Year 7 block opened in 2016. Built on pylons close to the creek, this three-storey building contains 16 flexible classrooms, drama and art rooms. The ground floor, known generally as 'Under S Block', was an open-sided break area for Year 7 students. This was a stark space with concrete walls and a concrete floor covered with artificial grass matting. There were bench seats around the edge and a large open space in the middle that students mainly used for handball.

Year 7 student perspectives

The following students' photos (Fig. 6) illustrate spaces around School B where they experienced wellbeing.

School B students identified under S Block (the Year 7 building) as their preferred space. During the mapping activity, there was a notable clustering of spaces they associated with wellbeing around S Block, such as the library, oval and the Activities Centre. In contrast, their spaces of limited wellbeing were widely spread across the campus and further away from the Year 7 area.

Fig. 6 Spaces of wellbeing for School B students

Collectively, the students associated S Block with all six aspects of wellbeing. They were keen to spend most of their time here and appreciated that it was away from busier parts of the campus. As newer members of the school, they found the familiarity of Year 7 space reassuring. Here they felt happy and safe:

That's where we are taught; we do practically everything.... It's great, nobody else is allowed to come here except for Year 7 s, so we feel safe.

The Library was another space where students liked to spend time with friends and feel part of the school community. They valued it as an alternative to the more crowded Year 7 space. While some associated it with fun or a space *where I can be me*, others experienced it as a quiet getaway space where they could be on their own to relax and read, think and learn.

The performing arts block was another popular space where Year 7 students could interact with others from across the school with a shared interest in music and art. One Year 7 student commented that here she *feels part of the school community*, another was *happy* here because he had fun with friends. Similarly, one student mentioned the activities centre (hall) as somewhere she was *happy* because she played sport with friends here. In addition, she felt part of the community here during whole school assembly.

While most of the students preferred indoor or covered spaces, two selected the oval (sports field). They associated it with being happy, active and having fun with friends and a sense of freedom:

Fig. 7 Spaces of limited wellbeing for School B students

> When you are on the oval you can almost do whatever you like.

The following photos (Fig. 7) represent spaces around School B where Year 7 students experienced limited wellbeing.

Three points stand out about Year 7 students' less preferred spaces at School B: there were fewer spaces of limited wellbeing than of wellbeing; they were mainly outdoors; and they were associated with feeling uncomfortable and unsafe.

The students were often anxious about narrow pathways between buildings, which they found 'too busy' with 'too many people' and difficult to 'push a way through'. An alleyway between S Block and the tuckshop was a site of particular discomfort as 'it looks like a dungeon'. An out of bounds path along the creek felt dangerous to some students as they were afraid both of people and physical features here:

> It seems a bit gloomy, because of the trees, and the bush around it, and it's sometimes where older kids hang around, and so I don't feel very comfortable around here.

Other places were unsettling because they just did not feel right:

> There's [a] really weird locker place … It's a building. But there's no doors or anything, so it's just open … it echoes in there.

Sometimes students associated feelings of limited wellbeing with particular events. For example, some students did not like the activities centre because assemblies were held there. It was uncomfortable and they cannot be me or talk with friends:

> You're overrun by other kids … at assemblies … I feel like I'm bored and—because it's hard to listen, because everybody's talking, and there's so much noise … It gets really hot.

Sensory responses were also related to some students' discomfort. One student did not feel happy in the learning centre because it has a 'weird smell' and she associated it with school photos and vaccinations. Another student did not like the area under S Block because of smelly toilets.

School B students' suggestions for enhancing the school environment highlighted a need for active play spaces and equipment including soccer posts, a climbing frame and a maze:

> A playground but it's like better, not like one of those kiddy things.

Some would welcome more variety in their classroom environment:

> For each lesson, a different teacher and a different classroom ... it would be more fun to just walk around the school.

Case Study 3: School C

School C was on a hilly site. The campus was quite densely built-up and included a mix of traditional brick and more contemporary buildings. There were established trees in the higher part of the campus and recently created gardens and a sandstone yarning circle on the slope down to the sports field.

Although a six-storey building was built as part of the Flying Start Infrastructure project, Year 7 classrooms were located in an older building near the school entry. The classroom we visited was in a large high-ceilinged space that contained another Year 7 classroom, with a computer room between them. These rooms opened onto an indoor walkway. The classrooms' openness allowed for collaboration but competing activities could be noisy and distracting. Old, formal furnishings were due to be updated with more contemporary flexible tables and chairs. The Year 7 classrooms were close to the supervised Year 7 eating area and handball courts, and the students were not allowed into other year level areas.

Year 7 student perspectives

The following photos (Fig. 8) show the students' *spaces of wellbeing* at School C.

The students nominated a mix of internal and external spaces, while the stone circle was associated with the widest range of wellbeing aspects. The performing arts block also featured prominently, perhaps reflecting the school's strength in this area.

The students most frequently associated spaces of wellbeing with feeling happy, having fun, being creative and doing things they enjoy with friends. For example, in the art room, a student felt she *can be me* because:

> I can do like painting that express my feelings, and I can draw. I can have fun at the same time.

Similarly, another student was happy in the music block because:

> It's just full of energy here, and there are a lot of things around here that make me feel great, as a person who loves music... It's just the idea that I'm surrounded by music.

Fig. 8 Spaces of wellbeing at School C

For this student, it had the added appeal of connection with outdoors and nature:

> And it's really nice because on the balcony, you've got the trees here, and it just feels really comforting… You're just, engulfed by nature while being at school and playing your instrument – it's amazing.

Being outdoors was important for students to get away from more formal areas to relax and socialise. They particularly appreciated the stone circle and surrounding grassed area:

> This place is really open, I don't feel closed in or trapped. And I can imagine a sunny day, and I'm hanging out with my friends, and having a great time, and I'm surrounded by these plants, and nature-y things that are really green and bright, and it just makes me feel really nice inside.

Another described it as 'a nice area where you can, kind of unwind'. It also offered a space to catch up with students from other classes. One student felt comfortable and safe at the outdoor swimming pool where there is a caring adult 'making sure I don't drown'. The Library was an indoor space where students liked to get away from the classroom and relax alone. In contrast, one student liked to be in the Hall where she felt part of the community because 'at assembly the whole middle school is here'.

The following photos (Fig. 9) represent spaces around School C where students experienced limited wellbeing.

The students most often associated corridors and stairwells with limited wellbeing because they tended to be hidden, enclosed, dark, even forbidding:

Fig. 9 Spaces of limited wellbeing at School C

> It just feels very secluded. And it just feels quite dark and it's not really open... It's almost
> like a building that's kind of hidden with some metal bars, and it's not really that nice.

The unsettling nature of these spaces was compounded by the presence of older somewhat sinister-seeming older students who 'kind of look at you creepy' and 'psych you out'.

Being alone in spaces like the stairwells caused a sense of limited comfort and safety:

> This place is kind of hidden from the outside areas... it can feel really scary at times because
> you are here alone... Nobody supervises it, so there is nobody here to watch anything happen
> here.

Alluding to another kind of social isolation, two students indicated that they are not happy in the new building's upstairs exterior corridors. Repelled by the mesh doors and stark metal railings, they expressed empathy for students from the Special Education centre who were required to spend their breaks here for supervision purposes:

> They're all like talking and sitting on the bag racks ... This feels so cold and unwelcoming
> because it's like bars and like grey and hard corners and stuff. ...Because of the corridors
> it's very dark.

A more personal sense of exclusion was felt by a student in the hall during assembly. While he felt part of the community, he missed recognition as an individual because:

I can't really be me because we have to like respect the person on stage.

Cross-Case Findings

While there were some individual differences among students and between schools, the study shows considerable similarities about Year 7 students' experience of high school spaces. Summed up by one student, spaces of wellbeing are 'happy and energetic'. Overall, the students' four most commonly mentioned wellbeing aspects were *feeling happy, feeling safe, feeling comfortable* and *having friends*. For example, during the discussion round, the segments diagram about what is 'wellbeing', students variously mentioned:

> When you feel comfortable and safe enough to be happy.
>
> Generally being happy, being comfortable. Blanket.
>
> Where you feel happy and safe with who you are.
>
> Being happy and having friends that support you.

Students often associated wellbeing spaces with favourite activities and having fun, as the two following quotes indicate:

> To be able to relax and read or draw. It also means a place where I can hang out with my friends.
>
> Wellbeing means to be HAPPY! and feel comfortable and safe and to have fun!

Only one student drew a connection with learning:

> When I feel safe, happy and I can learn without any distractions

The study's findings suggest that Year 7 students:

- Prefer their designated home area where they feel supported by peers and familiar teachers.
- Need fresh air and spaces to play with equipment where they can run, play games and generally have fun with friends.
- Gravitate towards informal spaces such as eating areas and stone circles.
- Get away from it all in the library to relax, read, study and enjoy some quiet time alone or with friends.
- Feel intimidated and unsafe in busy school-wide spaces such as thoroughfares (corridors, pathways, stairwells), the tuckshop and sports field.

Spatial characteristics that support Year 7 students' wellbeing needs are shown in Table 2 as follows.

In contrast, spaces that are less supportive of wellbeing fail to meet Year 7 students' needs for safety, interaction and emotional comfort. These include corridors and the tuckshop where they encounter older students, who tease or give them 'weird looks'; spaces where they risk being squashed like the bus queue or yelled at by teachers. Limited physical appeal of particular spaces diminishes their sense of wellbeing, in particular uninvitingly dark and characterless classrooms.

Table 2 Characteristics of spaces of wellbeing: Students' collective response

Wellbeing needs	Spatial characteristics
Friends: Social wellbeing	Social spaces where students can hang out with and feel safe around friends and have fun
Privacy: Psychological wellbeing	Private, quiet spaces where students can be by themselves
Happiness: Emotional wellbeing	Spaces where students feel happy, relaxed
Comfort: Physical wellbeing	Comfortably furnished spaces, with good ventilation and temperature control
Safety: Physical and psychological wellbeing	Spaces that are familiar. Spaces where students feel safe and able to walk, sit and play freely away from intimidating older students and protected from traffic, with supportive teachers nearby
Aesthetics: Physical and emotional wellbeing	Large, spacious, open rooms that are bright and colourful
Connections with nature: Physical, emotional, psychological and existential wellbeing	Classrooms that offer a pleasant view and fresh air. Big outdoor spaces that offer trees and wind, and seating areas shaded by greenery
Play and activity: Physical, social and psychological wellbeing	Spaces where students can be active and playful in different ways including: playing games, running around, handball, dancing and singing, skipping, chalk drawing and having lunch
Learning: Cognitive wellbeing	Spaces where there are good teachers and students can think and pay attention

Discussion

The study contributes further evidence of interrelationships between school environment, learning and student wellbeing as identified elsewhere (Blackmore et al., 2011; Brooks, 2011; Cardellino et al., 2009; Gislason, 2009; Harrison & Hutton, 2012; Rudd et al. 2008; Tanner, 2009; Woolner, 2015). In particular, the findings accord with another Australian study (Simmons et al., 2015) with regard to students' association of wellbeing with particular aspects of their learning environment, and their desire to have fun and access to nature. Similar to Luz (2008), we noted significant impacts, both positive and negative, that informal spaces such as eating areas and corridors have on students' sense of wellbeing. The implications of the findings are discussed below.

Implications of Case Study Findings

Mid-way through Year 7 most participants appeared to have settled quite well aided by the transition programs provided at each school. However, they had some ongoing space-related social and safety needs.

Overall, the findings show that Year 7 students are playful young people with energy to burn who enjoy being outdoors. Having come from more activity-based primary school environments, they are less accustomed to sitting and talking quietly during breaks. They are of an age where their bodies are growing rapidly with impulses to run and jump. While designated Year 7 areas offer conditions that enable students to feel comfortable and safe and hang out with friends, tensions can arise between boisterous adolescents in a confined space, leading to accidents. Many Year 7 students still crave space and equipment for physical activity, similar to their primary school playgrounds. While they need access to open spaces, it is important to create sports areas where younger students feel comfortable and less dominated by older ones.

Year 7 students also like spaces, such as the library, where they can escape the noise and busyness of the school day. This suggests an opportunity for teachers to take greater advantage of the library as a neutral social hub and context for informal learning.

While the strategy to keep Year 7 students separate with peers of similar age, size and interest is well founded, there is still a need to actively encourage Year 7 students' sense of belonging to the school community. Possibly Year 7 students would benefit from freedom to roam and experience the wider spaces and life of the school; and to get to know older students as 'normal' young people rather than scary 'others'. In part, this calls for greater awareness among older students about the safety and comfort needs of Year 7 students in communal spaces like pathways and the tuckshop.

The teachers and school leaders we met expressed surprise at some of the Year 7 students' comments or were unaware of particular concerns about their high school spaces. This highlights the benefit of attending to student voice and agency in the design of their school environment (Blackmore et al., 2011; Woolner, 2015). Student-sensitive design solutions, such as more active playgrounds and wider walkways, might reduce supervision needs and allow teachers to direct their energy elsewhere.

The findings draw attention to the individuality of Year 7 students. Different students prefer different spaces; and some prefer different spaces at different times depending on their mood or who they are with. These findings demonstrate the importance of providing a variety of high school spaces that nurture individuals and allow for differing personal preferences and needs, rather than inequitable one-size-fits-all solutions. This could be creatively addressed by enabling student and teacher participation in the ongoing evaluation and design of their learning environment (Bland et al., 2013; Clarke, 2011; Woolner, 2015).

Limitations of the study

As an exploratory qualitative study, the number of research sites and participants was relatively limited. Rather than generalisable, the findings are intentionally indicative of students' transitioning experience and space-related wellbeing implications. The participants who elected to be involved in the study tended to be highly engaged in school life and consequently, their views do not necessarily reflect the experience of the whole Year 7 cohort, particularly those students struggling to settle into high school. The case study schools varied in size and nature but are not representative of all Queensland state schools.

Contributions of the Study

This study is of potential interest to education facility planners, architects, school leaders, Year 7 teachers and students and researchers. The findings enhance understanding about how students respond to particular spaces in particular ways. Thus, they provide an evidence base to inform the design of high school spaces that support the wellbeing of transitioning students.

From a methodological perspective, the study offers an innovative approach for working with young people to investigate learning spaces and facets of wellbeing. The medley of data collection activities introduced an element of fun into the research, attracting students' interest and willingness to participate. They evidently enjoyed acting as guides to their school and the freedom to share thoughts and feelings about particular spaces. The wellbeing 'playing cards' and segmented diagram enabled participation by translating complex theory of wellbeing and learning space design into student-friendly language.

The study also provides a foundation for further research that includes additional school types and a more diverse range of students and other stakeholders. Specific attention may also be given to:

- The spatial experience of students for whom transition is challenging.
- A longitudinal study of students' expectations and experience of high school spaces as they transition through Years 6, 7 and 8.
- Participatory processes to empower students and teachers as designers of school spaces.

Enhancing Practice

While students wish for exciting new spaces at high school too often they experience what one student described as 'nothing different or unique'. Therefore, based on this study's findings, we offer the following suggestions (Table 3) for designing school

Table 3 Suggestions for enhancing the high school spaces and wellbeing of Year 7 students

Wellbeing needs	Suggestions
Feel comfortable and safe	1. Provide active playground areas for Year 7 students, with equipment such as climbing frames, basketball hoops and soccer posts for casual play; and open spaces where they can run free 2. Provide shaded outdoor areas with picnic seating 3. Create enticing walking tracks on campus, taking advantage of the natural environment
Can think and learn	4. Use a variety of formal and informal areas around campus to widen students' perceptions about what constitutes a 'learning space' 5. Promote the library as social learning hub for the whole community—a neutral space where students of differing ages and abilities can come together for serious leisure 6. Initiate a Year 7 awareness program for older students to understand and support Year 7 students' transition to high school, buddy relationships
Hang out with friends	7. Designate a range of spaces around the campus as Year 7-friendly spaces where students of different years are encouraged to interact 8. Provide an online space for Year 7 students to interact, share their transitioning stories, news and events; anonymous Q & A section
Feel happy	9. Develop activity programs for Year 7 students led by Year 12 students 10. Provide opportunities for Year 7 students to engage in informal creativity around campus, e.g. painting murals, artwork displays, busking 11. Involve Year 7 students in gardening and other projects to enhance the school environment
Can be me	12. Celebrate cultural diversity of Year 7 students around the school through displays, colour schemes, murals, mosaics, multilingual signs
Part of the school community	13. Create a campus way-finding quiz (online or print format), adding locations and clues at regular intervals 14. Foster inclusivity for students of all abilities; for example, provision of suitable play spaces and equipment, sensory garden, braille signage; universal design principles (NDA, 2014) 15. Formally assess the relative advantages of locating Year 7 students separately versus integration with other year level students 16. Enable Year 7 students to participate in ongoing evaluation and design of their high school spaces

spaces that enhance the wellbeing of Year 7 students. The wellbeing needs (column 1) relate to the concepts on the wellbeing cards that the students used during data collection activities (Table 3).

Conclusion

This study has revealed the complex relationship between student wellbeing, student transitioning and high school spaces. It is vital to continue exploring the associated student needs as transitioning is a common experience at all schools and for all students at various stages of their school career. For Year 7 students in particular, successful transition to high school and feeling at home in their new learning environment can have long-term implications for their social and educational wellbeing.

Acknowledgements Queensland Department of Education and Training (DET) supported this research through funding and allowing access to schools. The research was carried out with ethical clearance from QUT (1600000299) and permission from DET.
Sincere thanks to the students, school leaders and Year 7 teachers for so willingly collaborating in data collection and sharing insights and creative ideas.

References

Atkinson, S., Fuller, S., & Painter, J. (Eds.). (2012). *Wellbeing and place*. Surrey: Ashgate.
Australian Curriculum, Assessment and Reporting Authority (ACARA). (2016). *My school*. https://www.myschool.edu.au/.
Australian Institute of Health and Welfare (AIHW). (2012). *Social and emotional wellbeing: Development of a Children's headline indicator. Information Paper*. Canberra: AIWH. https://www.aihw.gov.au/reports/children-youth/social-emotional-wellbeing-development-of-chi/contents/table-of-contents.
Barber, B. K., & Olsen, J. A. (2004). Assessing the transitions to middle and high school. *Journal of Adolescent Research, 19*(1), 3–30.
Blackmore, J., Batemann, D., Loughlin, J., O'Mara, J. & Aranda, G. (2011). *Research into the connection between built learning spaces and student outcomes: Literature review. Paper No. 22*. Melbourne: Department of Education and Early Childhood Education.
Bland, D. (2012). Analysing children's drawings: Applied imagination. *International Journal of Research and Method in Education, 35*(3), 235–242.
Bland, D., Hughes, H., & Willis, J. (2013). *Reimagining learning spaces: A research report for the Queensland Council for Social Science Innovation*. Brisbane: Queensland University of Technology. https://eprints.qut.edu.au/109555/.
Brewin, M., & Statham, J. (2011). Supporting the transition from primary school to secondary school for children who are looked after. *Educational Psychology in Practice, 27*(4), 365–381.
Brooks, D. (2011). Space matters: The impact of formal learning environments on student learning. *British Journal of Educational Technology, 42*(5), 719–726.
Burke, C. (2014). Looking back to imagine the future: Connecting with the radical past in technologies of school design. *Technology, Pedagogy and Education, 23*(1), 39–55.
Byers, T., Imms, W., & Hartnell-Young, E. (2014). Making the case for space: The effect of learning spaces on teaching and learning. *Curriculum and Teaching, 29*(1), 5–19.
Cardellino, P., Leiringer, R., & Clements-Croome, D. (2009). Exploring the role of design quality in the building schools for the future. *Architectural Engineering and Design Management, 5*(4), 249–262.
Clark, A. (2011). Breaking methodological boundaries? Exploring visual, participatory methods with adults and young children. *European Early Childhood Education Research Journal, 19*(3), 321–330.

Cleveland, B., & Fisher, K. (2014). The evaluation of physical learning environments: A critical review of literature. *Learning Environment Research, 17,* 1–28.

Department of Education and Training (DET). (2018). *A flying start for Queensland children.* Brisbane: Queensland Government. http://flyingstart.qld.gov.au/Pages/home.aspx.

Desjardins, R. (2008). Researching the links between education and well-being. *European Journal of Education, 43*(1), 23–35.

Fraillon, J. (2004). *Measuring student well-being in the context of Australian schooling: Discussion paper.* Victoria: ACER/MCEETYA.

Franz, J. M. (2010). Arts-based research. In J. Higgs, N. Cherry, R. Macklin, & R. Ajjawi (Eds.), *Researching practice: A discourse on qualitative methodologies* (pp. 217–226). Rotterdam: Sense Publishers.

Gislason, N. (2009). Mapping school design: A qualitative study of the relations among facilities design, curriculum delivery, and school climate. *Journal of Environmental Education, 40*(4), 17–33.

Harrison, A., & Hutton, L. (2012). *Design for the changing educational landscape: Space, place and the future of learning.* Abingdon: Taylor & Francis.

Hughes, H., Franz, J., Willis, J., Bland, D., & Rolfe, A. (2016). *High school spaces and student transitioning: Designing for student wellbeing.* Research report for Queensland Department of Education and Training. https://eprints.qut.edu.au/109555/.

Lamb, S. Walstab, A., Teese, R., Vickers, M., & Rumberger, R. (2004). *Staying on at school: Improving student retention in Australia.* Queensland Department of Education and the Arts. http://www.curriculum.edu.au/verve/_resources/studentretention_main_file.pdf.

Luz, A. (2008). The [design of] educational space: A process-centred built pedagogy. In A. Clarke, M. Evatt, P. Hogarth, J. Lloveras & L. Pons (Eds.), *Proceedings of E&PDE 2008: International Conference on Engineering and Product Design Education* (pp. 339–344). Universitat Politecnica de Catalunya, Barcelona, Spain, 4–5 September, 2008.

Mackenzie, E., McMaugh, A., & O'Sullivan, K. (2012). Perceptions of primary to secondary school transition: Challenge or threat? *Issues in Educational Research, 22*(2), 298–314.

Marley, J., Nobe, M., Clevenger, C., & Banning, J. (2015). Participatory post-occupancy evaluation (PPOE): A method to include students in evaluating health-promoting attributes of a green school. *Children, Youth and Environments, 25*(1), 4–28.

Miles, M. B., Huberman, A. M., & Saldaña, J. (2014). *Qualitative data analysis: A methods sourcebook.* Thousand Oaks: Sage.

Ministerial Council on Education, Employment, Training and Youth Affairs. (MCEETYA). (2008). *Melbourne declaration on educational goals for young Australians.* http://www.curriculum.edu.au/verve/_resources/National_Declaration_on_the_Educational_Goals_for_Young_Australians.pdf.

National Disability Authority. Centre for Excellence in Universal Design. (NDA). (2014). *The 7 principles.* Dublin: NDA. http://universaldesign.ie/What-is-Universal-Design/The-7-Principles/.

Newton, C., & Fisher, K. (2009). *Take 8: Learning spaces: The transformation of educational spaces for the 21st century.* Canberra: Australian Institute of Architects.

O'Toole, L. (2008). Understanding individual patterns of learning: Implications for the well-being of students. *European Journal of Education, 43*(1), 71–86.

Pendergast, D., Flanagan, R., Land, R., Bahr, M., Mitchell, J., Weir, K., et al. (2005). *Developing lifelong learners in the Middle Years of Schooling.* Brisbane: The State of Queensland.

Queensland. Department of Education and Training (DET). (2015). *School enrolment management plans.* http://education.qld.gov.au/schools/catchment/.

Rudd, P., Reed., F. & Smith, P. (2008). The effects of the school environment on young people's attitudes towards education and learning. Summary Report. Berkshire: National Foundation for Educational Research.

Sanoff, H. (2001). *School building assessment methods.* Washington DC: National Clearinghouse for Educational Facilities.

Simmons, C., Graham, A., & Thomas, N. (2015). Imagining an ideal school for wellbeing: Locating student voice. *Journal of Educational Change, 16,* 129–144.

Simmons, R. G. (1987). Social transition and adolescent development. *New Directions for Child and Adolescent Development, 1987*(37), 33–61.

Simons, H. (2009). *Case study research in practice.* Los Angeles: Sage.

Soutter, K. (2011). What can we learn about wellbeing in school? *Journal of Student Wellbeing, 5*(1), 1–21.

Tanner, C. (2009). Effects of school design on student outcomes. *Journal of Educational Administration, 47*(3), 381–399.

Watson, D., Emery, C. & Bayliss, P. (2012). *Children's social and emotional wellbeing in schools: A critical perspective.* Bristol: Policy.

Wheeler, A., & Malekzadeh, M. (2015). Exploring the use of new school buildings through post-occupancy evaluation and participatory action research. *Architectural Engineering and Design Management, 11*(6), 440–456.

Woolner, P. (Ed.). (2015). *School design together.* Abingdon: Routledge.

Students Reimagining School Libraries as Spaces of Learning and Wellbeing

Jill Willis, Hilary Hughes and Derek Bland

Abstract School libraries contribute to student wellbeing as one of the few spaces at the school where students from different year levels can interact and engage in informal learning. Drawing on the case study findings, this chapter presents the perspectives of 44 students on their new or refurbished school library at 7 schools in Queensland, Australia. Students participated in interviews about their lived experience of their existing library, and drew their imagined ideal library spaces. In the existing libraries, they valued spaciousness, technology, social connectedness and choices and control; while in their ideal libraries, they imagined peacefulness, comfort, connectedness to the outside world through natural and technological links, and adventure. The findings support a *framework for fostering student wellbeing through the school library* that builds upon an apparent three-way synergy between the goals of the Melbourne Declaration, students' ideal library features and preferred spatial qualities.

Introduction

Rocket-powered libraries, a doorway to Narnia and reading books while riding horses were among the ideas primary school students drew when imagining their ideal school library. They wished for a library that engaged their imagination and connected them to learning, where they could be active, creative, empathetic and social people. These students' insights arise from the *Reimagining learning spaces* research project (Bland, Hughes, & Willis, 2013) discussed in this chapter. The findings reveal relationships between school libraries and wellbeing, and underpin a framework for designing school libraries as learning spaces that contribute to the wellbeing of students as confident and creative learners, and active and informed citizens.

J. Willis (✉) · H. Hughes · D. Bland
Queensland University of Technology, Brisbane, QLD, Australia
e-mail: jill.willis@qut.edu.au

Concepts of Wellbeing in Education

Wellbeing is a prominent focus of policy and research about Australian children (Hamilton & Redmond 2010). Wellbeing policy documents commonly emphasise social and emotional wellbeing with a focus on mental health and child safety protection, with less emphasis on other identified domains of wellbeing such as school culture and physical environment (Graham et al., 2014). Yet the physical environment is an enabling wellbeing factor. Children in an Australian study associated physical environments and wellbeing with spaces linked to a sense of personal agency, security and a positive sense of self (Fattore, Mason, & Watson, 2009, p. 62). A link between student agency and wellbeing is also evident within the *Melbourne declaration on educational goals for young Australians* (Ministerial Council on Education, Employment, Training and Youth Affairs, MCEETYA, 2008). The goal of students becoming confident and creative individuals is associated with 'maintaining physical and emotional wellbeing' and 'developing the knowledge, skills and values needed to lead healthy, satisfying lives' (p. 9). These elaborations reflect a whole child approach to wellbeing.

Holistic concepts of wellbeing consider the current and future experiences of children, as well as the type of adults children will become, and the type of society in which they will live (Hamilton & Redmond, 2010). When wellbeing is seen as developmental and influenced by ecological interactions, a child's commitment to learning and to their sense of belonging at school is supported by safe and caring environments across home, school and wider community settings (Australian Institute of Health and Welfare, AIHW, 2012). This chapter adopts such a holistic view of wellbeing with strong links between physical, social and material environments. Children are regarded as collaborative, reflexive and critical agents who can take action within these contexts both now and in the future.

Student Involvement in Reimagining School Spaces Linked to Wellbeing

The *Reimagining learning spaces* study considered children to be critical agents who was able to highlight relationships between learning spaces and their physical, social and imagined environments. We recognised that active participation in decisions about school has been linked previously to significant increases in student perceptions of wellbeing (Lloyd and Emerson, 2017), especially when children are viewed as competent and engaged in democratic ideals of developing citizenship (Simmons, Graham, & Thomas, 2015). When Australian primary students designed practical classroom spaces, they designed spaces that included choices about where to sit to concentrate and how to support peers (Willis, 2014, 2016). In Finland, students who co-designed their learning spaces experienced enhanced personal wellbeing through their participation in decision making, citizenship skills and increased knowledge of the interrelationships between learning and spaces (Mäkelä, Helfenstein, Lerkkanen, & Poikkeus, 2018). Consulting students in the design or imagined design of school learning spaces also leads to more general wellbeing benefits as students often bring an 'uninhibited fresh outlook' and 'unbridled creativity' to the design of learning spaces in schools (Brown, 1992, p. 33). As some of the main users of schools, students can identify local needs and design solutions (Woolner, Hall, Higgins, McCaughey, & Wall, 2007), help designers understand more about the social impacts of physical designs (Flutter, 2006) and can improve school culture through suggested improvements to school pedagogy, environment and relationships (Simmons, Graham, & Thomas, 2015). Despite the evident benefits, student participation in the design of learning spaces has generally been limited or overlooked (Flutter & Ruddock, 2004). Often, the tight timeframes of the building allow little time to involve students in the design of innovative spaces.

School Libraries as Spaces for Wellbeing

School libraries as learning spaces can make a considerable contribution to students' educational, social and emotional wellbeing. As well as supporting literacy and reading for pleasure and study, school libraries are inclusive hubs for active, social learning and personal development (Buchanan, 2012; Weeks & Barlow, 2017). Numerous studies in the USA, Canada, UK and Australia demonstrate that school libraries and teacher-librarians positively impact student learning (Hughes, Bozorgian, & Allan, 2014; Scholastic, 2016) and can promote students' wellbeing through 'development of positive and ethical values in relation to the use of information, feelings of success and accomplishment, resilience, developing positive self-concept, self-esteem, independence and collaborative learning' (Teravainen & Clark, 2017, p. 24). Qualified librarians and teacher-librarians lead informational–pedagogical environments that foster active learning and social engagement (Teravainen & Clark, 2017; Valenza, 2017) through inquiry, problem based, connected and flipped learning, and design thinking (McGrath, 2015; Valenza, 2017). With expertise in information, digital and data literacies, they also foster wellbeing in online environments by guiding students in safe, responsible, critical and productive practices for learning and digital citizenship (Stripling, 2017; Todd, 2017; Valenza, 2017).

As a site of social wellbeing, the school library is one of the few indoor school spaces where students of different year levels can interact during free times and engage in a range informal learning and shared interests. The school library offers a safe, neutral space for those who feel uncomfortable elsewhere at school or who seek a quiet space to relax (Libraries All Party Parliamentary Group, 2014; Todd, 2017). In response to contemporary trends in curriculum and pedagogy, many school library spaces are being redesigned as iCentres (Hay, 2015), learning commons (Buchanan, 2012; Loertscher, Koechlin, & Rosenfeld, 2012) and innovation labs (McGrath, 2015). Flexible designs are conducive to individual and collaborative study, display, performance, and media production (Hay, 2015). Many incorporate a makerspace that fosters shared experimentation, critical thinking and creativity (Preddy, 2013). In spanning physical and virtual environments, school libraries are becoming the hub of a 'globally connected information ecosystem' (Valenza, 2017). In these 'zones of innovation, centres for design thinking', the school librarians can support 'children's capacities for creation and contribution' by promoting intellectual freedom, social responsibility and 'possibilities for student leadership and agency' (Valenza, 2017, p. 129). In Australia, the Federal Government's Building the Education Revolution (BER) programme funded the construction of new school libraries and other facilities with varying cost effectiveness (Lewis, Dollery, & Kortt, 2014). Our study took this as an opportunity to explore how newly designed libraries support students' learning and wellbeing.

Research Design

The *Reimagining Learning Space*s study (Bland et al., 2013) investigated how the physical environment of school libraries influenced pedagogic practices and learning outcomes. While the whole study involved a range of school stakeholders, this chapter focuses on students' perspectives. The qualitative case study (Simons, 2009) focused on seven schools in Queensland, Australia that had recently gained a new or refurbished school library through the Building the Education Revolution (BER) project (Lewis, Dollery, & Kortt, 2014). The schools were purposefully selected to allow a varied range of primary and secondary, government and private schools, located in Brisbane and regional towns, with student enrolments ranging from 280 to 915 students.

At each school, the research team visited the library and conducted interviews with the principal, a teacher and the teacher-librarian. In addition, during the focus groups, we invited about 10 students to create and annotate an image of their imagined ideal library in response to the question: *If you could design a school library, what would it look like?* We also asked the students questions about how they use their actual newly built or refurbished library, which included:

- What are some of your favourite things to do in the library? Why?
- What is one word you would use to describe the library? Explain your choice.
- How might the library space be improved to help students learn?

Imaginative ideas as metaphors for what excites and engages children in learning can be a valuable point of entry for consultation with children. We encouraged the students to draw on their social imagination, that is 'the capacity to invent visions of what should be and what might be [...] in our schools' (Greene, 1995, p. 5). The student focus group data were analysed inductively using grounded theory techniques (Charmaz, 2006). Their images were analysed using a thematic categorisation approach developed by one of the researchers (Bland, 2012). Sharing their library using experiences and imaginings enabled the students to contribute towards a holistic vision for wellbeing that captured children's feelings about present realities and future possibilities.

Combining student drawings with verbal responses enabled students to combine the faculty of reason to operate in parallel with the power of imagination (Bland, 2014, 2016). Four types of imagination act both independently and in combination: creative imagination (the artistic application that is generally perceived as imagination); fantasy (hope, daydreams, wishful thinking); empathy (seeing from others' points of view); and critical imagination (perceiving the social/cultural/political forces that shape, support and limit us). All four imaginations need to be engaged to ensure that school design not only meets functional requirements, but also meets students' aspirations, and their wellbeing needs. The experiences that students reported about their actual new library and their imagined ideal library are outlined in the following section.

Students' Experience of Their New School Libraries

The students, who ranged in age from 8 to 12, valued the new school library as a place where they could spread out and relax, in contrast to their classrooms which were often crowded and associated with feeling stressed. Students most appreciated the library's range of soft seating options, colour and natural light, and would often gravitate to areas where they could connect with each other and see the outdoors and experience natural light, breeze and see plants growing.

The students highlighted the variety of learning activities that were happening in the new library spaces. Traditional school library activities such as research, personal reading, displays and promotion of readings schemes still occurred, but in the newly designed spaces, these were often expanded to occur more frequently. The new library spaces also enabled new activities that included formal learning activities organised by teachers or the teacher librarian, informal learning led by the students, or community events with the extended school community such as parents. Students reported making movies, running special interest clubs, listening to music, playing games, designing games, conducting science experiments and running whole school events such as concerts, graduation ceremonies, buddy reading programmes and a puppet show put on by older students for younger students.

The students were ready to offer critical insights into the new library spaces and to reimagine alternatives and make suggestions to improve the functionality of their school libraries. As outlined below, their responses reflect four wellbeing-related themes: *spaciousness*; *technology; social connectedness*; and *choice and control*. These are illustrated with individual quotes, and inform the framework at the end of the chapter.

Spaciousness

The students' responses suggest that spaciousness was linked to emotional wellbeing. Increased space in the new library seemed to reduce the stress of overcrowding, enable choices of activity or privacy in order to relax, and they provided increased flexibility for possible agentic action.

In the new libraries, students valued having more space as 'you can walk through without tripping someone else'. More space gave greater choice of where to sit and talk with friends, or to find a quiet space to read, relax or spread out in the library. It was often associated with increased light which was particularly valued by students whose previous library was dark and old, and so 'a bit scary'. Other students missed the feel of the old library and the 'cubby house' feel where they could 'get away from everyone else' and 'just read and sit in a corner by yourself'. Portable seating options contributed to a sense of spaciousness, with soft furnishings such as beanbags enabling individual reading in a corner in a patch of sun, or seating with friends. A frequent criticism was that there were not enough beanbags to go around so only a few people could take advantage of the option of creating a comfortable space.

Spaciousness was linked to flexibility. While tables on wheels enable flexible arrangements, they were unpopular with students when the rooms were too small for lessons where they were expected to rearrange furniture to work in different configurations for collaborative groups. One reported feeling 'all squished up and you'd have no space because there'd be too many tables'. Students were critical as 'people don't put the brake off. They just wheel it, and they break the brake…Then the tables just slide around. They won't stay still. It's very frustrating when they do that.' They suggested stackable chairs and tables with tops that could flip up so that the rooms could be more flexible and suit their small group research projects, drama productions, and family movie night fundraisers. In some of the schools where the library shelves were on wheels, and at low height to reduce weight, the mobility of the shelves enabled staff and students to shift furnishings to create open learning spaces. This occurred for special events such as a whole school puppet show put on by younger grades, or for wet weather days to enable the greater numbers of students to play some organised indoor sports.

Technology

Technology was linked to wellbeing when students were able to access and use it to relax and be comfortable and creative.

The students generally associated the new library learning spaces with 'way more technology' and increased access and permission to use it. In some schools, the IT helpdesk was located in the library, and the library was named the 'i-centre' or 'i-hub' to increase the relationship between information use through digital technology and the traditional research functions of a library. Students appreciated considerations such as many more power sockets available through floor hubs, or under the seating to enable them to charge their laptops or mobile devices. They also enjoyed going to the library to play games on their computer, create digital games. It was a space where they could listen to music together with friends, create photos, or movies, or relax and watch a movie with friends during lunchtime. For example, on a day to raise awareness of mental health, students could create group photos in the green screen room. A participant noted: 'the one I've got is of everybody in our group in Paris with the Eifel Tower behind us'.

Despite a general sense of 'more' technology, access to it was regulated through rosters and schedules. In some schools a roster gave students confidence about the shared expectations, and a sense that access to special opportunities was fair:

> We have to line up. Then you need a partner. They'll sign in your name…write down what number it is and then pass the iPad to you. Then once the bell rings to clear up and stuff you have to hand them back. They cross off your name and just check that's the right number.

In other schools with fewer devices to share, the students did not all expect to have access.

The potential of technology in the library to support students' wellbeing was sometimes overlooked. For example, large digital screens can generate a sense of belonging by advertising school events or achievements, yet students observed that they were rarely turned on. The library air conditioners were also seldom on at some schools, even in hot weather. As an indication of discomfort (and limited wellbeing) a student mentioned that when they were used there was a funny smell 'like wet socks'. Another explained that their use was for special events or when visitors came as they cost too much to use everyday. While students would have liked to see all of these facilities used, they were resigned to energy saving decisions as part of the adult control of their environment. In contrast, at another school, the passive energy saving aspects of the building such as cross ventilation and natural light were a source of student pride as they felt that they were contributing to global aims of sustainability.

Social Connectedness

The students seemed to experience social wellbeing through connectedness with other people in the library.

In each school, the students reported that they came to the library several times a week to socialise and relax: 'If you just want to hang with your friends you come here'. The teacher-librarian was important in establishing a welcoming culture and designing activities that promoted a sense of community. Students valued library spaces that were 'bright and airy' where there was something new to see or do every week. For example, in one school, the Spanish teacher put up a collection of phrases and gave prizes to those who could translate the phrases. Students valued displays social games, and a celebration of learning that was happening in other classes and year levels.

In the new libraries, students from multiple grades met together informally to chat or to play board games, or be part of formal social activities such as Anime, Writers or Chess clubs. However, the noise of socialising sometimes caused tensions for those who sought quietness or privacy. There was also a tension around the need for privacy in social conversation, as some students reported that 'everyone tries to book the small quiet rooms so there isn't as many people listening into your conversation.' Younger students would have liked to include some more toys and dress up props for social activities especially on rainy days. At one school, the students were proud to indicate that their new library had a lift to enable wheelchair access to the library, and valued the inclusiveness of the design.

Choices and Control

Wellbeing was apparently linked with opportunities for students to make choices about how to use the library spaces and have their preferences and opinions valued, including their requests for more manga books, e-books and technology like Xbox and Wii games. In some schools, there was greater opportunity for students to be involved in democratic decision making or action. Students appreciated being able to make suggestions for improvements to the library, for example through the Student Council.

In one school, teachers and students made choices about how to convene different spaces for events, using a 'return the room to this arrangement' chart to guide how the space needed to be left for the next users. Systems that enabled students to access, use and share resources were used in many of the libraries. Reading was a favourite activity and the students appreciated the variety of places they could choose to sit and read. Some of the students aimed to find the quietest place to read: 'If there's too much noise all I can hear is that and I can't - I'm not focused on the story. I've not actually got into the story'. They often chose to sit in hidden or out of the way place such as under a desk, under the library office overhang or 'out on the deck'.

While many of these same themes were evident in the imagined libraries drawn by students, there were significant gaps between the real spaces provided for them and their imagined ideal library, with students identifying a desire for more fun, nature and fantasy.

Imagining an Ideal Library

The drawings of imagined libraries were analysed and four key themes were identified: *connectedness*, *peacefulness*, *adventure and playfulness* and *technology*. Often the themes overlapped. For example, a Year 6 male student imagined a futuristic library (technology) that was situated partly in a grassy area with animals (connected to nature) whose role was to hand out books and provide advice (connectedness) to students who sat in bean bag chairs (peacefulness). While *connectedness* was similar to what students experienced within their existing library, *peacefulness, adventure and playfulness* were different themes and indicated some disparity between reality and the ideal. Across all of the themes, bright colours and natural light were important. The following examples illustrate the ways that students reimagined possibilities for learning in their ideal school library.

Connectedness

Students' images highlighted holistic wellbeing factors that link school learning and life experience. Connectedness reflected emotional and physical wellbeing, sometimes associated with a sense of peace.

Students desired to connect their learning with the natural world. As one year 5 student wrote, 'I don't see why we sit cooped up in a stuffy classroom all day when the sun is high in the sky'. Students drew pictures and described their ideal library as 'a garden where you can read in the sunshine' and with grassy areas where they could read, play and be near a pond that would 'make me feel happy and peaceful'. Common features included gardens and animals to look after, and water, with the idea that the 'library is on a river...like a boat'. Connectedness in learning was evident through links between real life observation and experience and reading and listening, so 'you could learn about animals by reading and looking' (Fig. 1). Frequent connections occurred between indoor and outdoor spaces and a connection between multiple sensory stimuli including sound, texture, breeze, warmth, light.

Peacefulness

Peacefulness was an important aspect of many students' imagined libraries, linked to wellbeing through their desire to refresh, rest and maintain a peaceful escape from the noise and bustle of a school day. It suggested that peacefulness was a positive wellbeing strategy for emotional self-regulation, linked to reduced anxiety and informed decisions about learning. As the illustration of the doorway to Book Narnia shows (Fig. 2), peacefulness was not always passive but was often linked to imagined adventure.

A sense of peacefulness in students' imagined library was associated with relaxing in comfortable and soft chairs, pillows and beds, in quiet places that could help students think. The imagined spaces were sometimes dark with sound-proofed reading spaces and cosy corners and sleeping rooms with furnishings such as 'pillows or beanbags if you like to work in comfort as I do'. These were not only for relaxing, but for learning and contemplation away from noise such as 'a study corner with a sound proof wall so you can think' or 'reading corner somewhere quiet for people to sit, relax and read a book'.

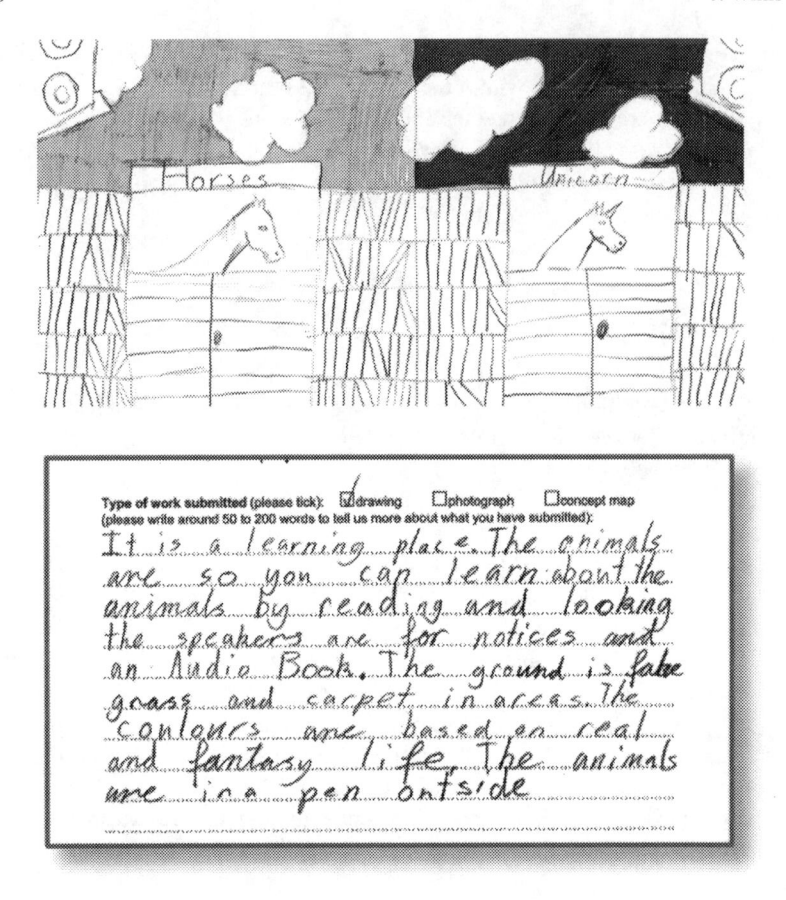

Fig. 1 Animals, audio books and colours of nature (Year 6 female student at a rural school)

Adventure and Playfulness

The student images of an ideal library often conveyed a sense of adventure and playfulness. There was a preference for being active decision makers, who could enjoy physical and intellectual adventures with friends and book characters. These preferences can be seen to be linked to physical, social and emotional wellbeing.

Adventure was an aspect of many of the student drawings, with slides connecting different levels of the library, or fanciful transport such as roller coasters to get around. Futuristic floating chairs and tables, and rockets point to a physical environment that could allow for movement, fun and discovery. Cafés and eating areas were often pictured with explanations that this would allow children and teachers to take breaks from working, or to eat while learning, or be a social space during break times. The

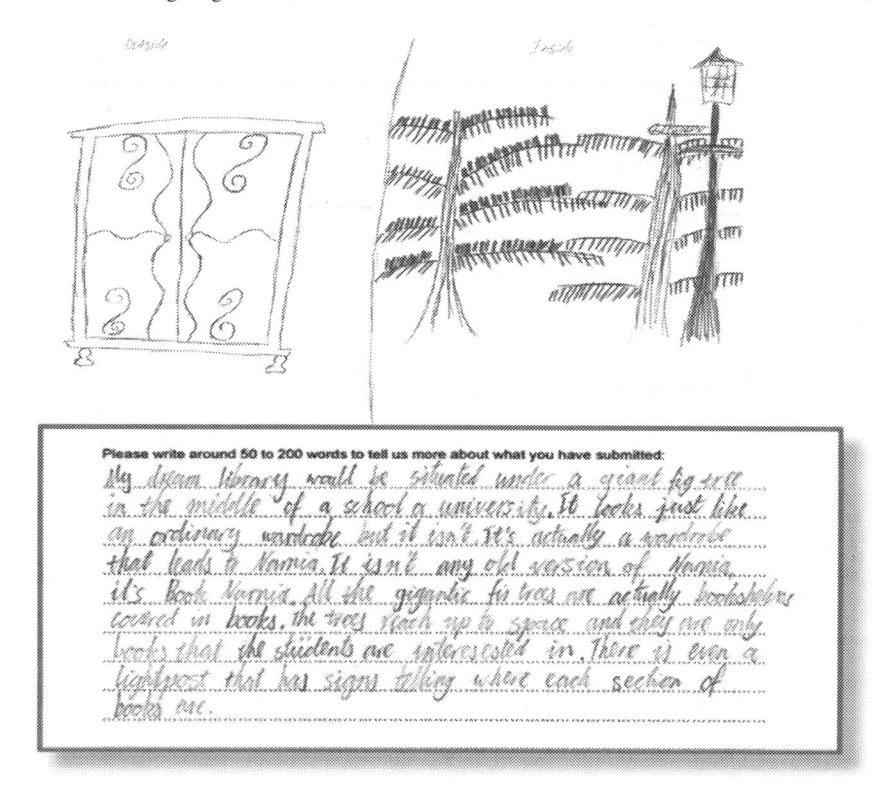

Fig. 2 A doorway to Book Narnia through a wardrobe under a giant tree (Year 6 female student at a suburban school)

idea of entering into the story world was mentioned by quite a few students who valued taking their minds on imaginative journeys. Their ideas included 'a teleporter to dream maker playground, tv room, make-a-books…that can teleport you into the book' and spaces where 'you can go in them and camp in them'.

Technology

The students' images of their ideal libraries often include technology and suggest awareness of the needs of others as well as optimism for the future. While many of their ideas could be dismissed as fantasy they also tell us something of their hope that schools might be places of imagination and educational adventure.

Technologies in students' imagined libraries included futuristic ideas such as a TARDIS and an observatory and a library that hovered in the air (Fig. 3). Students also designed libraries with more access to current technology, as one explained: 'If I could build my own library, it would have fun, but educational things like iPads,

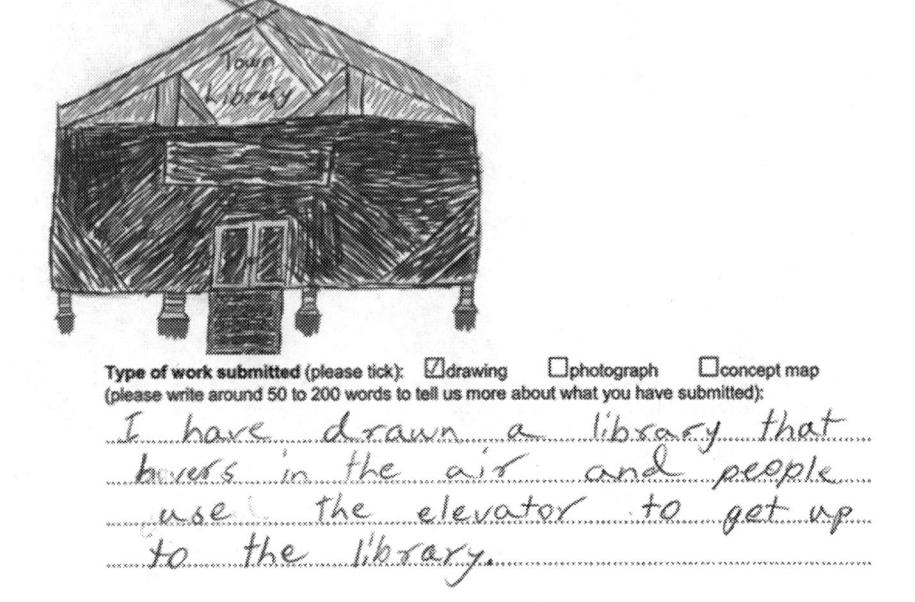

Type of work submitted (please tick): ☑drawing   ☐photograph   ☐concept map
(please write around 50 to 200 words to tell us more about what you have submitted):

I have drawn a library that hovers in the air and people use the elevator to get up to the library.

Fig. 3 A library that hovers in the air (Year 6 male student at a rural school)

e-readers, computers and plasma flat screen t.v.s'. Technology and playfulness were frequently linked together where technology would allow students to 'learn and have fun at the same time'. Students also recognised the need to plan for children of all ages and abilities, with 'different t.v.s for different age group with different games so a four year old doesn't end up playing Super Mario brothers with some stranger that's 20 years old'. Another technology was related to environmental sustainability such as 'lots of glass to let natural light in', and 'roof is made out of glass, so it offers UV protection and there is no need for lights'.

Discussion

The students were able to critically evaluate their current experiences of newly designed libraries, and through their imagination of an ideal library they provided insights into some of their preferences for learning in school library spaces. There were strong recurring themes in their responses about their actual and imagined libraries that indicate students desired places that inspired their imaginations, and wished to learn in physical environments that allow for flexibility, movement, fun and discovery. In particular, they longed for spaciousness, and for the external world to be almost seamlessly integrated into the internal library space.

Ideas of real-world environments with direct access to nature are typical of students' responses in the UK, USA and Australia (Bland & Sharma-Brymer, 2012; Burke & Grosvenor, 2003; Ghaziani, 2008). Natural settings are seen as not only providing refreshment and a quiet space, but as an opportunity to learn about and care for the environment and gardens both in the immediate and long term as part of a commitment to sustainability. The students in this study desired a balance between active spaces and quiet, private spaces. Mäkelä et al.'s study (2018) reflected similar outcomes as students indicated the need to balance individual needs for privacy and quiet, with needs for spaciousness, and being able to fit enough seating options into the learning spaces for collaboration and teacher-led instruction (p. 22).

The creative pedagogies that our participants imagined have also previously been identified by young people as an important aspect of wellbeing in schools (Simmons et al., 2015). The students' desire for greater control over choices and the routines that might govern the use of technology has been identified with increased student wellbeing. Gillett-Swan and Sargeant (2018) note that the digital learning spaces in schools are highly regulated by adults, and they advocate for students to be included in everyday decisions and governance of these online learning spaces.

Reimagining school library spaces assume that designing and learning are ongoing processes that involve the participation of everyday stakeholders. The interview responses and drawings highlight that students are insightful critics who have challenging ideas to share. While students were not consulted in the design of these new library spaces, their preferences could still inspire some ongoing designing and reimagining of existing school library spaces as well as inform future library and school design.

Libraries are just one of the school spaces that are constantly changing. A holistic view of student wellbeing includes helping students become confident and creative learners, and active and informed citizens, three student aims espoused by the *Melbourne declaration on educational goals for young Australians* (MCEETYA, 2008). Drawing on the findings from this study, Table 1 shows a three-way synergy between:

- The goals of the Melbourne Declaration
- Students' ideal library features; and
- Students' preferred library spatial qualities.

For example, a school library may realise the goal for students to become confident learners and promote wellbeing by enabling a group of students to:

- Collaboratively research and build an Arduino robot (learning activity);
- Create a video that documents their robot design process using animation software (library feature—access and use technology to be creative and have control);
- Share the robot and video with friends after school in the library's innovation corner (library spatial qualities—accessible technology and student friendly display space freely available).

Table 1 Framework for fostering student wellbeing through the school library

Learning activities in library linked to goals of the Melbourne Declaration	Students' ideal library features linked to wellbeing	Students' spatial preferences with links to support learning and wellbeing
Goal: Confident learners Activities: experiment, choose, try things in a supportive environment. Through accessing resources, celebrating learning through displays or events, writers club, conducting science experiments, sharing ownership of rooms and resources	**Technology** Wellbeing through: access and use of technology to relax and be comfortable, be creative, have control and a sense of agency **Varied spaces** Wellbeing through: choice about collaboration or privacy; support for positive social relationships as well as opportunity to relax, concentrate and have peacefulness	**Spaciousness** Wellbeing through: Spaces that are flexible and not crowded. Technology accessible and used daily not just for special occasions **Flexible and comfortable** Wellbeing through: furnishings and seating choices that can easily be rearranged without being damaged
Goal: Creative learners Activities: explore ways of authoring and communicating new ideas individually and collaboratively. Through games, technology, artwork, inviting guest authors or artists, supporting students to create	**Connectedness and peacefulness** Wellbeing through: attentiveness to multiple senses including sound, texture, breeze, warmth, light as well as body needs such as fun, friendship, movement, eating and rest **Creative environment** Wellbeing through: Imagination in all of its forms encouraged and valued both for the present and future self	**Colourful and collaborative** Wellbeing through: spaces that encourage playfulness, socialising, and games **Connections to nature** Wellbeing through: light, water, animals and outdoor elements visible from inside
Goal: Active and informed citizens Activities: investigate and plan actions in response to community needs. Through leadership roles for students, clubs, connections to inquiry sources both physical and virtual, community events. Games, movies and opportunities to innovate and imagine	**Welcoming environment** Wellbeing through: Feeling welcome and recognising students' choices were valued **Varied opportunities** Wellbeing through: Self-regulation, choices of activity or privacy in order to relax **Shared decision-making** Wellbeing through: being active decision makers about library design and use, who could enjoy physical and intellectual adventures with friends and book characters **Spaces for imagination and activity** Wellbeing through: Making links between real life experiences and reading and listening	**Inclusive and sustainable** Wellbeing through: cross ventilation, light; outdoor eating areas for community events are used and valued as a part of a community and future focused

The table identifies key considerations in (re)imagining school libraries as information-rich, inclusive learning spaces that entice active inquiry and creativity. It is a first step in representing the school library as a student wellbeing hub or ecosystem (Todd, 2017; Valenza, 2017). While this notion requires extensive further exploration, the table offers school communities and researchers a basic evidence-based framework for school designing that is both innovative and student-focused.

Implications for Designing Libraries that Foster Student Wellbeing

The findings of this research project suggest that the use of creative and critical imagination can increase the pedagogical potential of new library spaces, challenging what is, and inciting what could be, helping to 'imagine a world that is not yet imagined' (Fine, 1994, p. 30). For designers, being informed by empathetic understandings of potential end users may also produce more agile spaces, with the possibility that students' ideas could contribute to problem identification and solutions and lead to their genuine empowerment and wellbeing.

Key implications for practice arising from the findings is as follows:

- School libraries are responsive and hybrid spaces that enable students to develop their confidence, creativity and agency as learners.
- Interactive, learner centred, inclusive and flexible spaces extend students' learning opportunities, and contribute to their sense of wellbeing.
- Social and emotional wellbeing such as the need for relaxation, peacefulness, fun, choice and privacy can be enhanced by spatial designs.
- To ensure student wellbeing, school library designing must be inclusive of all students and their diverse educational, physical and emotional needs.
- As students are insightful and imaginative critics of school design they should be consulted and involved in the design, evaluation and continual redesign of school learning spaces.

Conclusion

Through presentation and discussion of select findings from the research project *Reimagining learning spaces*, this chapter has demonstrated the importance of including the experience and imagination of students in designing school libraries and other school spaces. In addition, it has expanded understanding about the connections between learning spaces and wellbeing, providing a foundation for further exploration about the design of school culture and the physical environment.

References

Australian Institute of Health and Welfare (AIHW). (2012). *Social and emotional wellbeing: Development of a children's headline indicator*. Information paper. Cat. No. PHE 158. Canberra: AIHW.

Bland, D. (2012). Analysing children's drawings: Applied imagination. *International Journal of Research and Method in Education, 35*(3), 235–242. https://doi.org/10.1080/1743727x.2012.717432.

Bland, D. (2014). Children's imagination at the centre of design for education. In P. Woolner (Ed.), *School design together* (pp. 153–166). Milton Park, UK: Routledge.

Bland, D. (2016). Introduction: Reimagining imagination. In D. Bland (Ed.), *Imagination for inclusion: Diverse contexts of educational practice* (pp. 1–12). New York, NY: Routledge.

Bland, D., Hughes, H., & Willis, J. (2013). *Reimagining learning spaces. Final report to the Queensland Centre for Social Science Innovation.* Retrieved from https://eprints.qut.edu.au/63000/.

Bland, D., & Sharma-Brymer, V. (2012). Imagination in school children's choice of their learning environment: An Australian study. *International Journal of Educational Research, 56*, 75–88.

Brown, R. (1992). Students as partners in library design. *School Library Journal, 38*(2), 31–34.

Buchanan, S. (2012). Designing the research commons: Classical models for school libraries. *School Libraries Worldwide, 18*(1), 56–69.

Burke, C., & Grosvenor, I. (2003). *The school I'd like: Children and young people's reflections on an education for the 21st century.* London: Routledge Falmer.

Charmaz, K. (2006). *Constructing grounded theory: A practical guide through qualitative analysis.* London: Sage.

Fattore, T., Mason, J., & Watson, E. (2009). When children are asked about their well-being: Towards a framework for guiding policy. *Child Indicators Research, 2*(1), 57–77.

Fine, M. (1994). Dis-stance and other stances: Negotiations of power inside feminist research. In A. Gitlin (Ed.), *Power and method: Political activism and educational research* (pp. 13–35). New York: Routledge.

Flutter, J., & Ruddock, J. (2004). *Consulting pupils: What's in it for schools?.* London: Routledge.

Flutter, J. (2006). 'This place could help you learn': Student participation in creating better school environments. *Educational Review, 58*(2), 183–193.

Ghaziani, R. (2008). Children's voices: Raised issues for school design. *CoDesign, 4*(4), 225–236.

Gillett-Swan, J. K., & Sargeant, J. (2018). Voice inclusive practice, digital literacy and children's participatory rights. *Children and Society, 32*(1), 38–49.

Graham, A., Fitzgerald, R., Powell, M. A., Thomas, N., Anderson, D. L., White, N. E., & Simmons, C. A. (2014). *Wellbeing in schools: Research project: Improving approaches to wellbeing in schools: What role does recognition play?* Final report: volume two. Lismore, NSW: Centre for Children and Young People. Southern Cross University. Retrieved from https://epubs.scu.edu.au/educ_pubs/1354/.

Greene, M. (1995). *Releasing the imagination: Essays on education, the arts, and social change.* San Francisco: Jossey-Bass.

Hamilton, M., & Redmond, G. (2010). *Conceptualisation of social and emotional wellbeing for children and young people, and policy implications: A research report for Australian Research Alliance for Children and Youth and the Australian Institute of Health and Welfare.* Canberra: Australian Research Alliance for Children and Youth. Retrieved from http://www.aracy.org.au/publications-resources/command/download_file/id/91/filename/Conceptualisation_of_social_and_emotional_wellbeing_for_children_and_young_people,_and_policy_implications.pdf.

Hay, L. (2015). The evolution of the iCentre model. *Teacher Librarian, 42*(4), 15–19.

Hughes, H., Bozorgian, H., & Allan, C. (2014). School libraries, teacher-librarians and student outcomes: Presenting and using the evidence. *School Libraries Worldwide, 20*(1), 29–50. https://doi.org/10.14265.20.1.004.

Lewis, C., Dollery, B., & Kortt, M. (2014). Building the education revolution: Another case of Australian government failure? *International Journal of Public Administration, 37*(5), 299–307. https://doi.org/10.1080/01900692.2013.836660.

Libraries All Party Parliamentary Group. (2014). *The beating heart of the school: Improving educational attainment through school libraries and librarians*. London: CILIP. Retrieved from https://archive.cilip.org.uk/cilip/advocacy-campaigns-awards/advocacy-campaigns/libraries-all-party-parliamentary-group/beating.

Lloyd, K., & Emerson, L. (2017). (Re)examining the relationship between children's subjective wellbeing and their perceptions of participation rights. *Child Indicators Research, 10*(3), 591–608.

Loertscher, D. V., Koechlin, C., & Rosenfeld, E. (2012). *The virtual learning commons: Building a participatory school learning community*. Salt Lake City, UT: Learning Commons.

Mäkelä, T., Helfenstein, S., Lerkkanen, M. K., & Poikkeus, A. M. (2018). Student participation in learning environment improvement: Analysis of a co-design project in a Finnish upper secondary school. *Learning Environments Research, 21*(1), 19–41.

McGrath, K. (2015). School libraries and innovation. *Knowledge Quest, 43*(3), 54–61.

Ministerial Council on Education, Employment, Training and Youth Affairs (MCEETYA). (2008). *Melbourne declaration on educational goals for young Australians*. Retrieved from http://www.curriculum.edu.au/verve/_resources/National_Declaration_on_the_Educational_Goals_for_Young_Australians.pdf.

Preddy, L. B. (2013). *School library makerspaces: Grades 6-12*. Santa Barbara, CA: Libraries Unlimited.

Scholastic. (2016). *School libraries work! A compendium of research supporting the effectiveness of school libraries*. Retrieved from http://www.scholastic.com/SLW2016/.

Simons, H. (2009). *Case study research in practice*. London: Sage.

Simmons, C., Graham, A., & Thomas, N. (2015). Imagining an ideal school for wellbeing: Locating student voice. *Journal of Educational Change, 16*(2), 129–144.

Stripling, B. K. (2017). Empowering students to inquire in a digital environment. In S. W. Alman (Ed.), *School librarianship: Past, present, and future* (pp. 51–63). Lanham, MA: Rowman and Littlefield.

Teravainen, A., & Clark, C. (2017). *School Libraries: A literature review of current provision and evidence of impact*. London: The National Literacy Trust. Retrieved from https://literacytrust.org.uk/documents/210/2017_06_30_free_research_-_school_library_review_XxR5qcv.pdf.

Todd, R. J. (2017). School libraries 4D: Disruption, design, data, dance. In S. W. Alman (Ed.), *School librarianship: Past, present, and future* (pp. 181–171). Lanham, MA: Rowman and Littlefield.

Valenza, J. K. (2017). Reimagining school libraries to lead future learning. In S. W. Alman (Ed.), *School librarianship: Past, present, and future* (pp. 109–133). Lanham, MA: Rowman and Littlefield.

Weeks, A. C., & Barlow, D. L. (2017). A brief look at the development of school libraries in the United States. In S. W. Alman (Ed.), *School librarianship: Past, present, and future* (pp. 1–13). Lanham, MA: Rowman and Littlefield.

Willis, J. (2014). Making space to learn: Leading collaborative classroom design. *Journal of Educational Leadership, Policy and Practice, 29*(1), 3–16.

Willis, J. (2016). Imagining ourselves as twenty-first-century learners: Making space to learn. In D. Bland (Ed.), *Imagination for inclusion: Diverse contexts of educational practice* (pp. 83–94). New York, NY: Routledge.

Woolner, P., Hall, E., Higgins, S., McCaughey, C., & Wall, K. (2007). A sound foundation? What we know about the impact of environments on learning and the implications for building schools of the future. *Oxford Review of Education, 33*(1), 47–70.

Creating Learning Spaces that Promote Wellbeing, Participation and Engagement: Implications for Students on the Autism Spectrum

Beth Saggers and Jill Ashburner

Abstract The developmental wellbeing of students is strongly influenced by their response to their environments (Frankish et al. in Health impact assessment as a tool for population health promotion and public policy. University of British Columbia, Canada 1996). Creating learning spaces that promote participation, engagement and wellbeing are therefore important for all students. In the case of students on the spectrum, evidence suggests that students on the spectrum have sensitivities to environmental stimuli that may affect their attention and academic performance in the classroom (Ashburner et al. in J Occup Ther 62:564–573 2008). As a result, consideration of the design elements of learning environments is essential to not only promote effective teaching and learning but also support wellbeing for this specific group of students. This chapter will explore some of the key issues for students on the spectrum identified in the research. An extensive review of the literature is used to inform the creation and design of learning spaces to address these key issues with the aim of positively influencing their learning, participation and engagement in educational settings. The benefits for all children will also be highlighted.

Introduction

Wellbeing focuses on a person's ability to adapt or respond to life events (Marshall, 2004) and relates to five key areas of development including: (i) social, (ii) physical, (iii) mental, (iv) emotional and (v) spiritual development (Masters, 2004). The developmental wellbeing of students is strongly influenced by their response to their environments (Frankish, Green, Ratner, Chomik, & Larsen, 1996). Evidence highlights the significant influence wellbeing has on students including their physical and mental health outcomes and academic success (World Health Organisation, 2017).

B. Saggers (✉)
Queensland University of Technology, Brisbane, Australia
e-mail: b.saggers@qut.edu.au

J. Ashburner
Austism Queensland, Sunnybank Hills, Australia
e-mail: jill.ashburner@autismqld.com.au

© Springer Nature Singapore Pte Ltd. 2019
H. Hughes et al. (eds.), *School Spaces for Student Wellbeing and Learning*,
https://doi.org/10.1007/978-981-13-6092-3_8

Creating learning spaces that promote participation, engagement and wellbeing are especially significant for students on the autism spectrum (hereafter referred to as 'students on the spectrum'). This chapter will explore some key factors that have been identified as influencing the learning of students on the spectrum. This information will help to inform the creation of learning spaces that support the learning, participation, engagement and wellbeing of school-aged students on the spectrum. The benefits for all children are highlighted.

Some Key Factors Influencing the Learning and Wellbeing of Students on the Spectrum

Globally, there has been a dramatic increase in the prevalence of students diagnosed with autism spectrum disorder. Approximately, 70% of school-aged students on the spectrum now attend mainstream settings worldwide (Department for Education, 2014). Evidence suggests that students on the spectrum have sensitivities to environmental stimuli that may affect their attention in the classroom and academic performance (Ashburner, Ziviani, & Rodger, 2008). Consideration of the design elements of learning environments is essential to not only promote effective teaching and learning but also support wellbeing. Students on the spectrum share difficulties in: (i) social communication and social interactions and (ii) restricted, repetitive patterns of behaviour, interests or activities, which can include unusual responses to the sensory aspects of the environment [American Psychiatric Association (APA), 2013]. These characteristics can present significant challenges for students on the spectrum, in that they often experience poorer educational and post-school outcomes than their peers (Australian Bureau of Statistics, 2015).

While an underutilised perspective in research, the studies that have focussed on personal accounts from students on the spectrum can help us to identify key aspects of the environment that influence learning (Roberts, & Simpson, 2016; Saggers, Hwang, & Mercer, 2011; Saggers et al., 2016). These studies highlight factors to consider when designing learning environments that may help support the specific needs of students on the spectrum while also promoting learning and wellbeing for all students in the classroom. A survey of 107 students on the spectrum aged 11–18 years about school tasks that they found most difficult (Saggers et al., 2016) revealed elements of the learning environment that they found problematic. These included challenges: (a) socially, (b) linked to the sensory environment, (c) coping with change and transitions, (d) with executive function aspects of learning and (e) with written expression. We can draw from these experiences when considering important elements in learning environment design that may benefit not just students on the spectrum but all students.

Robeyns (2016) highlights the absence of sensory overload, the need for communication to be explicit, and the need to be properly understood as dimensions of wellbeing that are especially pertinent to people on the spectrum. Anxiety is also commonly recognised to have a detrimental effect on the wellbeing of students on the spectrum (Vasa et al., 2013). Research suggests that intolerance of uncertainty (Boulter, Freeston, South, & Rodgers, 2014) and sensory sensitivities (Green & Ben-Sasson, 2010) can be significant contributors to anxiety in people on the spectrum. Our recommendations for the design of learning spaces, therefore, include ways to accommodate the need for predictability, and the sensory and communication challenges of students on the spectrum.

Social Challenges of Students on the Spectrum

The social difficulties experienced by students on the spectrum are recognised as core to the diagnosis (APA, 2013). Studies that have captured the voice of students on the spectrum suggest that social elements of school that they find challenging include: (i) positive relationships with peers, (ii) developing and maintaining friendships, (iii) coping with teasing and bullying, (iv) working as part of group, (v) emotional regulation (especially managing anxiety and stress in the learning environment) and (vi) negotiating difference (Humphrey & Lewis, 2008; Saggers et al., 2011). Loomis (2008) highlights a number of factors that can impact on the capacity of students on the spectrum to manage social situations, including sensory factors, predictability, the clarity of expectations, the communication demands and the number of people in the setting. These factors offer insight into environmental issues that may influence the social experiences of students on the spectrum. For example, social situations that are likely to be the most stressful include unstructured and unpredictable social contexts with large numbers of people (i.e. crowds) where sensory input that is overwhelming (i.e. high levels of noise and commotion), and social and communication expectations are unclear.

Challenges in Coping with Change and Transitions

Difficulty coping with change and a preference for 'sameness' are recognised as key features of autism spectrum disorder (APA, 2013). Intolerance of uncertainty is significantly correlated with anxiety in people on the spectrum (Boulter et al., 2014). Students on the spectrum have described difficulties coping with transition and change including: (i) changes in teachers, (ii) timetable changes and (iii) any activity involving unexpected or unpredictable changes (Saggers et al., 2016). Transitions and change, which typically occur frequently in the school day, maybe anxiety-provoking and can be a common antecedent to maladaptive behaviours.

Challenges Coping with Executive Function Demands

Our executive function skills help us to focus our attention on relevant aspects of the environment and to plan and organise our day and everyday tasks (Pellicano, 2012). The executive function demands of school often challenge students on the spectrum (Saggers et al., 2016). Students on the spectrum may have increasing difficulty in higher grades when planning and organisation become more essential to learning. Contributors to executive dysfunction in people on the spectrum are thought to include: (a) difficulties selectively attending to a task while ignoring irrelevant information, (b) difficulties disengaging attention from one stimulus to attend to another (described as 'sticky attention') and (c) language difficulties that impact their capacity to develop an internal plan for behaviour (Pellicano, 2012). Students themselves have highlighted the following executive function challenges: (i) planning assignments, (ii) organising themselves and their belongings, (iii) time management and (iv) homework (Saggers et al., 2016).

Challenges with Written Expression

Students on the spectrum often struggle to handwrite legibly due to difficulties with fine motor and perceptual skills (Kushki, Chau, & Anagnostou, 2011). Their frustration with an inability to write legibly often results in poor motivation, and an increasing avoidance and minimisation of writing (Broun, 2009). The conceptual aspects of written composition can also be challenging due to difficulties with abstract concepts and organisational skills, lack of imagination and literal thinking (Harbison & Alexander, 2009) and language comprehension and expression difficulties (Griswold, Barnhill, Myles, Hagiwara, & Simpson, 2002).

Sensory Challenges

Atypical sensory responses of individuals on the spectrum have recently been formally recognised in the revised diagnostic criteria for autism spectrum disorders (APA, 2013). Students on the spectrum may present with: (a) unusual sensory hypersensitivity to stimuli such as loud sounds, unexpected touch or bright lights, (b) unusual sensory hyposensitivity, such as indifference to others speaking to them, painful stimuli or extreme temperatures and (c) high levels of sensory seeking behaviours such as noise making, body rocking, smelling or touching objects and fascinations with lights or spinning objects (Ben-Sasson et al., 2009). Significant associations between sensory sensitivities and intolerance of uncertainty have been reported in people on the spectrum (Neil, Olsson, & Pellicano, 2016;). This may explain their tendency to overreact to unpredictable or unexpected sensory input, coupled with a preference for predictable and controllable input (Ashburner, Bennett, Rodger, & Ziviani, 2013; Pellicano, 2013). The self-stimulatory behaviours often seen in children on the spectrum (e.g. making noises, or body rocking) are thought to be a means of ensuring that incoming sensory input is predictable, particularly when overwhelmed by sensory input over which they have no control (Gomot, Belmonte, Bullmore, Bernard, & Baron-Cohen, 2008). Students on the spectrum may also find it difficult to 'filter' or selectively attend to relevant sensory input, while ignoring extraneous input. Auditory filtering issues which are reported in 78% of people on the spectrum can be particularly problematic (Tomchek & Dunn, 2007). Children on the spectrum have difficulty processing speech in noisy environments (Alcantara, Weisblatt, Moore, & Bolton, 2004) and are reported to have less than half the speech-in-noise perception of typically developing peers (Schafer et al., 2013). These children may therefore find it difficult to process their teachers' instructions in noisy classrooms (Nelson & Soli, 2000). Students on the spectrum are prone to becoming over aroused and overly emotional in classrooms with high levels of noise, visual clutter, movement and crowding (Ashburner, Rodger, Ziviani, & Hinder, 2014) and may present with distractible and repetitive behaviours in noisy environments (Kanraki, Shepley, Tassarinary, Varni, & Fawaz, 2017). Sensory processing differences including auditory processing difficulties (particularly auditory filtering issues), sensory seeking behaviours and touch sensitivity of these students have been found to be negatively associated with academic performance and attention (Ashburner et al., 2008). Students on the spectrum commonly describe feelings of distress in noisy crowded spaces at school (Humphrey & Lewis, 2008; Saggers et al., 2011).

Optimising the Learning Space Through Planning and Design: Considerations When Designing Learning Environments that Support the Learning Needs of Students on the Spectrum

The Salamanca Statement and Framework for Action on Special Needs Education (United Nations Scientific & Cultural Organisation, 1994) decreed that every child has the fundamental right to education: 'Those with special educational needs must have access to regular school which should accommodate them within a child-centred pedagogy capable of meeting these needs'. Australian education providers are legally required to make 'reasonable adjustments' to ensure students with disability are included unless it poses 'unjustifiable hardship' (Commonwealth of Australia, 1992). More recently, inclusive education has been recognised as a fundamental human right of all learners by the United Nations (2016) who reinforces the need to accommodate the differing requirements and identities of individual students and remove the barriers that impede their progress.

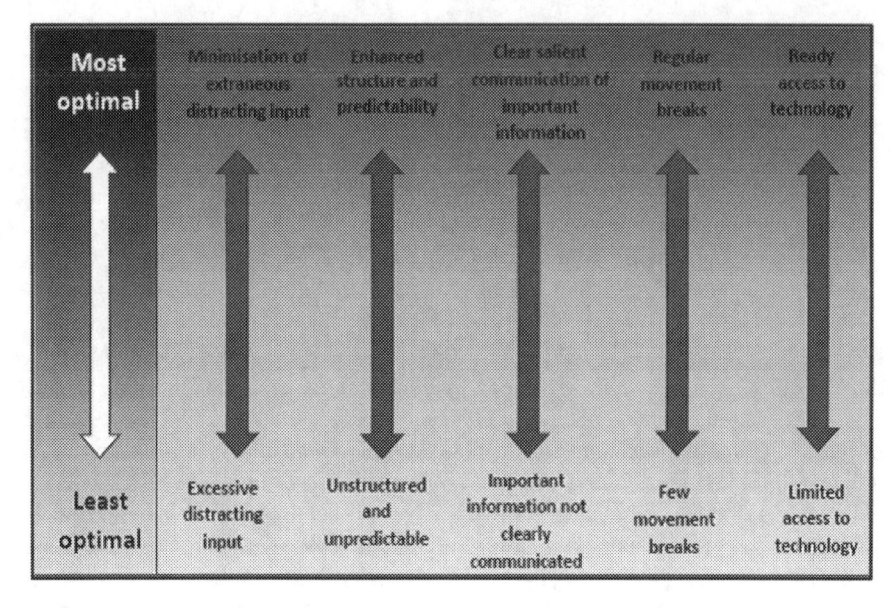

Fig. 1 Principles involved optimising the learning space for students on the spectrum

Universal Design is a philosophy advocating the design of products and environments to be as usable by as many people as possible. According to CAST (2017) 'Universal Design for Learning (UDL) is a research-based set of principles to guide the design of learning environments that are accessible and effective for all' (para 1). The review of the social, transition, executive function and sensory challenges of students on the spectrum described above, suggests some key UDL principles in relation to the optimisation of the learning environment to accommodate these students, as illustrated in Fig. 1.

Rather than retrofitting learning spaces and programmes for students with special needs, UDL advocates the design of classrooms and curricula from the outset to accommodate the needs of students with a wide range of learning needs. Classroom accommodations for students on the spectrum are also likely to suit other students, particularly those with other additional learning needs (Zehner, Chen, & Aladsani, 2017). This approach has two important advantages. First, if the curriculum and learning environment are designed from the beginning to incorporate options to suit a wide range of learning needs, the demand on teachers to make individualised adjustments is reduced. Second, students are less likely to feel stigmatised, if the environment is suited to their needs and/or they can avail themselves of a range of options available to all their classmates, rather than requiring an individualised approach that brands them as different. UDL is therefore likely to enhance feelings of inclusion of students on the spectrum. Details of the principles highlighted in Fig. 2 are discussed below. Operationalising these principles in classrooms can involve both adaptations to the physical environment, and pedagogical considerations. The relationship between

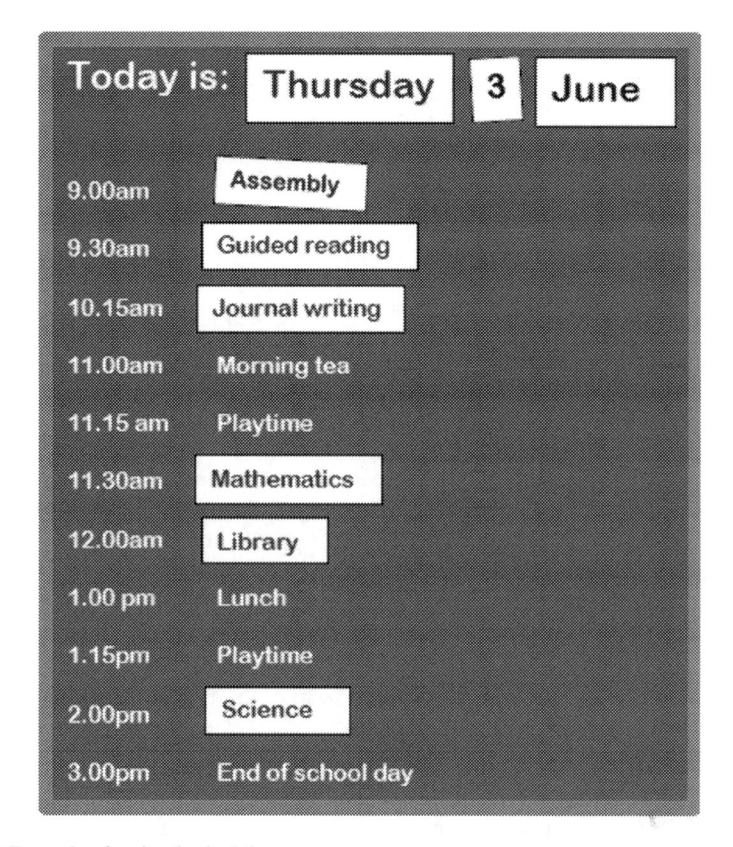

Fig. 2 Example of a visual schedule

the physical environment and pedagogy is therefore considered. For example, as movement breaks have been highlighted as beneficial, the design of the physical environment should accommodate whole-of-class movement opportunities.

Minimisation of Extraneous, Distracting Input

Given the difficulties of students on the spectrum in selectively attending to relevant rather than irrelevant input (Pellicano, 2012), a key consideration when designing a learning space is the reduction of extraneous, distracting sensory input in the environment including (a) auditory, (b) tactile, (c) visual, and (d) complex multisensory input.

Reducing Extraneous Noise and Auditory Distractions

Classroom noise can be especially challenging for students on the spectrum (Saggers et al., 2011). Unpleasant tactile input can be largely avoided by keeping a distance from others and wearing soft clothing, while distracting visual stimuli can often be avoided by moving away or averting gaze. However, as noise is almost impossible to avoid without leaving the environment altogether, it is imperative to consider strategies to reduce extraneous noise and auditory distractions. These adjustments will not only benefit students on the spectrum, but also other students who are challenged by classroom noise including those with (i) otitis media, (ii) auditory processing difficulties, (iii) attention difficulties, (iv) English as a second language and (v) any student under the age of 13, given that auditory figure-ground skills do not mature until adolescence (Crandell & Smaldino, 2000). Noisy environments may increase off-task behaviour in students on the spectrum (Kinnealey et al., 2012) and the risk of vocal fatigue in teachers (Urrutikoetxea, Ispizua, & Matellanes, 1995). Mostafa (2014) perceives classroom acoustics to be a key architectural consideration when designing for students on the spectrum. The examples of strategies to reduce auditory distractions are now described.

The installation of sound absorbing walls in classrooms has been found to benefit students on the spectrum by decreasing non-attending behaviours (Kinnealey et al., 2012) and increasing attending behaviours, and reducing response time and self-stimulatory behaviours (Mostafa, 2008). The use of sound absorbing materials, such as curtains, and carpet on the walls and floor, or the installation of sound absorbing panels should therefore be considered.

The use of either a 'low-tech' noise level meter (a chart that teachers can use to prompt students to quieten down) or a 'high-tech' noise level app (that records decibels of background noise) can be used. Relocation of communication situations away from the noise source should also be considered (e.g. direct teaching away from group activities). A structured turn-taking protocol may help to reduce simultaneous speaking (e.g. a 'talking stick'). Furthermore, noise reduction headphones have been used to improve the attention to task of students with sound sensitivities during independent learning tasks (Rowe, Candler, & Neville, 2011).

Reducing Extraneous Tactile Input

Students on the spectrum have highlighted difficulties with (a) the close proximity of others (where others crowd them or brush past them), (b) being touched by other students and (c) the textures of clothing including school uniforms (Saggers et al., 2011, 2016). Strategies to reduce extraneous tactile input and/or crowding, include: (i) positioning students with touch sensitivity at the front or end of lines and edge when sitting on the floor to minimise close proximity to others, (ii) sitting spots for circle time and (iii) the use of visual cues which help students to understand the need to respect the personal body space of their classmates.

Reducing Extraneous Visual Clutter and Distractions

Students on the spectrum may find it difficult to focus on key visual information if there is a lot of extraneous visual information or visual clutter (Hume, 2015). Other visual issues that students on the spectrum report as being problematic include: (a) sunlight, (b) bright lights (especially fluorescent lights) and (c) movement and/or people walking around (Saggers et al., 2016). Early research has suggested that fluorescent lights may increase the self-stimulatory behaviours of children on the spectrum (Fenton & Penney, 1985). First-hand accounts also suggest that people on the spectrum are unusually sensitive to the 'flicker' of fluorescent lighting (Robertson & Simmons, 2015). Kinnealey et al. (2012) found that the replacement of classroom fluorescent lights with halogen lights improved the attention, classroom performance, comfort and mood of students on the spectrum. As some people on the spectrum describe feelings of distress when moving from a dark room to bright sunlight (Elwin, Ek, Schröder, & Kjellin, 2012), the use of hats and sunglasses when leaving the classroom may be necessary for some students.

Strategies to reduce of visual clutter with the aim of improving visual clarity may include covering classroom resources and content when not in use, using room dividers to cover distracting areas, and covering computers screens when not in use (Hume, 2015). Design considerations for autism-friendly classrooms developed by McAllister and Maguire (2012) include the use of high-level glazing and attention to the sight lines within classrooms to prevent students being distracted by visual stimuli exterior to the classroom. Individual workstations facing the wall may help students to focus on learning tasks by minimising visual distractions (Hume & Reynolds, 2010). Where individual workstations are not a feasible option, portable screens on the student's desk may be used for independent learning tasks.

Complex Multisensory Environments

Crowded environments such as playgrounds, corridors, assemblies and group work activities typically involve complex multisensory input, including high levels of competing noise, the colour and movements of students moving within confined spaces and the unpredictable touch and proprioceptive input associated with being pushed along in a crowd. Students on the spectrum who describe feeling distressed in these environments may benefit from flexible access to quiet spaces to which they can withdraw, when they feel overwhelmed. The design considerations of Mostafa (2014) and McAllister and Maguire (2012) include the provision of a quiet room, or an escape space which can simply be a small partitioned area within the classroom. McAllister and Maguire (2012) also advocate flexible access to a quieter environment within the school playground so that students on the spectrum can control the balance between time spent socialising and time spent alone. Where availability of quieter spaces is limited, the school libraries can be used for this purpose. Consideration also needs to be given to reducing the exposure of students on the spectrum to crowding around bag racks or lockers (e.g. providing a locker at a distance from those of classmates). With respect to group activities, secondary school students on the spectrum have reported a preference for working in smaller, quieter groups with familiar students (Dillon, Underwood, & Freemantle, 2016). This finding has implications for the physical environment (e.g. access to a quiet space for group work involving students on the spectrum) and teaching strategies (e.g. smaller group sizes and the selection of familiar peers who are supportive of students on the spectrum).

Quill (1997) was the first of many practitioners to advocate the use of an 'I need a break' card to enable students on the spectrum to discretely indicate their need to retreat to a quieter environment. Students on the spectrum may also be permitted to leave the class early or later than other students, thereby avoiding crowding in corridors.

Enhanced Structure and Predictability

The need for structure and predictability is clearly a recurring theme pervading many of the challenges experienced by students on the spectrum described above. Humphrey and Lewis (2008, p. 37) observed that for the students on the spectrum: '*order and predictability appeared to act as a 'security blanket' that allowed them to function*'. Enhanced predictability can make many aspects of school life easier for the students on the spectrum, including social contexts, transitions, and the organisation involved in managing assignments, homework, time and belongings. *Structured Teaching* strategies, which focus on increasing predictability, were originally developed as a central component of the *Treatment and Education of Autistic and Related Communication Handicapped Children* (TEACCH) programme in 1972 (Mesibov, Shea, & Schopler, 2004).

The use of schedules is now widely recognised as an evidence-informed practice for students on the spectrum (National Autism Center, 2015). Visual supports that inform students of upcoming transitions from one activity to another can help to: (i) increase predictability, (ii) reduce the time needed for transitions, (iii) promote positive behaviour and participation during transitions, (iv) support shifting of attention to a new activity or task and (v) reduce student anxiety associated with transitions (Saggers & Beasley, 2017). Visual schedules make sequences of events predictable and give forewarning of anticipated changes. Predictability can also be enhanced using timers, checklists, apps, weekly, monthly and school term calendars, electronic diaries and formative feedback. Figure 2 below provides an example of a visual schedule.

A structured teaching strategy called the *Work System* that is routinely used to support students on the spectrum involves the use of physical and visual cues to indicate: (1) what task to do, (2) how much work to do, (3) when the task is finished and (4) what to do next (Mesibov et al., 2004). Although structured teaching approaches have traditionally been used in special education settings, visual schedules and work systems have recently been found to be effective in supporting students on the spectrum in mainstream classrooms to stay on task (Macdonald, Trembath, Ashburner, Costley & Keen, 2018).

Structured teaching also advocates the arrangement of the physical environment to support executive functioning, by clearly defining areas for different activities, clearly labelling and positioning materials, and minimising visual and auditory distractions (Hume, 2015). Information should be presented in ways that enhance visual clarity (e.g. ensuring the use of sufficient space to reduce clutter and the use of colour coding) (Hume, 2015). The distress caused by sudden unpredictable sensory input may be reduced through preparatory cues (e.g. a visual cue to pre-warn students of the impending sound of the school bell).

Clear, Salient Communication of Important Information

The salience of instructions and other important and/or relevant information in the environment is essential if students are to focus their attention on key information to be learned, while ignoring conflicting distracting stimuli. Three key ways of enhancing the salience of information include: (i) the use of visual instruction, (ii) the use of the structure of the learning space to communicate key information and (iii) amplifying the teacher's voice.

Enhancing the Salience of Information Through the Use of Visual Instruction

Verbal instructions involve rapid, sequential processing of transient information, which can pose difficulties for students on the spectrum (Quill, 1997). In contrast, visual instructions are highly predictable and concrete; can be referred to as often as needed (unlike verbal instructions which are transient); and can reduce the student's dependence on an adult prompting (Quill, 1997). Visual skill sequences are often used to support students on the spectrum (e.g. steps involved in hand washing) (Ganz, 2007). Modelling and video modelling are also well-established as effective evidence-based strategies for children on the spectrum that enable information to be communicated in the same way each time (National Autism Centre, 2015).

Enhancing the Salience of Information Through the Use of Classroom Structure

Classroom structure can be used to communicate what students are expected to do in each space in the classroom (Hume, 2015). A classroom design feature for students on the spectrum recommended by Mostafa (2014) is 'compartmentalisation', which involves sections of classrooms having a clearly designed function and sensory quality. The classroom may be segmented into areas related to learning activities, such as teacher-directed activities, group activities, a reading corner, and/or an area for independent or individual instruction. Boundaries or visual cues can be used to demarcate different areas (e.g. furniture such as book shelves, taping lines on the floor, coloured rugs, labels, colour coding or placemats).

Enhancing the Salience of Information Through Amplification of the Teacher's Voice

A review by van Der Kruk et al. (2017) concluded that an improved classroom signal-to-noise ratio (i.e. improving the ratio of the teacher's voice volume to background classroom noise) can improve the performance of students on the spectrum through enhanced speech recognition, listening and on-task behaviours. Important auditory information can be made more salient by amplifying the teacher's voice. Two commonly used methods of amplifying the teachers' voice include (a) frequency modulation (FM) systems for individual students and (b) sound field amplifications that enable the teacher's voice to be heard clearly by all students in all areas of the classroom. Both systems include a microphone and transmitter worn by the teacher. FM systems involve earphones worn by the student, whereas sound field amplification systems include loudspeakers that are placed around the classroom. Personal FM systems have been shown to result in improvements for students on the spectrum including (a) improved listening (Rance, Saunders, Carew, Johansson, & Tan 2014; Schafer et al., 2016), (b) improved speech-in-noise recognition in noise (Schafer et al., 2013, Schafer et al., 2016) and (c) improved on-task behaviours (Schafer et al., 2013). However, these three studies also reported that a few students on the spectrum were unable to tolerate the ear pieces due to tactile sensitivity (Schafer et al., 2013, 2016; Rance et al., 2014). Anecdotally, another potential disadvantage of FM system is that some students may feel embarrassed about appearing different to their classmates. Although sound field amplification systems have been reported to be helpful for students without autism (Dockrell & Shield, 2012; Massie & Dillon, 2006), as yet research on their use by students on the spectrum has been limited. Rance et al. (2017) reported that listening stress (measured using salivary cortisol levels) of students on the spectrum reduced when sound field amplification systems were used. Further research is required, however, on their efficacy in improving listening behaviours of these students.

Ensure Movement Needs of Students Are Met

A range of sensory strategies are commonly embedded within school routines with the aim of optimising a child's level of arousal. These strategies vary, however, in terms of the evidence to support them. Commonly used strategies include (a) fidget toys and oral motor gadgets, which have limited available evidence, (b) inflated cushions or fitness balls, which have inconsistent evidence (Bagatell, Miriglini, Patterson, Reyes & Test, 2010; Schilling & Shwartz, 2004; Umeda & Deitz, 2011), (c) weighted vests which are not considered an evidence-based (Stephenson & Carter, 2009; Taylor, Spriggs, Jones Ault, Flanagan, & Sartini, 2017) and (d) exercise or movement breaks. Of these strategies, only exercise is considered a well-established evidence-informed practice, with systematic reviews concluding that the use of exercise in children on the spectrum is effective in reducing, aggression and off-task behaviour, and in improving their on-task behaviour, engagement and academic performance (Lang et al., 2010; Wong et al., 2013).

An extensive review of interventions for people on the spectrum (Wong et al., 2013) has listed exercise as evidence-based. Movement breaks are effective, low cost and non-stigmatising. Both the classroom schedule and physical environment should, therefore, be designed to accommodate the movement needs of all students, particularly students on the spectrum who describe difficulties with sitting still in class (Saggers et al., 2016).

The review by Lang et al. (2010) indicated that: (i) the positive effects of exercise last 40–90 min and (ii) vigorous exercise is more effective than less strenuous exercise. These findings suggest that movement breaks need to be regularly implemented throughout the school day, and that more vigorous exercise such as jogging on the spot or star jumps may be more likely to be more effective than less vigorous exercise such as walking. Ideally, fun- and age-appropriate movement should be embedded into the school routine, followed by 'calm down' activities. Preliminary evidence suggests that classroom yoga may be helpful in reducing maladaptive behaviours in students on the spectrum (Koenig, Buckley-Reen, & Garg, 2012) although recent reviews suggest that more research is needed (Gwynette & Warren, 2015). The implication of these findings is that classrooms should be designed with adequate space to allow students to participate in movement activities.

Ready Access to Technology

The use of technology may assist students on the spectrum in overcoming some of their challenges with written expression. Ashburner et al. (2012) found that students on the spectrum were much more motivated to type than to handwrite. An extensive review of interventions for young people on the spectrum by Wong et al. (2013) has recognised technology-aided instruction and intervention, as evidence-based. Students on the spectrum often have a natural affinity for technology, possibly because computer-based information tends to be structured and predictable with minimal distractions and because it is presented visually. Computer-based instruction also allows students to work at their own pace. A review by Asaro-Saddler (2016) concludes that the use of learning technologies can improve spelling ability and sentence construction of students on the spectrum. Technology offers many options that can support students on the spectrum to write including graphic organisers to help plan a written composition, and features such as spell check, grammar check, editing functions, word prediction, text-to-speech and speech-to-text options. These features can allow students to focus on content generation and revision rather than the mechanics of writing (Asaro-Saddler, 2016). Learning environments should, therefore, include ready access to devices such as laptops or computer tablets, a range of learning support software and access to the internet.

Conclusion

Students on the spectrum often experience significant barriers to learning, participation and engagement within the classroom. Inclusive policies reinforce the need for educators to accommodate the differing requirements and identities of individual students and remove any barriers that limit their progress. The potential of learning space design to promote inclusive education practices and maximise the wellbeing, participation and engagement of students on the spectrum is often overlooked. To date, research on the behavioural outcomes of adjustments to the physical classroom environment for students on the spectrum has been limited, and restricted to special education classrooms (Kinnealey et al., 2012; Mostafa, 2008). Consequently, further research is required in mainstream school contexts. Further research is also needed to explore the perspectives of students on the spectrum on their learning environments. Listening to the voice of students on the spectrum has been an underutilised resource when designing learning spaces. The importance of practitioners, researchers and policymakers listening to the voice of people on the spectrum is clear when one considers this eloquent description of an ideal learning environment by Donna Williams (1996) an adult on the spectrum:

> My ideal educational environment would be one where the room had very little echo or reflective light… It would be one where the physical arrangements of things in the room was cognitively orderly and didn't alter and where everything in the room remained in routine-defined areas. It would be an environment where only what was necessary to learning was on display and there were no unnecessary decorations or potential distractions…. It would be one where learning was through objects, nature and doing, not through having to rely on the interpretation of written or spoken words, or having to watch someone's constantly moving, constantly changing face or body…. If it was less noisy and without bright lighting or unpredictable touch, it would probably create less aversion. If it was without visual or auditory disorder and predictable and full of routine structures and patterns, it would probably create less aversion (p. 284).

This chapter has discussed learning spaces characterised by designs that (a) minimise extraneous distracting input, (b) enhance structure and predictability, (c) provide clear salient communication of important information, (d) give opportunities for regular movement breaks and (e) provide ready access to technology. Many of these recommended adjustments are relatively simple and achievable. Schools will ultimately be rewarded by the creation of environments that accommodate rather than distress students on the spectrum and in turn promote wellbeing. Learning space designs that address these key elements are likely to benefit all students, rather than just those on the spectrum.

References

Alcantara, J. I., Weisblatt, E. J., Moore, B. C., & Bolton, P. F. (2004). Speech-in-noise perception in high-functioning individuals with autism or Asperger's syndrome. *Journal of Child Psychology and Psychiatry, 45*(6), 1107–1114. https://doi.org/10.1111/j.1469-7610.2004.t01-1-00303.x.

American Psychiatric Association (APA). (2013). *Diagnostic and statistical manual of mental disorders* (5th ed.). Washington, DC: Author.

Asaro-Saddler, K. (2016). Using evidence-based practices to teach writing to children with autism spectrum disorders. *Preventing School Failure: Alternative Education for Children and Youth, 60*(1), 79–85. https://doi.org/10.1080/1045988X.2014.981793.

Ashburner, J., Ziviani, J., & Rodger, S. (2008). Sensory processing and classroom emotional, behavioural, and educational outcomes in children with autism spectrum disorder. *American Journal of Occupational Therapy, 62*(5), 564–573.

Ashburner, J., Ziviani, J., & Pennington, A. (2012). The introduction of keyboarding to children with Autism Spectrum Disorders with handwriting difficulties: A help or a hindrance? *Australasian Journal of Special Education, 36*(1), 32–61. https://doi.org/10.1017/jse.2012.6.

Ashburner, J., Bennett, L., Rodger, S., & Ziviani, J. (2013). Understanding the sensory experiences of young people with autism spectrum disorder: A preliminary investigation. *Australian Occupational Therapy Journal, 60*(3), 171–180. https://doi.org/10.1111/1440-1630.12025.

Ashburner, J. K., Rodger, S. A., Ziviani, J. M., & Hinder, E. A. (2014). Optimizing participation of children with autism spectrum disorder experiencing sensory challenges: A clinical reasoning framework. *Canadian Journal of Occupational Therapy, 81*(1), 29–38. https://doi.org/10.1177/0008417413520440.

Australian Bureau of Statistics. (2015). Autism in Australia. http://www.abs.gov.au/ausstats/abs@.nsf/Latestproducts/4430.0Main%20Features752015.

Bagatell, N., Mirigliani, G., Patterson, C., Reyes, Y., & Test, L. (2010). Effectiveness of therapy ball chairs on classroom participation in children with autism spectrum disorders. *American Journal of Occupational Therapy, 64,* 895–903. https://doi.org/10.5014/ajot.2010.09149.

Ben-Sasson, A., Hen, L., Fluss, R., Cermak, S. A., Engel-Yeger, B., & Gal, E. (2009). A meta-analysis of sensory modulation symptoms in individuals with autism spectrum disorders. *Journal Autism and Developmental Disorders, 39*(1), 1–11. https://doi.org/10.1007/s10803-008-0593-3.

Boulter, C., Freeston, M., South, M., & Rodgers, J. (2014). Intolerance of uncertainty as a framework for understanding anxiety in children and adolescents with autism spectrum disorders. *Journal of Autism and Developmental Disorders, 44*(6), 1391–1402. https://doi.org/10.1007/s10803-013-2001-x.

Broun, L. (2009). Take the pencil out of the process. *Teaching Exceptional Children, 42*(1), 14–21.

CAST. (2017). *Universal design for learning.* http://www.cast.org/.

Commonwealth of Australia. (1992). *Disability Discrimination Act 1992.* https://www.legislation.gov.au/Details/C2017C00339.

Crandell, C. C., & Smaldino, J. J. (2000). Classroom acoustics for children with normal hearing and hearing impairment. *Language, Speech and Hearing Services in Schools, 31,* 362–370. https://doi.org/10.1044/0161-1461.3104.362.

Department for Education. (2014). *Statistical first release: Special educational needs in England: January 2014.* London: UK Government. https://www.gov.uk/government/uploads/system/uploads/attachment_data/file/362704/SFR26-2014_SEN_06102014.pdf.

Dillon, G. V., Underwood, J. D. M., & Fremantle, L. J. (2016). Autism and the U.K. secondary school experience. *Focus on Autism and Other Developmental Disabilities, 31*(3), 221–230. https://doi.org/10.1177/1088357614539833.

Dockrell, J. E., & Shield, B. (2012). The impact of sound-field systems on learning and attention in elementary school classrooms. *Journal of Speech, Language, and Hearing Research, 55*(4), 1163–1176.

Elwin, M., Ek, L., Schröder, A., & Kjellin, L. (2012). Autobiographical accounts of sensing in Asperger syndrome and high-functioning autism. *Archives of Psychiatric Nursing, 26*(5), 420–429. https://doi.org/10.1016/j.apnu.2011.10.003.

Fenton, D. M., & Penney, R. (1985). The effects of fluorescent and incandescent lighting on the repetitive behaviours of autistic and intellectually handicapped children. *Australia and New Zealand Journal of Developmental Disabilities, 11*(3), 137–141. https://doi.org/10.3109/13668258508998632.

Frankish, J., Green, L., Ratner, P., Chomik, T., & Larsen, C. (1996). *Health impact assessment as a tool for population health promotion and public policy. Report for the Institute for Health Promotion Research.* Vancouver, Canada: University of British Columbia.

Ganz, J. (2007). Classroom structuring methods and strategies for children and youth with autism spectrum disorder. *Exceptionality, 15*(4), 249–260. https://doi.org/10.1080/09362830701655816.

Gomot, M., Belmonte, M. K., Bullmore, E. T., Bernard, F. A., & Baron-Cohen, S. (2008). Auditory novel targets in children with high-functioning autism. *Brain, 131*(9), 2479–2488. https://doi.org/10.1093/brain/awn172.

Green, S. A., & Ben-Sasson, A. (2010). Anxiety disorders and sensory over-responsivity in children with autism spectrum disorders: Is there a causal relationship? *Journal of Autism and Developmental Disorders, 40*(12), 1495–1504. https://doi.org/10.1007/s10803-010-1007-x.

Griswold, D. E., Barnhill, G. P., Myles, B. S., Hagiwara, T., & Simpson, R. (2002). Asperger syndrome and academic achievement. *Focus on Autism and Other Developmental Disabilities, 17*(2), 94–102. https://doi.org/10.1177/10883576020170020401.

Gwynette, M.F., & Warren, N.J., (2015). Yoga as an intervention for patients with autism spectrum disorder: A review of the evidence and future directions. *Autism Open Access, 5*(3). https://doi.org/10.4172/2165-7890.1000155.

Harbinson, H., & Alexander, J. (2009). Asperger syndrome and the English curriculum: Addressing the challenges. *Support for Learning, 24*(1), 10–17. https://doi.org/10.1111/j.1467-9604.2009.01392.x.

Hume, K. (2015). *Structured teaching strategies: A series.* http://www.iidc.indiana.edu/?pageId=3520.

Hume, K., & Reynolds, B. (2010). Implementing work systems across the school day: Increasing engagement in students with autism spectrum disorders. *Preventing School Failure, 54*(4), 228–237. https://doi.org/10.1080/10459881003744701.

Humphrey, N., & Lewis, S. (2008). 'Make me normal': The views and experiences of pupils on the autistic spectrum in mainstream secondary schools. *Autism, 12*(1), 23–44. https://doi.org/10.1177/1362361307085267.

Kanraki, S. M., Shepley, M., Tassarinary, L. G., Varni, J. W., & Fawaz, H. M. (2017). An observational study of classroom acoustical design and repetitive behaviors in children with autism. *Environment and Behavior., 49*(8), 847–873. https://doi.org/10.1177/0013916516669389.

Kinnealey, M., Pfeiffer, B., Miller, J., Roan, C., Shoener, R., & Ellner, M. L. (2012). Effect of classroom modification on attention and engagement of students with autism or dyspraxia. *American Journal of Occupational Therapy, 66*, 511–519. https://doi.org/10.5014/ajot.2012.004010.

Koenig, K. P., Buckley-Reen, A., & Garg, S. (2012). Efficacy of the get ready to learn yoga program among children with autism spectrum disorders: A pretest-posttest control group design. *The American Journal of Occupational Therapy, 66*(5), 538–546.

Kushki, A., Chau, T., & Anagnostou, E. (2011). Handwriting difficulties in children with autism spectrum disorders: A scoping review. *Journal of Autism and Other Developmental Disorders, 41*(12), 1706–1716. https://doi.org/10.1007/s10803-011-1206-0.

Lang, R., Koegel, L. K., Ashbaugh, K., Regester, A., Ence, W., & Smith, W. (2010). Physical exercise and individuals with autism spectrum disorders: A systematic review. *Research in Autism Spectrum Disorders, 4*(4), 565–576. https://doi.org/10.1016/j.rasd.2010.01.006.

Loomis, J. W. (2008). *Staying in the game: Providing social opportunities for children and adolescents with autism spectrum disorders and other developmental disabilities.* Kansas: Autism Asperger Publishing Company.

Marshall, S. (2004). Strengthening learning through a focus on wellbeing. In Australian Council for Educational Research (ACER), *Supporting student wellbeing: What does the research tell us about the social emotional development of young people? Conference proceedings,* 2004). Retrieved from http://research.acer.edu.au/cgi/viewcontent.cgi?article=1000&context=research_conference_2004.

Massie, R., & Dillon, H. (2006). The impact of sound-field amplification in mainstream cross-cultural classrooms. Part 1. Educational outcomes. *Australian Journal of Education, 50*(1), 62–67.

Masters, G. (2004). Opening address: Conceptualising and researching student wellbeing. In Australian Council for Educational Research (ACER), *Supporting Student wellbeing: What does the research tell us about the social emotional development of young people? Conference proceedings* (pp. 2–6). 24–26 October, 2004, Adelaide, South Australia. http://research.acer.edu.au/cgi/viewcontent.cgi?article=1000&context=research_conference_2004.

Macdonald, L., Trembath, D., Ashburner, J., Costley, D., & Keen, D. (2018). The use of visual schedules and work systems to increase the on-task behaviour of students on the autism spectrum in mainstream classrooms. *Journal of Research in Special Educational Needs*. Advance online publication. https://doi.org/10.1111/1471-3802.12409.

McAllister, K., & Maguire, B. (2012). Design considerations for the autism spectrum disorder-friendly Key Stage 1 classroom. *Support for Learning, 27*(3), 103–112. https://doi.org/10.1111/j.1467-9604.2012.01525.x.

Mesibov, G. B., Shea, V., & Schopler, E. (2004). *The TEACCH approach to autism spectrum disorders*. New York: Springer.

Mostafa, M. (2008). An architecture for autism: Concepts of design intervention for the autistic user. *International Journal of Architecture Research, 2*(1), 189–211.

Mostafa, M. (2014). Architecture for autism: Autism ASPECTSS™ in school design. *International Journal of Architectural Research, 8*(1), 143–158.

National Autism Center. (2015). *Findings and conclusions: National standards project, phase 2.* Randolph, MA: National Autism Center.

Neil, L., Olsson, N. C., & Pellicano, E. (2016). The relationship between intolerance of uncertainty, sensory sensitivities, and anxiety in autistic and typically developing children. *Journal of Autism and Developmental Disorders, 46*(6), 1962–1973.

Nelson, P. B., & Soli, S. (2000). Acoustical barriers of learning: Children at risk in every classroom. *Language, Speech and Hearing Services in Schools, 31*(4), 356–361.

Pellicano, E. (2012). The development of executive function in autism. *Autism Research and Treatment.* Article ID 146132, n.p. http://dx.doi.org/10.1155/2012/146132.

Pellicano, E. (2013). Sensory symptoms in autism: A blooming, buzzing confusion? *Child Development Perspectives, 7*(3), 143–148. https://doi.org/10.1111/cdep.12031.

Quill, K. A. (1997). Instructional considerations for young children with autism: The rationale for visually cued instruction. *Journal of Autism and Developmental Disorders, 27*(6), 697–714.

Rance, G., Saunders, K., Carew, P., Johansson, M., & Tan, J. (2014). The use of listening devices to ameliorate auditory deficit in children with autism. *Journal of Pediatrics, 164*(2), 352–357.

Rance, G., Chisari, D., Saunders, K., & Rault, J.-L. (2017). Reducing listening-related stress in school-aged children with autism spectrum disorder. *Journal of Autism and Developmental Disorders, 47*(7), 2010–2022. https://doi.org/10.1007/s10803-017-3114-4.

Roberts, J., & Simpson, K. (2016). A review of research into stakeholder perspectives on inclusion of students with autism in mainstream schools. *Journal of Inclusive Education., 20*(10), 1084–1096. https://doi.org/10.1080/13603116.2016.1145267.

Robertson, A. E., & Simmons, D. R. (2015). The sensory experiences of adults with autism spectrum disorder: A qualitative analysis. *Perception, 44*(5), 569–586. https://doi.org/10.1068/p7833.

Robeyns, I. (2016). Conceptualising well-being for autistic persons. *Journal of Medical Ethics, 42*(6), 383–390. https://doi.org/10.1136/medethics-2016-103508.

Rowe, C., Candler, C., & Neville, M. (2011). Noise reduction headphones and autism: A single case study. *Journal of Occupational Therapy, Schools & Early Intervention, 4*(3–4), 229–235. https://doi.org/10.1080/19411243.2011.629551.

Saggers, B., & Beasley, T. (2017). Students on the autism spectrum: Influences on the middle years learner. In B. Saggers (Ed.), *Developing positive learning environments: Nurturing adolescent learning* (pp. 295–307). New South Wales: Allen and Unwin.

Saggers, B., Hwang, Y.-S., & Mercer, L. (2011). Your voice counts: Listening to the voice of high school students with autism spectrum disorder. *Australasian Journal of Special Education, 35*(2), 173–190.

Saggers, B., Klug, D., Harper-Hill, K., Ashburner, J., Costley, D., Clark, ... Carrington, S. (2016). *Australian autism educational needs analysis – What are the needs of schools, parents and students on the autism spectrum? Full report.* Cooperative Research Centre for Living with Autism, Brisbane.

Schafer, E. C., Mathews, L., Mehta, S., Hill, M., Munoz, A., Bishop, R., et al. (2013). Personal FM systems for children with autism spectrum disorders (ASD) and/or attention-deficit hyperactivity disorder (ADHD): An initial investigation. *Journal of Communication Disorders, 46*(1), 30–52.

Schafer, E. C., Wright, S., Anderson, C., Jones, J., Pitts, K., Bryant, D., et al. (2016). Technology evaluations: Remote-microphone technology for children with autism spectrum children. *Journal of Communication Disorders, 64*, 1–17. https://doi.org/10.1016/j.jcomdis.2012.09.002.

Schilling, D. L., & Schwartz, I. S. (2004). Alternative seating for young children with autism spectrum disorder: Effects on classroom behavior. *Journal of Autism and Developmental Disorders, 34*(4), 423–434. https://doi.org/10.1023/B:JADD.0000037418.48587.f4.

Stephenson, J., & Carter, M. (2009). The use of weighted vests with children with autism spectrum disorders and other disabilities. *Journal of Autism and Developmental Disorders, 39*(1), 105–114. https://doi.org/10.1007/s10803-008-0605-3.

Taylor, C. J., Spriggs, A., Jones Ault, M., Flanagan, S., & Sartini, E. C. (2017). A systematic review of weighted vests with individuals with autism spectrum disorder. *Research in Autism Spectrum Disorders, 37*(May), 49–60. https://doi.org/10.1016/j.rasd.2017.03.003.

Tomchek, S. D., & Dunn, W. (2007). Sensory processing in children with and without autism: A comparative study using the Short Sensory Profile. *The American Journal of Occupational Therapy, 61*(2), 190–200.

Umeda, C., & Deitz, J. (2011). Effects of therapy cushions on classroom behaviors of children with autism spectrum disorder. *American Journal of Occupational Therapy, 65*, 152–159. https://doi.org/10.5014/ajot.2011.000760.

United Nations Educational, Scientific and Cultural Organization. (1994). *The Salamanca statement and framework for action on special needs education.* http://www.unesco.org/education/pdf/SALAMA_E.PDF.

United Nations (2016). *Convention on the rights of persons with disabilities. General comment number 4 (2016). Article 24: Right to inclusive education.* https://www.ohchr.org/en/hrbodies/crpd/pages/gc.aspx.

Urrutikoetxea, A., Ispizua, A., & Matellanes, F. (1995). Vocal pathology in teachers: A videolaryngostroboscopic study in 1046 teachers. *Revue de Laryngologie - Otologie - Rhinologie., 116*(4), 255–262.

van Der Kruk, Y., Wilson, W., Palghat, K., Downing, C., Harper-Hill, K., & Ashburner, J. (2017). Improved signal-to-noise ratio and classroom performance in children with autism spectrum disorder: A systematic review. *Review Journal of Autism and Developmental Disorders, 4*(3), 243–253. https://doi.org/10.1007/s40489-017-0111-7.

Vasa, R. A., Kalb, L., Mazurek, M., Kanne, S., Freedman, B., Keefer, A., et al. (2013). Age-related differences in the prevalence and correlates of anxiety in youth with autism spectrum disorders. *Research in Autism Spectrum Disorders, 7*(11), 1358–1369. https://doi.org/10.1016/j.rasd.2013.07.005.

Williams, D. (1996). *Autism: An inside-out approach.* London: Jessica Kingsley.

Wong, C., Odom, S. L., Hume, K., Cox, A.W., Fettig, A., Kucharczyk, S., … Schultz, T.R. (2013). *Evidenced based practices for children, youth and young adults with autism spectrum disorder.* Chapel Hill: The University of North Carolina, Frank Porter Graham Child Development Institute, Autism Evidence-Based Practice Review Group. http://cidd.unc.edu/Registry/Research/Docs/31.pdf.

World Health Organization. (2017). *Mental health: A state of wellbeing.* http://www.who.int/features/factfiles/mental_health/en/.

Zehner, A., Chen, X., & Aladsani, M., (2017). Implementing universal design for learning in classrooms with minorities with autism. *Journal of Childhood and Developmental Disorders, 3*(2), n.p. https://doi.org/10.4172/2472-1786.100048.

Enhancing Wellbeing Through Broadening the Primary Curriculum in the UK with Open Futures

Pamela Woolner and Lucy Tiplady

Abstract Based on data collected when evaluating the UK Open Futures program, this chapter argues for altering school space to enable and imbed curriculum broadening to enhance student wellbeing. Such enriched school experience is under threat in the UK and elsewhere through curriculum narrowing in face of performativity and standardised testing, particularly in schools serving the most deprived communities. To counter this tendency, we investigate how the success of Open Futures in terms of impact on wellbeing can inform other school level change. Our analysis, based on student and teacher voices and our observations in school, suggests the importance of material changes alongside organisational and cultural developments. Changes that are powerful both pragmatically and symbolically, such as learning outside and developing spaces beyond traditional classrooms, can support changed relationships and the variety of learning opportunities that wellbeing literature promotes. However, alterations to curriculum, school organisation and the physical environment need to be held together through an overarching rationale that is articulated by school leaders and understood across the school community.

Open Futures, School Space and Student Wellbeing

This chapter considers the effects of a program aiming to produce more autonomous and successful learners through their development of skills and enquiry, partly to counter recent tendencies to narrow the primary curriculum. Berliner (2011) has argued that American and British school reform policies that are focused upon high stakes testing in 'core' subjects result in an inevitable restriction in creative and enjoyable school activities. We would add that these extracurricular activities and parts of the curriculum outside the core subject areas often provide opportunities for a range of students thought to be talented to develop many of the skills judged to be

P. Woolner (✉) · L. Tiplady
Newcastle University, Newcastle upon Tyne, UK
e-mail: pamela.woolner@newcastle.ac.uk

L. Tiplady
e-mail: lucy.tiplady@newcastle.ac.uk

© Springer Nature Singapore Pte Ltd. 2019
H. Hughes et al. (eds.), *School Spaces for Student Wellbeing and Learning*,
https://doi.org/10.1007/978-981-13-6092-3_9

most useful in the twenty-first century. Thus, any narrowing of opportunities can only threaten the wellbeing of children and young people. With the last available statistics in the UK revealing that one in ten young people (aged 5–16 years) has a clinically diagnosable mental health problem (Green, McGinnity, Meltzer, Ford, & Goodman, 2005), many are asking what more can be done to enrich lives? Open Futures (https://openfutures.com/), which ran in the UK between 2006 and 2017 was not specifically conceived as a program to enhance wellbeing. However, it centred on a holistic understanding of learners and a desire to develop a more comprehensive learning experience, which could be, and indeed was by many of those involved, expected to result in healthier, happier students. The emphasis on developing children's ability 'to think and to do', together with the 'acquisition of fundamental life skills and knowledge' was not only concerned with children's lives whilst at school but also beyond into their adult futures. Before discussing the experience and outcomes of the program that appear to relate to wellbeing, we will clarify our understanding of this concept and its relationship to education and school space, then introduce the Open Futures program and the educational policy context within which it was developed and enacted.

Defining, Assessing and Enhancing Wellbeing

Wellbeing as a concept has become increasingly topical and of political interest both in the UK and internationally. The UK government launched the National Wellbeing Programme in 2010 and subsequent reports such as *Measuring National Wellbeing: Life in the UK* (United Kingdom, Office for National Statistics, 2017) reports twice a year on a range of measures which include objective statistics (such as life expectancy, recorded crime and unemployment) as well as subjective measures (such as how people feel about a range of issues). Childhood wellbeing is often considered to be of particular concern, in part in a response to the principles articulated through the United Nations Convention on the Rights of the Child (1989). UNICEF has produced a number of reports on child wellbeing in rich countries, most recently the *Innocenti Report Card 11* (United Nations Children's Fund, UNICEF Office of Research, 2013), and, in the UK, The Children's Society has consulted with young people about their subjective wellbeing (Pople & Rees, 2017). In education, reports such as that produced by Public Health England *The link between pupil health and wellbeing and attainment: A briefing for head teachers, governors and staff in education settings* (Brooks, 2014) emphasise the possible links between some measures of wellbeing and attainment. The report goes on to state that 'maintained[1] schools have statutory duties to promote children and young people's wellbeing and statutory responsibilities to provide a curriculum that is broadly based, balanced and meets the needs of all pupils' (p. 5).

---

[1]UK term, meaning state funded schools.

Nevertheless, despite such strong rhetoric, the concept of wellbeing is not easily defined and this has led to the term being used to address a multitude of issues and measured in a variety of ways (McLellan & Steward, 2015; Spratt, 2016). Spratt (2016) argues that Scottish education policy assumes that health and wellbeing are prerequisites to learning and whilst not entirely unsympathetic to this, she argues that 'a fuller consideration of health and wellbeing would move beyond its supporting role in schooling and look to the role of education itself in enhancing human flourishing' (p. 237). This view that increased wellbeing is an outcome of an enriched curriculum, participated in a joint endeavour with fellow students and staff, conceptualises wellbeing from an eudaimonic perspective (originating from Aristotle's view of wellbeing as leading a virtuous life) whereby education can be viewed as a means by which an individual can fulfil his/her potential (Waterman, 1993). For the purposes of this chapter, we will be conceptualising wellbeing from such a perspective as we consider the potential for enhancing wellbeing through the broadening of the primary curriculum facilitated through the development of school space.

School Space and Student Wellbeing

To clarify how we see wellbeing relating to school space, we start from a review article that presents evidence that student 'health and wellbeing' (Bell & Dyment, 2008, p. 77) can be improved and promoted through the development of 'green' school grounds. A recently published guide to 'greening' schools in the US (Kensler & Uline, 2017) presents an argument that progresses in the other direction, establishing that the benefits of a school guided by a sustainability agenda include enhanced 'human wellbeing' (p. 5). Both sets of authors proceed from understandings of how educational space relate to practices that parallel our own, and can be justified in relation to the established evidence base resulting from research into the physical learning environment. In essence, the school premises should be recognised as significant, exerting an important influence on activities, attitudes and behaviour, and ultimately contributing to outcomes (for example see Maxwell, 2016; Woolner, Hall, Higgins, McCaughey, & Wall, 2007; Weinstein, 1979). Yet this relationship is not deterministic or static: settings facilitate certain practices, rather than mandating them, and can be adjusted to support different practices and so enable educational change (Woolner, Thomas, & Tiplady, 2018; Uline, Tschannen-Moran, & De Vere Wolsey, 2009).

In relation to wellbeing, more environmentally responsible schools can aspire to make a positive contribution: Bell and Dyment (2008) argue that educationalists concerned with health and wellbeing need to move from a deficit view of the physical school environment where the 'emphasis… is… on accident/illness prevention' (p. 86), while Kensler and Uline (2017) similarly envisage green schools as 'part of the solution rather than the problem' (p. 14). In terms of how this might happen, the conceptualisation of the physical setting facilitating, not determining, actions requires us to look for ways to understand the mediating factors and events that potentially bridge between designed space and intended student outcomes. A classic article examining ways that classroom space might support pedagogical innovation suggests a useful distinction between the *'pragmatic* role played by features of the setting and the *symbolic* message of what one expects to happen in a particular place' (Proshansky & Wolfe, 1974, pp. 558–559, italics in original). Thus, a school garden of wild flowers will practically facilitate interactions with nature but may also, through its existence, signal certain values and suggest further ecological activities. A related characterisation of different means for schools to enact educational change distinguishes between structural and cultural aspects (Priestley, Millera, Barratt, & Wallace, 2011; Woolner et al., 2018). Enhancing wellbeing can be expected to involve structural changes, such as overhauling pastoral arrangements or changing how informal social time is organised, but to be successful these will need to be experienced as part of a coherent, shared school culture that is clear about the importance of wellbeing. As will become evident, Open Futures did generally involve both structural and cultural change, with school spaces and organisation being altered to enable a new school culture to develop.

Enhancing Wellbeing Through Open Futures

Open Futures described itself as a teacher continuing professional development (CPD) program that intended to enable teachers to build children's ability 'to think and to do'. It developed skills of enquiry, both as an end in itself and to underpin learning in the Open Futures 'strands'. These four strands were *askit* (Philosophy for Children), *growit* (gardening focused on growing fruit and vegetables), *cookit* (preparing and cooking food) and *filmit* (making and editing films). They were intended to be delivered as part of a school's existing curriculum. Open Futures on their website claimed that 'by integrating engaging, practical and relevant activities into the learning environment, children have access to contexts which enable independent learning and the acquisition of fundamental life skills and knowledge'. Whilst claiming that Open Futures provided opportunities to raise attainment, the providers additionally emphasised the opportunities for 'all learners to engage and contribute positively to the classroom, the school and the community'. This holistic focus was designed to enrich children's lives within school and beyond. The CPD program drew upon expertise in each of the four strands (SAPERE, the UK charity for the Philosophy for Children, The Royal Horticultural Society and Focus on Food, as well as specialist media advisers) and combined modular courses, cross-curricular workshops, in-school support days and leadership and implementation workshops. Open Futures was designed as a whole school program and whilst individual schools were encouraged to make it their own, implementation necessitated certain key school spaces to be developed: most notably a garden and cooking space (see Figs. 1 and 2), but in some cases also a media space.

Fig. 1 Developing school space to accommodate growing

This chapter draws on data collected in collaborative research between the research team and seven Open Futures case study schools in 2011–2013, informed by formative evaluations during the development of the program from 2006 to 2010. These primary schools (children aged 4 to 11 years) were from three areas of England (two northern and one from the capital city) which faced significant challenges in relation to community deprivation. This was a deliberate decision as the program funders were keen to understand the challenges of implementation and impact in such urban, economically disadvantaged school settings. The overarching aim of the research was to consider change so the research team worked with each case study school to collaboratively produce individual Theories of Change (Dyson & Todd, 2010) which articulated school contexts and aims, in addition to the steps of change which the school expected to travel along to their desired outcomes. Research data, which was

Fig. 2 Developing school space to accommodate cooking

used to assess this intended progress, included a combination of school collected evidence (such as curriculum and organisational documentation, school statistical data, parent and pupil questionnaires) and researcher collected evidence (such as interviews with leadership and staff, a staff questionnaire issued to all schools and pupil interviews facilitated by visual methods). This data was used to produce an evaluation report for the Open Futures trustees (Woolner, Tiplady, & Leat, 2013).

For the purposes of the evaluation, much of the data analysis proceeded at a surface level, seeking to understand whether and how the strands of Open Futures were being implemented, and note effects of the program on schools, teachers and students. However, we were aware of aspects of the participants' experiences of the program involving student wellbeing, and have returned to the data to investigate. This is discussed in relation to four themes, which we relate to ideas from the wellbeing literature, and use to consider the contribution of school space to enhancing wellbeing. These themes are:

- Benefits of learning outside;
- Developing life skills for a healthy life;
- Different relationships—with peers, staff and beyond school; and
- Confidence through success—varied activities create more opportunities.

Benefits of Learning Outside

There is a general consensus that children and young people should be given the opportunity to learn outside of the classroom and in England the *Learning Outside the Classroom Manifesto* (United Kingdom, Department for Education and Skills, 2006) articulated just this. The arguments in favour include research suggesting specific benefits for specific children, such as the findings of Taylor and colleagues (Taylor, Kuo, & Sullivan, 2001) that regular contact with outdoor spaces reduced the symptoms of a group of young people diagnosed with attention deficit disorder and that the greener the space the greater the benefit. Other research has shown that access to nature can more generally support young people's wellbeing and ability to manage stress both now (Wells & Evans, 2003) and in their adult lives (Ward Thompson, Aspinall, & Montarzino, 2008). Others have argued that the development of green school grounds with 'the rules that govern them, their role in school and community life, and the types of play and social interactions that they invite and support' combine to meaningfully promote health and wellbeing for all (Bell & Dyment, 2008, p. 78), enacting cultural as well as physical change.

Given such established understanding about the benefits for children of getting outdoors for exercise and experiential learning, the *growit* strand constitutes a fundamental contribution of Open Futures to student wellbeing. As a result of involvement in the program, new school garden spaces were developed and curriculum time set aside for a range of activities, some centred on gardening, but some linked to the other strands (e.g. harvesting produce to cook) and to the wider school curriculum (e.g. growing plants featured in stories). The benefits were clearly and frequently expressed by teachers and other staff in terms of student enjoyment: 'children love gardening' (teacher questionnaire). This was often linked to the experience of being outside and being physically active:

> The children absolutely love it. I mean, let's face it, it's active, which children tend to love; it's outside, which children tend to love (teacher interview).

The students we met during this and previous evaluations of Open Futures similarly emphasised this aspect of the program, often expressed as liking 'getting outside' or 'getting fresh air'.

However, it is not just about enjoyment. As one child commented, 'you get the breeze and you can run around but you still do your work.' Comments from staff also referred to learning about the lifecycles of plants, plant needs and the origins of fruit and vegetables. Some of the learning occurred in the overlap between *growit* and other strands or curricular areas, as for example in the school where the lead teacher on languages had labelled the growing vegetables in French. This integration of subjects and approaches is characteristic of Open Futures and will be returned to. In addition, it is worth noting that both staff and students also valued the learning of gardening skills themselves, and this reference to life skills, frequently made in relation to *growit* and other strands, will be explored in the following section.

The articulations of enjoying or learning from gardening sometimes included the idea specifically of being in the garden: 'Children enjoy the school garden' (teaching

Fig. 3 Centrally positioned school growing space enables children with less access to natural environments to enjoy gardening

assistant, TA, questionnaire). The point was additionally made by staff in some schools that 'many children don't have a garden or opportunities to grow things for themselves' (teacher questionnaire). Thus, the planted spaces (see Figs. 1, 2 and 3 for examples) were enhancing their school experience but also widening opportunities beyond those typically available to children growing up in densely populated urban environments. This is important because access to natural environments, and thus the associated benefits, are not equitably distributed with those children and young people from areas of high deprivation that are most likely to be disadvantaged (Malone & Waite, 2016; Morris et al., 2011).

Developing Life Skills for a Healthy Life

That primary education should be concerned not only with the needs of children and young people whilst at school but beyond into their adult futures was conveyed in the UK *Cambridge Primary Review* which stated 'Fostering children's wellbeing requires us to attend to their future fulfilment as well as their present needs and capabilities' (Alexander, 2010). Open Futures was designed to develop children's ability 'to think and to do' now and in the future. Through developing children's skills in a variety of contexts, including the garden, kitchen and media suites as well as within the classroom, it was intended that children would cultivate learning approaches that would transcend the school gates. The more practical nature of some of the strands was also felt to be popular with children and this echoes findings by Layard and Dunn (2009) who reported that in a survey of 14–16 year olds from the UK 'learning by doing rather than listening' was considered to be important for 'the good life'.

Across the questionnaire and interview responses, there are many mentions of 'life skills' as a benefit staff see for students involved in Open Futures. These comments refer to a diverse range of perceived benefits, not always consistently articulated, and some consideration of the ideas and experiences that underpin these assertions is informative. One teacher mentioned 'life skills' twice, once elaborating as 'understanding their world' for *growit* and then as 'healthy lifestyles' for *cookit* (teacher questionnaire). A link to healthy eating is also apparent in other responses, such as 'knowledge of where food comes from' (teacher questionnaire). The suggestion of these skills being widely applicable, learnt and useful beyond the classroom with the inevitable implications for physical space in schools (for example see Fig. 4), is inherent in references to 'real life skills' (teacher questionnaire). Another questionnaire response referring to 'hands on, practical skills which will be useful in everyday life' echoes this idea of utility but adds an emphasis on practicality, contrasting presumably with the more abstract, academic knowledge of the core curriculum. Yet, many teachers also valued the links they were developing between these practical skills and the wider curriculum. As one teacher explained during an interview:

> It's a really valuable thing to be able to cook and you might even make it so that you're cooking something you've grown in the garden so that it links with something they've done in the Second World War [i.e. history content].

A sense of equipping the children for their future lives is evident in many of the mentions of life skills, and we have also noted children talking in these terms about their Open Futures experiences. A particularly thorough reference to this idea was provided by the teacher who responded that their expectations of the program for the students were, 'To prepare them for life in the 21st century. To provide them with skills necessary to achieve success within the workplace and within the family and community life' (teacher questionnaire). That this use of skills outside school was already happening was evident from some student and parent comments. For example, a parent wrote that their child 'likes to grow at home', while a child at a different school explained that 'granddad applied to do the allotment and now I can help him'. These ideas overlap considerably with our next theme of relationships.

Different Relationships—With Peers, Staff and Beyond School

Philosophy for Children (P4C) is specifically designed to develop social aspects of wellbeing through working collaboratively with peers, reducing initial teacher

Fig. 4 Authentic kitchen space to learn 'life skills'—note also the posters relating to the English curriculum

scaffolding and leading to self-regulated peer interactivity (Topping & Tricky, 2007). Within Open Futures, this approach was further encouraged through the three more practical strands (*growit, cookit* and *filmit*) and was thought to enable and support qualitatively different relationships with peers, teachers and other school staff. This resulted in Open Futures changing and developing relationships within school. It was noticed by children that Open Futures activities, across all the strands, tended to require cooperation and team work by the students (see Fig. 5), contrasting dramatically with the individualised learning they were accustomed to in much of their school work. The different role of the teacher, as collaborator on a joint project rather than isolated bastion of knowledge, was also remarked upon.

Reports of changes in the ways in which children and young people are perceived by adults, both school staff and parents, and by their peers have similarly been reported as an outcome of the Forest Schools approach, leading to 'new perspectives' (O'Brien, 2009; Slade, Lowery & Bland, 2013). Within Open Futures, staff reported children initiating cooking, gardening or filming at home with parents and other family members, and there are suggestions of altered relationships within families. A student explained that 'when you cook you can teach other people what you've done, like your family.'

A teacher at another school was very clear in her opinion that relationships between children and their parents were being enhanced through 'one to one' time doing

Fig. 5 Working together, and also integrating the strands through filming the potato harvest

activities inspired by Open Futures. In her view, this is beneficial for the families but is also 'like gold' for the school in terms of linking together children's in and out of school experiences. Elaborating on this parental involvement, the teacher went on to discuss how the *cookit* and *growit* strands in particular facilitated a range of community links and relationship building, 'so the community's becoming more together.' Specific events to facilitate intergenerational relationships included a Christmas cake competition that culminated in a cake decorating event which she described as 'such a lovely environment of children and adults doing something together' (teacher interview). In another school, the teachers noticed parents and children gathering to look at and discuss the school garden together during pick up and drop off times.

Confidence Through Success—Varied Activities Create More Opportunities

It was asserted by many adults involved in Open Futures that the program developed children's confidence. A range of routes to this change were suggested, often linked to the different relationships and life skills elements discussed above, but centring on achieving success through being offered varied opportunities to learn and succeed. In a related way, increased self-confidence and self-esteem have been reported as outcomes of Forest Schools, often thought to be partly attributable to children being encouraged to develop independent learning and to take risks (Swarbrick, Eastwood, & Tutton, 2004; O'Brien & Murray, 2007; O'Brien, 2009). However, since these concepts are difficult to define and assess, others have questioned the robustness of evidence presented and asked whether the significance of the effect on self-esteem has been over emphasised (Leather, 2017; Maynard & Waters, 2007).

In the rather different context of secondary mathematics learning, Boaler (2008) has argued for the significance of approaches that are 'multidimensional': classrooms where both teachers and students value a wider range of practices than the accurate performance of procedures required in standardised assessments. Within these classes, 'because there were more ways to be successful, many more students were successful' (Boaler, 2008, p. 185), but this also made the students more confident and positive about mathematics and ultimately led to them being more successful in the narrower set of skills needed for exams and tests. Our evaluation of Open Futures appealed to this idea of multidimensionality as underpinning its success since the diverse activities of the program provide many different ways to learn and to succeed compared to a narrow interpretation of the core curriculum. Recognising the strength of this range was probably important for staff as well as for students, given the context of pressure to narrow the curriculum, which is often felt more keenly by schools in economically disadvantaged areas (Berliner, 2011).

A questionnaire response from a teaching assistant articulated this key idea of different ways to learn: 'Pupils can see that to understand something you can learn in different ways and make links to different things' (TA questionnaire). During interview, one teacher talked at length about Open Futures engaging the children through appealing to diverse interests, 'celebrating their individual skills' and enabling children to become 'experts' in particular areas. In relation to developing such expertise, the student above who mentioned that 'when you cook you can teach other people what you've done' suggests how the practices of Open Futures are valued by the students. The teacher went on to exemplify the potential for consequential success in the mainstream curriculum by describing how cooking experience helped students understand ratio in maths. Similarly, and linking back to the idea of confidence, in another school, gardening was praised because it had 'given them [students] practical science experience and they have found it empowering' (teacher questionnaire).

For an idea of how this is experienced by the students, in addition to the comment above about teaching others, we noted a child remarking that through Open Futures 'you get to choose more'. There were also comments from a number of children at this school about being able to make mistakes, with one child adding that in *askit* 'no one will make fun of you'. It was the *askit* strand that many members of staff saw as being pivotal for confidence building through ensuring that 'Every child has the chance to speak, listen and gain confidence' (TA questionnaire). Overall, it is apparent that the Open Futures program widened opportunities for children to succeed through offering different skills as valued, and supporting children to develop them. This was initially in the 'safe' setting of the *askit* session or the kitchen, but the intention was that these skills could then be drawn upon with confidence in core curriculum lessons.

Understanding the Impact of Open Futures

In completing our evaluation of Open Futures, we were struck by the way that change could be seen to be happening in many different areas of school functioning, and in this chapter, we have explored the impact on wellbeing. The success of Open Futures in this and other respects needs to be considered in the context of contemporary school teaching and management in the UK. Against a backdrop of concerns about the wellbeing of children and young people, there have been a number of projects and initiatives related to wellbeing in schools, but these tend not to gain holds within a context characterised by pressure to narrow student experience. Yet Open Futures became established. Notably, progress was made quickly for a program of this complexity, with the majority of the evaluation schools well on the way to the 'institutionalisation' of Open Futures after the 2 years that Fullan (2007) proposes as a minimum for even a relatively simple innovation.

We concluded that Open Futures endured and became a way of life in most program schools through cyclical development, where tangible changes embedded the initiative (see Fig. 6). These changes, made to school organisation, space and curriculum, are interlinked, becoming increasingly coherent and mutually interdependent. A central strength is that the diverse activities are aligned in their intentions and requirements, held together by an overarching culture, so that the changes made are understood to be more than superficial structural alterations. Another important aspect of the program is the balance of prescription and flexibility. The extensive support, which was especially useful to schools at the beginning of their involvement, came together with clear requirements and obligations in terms of staff attending training and implementing the strands. Yet, there is also plenty of opportunity for staff and schools to 'make it their own', which enhances ownership in a way that is appreciated by schools, and contributes to the development of the overarching Open Futures culture within the school, as this head teacher explains:

> No two Open Futures schools look alike and when you think... am I you know just going off track here or you know is this what it's supposed to look like, you realise there is no model for what it's supposed to look like and it's what works for individual schools... we've found a model that works for this school you know (Head teacher, interview).

Fig. 6 Tangible changes enabled, supported and embedded the program

Using School Space to Enhance Wellbeing

The intention of this final section is to move back from the detail of the Open Futures program to question how the experience of this unique approach can inform very different attempts to enhance wellbeing. We will argue that the school space is a key element of a successful approach, and that there do appear to be some essential components of any development. Yet there is room for variety, and it is important that both the underpinning environmental changes and other developments are all understood as part of a dynamic learning environment that depends on social, cultural and organisational, as well as material, elements. To conceptualise this, we return to the two different, but complementary, aspects to the use of school space to support change, which were introduced earlier. These can be understood as making structural changes to the physical and material school environment to enable and support particular behaviour and activities—the pragmatic role of the setting in the terms of Proshansky and Wolfe (1974); and as recognising the entwined meanings and consequences of school space—its symbolic role. Through attending to this second aspect, and ensuring the alignment of physical and other alterations, the chances of achieving a more robust cultural change are raised, while the identification of 'bigger' ideas of a new school culture can act to bind together changes made to school space, organisation and procedures.

Structural Change: Specific Requirements for School Space to Enhance Wellbeing

The literature related to wellbeing, together with the Open Futures experience, makes abundantly clear that the more holistic approach to learning being proposed will require school space other than traditional classrooms. The detailed requirements of this space will vary depending on the particular intentions of the wellbeing program adopted, but the development of life skills, important for future healthy lives, to enhance existing relationships and to offer students more ways to be successful, needs authentic space for hands-on experiences. Within Open Futures, the requirements of the *cookit* and *growit* strands demanded areas for gardening and cooking: as one head teacher explained to us, '... so we decided if we were going to increase the volume of cookery that we needed a proper space for it' (Head teacher, interview).

As has been discussed, there is plenty of evidence of the benefits to children of learning outside so a development of outdoor space is likely to be part of any wellbeing initiative. In addition to demonstrating many of these proposed benefits in relation to gardening, Open Futures also suggests the advantages of requiring some quite specific physical changes, particularly in the early stages of a new initiative: their purpose can be clearly articulated and their achievement is tangible and visible to all. Some of the physical changes suggested by proponents of 'green' schools, such as installing renewable energy generation systems (Kensler & Uline, 2017, p. 145), similarly entail bounded and comprehensible demands that can be seen to be fulfilled.

Once these physical changes are in place, their visibility makes development in their usage beyond the original activities more likely. Kensler and Uline remark on the potential to link the curriculum with environmentally sound facilities management through student projects to measure energy use. This expansion in ideas for use of the garden space was seen in a number of the Open Futures schools, where science, language and other teaching drew on the resources offered by the garden, convincing us of the importance of growing spaces being developed in places visible to students, staff and parents.

Symbolic Role of Space: Aligning and Integrating to Achieve Cultural Change

Despite the diversity of activities and new skills inherent in Open Futures, we noted the overall cohesion of the program within each school. The diversity provided different ways into the program for members of staff and students with different interests and existing skills, but the encouragement to link strands with each other and with existing curriculum areas ensured coherence and avoided the program being experienced as a random collection of activities. It seems clear that such coherence could be provided by a different 'big idea' to link a series of changes and initiatives. The idea of 'greening' your school would seem to fulfil this need and offer a different, but potentially powerful, banner under which to guide a wellbeing initiative (Bell & Dyment, 2008).

Without such an overarching aim, it seems likely that developments will be fragmented and more likely to become exhausted. Scholars of educational change suggest that this is indeed what happens if structural changes occur without complementary cultural change (Priestley et al., 2011), and when schools develop outdoor growing space without a bigger agenda, it can become hard to justify the staff time and financial cost of a space just to do some gardening. Such neglect of newly established garden space was not seen during our research and development relationship with Open Futures, even when we visited schools who had become involved in the program some years previously.

The relationship between the big cultural idea and the structural changes can be seen to be reciprocal. Through enacting physical, curricular and organisational changes, school communities demonstrated their commitment and became better Open Futures schools, but the overarching aims of the program provided courage to make alterations. Both directions of influence were apparent in the head teachers' understandings of what they were doing. In one school, the head teacher established a space for *filmit* to convey that the strand was valued in school (Woolner & Tiplady, 2016), but she also explained the school's commitment to the program in a way that suggested she took strength from Open Futures alternative conception of primary school learning (Woolner & Tiplady, 2016, p. 79). Again, it seems likely that a commitment to environmental sustainability could fulfil these roles in the case of 'green' schools, guiding physical changes, but also providing the rationale for making them. This suggests that any initiative to enhance student wellbeing would be advised to underpin changes with an overarching rationale or big idea. Wellbeing itself, being defined in various ways as discussed above, might require considerably more explicit conceptualisation before it could fulfil this role for a school.

The observation of Open Futures succeeding through a balance of prescription and flexibility can also be seen as founded on this reciprocal relationship between structure and culture. Furthermore, it is inherent in the way Proshansky and Wolfe define the 'symbolic message' of school spaces and furnishings as conceptually distinct from their 'pragmatic role', but overlapping in practice in schools (1974, pp. 558–9). Finally, it is perhaps the case that learning environments succeed, whatever their particular intentions, when the space imposes some limits to activities through being properly designed for a purpose but leaves room for innovation and subsequent development. In order to use school space to enhance wellbeing, these understandings of the ways that physical settings function within the school need to be returned to and explored for each initiative.

The implications of our analysis for policy and practice can be summarised as follows:

- Spaces other than traditional classrooms enhance wellbeing through facilitating the development of different relationships and enabling a variety of learning opportunities.

- Outdoor space appears key for wellbeing and can improve equity through offering access for all.
- Individual changes made to curriculum, organisation and the physical environment need to be held together through an overarching rationale that is articulated by school leaders and understood across the school community.
- Within this scheme and across the school spaces, there should be opportunities for individual innovations and the possibility of new directions.

References

Alexander, R. J. (Ed.). (2010). *Children, their world, their education: Final report and recommendations of the Cambridge Primary Review.* London: Routledge.

Bell, A., & Dyment, J. (2008). Grounds for health: The intersection of green school grounds and health-promoting schools. *Environmental Education Research, 14*(1), 77–90 (2008). https://doi.org/10.1080/13504620701843426.

Berliner, D. (2011). Rational responses to high stakes testing: The case of curriculum narrowing and the harm that follows. *Cambridge Journal of Education, 41*(3), 287–302 (2011). https://doi.org/10.1080/0305764x.2011.607151.

Boaler, J. (2008). Promoting 'relational equity' and high mathematics achievement through an innovative mixed-ability approach. *British Educational Research Journal, 34*(2), 167–194. https://doi.org/10.1080/01411920701532145.

Brooks, F. (2014). *The link between pupil health and wellbeing and attainment: A briefing for head teachers, governors and staff in education settings.* London: Public Health England. Retrieved June 7, 2018, from https://www.gov.uk/government/publications/the-link-between-pupil-health-and-wellbeing-and-attainment.

Dyson, A., & Todd, L. (2010). Dealing with complexity: Theory of change evaluation and the full service extended schools initiative. *International Journal of Research and Method in Education, 33*(2), 119–134. https://doi.org/10.1080/1743727x.2010.484606.

Fullan, M. (2007). *The new meaning of educational change* (4th ed.). New York/Abingdon: Routledge.

Green, H., McGinnity, A., Meltzer, H., Ford, T., & Goodman, R. (2005). *Mental health of children and young people in Great Britain, 2004.* Basingstoke: Palgrave Macmillan and U.K Office for National Statistics.

Kensler, L. A. W., & Uline, C. (2017). *Leadership for green schools.* New York: Routledge.

Layard, R., & Dunn, J. (2009). *A good childhood: Searching for values in a competitive age.* London: Penguin Books.

Leather, M. (2017). A critique of "Forest School" or something lost in translation. *Journal of Outdoor and Environmental Education, 21*(1), 5–18. https://doi.org/10.1007/s42322-017-0006-1.

Malone, K., & Waite, S. (2016). *Student outcomes and natural schooling: Pathways from evidence to Impact Report 2016.* Plymouth, U.K.: Plymouth University. Retrieved June 3, 2018, from https://www.plymouth.ac.uk/uploads/production/document/path/6/6811/Student_outcomes_and__natural_schooling_pathways_to_impact_2016.pdf.

Maxwell, L. (2016). School building condition, social climate, student attendance and academic achievement: A mediation model. *Journal of Environmental Psychology, 46*, 206–216. https://doi.org/10.1016/j.jenvp.2016.04.009.

Maynard, T., & Waters, J. (2007). Learning in the outdoor environment: A missed opportunity? *Early Years: An International Research Journal, 27*(3), 255–265. https://doi.org/10.1080/09575140701594400.

McLellan, R., & Steward, S. (2015). Measuring children and young people's wellbeing in the school context. *Cambridge journal of education, 45*(3), 307–332. https://doi.org/10.1080/0305764x.2014.889659.

Morris, J., O'Brien, E., Ambrose-Oji, B., Lawrence, A., Carter, C., & Peace, A. (2011). Access for all? Barriers to accessing woodlands and forests in Britain. *Local Environment, 16*(4), 375–396. https://doi.org/10.1080/13549839.2011.576662.

O'Brien, L. (2009). Learning outdoors: The Forest School approach. *Education 3–13: International Journal of Primary, Elementary and Early Years Education, 37*(1), 45–60. https://doi.org/10.1080/03004270802291798.

O'Brien, L., & Murray, R. (2007). Forest School and its impacts on young children: Case studies in Britain. *Urban Forestry & Urban Greening, 6*(4), 249–265. https://doi.org/10.1016/j.ufug.2007.03.006.

Pople, L., & Rees, G. (2017). *The good childhood report 2017.* London: The Children's Society. Retrieved June 7, 2018, from https://www.childrenssociety.org.uk/the-good-childhood-report-2017.

Priestley, M., Millera, K., Barrett, L., & Wallace, C. (2011). Teacher learning communities and educational change in Scotland: The Highland experience. *British Educational Research Journal, 37*(2), 265–284. https://doi.org/10.1080/01411920903540698.

Proshansky, E., & Wolfe, M. (1974). The physical setting and open education. *The School Review, 82*(4), 556–574. https://doi.org/10.1086/443150.

Slade, M., Lowery, C., & Bland, K. (2013). Evaluating the impact of forest schools: A collaboration between a university and a primary school. *Support for Learning, 28*(2), 66–72. https://doi.org/10.1111/1467-9604.12020.

Spratt, J. (2016). Childhood wellbeing: What role for education? *British Educational Research Journal, 42*(2), 223–239 (2016). https://doi.org/10.1002/berj.3211.

Swarbrick, N., Eastwood, G., & Tutton, K. (2004). Self-esteem and successful interaction as part of the forest school project. *Support for Learning, 19*(3), 142–146. https://doi.org/10.1111/j.0268-2141.2004.00337.x.

Taylor, A., Kuo, F., & Sullivan, W. (2001). Coping with ADD: The surprising connection to green play settings. *Environment and Behavior, 33*(1), 55–77. https://doi.org/10.1177/00139160121972864.

Topping, K., & Trickey, S. (2007). Collaborative philosophical inquiry for schoolchildren: Cognitive gains at 2-year follow-up. *British Journal of Educational Psychology, 77*(4), 787–796. https://doi.org/10.1348/000709907x193032.

Uline, C. L., Tschannen-Moran, M., & De Vere Wolsey, T. (2009). The walls still speak: The stories occupants tell. *Journal of Educational Administration, 47*(3), 400–426. https://doi.org/10.1108/09578230910955818.

United Kingdom Department for Education and Skills. (2006). *Learning outside the classroom manifesto.* http://www.lotc.org.uk/wp-content/uploads/2011/03/G1.-LOtC-Manifesto.pdf.

United Kingdom, Office for National Statistics (2017). *Measuring national wellbeing: Life in the UK, April 2017.* https://www.ons.gov.uk/releases/measuringnationalwellbeinglifeintheukapr2017.

United Nations Children's Fund. UNICEF Office of Research. (2013). *Child well-being in rich countries: A comparative overview (Innocenti Report Card 11).* Florence: UNICEF Office of Research.

United Nations Convention on the Rights of the Child. (1989). http://www.ohchr.org/Documents/ProfessionalInterest/crc.pdf.

Ward Thompson, C., Aspinall, P., & Montarzino, A. (2008). The childhood factor: Adult visits to green places and the significance of childhood experience. *Environment and Behaviour, 40,* 111–143. https://doi.org/10.1177/0013916507300119.

Waterman, A. (1993). Two conceptions of happiness: Contrasts of personal expressiveness (Eudaimonia) and hedonic enjoyment. *Journal of Personality and Social Psychology, 64*(4), 678–691. https://doi.org/10.1037//0022-3514.64.4.678.

Weinstein, C. S. (1979). The physical environment of the school: A review of the research. *Review of Educational Research, 49*(4), 577–610. https://doi.org/10.2307/1169986.

Wells, N., & Evans, G. (2003). Nearby nature: A buffer of life stress among rural children. *Environment and Behaviour, 35,* 311–330. https://doi.org/10.1177/0013916503035003001.

Woolner, P., Hall, E., Higgins, S., McCaughey, C., & Wall, K. (2007). A sound foundation? What we know about the impact of environments on learning and the implications for building schools for the future. *Oxford Review of Education, 33*(1), 47–70. https://doi.org/10.1080/03054980601094693.

Woolner, P., Thomas, U., & Tiplady, L. (2018). Structural change from physical foundations: The role of the physical environment in enacting school change. *Journal of Educational Change, 19*(2), 223–242. https://doi.org/10.1007/s10833-018-9317-4.

Woolner, P., & Tiplady, L. (2016). Adapting school premises as part of a complex pedagogical change programme. In U. Stadler-Altmann (Ed.), *Lernumgebungen: Erziehungswissenschaftliche Perspektiven auf Schulgebäude und Klassenzimmer* (pp. 69–78). Opladen, Berlin, Toronto: Barbara Budrich.

Woolner, P., Tiplady, L., & Leat, D. (2013). *Open Futures evaluation 2011–2013: Report to the trustees*. Newcastle upon Tyne: Research Centre for Learning and Teaching, Newcastle University. http://www.ncl.ac.uk/media/wwwnclacuk/cflat/files/OFReportFinal.pdf.

A Third Teacher?

Derek Bland, 2017

Part III
Participatory Designing of School Spaces for Wellbeing and Learning

Fostering Educator Participation in Learning Space Designing: Insights from a Master of Education Unit of Study

Hilary Hughes and Raylee Elliott Burns

Abstract Educators can play a vital role in creating environments that enhance student learning and wellbeing. Consequently, there is a teacher education need to empower teachers as learning space designers. The Master of Education program at Queensland University of Technology offers a unit entitled *Designing Spaces for Learning* which enables students to explore and practice the principles of consensus values-based designing. This chapter outlines the conceptualisation and ongoing development of the unit, which builds upon the doctoral research of Dr Raylee Elliott Burns. By outlining the design and implementation of the unit, the chapter models an innovative pedagogical approach that engages educators (as learners) in the evaluation and conceptual redesigning of learning spaces. The learning experience includes site visits, a charrette (collaborative designing workshop) and the compilation of a theoretically justified design brief and online portfolio. The chapter concludes by discussing how this unit fosters the learning and wellbeing of the educators who undertake the unit, and often also that of their students who engage in school-based designing projects.

Introduction

Educators seldom participate in the designing of learning spaces despite their situated professional experience of them (Cleveland & Fisher, 2014). In part this is attributable to limited formal learning opportunities, either pre-service or in-service, for educators to develop designing knowledge and practices (Blackmore, Bateman, Loughlin, O'Mara, & Aranda, 2011). Therefore, this chapter focuses on the Master of Education unit of study Designing Spaces for Learning as a pedagogical model for developing educators' capacity for participatory designing to foster learner wellbeing. The concepts and processes discussed are applicable to a wide range of educational contexts.

H. Hughes (✉) · R. Elliott Burns
Queensland University of Technology, Brisbane, QLD 4000, Australia
e-mail: h.hughes@qut.edu.au

© Springer Nature Singapore Pte Ltd. 2019
H. Hughes et al. (eds.), *School Spaces for Student Wellbeing and Learning*,
https://doi.org/10.1007/978-981-13-6092-3_10

Wellbeing Through Participation

This chapter highlights *participation* as a contributor to the wellbeing of those who design and use learning spaces: students, educators, administrators, architects and accredited designers, and the wider community. Participation is a connecting thread between learning and designing and supports social inclusion in both fields. We define participation broadly as active engagement in a collaborative creative process that involves stakeholders with varying experience. A participatory approach to designing learning spaces is values-based and assumes that the inclusion of diverse viewpoints and practices contributes to social, emotional and educational wellbeing. This understanding is reflected in the design and implementation of the Designing Spaces for Learning unit. Attention to wellbeing through participation is inherent in the unit's two guiding questions: *Who and what is valued here? Is this the best we can do?* These interrelated questions prompt continuous reflection on the nature and impacts of particular learning spaces and opportunities for enhancing users' experience of these spaces through participatory designing.

Participatory Designing

As discussed in the following brief literature review, participatory designing draws upon the experience of diverse stakeholders to ensure alignment of design outcomes and user needs. Similar principles apply to both the creation of new spaces and the refurbishment of existing ones. In educational contexts, potential participants include teachers and their students who bring insider perspectives on learning spaces. However, while educators can make specialist contributions to learning space designing, they often lack opportunities to learn the relevant language, principles and practices to support their participation in this complex process.

Why is Participation Important in Learning Space Designing?

The potential benefits of multiple stakeholder participation in learning space designing, across all educational sectors, are increasingly acknowledged (Day & Parnell, 2003; Ellis & Goodyear, 2016; Könings, Bovill C., & Woolner, 2017). Understandings developed through wide representation enable a designing approach that responds to contemporary educational policy, pedagogy and expected learning outcomes. This is important as:

changes in educational vision that necessitate curricular change require corresponding changes to the spaces. (Könings et al. 2017, p. 306)

Physical renovations of school buildings do not necessarily lead to change in learning and teaching unless educators have some involvement in their design (Lippincott, 2009). A participatory approach shifts the emphasis from 'building project' to the realisation of a shared pedagogical vision in which school managers, teachers, students, parents, architects, interior designers and ICT specialists all play a part (van Merriënboer, McKenney, Cullinan, & Heuer, 2017). It enables the sharing of expertise from professional and everyday practice across education and designing. It recognises interrelationships between organisational planning, school culture and leadership, the use and meaning of learning spaces, and student academic outcomes (Blackmore et al., p. 19). Thus, participation supports the creation of learning environments where physical, pedagogical and organisational elements align (Gislason, 2010). Involvement of multiple stakeholders fosters collective understanding of design goals, and this in turn can assist the achievement of successful outcomes in terms of buildings fit for the purpose of learning (Clark, 2010).

From a practical perspective, participatory designing has the potential to free innovative ideas in people's minds, allowing the exchange of creative possibilities while limiting 'groupthink' or rejection (Könings et al., 2017). It also allows the development of a shared educational vision to guide the design process. Stakeholders with differing backgrounds, such as teachers, education administrators and architects, can participate in differing ways and times:

In this continuous process, the key stakeholders are likely to change, with teachers and students becoming the most important agents to maximise learning within the new environment, whilst the professionals and the government will focus on evaluating the outcomes of the design process. (Könings et al., 2017, p. 310)

A participatory design process allows for experimentation and exploration of various options, thus minimising costly design errors. Growing student populations and changing pedagogies require huge investment in school buildings. However, some projects fail to achieve educational facilities that are fit for purpose and adaptation when the design process has overlooked the expert insights of teachers and other stakeholders (Könings et al., 2017). For example, some new school buildings in The Netherlands proved unsuitable because they were designed without a collectively defined pedagogical goal (van Merriënboer et al., 2017). Meanwhile, some schools gained inadequately or inappropriately planned facilities through the Australian government's Building the Education Revolution project due to limited consultation and choice (Bland, Hughes, & Willis, 2013; Lewis, Dollery, & Kortt, 2014).

Why is Educator Participation Important in Learning Space Designing?

The professional insights that educators contribute to an ongoing design process are important as relationships between learning spaces and pedagogy are complex and as yet not fully understood (Blackmore et al., 2011). In addition, educators' narratives or 'small stories' (Geogakopulus, 2007) concerning their lived experience of learning spaces can inform a creative process that respects those affected by long-term influences of the design outcomes.

Educators can play a 'pivotal role' in managing educational change, and encouraging student participation, as long as they themselves gain authentic opportunities to contribute, and recognition that '*they* matter' (Rudduck & Fielding, 2006, p. 227). They can help alleviate discrepancies between multiple stakeholder viewpoints by directing the attention to educational goals (Könings et al., 2017; van Merriënboer et al., 2017). Their practice-based insights complement the expertise of professional designers (Könings et al., 2017; Cober, Tan, Slotta, So, & Könings, 2015).

Educators contribute specialist knowledge about contemporary learning and learners to inform the designing of fit-for-purpose spaces. This knowledge can guide the creation of learning spaces that align with contemporary curriculum and pedagogy (van Merriënboer et al., 2017). As 'active agents', educators contribute authentic insights about learning spaces as 'living places' and how educators inhabit and alter them (Tondeur, Herman, De Buck, & Triquet, 2017, p. 281). In addition, they can assist other stakeholders, including teaching colleagues and design professionals, to learn about educational practices. By explaining their pedagogical practices, they clarify understandings about the varied activities new spaces need to support (Janssen, Könings, & van Merriënboer, 2017). Educators may promote further learning by attending to the voices of learners and enabling their students to participate in designing their learning spaces (Könings et al., 2017; Rudduck & Fielding, 2006). Participatory designing aligns with twenty-first century learning imperatives such as collaboration, critical thinking and creative problem solving (Luna Scott, 2015).

Another benefit of involving educators is that they often have an enduring relationship with a learning space, whereas professional designers generally move on once the building project is completed. Ideally, they can participate over an extended period in planning, implementing and reflecting on changes to a particular learning space (Woolner & Clark, 2015). Thus, they can support the necessary evaluation and (re)design of learning spaces to ensure their continuing fit in line with changes in pedagogy and curriculum (van Merriënboer et al., 2017).

Why is Learning About Designing Important for Educators?

Productive involvement in the designing process depends upon the ability to use appropriate tools and understand other stakeholders' contexts (Janssen et al. 2017,

p. 269). However, the literature offers limited guidance to support educators as participatory designers; and learning space designing is seldom present in formal teacher education programs, either pre-service or ongoing professional development (Blackmore et al., 2011; Könings et al., 2017).

For educators, while there is a substantial body of literature about designing curriculum and virtual environments (for example, Cober et al., 2015), there is little published guidance about designing physical spaces. Learning environment is often discussed without consideration of the physical environment, for example as 'an organic, holistic concept—an ecosystem that includes the activity and the outcomes of the learning' (OECD, 2013, p. 11). Learning environment tends to be associated with pedagogical practices such as fostering active engagement and positive relationships (Conner & Sliwka, 2014). Moreover, teachers gain limited preparation in their pre-service education with regard to the nature, processes and benefits of participatory learning space designing (Blackmore et al., 2011).

Without relevant professional learning opportunities, educators may lack necessary knowledge, skills and confidence to bring about physical design changes. Learning space designing calls for particular disciplinary learning, as it is a complex and 'very particular form of design' (Könings et al., 2017, p. 315). Research shows that it is important not simply to engage in a participatory process but to adopt an appropriate approach (Könings et al., 2017). Thus, participatory designing draws educators into a sphere of practice beyond their professional expertise where they may need to develop new knowledge and language in order to work with stakeholders of differing backgrounds.

Educators' learning needs include interpersonal skills to handle possible tensions among multiple stakeholders with varied experience and sociocultural backgrounds and divergent views (Könings et al., 2017). They also need the ability to negotiate educational policy and administrative processes, especially when they conflict with the goals of other stakeholders such as architects and facility planners. Moreover, attending to students' wishes and expectations in the designing process can bring particular challenges (Woolner & Clark, 2015).

In addition to design principles and practices, educators may need to develop new pedagogical approaches that support learning in innovative spaces. The physical environment can have a significant influence on teachers' practice, with potential to both enable and hinder the ways they manage student learning (van Merriënboer et al., 2017). Thus, teachers need particular understanding and skills to conjure the inherent benefits:

> Unless teachers are prepared and are provided with the necessary professional skills, tools and resources to change their practices, then new built spaces will not move them to innovative pedagogies. (Blackmore et al., 2011, p. 38)

Without professional development to support change, teachers in new or refurbished spaces often revert to their previous teaching practices (Lippincott, 2009). Therefore, learning opportunities need to be ongoing so that educators can respond to changing educational and spatial needs. These opportunities need to meet the varying circumstances of educators who may be 'initiators' with some involvement in the design; or newcomers who are required to maintain current pedagogical approaches and use of the space; or newly qualified teachers who expect but in reality do not find contemporary pedagogies and learning environments to be in place (Blackmore et al., 2011).

Participatory designing projects provide a fruitful context for inter-professional learning. It is also incumbent on teacher educators to maintain current knowledge of learning space theory and practice to enable graduates to apply current pedagogies in a varied range of learning environments (Blackmore et al., 2011). Through collaboration and knowledge sharing, educators may grasp designing concepts, while professional designers may become more familiar with contemporary education beyond more traditional perceptions or memories of school (Bland et al. 2013; Nordquist and Laing, 2014).

Tools for Participation

Various tools and strategies support participation, allowing stakeholders to contribute in differing ways through the designing process (Könings et al., 2017; van Merriënboer et al., 2017). Of potential usefulness in this regard are: the interdisciplinary model recently developed by Könings et al. (2017); the generic approach to aligning pedagogical vision and enactment that is mutually acceptable among school and designer stakeholders (van Merriënboer et al., 2017); new designing tools (Janssen et al., 2017); and the application of visual images to promote discussion and idea sharing (Woolner & Clark, 2015). In addition, the MEd unit of study outlined below is a postgraduate response to the limited attention to learning space designing in pre-service teacher education.

Participatory Designing of the Unit: A Small Story

The design and implementation of the unit Designing Spaces for Learning embody participatory principles through the authors' ongoing collaboration, which we relate here as a *small story*. Small stories, as conceptualised by Geogakopulu (2007), arise from participants' lived experience of particular incidents or processes. While these narratives may be quite brief or fragmentary, they are individually meaningful and contribute understanding about the wider context. In participatory designing, small stories can represent *voices of experience* from the diverse perspectives of multiple stakeholders, including educators and students who are often under represented (Elliott Burns, 2011). The following small story highlights individual and collegial experience in creating a unit to foster educators' learning about participatory designing.

Raylee Elliott Burns originally designed and taught the unit from 2004 until her retirement in 2008 when Hilary Hughes inherited it. For both of us, participatory designing is a focus of fascination in our research and teaching. While neither of us hold architecture or design qualifications, we bring the insights of experienced educators and information professionals to this interdisciplinary field.

Raylee Reflects ...

Taking a long view, from the 1960s, the pathway to my doctoral project and the Designing Spaces for Learning unit began as a fairly experiential, practical journey—maybe attached to my earliest experiences of school and public libraries and to an ever-increasing awareness of spaces and places with particular purposes. Thus, I experienced a curiosity about the capacity of spaces such as libraries to enable learning, and an appreciation of the relationships between physical site and space.

My later experiences as teacher, teacher-librarian and school library consultant augmented my curiosity about spaces for living and working. Involvement with school principals, teacher-librarians and school system representatives revealed multiple constraints on the designing of energising, responsive learning spaces. In the 1990s, it appeared to me that a 'parachute principle' operated in school designing. School system policies and practices seemed to collude with accredited designers/architects to 'parachute' buildings into school sites and subsequently to 'parachute' students and educators into the schools without seeking their viewpoints as the people who would live and work in these spaces. As I observed newly built schools in which educators struggled with precast spaces in adapting them to learners' needs and changing learning requirements, I began to question 'who and what is valued here?' It seemed to me that school building policies and practices afforded architects and accredited designers an almost exclusive and largely taken-for-granted position. I noted that beyond the school principal and financial administrators, educators and student learners were rarely consulted about matters such as learner diversity, learning theories and practices, or the scope of desired learning within communities. Rather, schools acquired ready-made spaces and were expected to make the best use of them.

The absence of educators in school designing seemed to be traceable to 'gaps and silences' in their knowledge and experience, and thence to a void in their foundation teaching qualifications. In other words, designing knowledge, skills and practical experience were not visible or valued enough to include in pre-service or postgraduate teacher education courses. Such puzzling observations and experiences provoked my doctoral research *Voices of Experience: Opportunities to Influence Creatively the Designing of School Libraries* (Elliott Burns, 2011). In this, I studied the *small stories* (Georgakopoulu, 2007) and values of educators and learners who occupy school spaces. My doctoral findings illustrate the multidimensional potential of consensus in (re)designing spaces for learning, when all stakeholders including students, teachers and accredited designers work towards a shared learning space vision.

An influential outcome of my doctoral study is the unit Designing Spaces for Learning. Invaluable in developing the unit was the support of QUT's then Dean of Education and the Teacher-Librarianship Co-ordinator; and the wisdom and experience of my Phd supervisors. I was also inspired by the experience of several teacher-librarian colleagues who, as school-based designer-educators, pioneered participatory approaches to designing libraries.

A key intention of this unit is for the participating student-educators to question things like the persistence of traditional school spaces, and to critically evaluate emerging pedagogies and leaner needs. Beyond developing students' theoretical knowledge, the unit aims to enable them to connect the theory with their own pedagogical experience; and then based on these new understandings, to start applying their ideas in practical contexts. I sought to set people on a course of possibility for their future work, to sow seeds for designing adventures.

Hilary Reflects…

My involvement in the Designing Spaces for Learning unit arose through keen interest and serendipity. After extensive experience as librarian and information literacy educator in academic and public libraries, I embarked on an academic career at QUT in

2005. Raylee became an essential mentor in my transition from librarian-educator to educator-researcher. Through close collaboration with Raylee in the Med (Teacher-librarianship) program, I learned the craft that underpins my academic work. In addition, her research and teaching opened my awareness of learning space designing as a socially enriching process. Through conversations and formal presentations, I developed a deep appreciation for the concepts and practices of values-based participatory designing that Raylee espouses. From my learner-focused perspective, it made perfect sense to ask intended users of a space about their wants and needs before embarking on a costly building project. So I was surprised to discover that the voices of students and teachers are seldom heard in the process of designing school facilities. This devaluing of the rich information of human experience seemed risky both socially and economically. Thus when Raylee retired, I was primed to take on the unit and the opportunities it offered me for fresh learning and research.

The Unit of Study: Designing Spaces for Learning

The unit of study Designing Spaces for Learning formed part of QUT's Master of Learning Innovation (MLI) which commenced in 2005 and later evolved into the Master of Education (MEd). The unit is intentionally relevant to educators in any context. It is offered as a core unit for Teacher-Librarianship students and as an elective unit for other study areas (majors) within the MLI/MEd and other postgraduate programs across the university. Each year, the unit attracts 60–80 students, most of whom are enrolled externally (and study online) while about 12% attend classes internally (on-campus).

The doctoral research of Raylee Elliott Burns shaped the unit's conceptual framework and pedagogical approach (Elliott Burns, 2011, 2016). Thus, the unit fosters participatory values-based designing in response to two questions: *Who and what is valued here?* and *Is this the best we can do?* These provocations prompt critical awareness of the nature and potential of spaces for learning, and the replacement of taken-for-granted assumptions with creative possibilities. Since its inception, the unit has continued to evolve in line with current educational practice. More recently introduced charrettes, online peer learning communities and digital portfolios promote further participation and inquiry. Thus, the participatory emphasis of the unit promotes the educational and social wellbeing of educators, their students and the professional colleagues they interact with.

Conceptual Underpinning

The unit builds upon an understanding of *learning space* that encompasses formal and informal sites of learning including schools, universities, libraries, workplaces and cultural venues (Elliott Burns, 2016; Ellis & Goodyear, 2016). On a practical level, learning spaces include external and internal built spaces, natural landscapes, shared community facilities and associated technologies—all of which shape the social relations of teaching and learning (Blackmore et al, 2011; Dovey & Fisher, 2014; Painter et al. 2013). Conceptually, the unit adopts the sociocultural perspective that space is dynamic and socially constructed. Thus, learning space has three inter-related physical, mental and social elements that people produce and inhabit: *spatial practice* relates to a perceived view of the material world and physical features; *representations of space* relates to conceived or imagined views, as presented in maps and plans; and *representational spaces* relates to lived experience and social relations that occur within a space (Lefebvre, 1991). The unit draws on this conceptual *triad* to ensure that students are alert to the multifaceted possibilities of learning spaces that they use and design.

The unit's values-based participatory approach is influenced by the work of three design practitioner-theorists: Tom Heath, an architect and educator; Christopher Day, a design consultant and architect; and Christopher Alexander, a design theorist and architect. In different ways all three foster connections with the *spirit of place* as experienced in the built spaces of life and work (Day & Parnell, 2003). Thus, their work focuses attention on peoples' experience of spaces rather than physical details. It supports a human-oriented designing process of collaboration between vernacular and accredited designers.

Heath urged students to consider designing as a cyclical creative learning process of evidence gathering, problem solving and discovery (Heath, 2010). He conceived an approach to designing which interrogates the community's beliefs and values and associated characteristics and activities, the nature of the site and the technical aspects of the building. Based on Heath's work, Elliott Burns developed the self-questioning *VAST heuristic* to support an 'interrogative, participative exploratory approach' to learning space evaluation and designing (Elliott Burns, 2011, p. 254). VAST is an acronym that represents the four key aspects of Values, Activities, Site/System and Technology. The underpinning thesis is that: 'people have Values, in relation to aspects [Activities] of buildings [Site/System] which must be expressed in built form [Technology]' (Elliott Burns, 2016, p. 197).

Day calls attention to physical, temporal and social considerations in learning space designing. He proposes that 'meaningful design depends on synthesised out-looks and inputs from professionals and community' (Day & Parnell, 2003, p. 18). Thus, Day encourages participatory designing through a consensus approach: stake-holders trace the *biography of a place* in developing designs that support the health and wellbeing of those who live and work there (Day & Parnell, 2003). To support evaluation, his assessment matrix focuses attention on a place's physical situation and biography, the mood that it generates and the ideals (or core spirit values) that it inspires (Day & Parnell, 2003, p. 219). A decision-making matrix for 'turning inspiration into action' (p. 220) integrates practical considerations about time and materials required to bring about the design. Elliott Burns (2011, 2016) created another self-questioning heuristic based on Day's *biography of a place*.

These *VAST* and *biography of place* tools offer researchers and students a stimulus for exploring experiential-existential values in the designing process. They enable understanding about users as designers, the dimensions of designing related to being and becoming, and subsequent practical-functional and structural-instrumental matters. These tools enable educator-designers to view spaces through fresh eyes, overcoming the taken-for-grantedness of particular features that can inhibit change.

Alexander's *pattern language* provides guidance for designing spaces that takes account of both the physical environment and human activity, ensuring that people can live with ease and amenity (Alexander, Ishikawa, & Silverstein, 1977). Spatial qualities such as *alive, holistic, balanced, self-sustaining, timeless* and *appropriate* are linked with the notion that 'the life and soul of a place depends not simply on the physical environment, but on the patterns of events that happen there' (Alexander et al., 1977, p. 167). *Patterns,* which can be used in any combination, are useful in suggesting possible responses to identified design problems.

While the work of these designing practitioners supports the practice aspects of the unit, a broader field of research underpins it theoretically. Foucault's notion of *heterotopia* prompts consideration of learning spaces as evolving entities (Foucault, 1997; O'Farrell, 2005). Like libraries and museums, they are the product of human actions and decisions and thus subject to change over time. Retrospective examination of spaces and their history enables understanding about how they are currently ordered, and indicates the possibility of overcoming the status quo. By challenging the way things are, designers have the power to bring about change in the learning environment.

From a sociological perspective, the unit views learning spaces as being imbued with symbolic and cultural capital (Bourdieu, 2005). Therefore, the unit promotes awareness of *habitus* and the potential influence that stakeholders' differing dispositions and practices might bring to the designing process. Thus, for example, students reflect on differing ways that educators and architects might understand the concept and intended use of a particular learning space, such as a school library.

Unit Aim

The unit aims to develop educators' capacity to contribute to values-based participatory learning space designing. Through engagement with key theory and contemporary practice, students gain the 'creative possibility' (Boyce, 2006) to develop learning spaces that respond to social, cultural, technological and pedagogical influences, and support users' wellbeing. The current unit outline justifies this aim as follows:

> Purposefully designed spaces contribute to the quality and outcomes of learning. Theoretical principles of learning and designing are widely applicable but changing social and educational conditions influence the needs of learners in particular contexts. (QUT, 2017)

The unit considers learning spaces in a wide range of educational contexts including schools, universities, early childhood centres, libraries, workplace training and cultural venues. Students' disciplinary fields are similarly diverse and include educational leadership, second language English teaching, information science and business. This interdisciplinarity enables designing conversations and collaboration across multiple educational perspectives.

The unit design assumes that students come with an interest in, but limited prior knowledge or experience of learning space designing. They are encouraged to consider themselves as vernacular designers whose everyday experience of learning spaces enables them to contribute to an inclusive designing process alongside professional designers and other key stakeholders such as their students, parents and teaching colleagues (Day & Parnell, 2003).

According to the current the unit outline, the aim is to enable students to 'view familiar educational environments, both physical and virtual, in different and creative ways' by exploring collaborative design principles and approaches, and developing innovative solutions to design problems for their own learning contexts (QUT, 2017). The intended learning outcomes include:

- Knowledge and understanding of recent developments in learning space design;
- Critical and reflective approach to theory and professional practice of learning space designing;
- Research capabilities to investigate and evaluate the design of learning spaces and creative capacity to apply this evidence to addressing learning space design problems;
- Written, oral, visual and digital communication capabilities to design, represent and justify learning space designs; and
- Creativity and initiative to translate design knowledge and practices to new professional or learning situations with high level personal autonomy and accountability.

Learning and Assessment

In the unit, students engage with concepts and practices of participatory values-based designing which they apply to familiar learning spaces. They engage in discourses and processes that develop a language of designing.

Throughout the unit, students engage with scholarly and professional literature that introduces key theoretical perspectives and research, as a foundation for practical designing. They also study the wider educational context and prevailing social, political, technological and cultural influences. Thus, they come to understand the complex interrelationships between physical and virtual spaces, designers and users. They develop awareness of the spatial relationships which shape the ways in which educators and learners are positioned and the ways in which learning takes place. They critically consider the impacts of sociocultural influences and emerging pedagogies on learners in particular learning contexts. They also become familiar with contemporary design theory and practice through readings and videos.

Online presentations by educators and architects with experience of learning space designing complement the theoretical content. In addition, students undertake site visits to innovative learning spaces such as recently completed new school buildings, libraries and a university science precinct. Brisbane-based students can attend organised group visits, while distance students undertake individual visits to convenient learning spaces.

Learning and assessment revolve around an individual project where students investigate participatory design principles and their practical application in a real-world learning space. In the first stage of the project (Weeks 1–6), students explore the design of a self-selected learning space (e.g. school library, lecture theatre, training room) within a wider educational context (e.g. primary school, university, public library). The students review literature and relevant policy, considering the implications for learning space design. Students then evaluate a self-selected learning space. Following the *Mosaic* designing approach (Clark, 2010) they:

- Undertake an evaluative 'tour' of their learning space using the VAST heuristic (Heath, 2010; Elliott Burns 2016) to identify 'who and what is valued here' and identify particular design problem(s);
- Create a 'map' (using photos, drawings or video) to illustrate the tour findings; and
- Write a 'meaning-making' commentary that considers the implications for learning space design of the tour findings in light of current educational policy and practice.

In the second project stage (Weeks 7–13), students develop a design that creatively responds to learning space problem(s) identified during the tour. They develop the design through a *charrette* (collaborative designing process) and represent it visually using drawings, photos, mindmaps, videos or free web-based software. As it is intended to be a low-tech conceptual design, detailed technical plans are not required. The students then prepare a proposal that presents and justifies their design. Drawing on scholarly references and policy documents they demonstrate how the design: is appropriate to the education context and reflects the values and needs of the intended users of the learning space; addresses universal design principles; and enables the creation of a future-focused learning space.

To document their learning and designing, the students compile a digital design portfolio. This is assessed at two points during semester: after the students have identified design problems(s) in their selected learning space; and on completion of their design proposal. The portfolio is intended to be a living document that reflects students' developing theoretical knowledge and practical capacity as participatory learning designers, during and beyond the unit.

Charrettes to Foster Participation

A participatory focus of the unit is the charrette which was introduced in 2014, inspired by one Hughes observed at University of Colorado Denver (Howard and Somerville, 2014; Hughes, 2017a). A *charrette* is a collaborative designing process most often used in architecture, interior design and urban planning (Roggema 2014). It supports community-based design of shared spaces, including schools and other educational sites (Sutton & Kemp, 2006). While it is used in higher education design disciplines (Webber, 2016), we are unaware of its use elsewhere as a pedagogical tool in teacher education.

In this unit, students participate in a charrette either at QUT Library, or at another learning space with their own students or colleagues. The charrette enables students to experience participatory designing in practice and contributes to their project work by supporting the development of creative designs. To ensure that everyone can participate without specialist design knowledge or skills, the charrette involves low-tech methods and discarded materials. Students engage in multi-modal learning that involves:

- Scholarly inquiry through charrette-related readings, videos, web-based examples;
- Shared exploration through face-to-face and online discussion, brainstorming and co-creation of designs;
- Creative visual expression of designs as drawings, mindmaps, 3D models; and
- Reflection on the charrette process and outcomes, in which students consider possible applications of a charrette for creating fit-for-purpose, learner-friendly spaces in other educational contexts.

Online Participation

The unit also promotes social wellbeing through active online participation among internal and external students. Initially, students communicated via typed discussion forums. More recently, the unit's Google + community offers students a shared space for discussion of weekly topics, exchanging design ideas, and reporting on-site visits and project progress. A Diigo account allows students to share additional unit-related resources, while a Pinterest board displays inspiring design concepts. In addition, for learning and assessment purposes, the students compile digital portfolios using free social software such as Edublogs or Weebly. Beyond the unit, students use their digital portfolio to showcase their designing work to colleagues, employers and the wider community. These digital technologies enable students to build peer networks to support ongoing initiatives as participatory learner-educator-designers.

Continuing Impacts

Continuing impacts of the unit are revealed in students' formal and unsolicited feedback. In several cases, students have gone on to realise their conceptual design solution at their own school, often engaging their own students in the process (Hughes, 2017a). Some have used their portfolio to support successful funding applications from their school or a government agency. For example, one student reported:

> The builders and landscapers have been working over the last 2 weeks and it is amazing… as an end to the charrette process I am now conducting training in the next weeks for staff and students and rolling out the space in an organised manner (MEd student, unsolicited email 5/7/2016).

There are opportunities for ongoing development of unit as well as associated research. Fruitful areas include enhancing teacher professional identity as designer and the impacts of new physical spaces on their pedagogy (Blackmore et al., 2011).

Implications for Practice

The Designing Spaces for Learning unit models a multifaceted participatory learning approach for educators that fosters the wellbeing of learners and other stakeholders. The participatory learning framework outlined below could be transferable wholly or in part to other education contexts.

- *Participatory unit design*: As exemplified in the authors' *small story* (Georgakopoulu, 2007) of collaboration, learning design can continue to evolve through educator-researcher collaboration, and enhance practice through shared insights and co-authorship.
- *Participatory pedagogy*: Participatory learning and designing is fostered through online and face-to-face interaction including discussion forums, Google + communities and site visits. Educators enrich their students' learning through collaborative designing projects or a charrette (at school or university). A charrette also has potential in higher education to support academic discourse (Hughes, 2017a) and action learning (Hughes, 2017b).

- *Participatory learning*: Participatory design projects provide opportunities for diverse stakeholders to learn from and with each other. For example, educators might learn to read technical drawings while architects might develop understanding about twenty-first-*century learning*.
- *Participatory inquiry*: Educators challenge the persistence of traditional educational spaces and innovative alternatives through shared evaluation, reflection and discussion around the two interrelated critical questions: *Who and what is valued here? Is this the best we can do?* The first question reviews the current space, while the second considers design possibilities. Thus, researching and visiting innovative spaces informs educators' creative design responses and focuses attention on learner wellbeing.
- *Participatory design theory and practice*: Sharing varied scholarly and professional resources allows exploration of current design thinking and practice, in education and wider contexts (e.g. journal articles, policy documents, websites and Pinterest boards).
- *Participatory designing*: A charrette and associated learning space evaluation and design activities supports active engagement with various design tools and creative processes that can be applied to designing, learning and teaching in various educational contexts. (e.g. digital tools like Google + communities and VAST heuristic). As the charrette involves low-tech methods, it engenders not only participatory but inclusive designing.
- *Participatory designing communities*: The development of participatory designing communities through online communities or face-to-face forums raises awareness of various stakeholder viewpoints and generates knowledge and common language for active participation in the design process.
- *Participatory media*: Preparation of an e-portfolio provides a contemporary and potentially far-reaching means for educators to showcase their evaluative and creative designing prowess to colleagues, employers and the wider designing community. It provides a focus for extending information, digital and visual literacies

A participatory approach, as outlined above, has the potential to empower educators as key contributors to learning space designing. Attending to human values and relationships in this way will enable consensus-based design outcomes that respect the wellbeing of all intended users. However, productive relationships require perseverance. Designing conversations that involve deep listening, clarification, imagination and shared decision-making open possibilities for learning spaces that enrich the lives and work of users.

Conclusion

Of potential interest to educators and designers beyond QUT, this chapter has presented a postgraduate unit that models a participatory, values-based approach to learning space designing. As discussed, exploration of relationships between physical environment and pedagogy enables educators to learn about designing, innovatively using and reimagining spaces that foster collective learning and wellbeing.

References

Alexander, A., Ishikawa, S., & Silverstein, M. (1977). *A pattern language: Towns, buildings, construction*. Oxford: Oxford University Press.

Blackmore, J., Bateman, D., Loughlin, J., O'Mara, J., & Aranda, G. (2011). *Research into the connection between built learning spaces and student outcomes: Literature review Paper No. 22*. Melbourne: Department of Education and Early Childhood Development. Retrieved February 11, 2018, 2016, from http://www.education.vic.gov.au/Documents/about/programs/infrastructure/blackmorelearningspaces.pdf.

Bland, D., Hughes, H., & Willis, J. (2013). *Reimagining learning spaces: A research report for the Queensland Council for Social Science Innovation*. Brisbane: Queensland University of Technology. Retrieved February 11, 2018, from https://eprints.qut.edu.au/63000/.

Bourdieu, P. (2005). Habitus. In J. Hillier & E. Rooksby (Eds.). *Habitus: A sense of place* (2nd. ed., pp. 43–52). Aldershot: Ashgate.

Boyce, S. (2006). Literacy spaces–library design. In C. Kapitzke & B. Bruce (Eds.), *Libr@ries: Changing information space and practice* (pp. 17–36). London: Lawrence Erlbaum.

Clark, A. (2010). *Transforming children's spaces: Children's and adults' participation in designing learning environments*. Abingdon, Oxon, UK: Routledge.

Cleveland, B., & Fisher, K. (2014). The evaluation of physical learning environments: A critical review of the literature. *Learning Environments Research, 17*(1), 1–28. https://doi.org/10.1007/s10984-013-9149-3.

Cober, R., Tan, E., Slotta, J., So, H.-J., & Könings, K. D. (2015). Teachers as participatory designers: Two case studies with technology-enhanced learning environments. *Instructional Science, 43*(2), 203–228.

Conner, L., & Sliwka, A. (2014). Implications of research on effective learning environments for initial teacher education. *European Journal of Education, 49*(2), 165–177. https://doi.org/10.1111/ejed.12081.

Day, C., & Parnell, R. (2003). *Consensus design: Socially inclusive process*. Oxford: Architectural Press.

Dovey, K., & Fisher, K. (2014). Designing for adaptation: The school as socio-spatial assemblage. *The Journal of Architecture, 19*(1), 43–63. https://doi.org/10.1080/13602365.2014.882376.

Elliott Burns, R. A. (2016). Voices of experience: opportunities to influence creatively the designing of school libraries. In K. Fisher (Ed.), *The translational design of schools: An evidence-based approach to aligning pedagogy and learning environments* (pp. 179–198). Rotterdam: Sense Publishers.

Elliott Burns, R. A. (2011). Voices of experience: Opportunities to influence creatively the designing of school libraries. *Doctoral Dissertation, Queensland University of Technology, 2011*. Retrieved from https://eprints.qut.edu.au/48974/.

Ellis, R. A., & Goodyear, P. (2016). Models of learning space: Integrating research on space, place and learning in higher education. *Review of Education, 4*(2), 149–191. https://doi.org/10.1002/rev3.3056.

Foucault, M. (1997). Space, knowledge and power (interview with Paul Rabinow). In N. Leach (Ed.), *Rethinking architecture: A reader in cultural theory* (pp. 367-380). London: Routledge.

Georgakopoulu, A. (2007). *Small stories, interaction and identities*. Amsterdam: John Benjamins.

Gislason, N. (2010). Architectural design and the learning environment: A framework for school design research. *Learning Environments Research, 13*(2), 127–145. https://doi.org/10.1007/s10984-010-9071-x.

Heath, T. (2010). *Learning architecture/Teaching architecture: A guide for the perplexed*. Brisbane: Denarius Design Books.

Howard, Z., & Somerville, M. M. (2014). A comparative study of two design charrettes: Implications for codesign and participatory action research. *CoDesign, 10*(1), 46–62.

Hughes, H. (2017a). Charrette as context and process for academic discourse in contemporary higher education. In T. Miranda & J. Herr (Eds.), *The value of academic discourse: Conversations that matter* (pp. 79–102). Lanham, Md.: Rowman and Littlefield.

Hughes, H. (2017b). Charrette: Case study of participatory library space designing in a postgraduate course. In *Proceedings of RAILS-Research Applications, Information and Library Studies*, 2016, School of Information Management, Victoria University of Wellington, New Zealand, 6–8 December, 2016. Retrieved from http://www.informationr.net/ir/22-4/rails/rails1602.html (*Information Research, 22*(4), n.p).

Janssen, F. J. J. M., Könings, K. D., & van Merriënboer, J. J. G. (2017). Participatory educational design: How to improve mutual learning and the quality and usability of the design? *European Journal of Education, 52*(3), 268–279. https://doi.org/10.1111/ejed.12229.

Könings, K. D., Bovill C., & Woolner, P. (2017). Towards an interdisciplinary model of practice for participatory building design in education. *European Journal of Education, 52*(3), 306–317. https://doi.org/10.1111/ejed.12230.

Lefebvre, H. (1991). *The production of space*. Malden, MA: Blackwell.

Lewis, C., Dollery, B., & Kortt, M. A. (2014). Building the Education Revolution: Another case of Australian government failure? *International Journal of Public Administration, 37*(5), 299–307. https://doi.org/10.1080/01900692.2013.836660.

Lippincott, J. K. (2009). Learning spaces: Involving faculty to improve pedagogy. *Educause Review, 44*(2), 16–25. Retrieved from https://er.educause.edu/articles/2009/3/learning-spaces-involving-faculty-to-improve-pedagogy.

Luna Scott, C. (2015). *The futures of learning 2: What kind of learning for the 21st century?*. Paris: UNESCO.

Nordquist, J. & Laing, A. (2014). Spaces for learning–A neglected area in curriculum change and strategic educational leadership. *Medical Teacher, 36*(7), 555–556. https://doi.org/10.3109/0142159x.2014.917288.

OECD. (2013). *Innovative learning environments*. Paris: OECD. Retrieved from http://www.oecd.org/edu/ceri/innovativelearningenvironmentspublication.htm.

O'Farrell, C. (2005). *Michel Foucault*. London: Sage.

Painter, S., Fournier, J., Grape, C., Grummon, P., Morelli, J., Whitmer, S., et al. (2013). *Research on learning space design: Present state, future directions*. Ann Arbor, MI: Society of College and University Planning.

Roggema, R. (Ed.). (2014). *The design charrette: Ways to envision sustainable futures*. Dordrecht: Springer.

Rudduck, J., & Fielding, M. (2006). Student voice and the perils of popularity. *Educational Review, 58*(2), 219–231. https://doi.org/10.1080/00131910600584207.

Queensland University of Technology (QUT). (2017). *Unit outline: LCN601 Designing spaces for learning*. Retrieved from https://qutvirtual3.qut.edu.au/qvpublic/unout_search_p.show_public.

Sutton, S. E., & Kemp, S. (2006). Integrating social science and design inquiry through interdisciplinary design charrettes: An approach to participatory community problem solving. *American Journal of Community Psychology, 38*(1–2), 51–62.

Tondeur, J., Herman, F., De Buck, M., & Triquet, K. (2017). Classroom biographies: Teaching and learning in evolving material landscapes (c. 1960–2015). *European Journal of Education, 52*(3), 280–294. https://doi.org/10.1111/ejed.12228.

van Merriënboer, J. J. G., McKenney, S., Cullinan, D., & Heuer, J. (2017). Aligning pedagogy with physical learning spaces. *European Journal of Education, 52*(3), 253–267. https://doi.org/10.1111/ejed.12225.

Webber, S. B. (2016). The charrette design model provides a means to promote collaborative design in higher education. *Systemics, Cybernetics and Informatics, 14*(1), 84–91.

Woolner, P., & Clark, A. (2015). Developing shared understandings of learning environments: Interactions with students, teachers and other professionals. In P. Woolner (Ed.), *School design together* (pp. 167–183). Abingdon, Oxon.: Routledge.

Participatory Principles in Practice: Designing Learning Spaces that Promote Wellbeing for Young Adolescents During the Transition to Secondary School

Christopher Nastrom-Smith and Hilary Hughes

Abstract With a view to informing school designing projects that foster the wellbeing of Middle Years students, this chapter explores the participatory designing process of the Junior Secondary Precinct at Cannon Hill Anglican College in Brisbane, Australia. The chapter highlights the importance of including *student voice* in the designing process and the benefits of collaboration between school community members and architects. The Cannon Hill College design project sought to create a learning environment that would respond to the wellbeing needs of Middle Years students who experience various challenges in their transition from primary to lower secondary school. The project members recognised that student-focused spatial design can enhance their motivation, learning engagement, changing relationship dynamics and developing self-identity. As demonstrated, the participatory designing process approach led to positive wellbeing and pedagogical outcomes.

Introduction

Schools face complex challenges in providing learning environments that are responsive to the needs and wellbeing of Middle Years students. For these young adolescents, transition from primary to secondary school coincides with a period of change and uncertainty associated with the complexities of puberty. During this crucial phase of their education, students need spaces that support motivation, school engagement, changing relationship dynamics and developing self-identity.

Revealing how one school addressed such challenges, this chapter presents an inside view of the participatory approach used at Cannon Hill Anglican College to design a Junior Secondary Precinct. After introducing the College context, the chapter discusses three key concepts that underpinned the design project, namely, contem-

C. Nastrom-Smith (✉)
Cannon Hill Anglican College, Brisbane, Australia
e-mail: cnastrom-smith@chac.qld.edu.au

H. Hughes
Queensland University of Technology, Brisbane, Australia
e-mail: h.hughes@qut.edu.au

© Springer Nature Singapore Pte Ltd. 2019
H. Hughes et al. (eds.), *School Spaces for Student Wellbeing and Learning*,
https://doi.org/10.1007/978-981-13-6092-3_11

porary pedagogy, student wellbeing and participatory designing. Then it presents an illustrative overview of the design project process and outcomes, highlighting the involvement of a wide range of school community and professional stakeholders, and attention to student voice. The chapter concludes by discussing the wider implications of the project with regard to student wellbeing and participatory designing in contemporary school contexts.

Context: Cannon Hill Anglican College

Cannon Hill Anglican College is located in the southeast of Brisbane, Australia. The College's gently sloping 11.5 hectare campus features giant eucalyptus trees and an extensive wetlands area rich in wildlife. By design, this is a 'College based on pathways rather than corridors, and trees for natural shade rather than man-made structures' (Cannon Hill Anglican College, 2018). From Preparatory through to Senior Secondary the College provides:

> A dynamic Christian learning community which strives to offer a balanced and holistic educational environment, in order to develop the intellectual, social, physical, emotional, aesthetic and spiritual dimensions of each of its members. (Cannon Hill Anglican College, 2018).

This holistic educational approach is founded on the concept of Next Practice which aims to develop knowledge and skills for the real world, enabled by technology and underpinned by neuroscience research (Cannon Hill Anglican College, 2018).

In 2015, the College partnered with Brisbane firm PW Architecture to create a new Junior Secondary Precinct. This project coincided with Queensland Government policy that transferred Year 7 from primary to secondary school (ACER, 2011). It was shaped by the College's desire to align physical design with a future-focused, balanced pedagogy that promotes the active learning and wellbeing of adolescent students when transitioning between primary and high school.

As Director of Junior Secondary (Years 7–9), principal author Nastrom-Smith was part of the College leadership and the Precinct design teams. His concurrent Master of Education study contributed insights about the theory and practices of contemporary pedagogy, wellbeing and participatory designing that underpinned the project. These three key concepts are discussed below.

Key Concepts

Contemporary Pedagogy

Within contemporary pedagogy, there is a close association between the concepts of twenty-first century and Middle Years learning. Both emphasise the development of lifelong learners with higher-order capabilities such as autonomy (Garrison, 2011; Wang & Holcombe, 2010), problem-solving (Pendergast, 2006; Salpeter, 2003), creativity (Chadbourne, 2003; Silva, 2009) and critical thinking (Breivik, 2005; Williamson, 2001).

Middle Years learning in Australia spans Years 5–9. It offers age-appropriate educational contexts and student-centred approaches that address outcomes linked to successful adolescent learning, such as student engagement and the development of higher-order capacities (Bahr & Crosswell, 2011). Thus, Middle Years learning is defined as:

> A progressive approach to curriculum, pedagogy and assessment (and sometimes organisational) practices that are responsive to the developmental needs of young learners in their societal context, and typically aged from approximately 11-12 to 14-15 years of age (Chadbourne & Pendergast as cited in Pendergast, 2006, p. 13).

The concept of twenty-first-century learning is similar to Middle Years philosophy, although not confined to one particular stage of schooling. It assumes that schools need to equip students with a suite of skills and capabilities that will be 'absolutely necessary for future professional flexibility and successful citizenship' (Breivik, 2005, p. 26). The influence of twenty-first-century learning on the junior secondary context is reinforced by key educational policy documents: *The Melbourne declaration on educational goals for young Australians* (MCEETYA, 2008), *Australian curriculum* (ACARA, n.d.) and the Queensland-focused *Junior secondary—theory and practice* (ACER, 2012).

Wellbeing

While wellbeing lacks a commonly accepted definition (Allison, Gray, Nash, Martindale, & Wong, 2015), there is growing recognition that it is a holistic concept dependent upon the presence of a range of interrelated capacities that influence an individual's success at school and in life (Allison et al., 2015; Cohen, 2006; Thorburn, 2015). Accordingly, this project was based on an understanding of wellbeing as a psychological construct made up of four components: mental, emotional, social and intellectual.

Mental wellbeing is a multidimensional concept, described as a 'combination of a subjective state of relaxation, the presence of a positive mood and an absence of negative mood, satisfaction with life, and a psychological state of personal growth, autonomy and personal relatedness' (Khawaja, Ibrahim, & Schweitzer, 2017, p.285). Indicators of positive mental wellbeing during adolescence closely reflect characteristics synonymous with twenty-first-century learning and Middle Years education. Capacities such as problem-solving, critical thinking and creativity encourage adolescents to remain open to new ideas and seek out new challenges (Kuhn, Black, Keselman, & Kaplan, 2000). The intrinsic motivation that is fostered by these capacities is linked to increased school engagement (Daniels, 2010) and positive wellbeing (Burton, Lydon, D'alessandro, & Koestner, 2006). Identity development and self-concept are also important for maintaining mental wellbeing in adolescence. Negative self-identity is often linked to anxiety and negative coping strategies (Žukauskienė, 2014), whereas positive self-concept is known to build confidence, autonomy, resilience and positive coping strategies (Hawkey, 2006; Ryan & Deci, 2006). Individuals with a positive state of mental wellbeing tend to have coping skills that enable them to adapt to new and unfamiliar environments, such as the transition to secondary school (Mander, Lester, & Cross, 2015).

Emotional wellbeing relates to an individual's ability to understand and express their own and others' emotions, and is closely linked to an individual's mental wellbeing. Emotional wellbeing can be enhanced through a strong sense of school connectedness (Frydenberg, Care, Freeman, & Chan, 2009), self-awareness (Lampert, 2005), personal values (Waters, Lester, Wenden, & Cross, 2012) and reflective practices (Thorburn & MacAllister, 2013). The ability to develop strategies to cope with stressful situations, regulate behaviour and engage in effective problem-solving is important during adolescence (Sabiston, Sedgwick, Crocker, Kowalski, & Mack, 2007). These complex skills are tied to identity-forming activities that characterise adolescence (Žukauskienė, 2014). However, most students are underprepared for the emotional challenges that occur during the transition to secondary school (Montemayor, Adams, & Gullotta, 2000).

Social wellbeing relates to 'how one gets along with others, how other people respond to one's being and more broadly how one engages with social institutions and societal mores' (Mander et al., 2015, p. 133). For adolescents in an unfamiliar school environment, social wellbeing is tested by the complexities of new relationships with peers and teachers, and changing academic expectations. Many authors have identified key influences on student social wellbeing which include peer acceptance (Osterman, 2000), connectedness (Lampert, 2005) and a strong sense of belonging (Daniels, 2005; Žukauskienė, 2014). To successfully develop and nurture these relationships, young adolescents require skills such as teamwork, problem-solving, collaboration, empathy and respect for others' points of view (Allison et al., 2015; Van den Berghe, Vansteenkiste, Cardon, Kirk, & Haerens, 2014). The development of these higher-order capacities will not only support an adolescent's social wellbeing, they will enable young people to fully engage as twenty-first-century citizens (McWilliam, 2011; Pink, 2005).

Intellectual wellbeing is described as cognitive competence and includes feelings of academic success (Bacete, Perrin, Schneider & Blanchard, 2014), an increase in academic autonomy (Žukauskienė, 2014) and engagement in cognitive risk-taking (Groundwater-Smith, 2004). Consideration of intellectual wellbeing is important as the transition to secondary school is often linked to declining academic performance (Benner, 2011; McGee, Ward, Gibbons, & Harlow, 2003), lower levels of intrinsic motivation (Wigfield & Eccles, 2002) and a lack of engagement (Dinham & Rowe, 2009). With these factors in mind, educators can support students' intellectual wellbeing by providing educational experiences that are challenging, yet achievable (Akos & Galassi, 2004), and allow students to have some control over their learning (Groundwater-Smith, 2004). Thus, to support student wellbeing during transition, schools should seek to create learning environments that inspire students' 'cognitive abilities, creativity and self-learning, and foster personal growth and social involvement', thereby encouraging the development of twenty-first-century skills (Shussman, 2017, p. 48).

The challenge for Cannon Hill College was to design a series of learning spaces that promoted the capacities associated with student wellbeing, while at the same time permitting twenty-first century and Middle Years learning to be integrated successfully into authentic classroom experiences. This challenge was addressed through participatory designing.

Participatory Designing

Participatory designing is a collaborative and iterative process that involves the active engagement of a range of stakeholders, with varied professional and lived experience. In an educational context, it includes teachers, students and school administrators working in partnership with architects and designers. While participatory designing can be a complex, time-consuming process, potential benefits include commitment to the process and likelihood that the final design will meet the stakeholders' needs (Woolner & Clark, 2015).

An effectively managed participatory designing approach is likely to 'produce a space that is organically connected to the needs and aspirations of some actual users' (Woolner, Hall, Wall, & Dennison, 2007, p. 237). It has the potential to achieve a synergy between pedagogy and innovative learning spaces, and foster a community of educators who embrace creative approaches to teaching and learning (van Merriënboer, McKenney, Cullinan, & Heuer, 2017). Thus, a participatory approach can enable school stakeholders to complement the design ideas of architects, who are often less familiar with the particular requirements of an educational environment. Participation enables multiple individual views and personalities to be balanced, particularly when agendas conflict (Woolner et al., 2007).

In an educational environment, an authentic designing participatory process recognises the voices of the students whose needs and wellbeing may be influenced by their physical surroundings (Woolner & Clark, 2015). While student consultation is frequently neglected in teaching and learning (McIntyre, Pedder, & Rudduck, 2005), the United Nations *Convention on the rights of the child* (1989) states that students are entitled to have a say in matters and decisions affecting them (Ruck, Keating, Saewyc, Earls, & Ben-Arieh, 2016). Thus, participatory designing provides opportunities for students to contribute ideas and share in decision making about matters that directly impact their learning (McIntyre et al., 2005; Pedder & McIntyre, 2006; Sinclair, 2004; Woolner et al., 2007). Moreover, research shows that that young people are capable of insightful analysis of their learning experiences (Flutter & Rudduck, 2004) and are able to demonstrate an awareness of how they and their peers prefer to learn (Pedder & McIntyre, 2006). This capacity to offer valuable contributions reinforces the need to position student voice alongside the views of other educational stakeholders when determining the direction of school learning spaces (Woolner & Clark, 2015; Woolner et al., 2007).

The range of wellbeing benefits which young adolescents gain through the participatory process include citizenship, social inclusion, improved relationships with adults and communication skills (Kirby, Lanyon, Cronin, & Sinclair, 2003). In addition, increased confidence and a sense of belonging can arise when students know that they are occupying learning spaces that reflect their own needs as adolescent learners (Kirby et al., 2003; Pedder & McIntyre, 2006).

The Project: Designing the Junior Secondary Precinct at Cannon Hill Anglican College

Informed by the research outlined above, the Junior Secondary Precinct project aimed to create a learning environment that would meet the needs of young adolescent learners, positively influence their wellbeing during the transition into secondary school, and support their academic performance during the Middle Years of learning. Therefore, the project adopted a participatory approach to ensure that the designing process and product would foster a sense of community, belonging and ownership amongst the College community (Lackney, 2000; Osterman, 2000; Tanner, 2008). This participatory approach drew on Day's *consensus design* philosophy and an awareness of the *spirit-of-place* which recognises 'the values, thoughts, emotions and actions of people who live in, work in and use the place' (Day & Parnell 2003, p. 40). The *spirit-of-project* (Day & Parnell 2003), or collective sense of direction, flowed from the commitment to create a space that would foster young adolescents' wellbeing.

Participatory Designing Cycles

The Junior Secondary Precinct design team included a wide range of stakeholders who comprised the two groups designated in Fig. 1 as College Collaborators and Architect's Collaborators. Throughout the project, separate participatory cycles for each group occurred simultaneously, with the outcomes shared between both groups at joint design project meetings. Multiple participatory cycles continued until all parties agreed on a design that aligned with College's vision, was structurally achievable and complied with all necessary building codes.

The Architect's Collaborators group formed a professional network that brought together the expertise of town planners, certifiers, structural engineers (who also engaged the soil engineer for soil testing), a civil engineer (who engaged a surveyor), hydraulic engineers, electrical engineers and mechanical engineers. The architects also worked with Queensland Fire and Emergency Services on stormwater flow, and

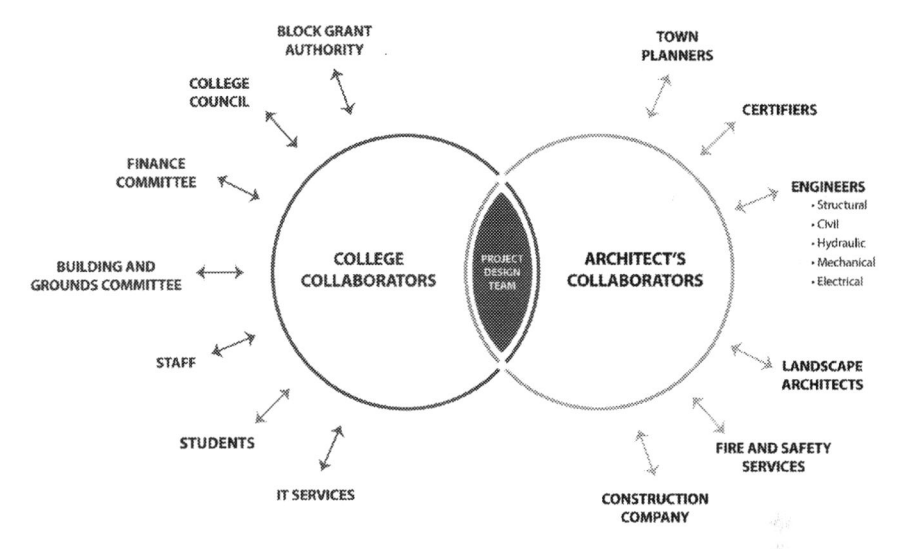

Fig. 1 Cannon Hill Anglican College's dual cycle participatory process model (Peta Prestidge, Cannon Hill Anglican College)

with a landscape architect regarding protection of the natural environment and re-vegetation. Drawing on all this collaborative activity, the architect regularly reported back to the school on the feasibility of their proposed design ideas. Meanwhile, members of the College Collaborators group considered design needs, evaluated the architect's plans and proposed changes. In line with *consensus design* (Day & Parnell, 2003) an explicit *student-focused* approach became the *spirit* with which the design plans were evaluated.

Initial Plans and Evaluation

The architect prepared an initial design in response to the College's brief for a building that would facilitate twenty-first-century learning and reflect the developmental and educational needs of young adolescent learners. The initial ground floor plan is shown in Fig. 2.

The College stakeholder group evaluated the initial design and considered the positioning of the learning spaces and their alignment with the College's teaching and learning philosophy (Oblinger, 2005). The school leadership team identified elements of the building design that did not appear to cater for the developmental and educational needs of young adolescents and they made a series of recommendations to better cater for these needs.

A group of Junior Secondary students (Years 7 to 9) also participated in a two-stage design evaluation. First, as an 'envisioning process', students visited the site

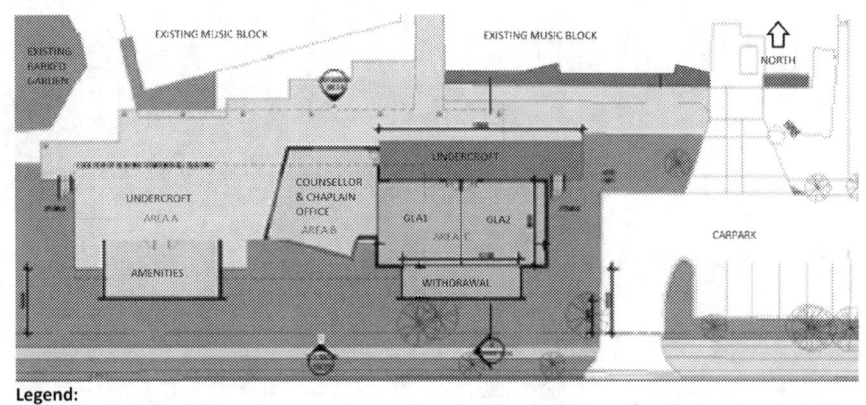

Legend:
GLA = General learning area
Barked garden = Lightly landscaped area (with bark mulch)

Fig. 2 Initial ground floor plan of the Junior Secondary Precinct (PW Architecture, copied with permission)

of the proposed building and evaluated the design plans in situ. They recorded their responses in free-hand notes and diagrams (e.g. Fig. 3). Then they evaluated an existing open learning space in the College. For this they used an evaluative tool called *the VAST heuristic* to identify *who and what is valued* in the existing space and gain feedback on what elements of the space enhanced or impaired learning (Elliott Burns, 2016). While relatively simple to complete, this evaluation was an important stage in the participatory process as it ensured that student perspectives were represented in the design project. This inclusion of student voice Woolner et al. (2007) revealed what the students value about their learning environment and thus informed the project about contributors to wellbeing during the transition to secondary school.

Revised Design

The College stakeholders' evaluation indicated that the initial design (Fig. 2) and positioning of the spaces on the ground floor failed to provide a 'complex of spaces' (Dittoe, 2006, p. 3.9) that adequately reflected the College's strategic direction and *spirit-of-project* (Day & Parnell, 2003). There was consensus that the design of the two general learning areas (GLAs) (Area C) appeared too conservative as a more traditional rectangular classroom structure, while the undercroft space (Area A) did not appear to effectively integrate pedagogical, social and physical environmental aspects. The College stakeholders felt that the spaces in the initial design lacked flexibility and variety and therefore failed to meet the needs of young adolescent learners.

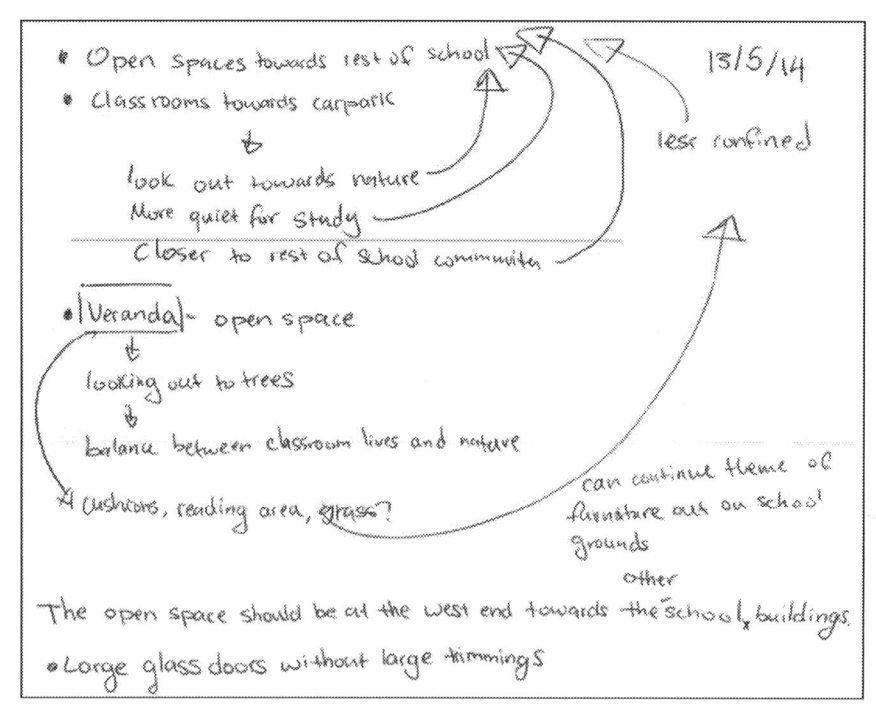

Fig. 3 Sample student response to the envisioning process

In response to these concerns about the initial design, the two project groups engaged in further participatory planning. They paid particular attention to aspects identified by students in the envisioning process with regard to repositioning the general learning areas and undercroft, and creating quiet spaces. The resultant revised plan is shown in Fig. 4.

To ensure that the design took full advantage of the College's physical environment and existing garden areas, the project team decided to move the two general learning areas (GLAs) from the eastern to the western end of the site, offering extensive views of the College's wooded landscape. Large glass doors and windows along the northern wall would allow access to a garden area with outdoor seating. These views and access to the outdoors were intended to connect the building with the existing natural environment and incorporate open learning areas of College grounds into the *flow* of the built space.

To create a space that the students could readily identify as their own, the two GLAs were converted into one open, flexible learning space, with an operable partition replacing the originally planned central wall. This conversion created a place for social collaboration during lunch breaks and doubled as a flexible learning area for shared teaching. The school team considered that this central hub would better cater for the developmental and educational needs of young adolescents, as its flexibility

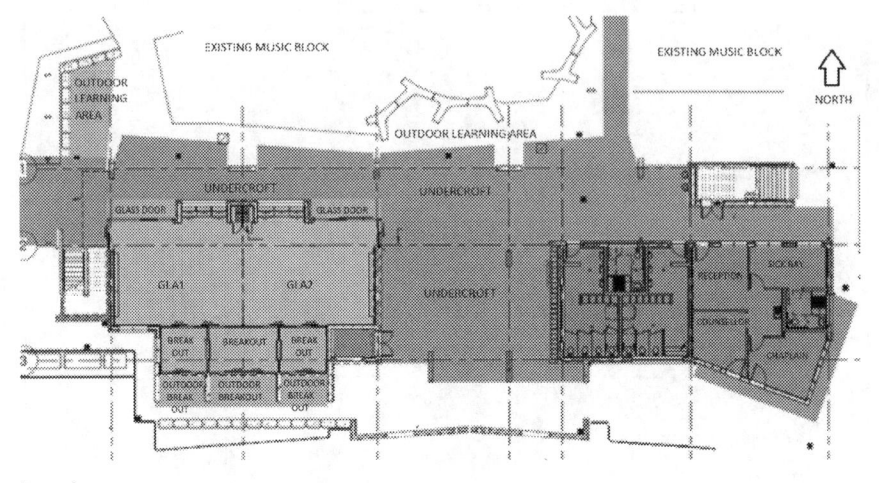

Legend:

GLA = General learning area

Fig. 4 Final ground floor plan of the Junior Secondary Precinct (PW Architecture, copied with permission)

created the potential for learning opportunities that transcend traditional classroom barriers (McWilliam, 2011).

With the relocation of the two GLAs to the western end of the site, further flexibility could be gained by moving the undercroft to the centre of the ground floor. Moreover, the revised plan provided a large doorway and floor to ceiling windows in the eastern wall of the GLAs that would open out to the undercroft area. This would increase the perceived size of the space and maximise opportunities for teaching and learning to spill out into these outside areas.

To ensure the building design provided a variety of learning spaces, the decision was made to replace the solid wall along the southern side of the two GLAs with glass doors and to split the withdrawal room (Area C in Fig. 2) into a series of break-out spaces. These were framed by writable glass surfaces that could provide a variety of learning and teaching spaces, and quiet areas for students when needed (Fig. 5).

Project Outcomes

The Junior Secondary Precinct project was successful in generating a range of important outcomes related to the design itself, student wellbeing and pedagogical variation. Moreover, the project continues to influence innovative learning space design and use at Cannon Hill Anglican College.

Fig. 5 A break-out space of the junior secondary precinct (Anne Andrew, Cannon Hill Anglican College)

Design Outcome

The design of the Junior Secondary Precinct addresses a recurring concern at Cannon Hill Anglican College, and in the literature, with enabling students' academic performance and social engagement throughout their transition to secondary school. This concern aligns with the inclusive *spirit-of-project* (Day & Parnell, 2003) that guided the participatory designing process. The design outcome exemplifies learning space that supports contemporary pedagogy, and values adolescent learners by responding to their wellbeing needs.

The new Junior Secondary Precinct offers a social learning hub with multiple indoor and outdoor spaces. This 'complex of spaces' (Dittoe, 2006, p. 3.9) caters to a diverse range of student needs and enables authentic twenty-first-century learning (McWilliam, 2011). As evidence of a positive design outcome, students' responses to a school-run evaluative survey indicate that they generally find this new environment to be inviting, positive and exciting. These responses from the intended Precinct occupants suggest the likelihood that they will 'engage with the experiences that the environment affords' (McWilliam, 2011, p. 265).

From a practical perspective, the building's orientation and the extensive use of glass walls and doors contribute significantly to its appeal. They ensure plentiful daylight and ventilation, and visual and physical connection with the surrounding natural environment. In addition, the brightly coloured, reconfigurable furniture allows flow between different areas and activities, both inside and outside.

The participatory nature of the project, in particular, attention to the views of school community members, was critical to achieving positive outcomes. The involvement of multiple stakeholders ensured that physical, social and pedagogical aspects were all considered in the designing process (McWilliam, 2011). For example, it was student and staff feedback on the initial plans that led to the re-orientation of the two general learning areas and opening up to the outdoors for informal learning activities. The inclusion of students in this process was particularly important for ensuring that the design outcomes were informed by authentic insights about how adolescent learners at Cannon Hill Anglican College envisage their preferred learning environment.

Wellbeing Outcomes

The Junior Secondary Precinct project illustrates the potential of purposefully designed learning spaces to enhance students' mental, emotional, social and intellectual wellbeing during transition to secondary school. With regard to intellectual wellbeing, the Precinct offers settings for collaborative and independent learning, and pedagogical opportunities for teachers to engage students in cognitively challenging activities. Students' participation in the designing process has contributed to the development of skills such as teamwork, problem-solving and collaboration which also contribute to social wellbeing (Allison et al., 2015; Van den Berghe et al., 2014).

The provision of several interconnected spaces in Junior Secondary Precinct positively impacts students' intellectual and mental wellbeing by offering them choices about how and where they learn, and therefore allowing an element of control over their learning (Groundwater-Smith, 2004). The fluid, student-welcoming character of these spaces also promotes social wellbeing by enabling peer connections to flourish (Lampert, 2005). In addition, the extensive use of glass for walls and doors lets in ample natural light, which is a known enhancer of emotional and physical wellbeing (Barrett, Barrett, Davies, & Zhang, 2015) and academic achievement (Nair, 2009; Tanner, 2008, 2009).

The inclusion of student voice in the designing process also contributed to social wellbeing. In particular, the envisioning activity was beneficial in fostering a strong sense of student ownership of the Precinct as it brought their input into the design of the general learning areas, break-out spaces and undercroft area. This inclusive approach also recognised that a sense of belonging is a strong predictor of mental wellbeing (Kirby et al., 2003; Pedder & McIntyre, 2006). From the emotional well-being perspective, student particpation generated positivity and confidence around learning and feelings of safety for students in the school environment (Coffey et al., 2011).

The focus on student inclusion accorded with the College's aim to generate school connectedness (Frydenberg et al., 2009) and a positive orientation towards schooling (Osterman, 2000). More widely, the project outcomes demonstrate that participatory designing presents a powerful strategy for engaging students during the Middle Years of schooling, thus minimising risks of academic or social alienation that can challenge student wellbeing at this critical stage in their education (Benner, 2011; Dinham & Rowe, 2009; MCEETYA, 2008).

Pedagogical Outcomes

The Precinct design draws strength from a two-way influence between school's physical environment and educational purpose (Tanner, 2008). From initial planning to final construction, the project focused on providing Cannon Hill Anglican College with a future-focused building conducive to evolving pedagogy. The flexible layout and reconfigurable furniture will ensure longevity of the space (Oblinger, 2005) and adaptability in line with future educational trends (Harris, 2010).

With its interconnected 'assortment of spaces' that can be used together or independently, the Precinct provides purposefully designed twenty-first-century learning environment for large and small group work and quiet nooks where 'students can think and work independently' (Tanner, 2008, p. 456). The glass doors provide easy access to the outside learning areas, allowing the class to easily spill out to the tables positioned amongst the nearby woodlands and gardens. Imaginative use of garden areas and the first floor balcony as outdoor rooms (Fig. 6) has achieved a blurring of the boundaries between the natural collaboration that occurs at lunch time and the collaboration that is associated with twenty-first-century learning, Middle Years education and student wellbeing.

The flexibility inherent in the Precinct design is already supporting pedagogical variation. For example, the operable partition between the general learning areas and the glass-enclosed break-out spaces allow different group formations and ways of working, with students demonstrating greater independence in their learning. Students frequently draw and write on the glass panels to creatively express their ideas when collaborating with others and brainstorming ideas. In these ways they are demonstrating ownership of individual learning styles.

Fig. 6 Indoor and outdoor rooms promote collaboration (Jason Waters, PW Architecture)

Continuing Outcomes

Since completion of the Junior Secondary Precinct at the end of 2015, the College has undertaken renovation of the Language Faculty classrooms and refurbishment of the Mathematics classrooms. In these projects, the College has drawn on a range of key learnings from the Junior Secondary Precinct design process and subsequent experiences of using its learning spaces and furnishings. For example, visual and physical access to natural elements such as the surrounding melaleuca woodlands has proved so successful in the Junior Secondary Precinct design that it has become a feature of the College's Language Faculty classroom renovation. In addition, the effective use of large glass doors and writable glass panels in the Junior Secondary building led to their addition in other classrooms for use by a wider range of students beyond Year 7.

The colourful, flexible furniture used in the Junior Secondary building has become the preferred option. Strong support for these contemporary furniture types in the College's annual *Year 7 student wellbeing and transition survey* provided the school leadership team with sufficient evidence to extend their provision throughout the College. The ability to easily move the Junior Secondary desks into a range of formations for student collaboration has led to their inclusion in the suite of furniture in the renovated Languages classrooms and Maths block. Height adjustable standing desks have also been adopted as part of each subsequent classroom refurbishment. The addition of a fidget bar on the standing desks promotes student engagement with learning for more active students and limits distractions for others. The provision of choice for students in how and where they are learning (standing, sitting, individually or in small groups) aims to foster a sense of autonomy and ownership of learning and enhanced student wellbeing.

Post-occupation: Project Outcomes from a School Leader's Perspective

Reflecting on the project post-occupation, lead author Nastrom-Smith shares the following insights on the designing process and outcomes from a school leader's perspective.

Ongoing evaluation of the effectiveness and success of the design decisions and resultant classroom learning spaces revealed several strengths of the participatory process and several key learnings to enhance future building projects. If I were involved in future projects, I would create more formal opportunities for staff and student representatives to participate in the design process, so that these views could be taken back to the table at the various project design team meetings. Involvement in subsequent projects has highlighted how senior leaders can allow key stakeholders from the school community to provide these feedback opportunities and how the resultant outcomes promote a greater sense of community around learning spaces.

A key aspect of an effective participatory designing process is the identification and engagement of the *right* stakeholders, without becoming so broad that the process is ineffective and no consensus can be achieved. A design approach that excludes the primary users of the learning space and relies on the views of only architects and school leaders risks becoming a white elephant, proclaiming itself as an innovative learning space, while not meeting the needs of teachers and students.

Creating more formalised opportunities for student voice to be heard in matters that directly impact their learning and wellbeing should be a continuing focus. This participatory project has shown me that without the inclusion of the student envisioning process, the explicit views of the students may not have been included in the Junior Secondary Precinct design. The outcomes may have been similar given the involvement of educators with significant teaching and learning experience. However, the inclusion of students in the envisioning activity, gave them a profound sense of connection with the building and its design.

These thoughts are borne out by results of the College's annual Year 7 Student Wellbeing and Transition Survey which provide senior leaders with feedback on how the learning spaces are influencing the educational experiences of the Junior Secondary students during their first year of secondary school. Students' generally positive responses indicate that they are experiencing known influences on successful transition, such as engagement, motivation, confidence, enjoyment and feelings of academic success. They also report that various elements of the learning spaces are contributing to a positive sense of wellbeing. Therefore, it is evident that the College can promote the Junior Secondary Precinct as representative of student wishes and needs, as what they value about their learning has been incorporated into the learning spaces. In this way, it supports their mental, emotional, social and intellectual wellbeing.

One of the key challenges of working in a College without a set of dedicated Middle Years staff is fostering pedagogical approaches that recognise the developmental stage and specific educational needs of young adolescent learners. The expansion of secondary school to include the younger Year 7 cohorts magnified the distinctive needs of Middle Years students as they transition from primary to secondary school. The feedback gained from the Year 7 Student Wellbeing and Transition Survey and the flexibility of the Junior Secondary learning spaces have provided significant impetus in the growth of a distinctive pedagogical approach amongst the secondary staff at Cannon Hill Anglican College. The feedback highlighting spatial elements that the students value and enjoy has resulted in further incorporation of these elements into each teacher's suite of pedagogical skills and has seen these elements become features of subsequent renovations and refurbishments.

Implications for Practice

Student and staff feedback and Nastrom-Smith's personal observations indicate that the Junior Secondary Precinct has significant influence on student learning and wellbeing during transition to secondary school. Based on this evidence, the following visual construct (Fig. 7) identifies three interconnected areas for enhancing student wellbeing at this critical stage of their education, namely: the design of student-friendly learning spaces; the design of pedagogy and curriculum suited to contemporary learners; and the provision of a pastoral care and transition program. Individually, each area supports student wellbeing to a degree. However, if a school could achieve synergy across these three areas, then student wellbeing would be optimised throughout the Middle Years of learning. While pedagogical and pastoral areas have traditionally gained greater attention, the visual construct highlights the significant yet less recognised role that learning space design plays in developing student wellbeing.

Along with several key learnings that have benefitted the College in its ongoing building and infrastructure projects, the participatory process and associated exploration of the literature has identified some wider implications for learning space designing that are worth further consideration by school leaders and architects alike. Given the permanency of building design decisions, it is imperative that decisions made by those involved in learning space design consider the impact that design choices may have on student wellbeing by:

- Actively involving the primary users of school learning spaces, namely, students and teachers, in the design process through meaningful participatory activities;

Fig. 7 Influences on student wellbeing during the transition to secondary school

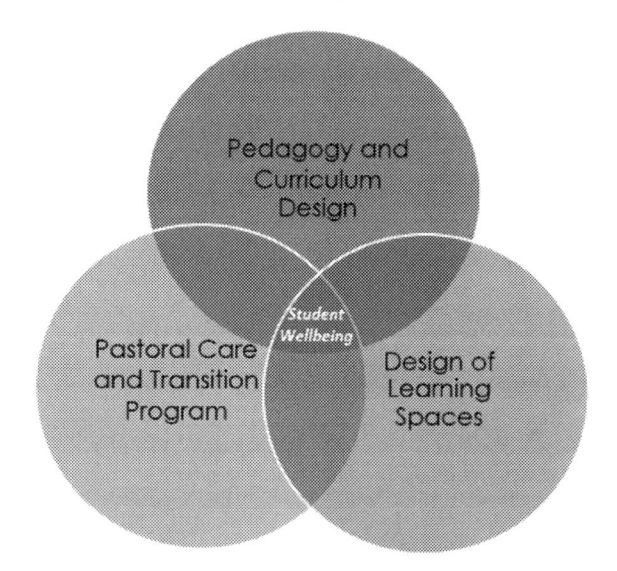

- Developing a strong relationship between school and architects that allows for a consultative approach and robust discussion around the design of any learning space;
- Designing spaces that are flexible and where possible are made up of a series of interconnected spaces;
- Capitalising on the surrounding natural environment of a school and incorporating it into the design of learning spaces;
- Including elements within the learning space that allow students to demonstrate ownership of their learning and give them a choice of how and where they learn. This extends to the furniture selection.

Conclusion

As discussed in this chapter, Cannon Hill College's Junior Secondary Precinct represents a purposefully designed twenty-first-century learning environment where students can build the capacities necessary for future citizenship. A varied range of spaces has been created to support innovative pedagogy that addresses the specific needs of Middle Years students and the transition to secondary school. In addition, this exploration of the Junior Secondary Precinct project has revealed the potential of a participatory designing approach to support students' learning and mental, emotional, social and intellectual wellbeing. As demonstrated, participatory designing can enhance students' engagement, motivation, confidence, safety, enjoyment and feelings of academic success. More widely, insights from this project could inform the initiatives of other school communities that seek to create engaging social learning spaces for contemporary learners.

References

Australian Curriculum, Assessment and Reporting Authority (ACARA). (n.d.). Retrieved May, 18, 2018, from https://www.australiancurriculum.edu.au.

Australian Council for Educational Research (ACER). (2012). *Junior secondary—theory and practice. Report to Queensland Department of Education and Training.* Brisbane: Queensland Government.

Australian Council for Educational Research (ACER). (2011). *Elaborations of the flying start junior initiative.* Brisbane: Queensland Government.

Akos, P., & Galassi, J. P. (2004). Middle and high school transitions as viewed by students, parents, and teachers. *Professional School Counselling, 7*(4), 212–221.

Allison, P., Gray, S., Sproule, J., Nash, C., Martindale, R., & Wong, J. (2015). Exploring contributions of project-based learning to health and wellbeing in secondary education. *Improving Schools, 18*(3), 207–220. https://doi.org/10.1177/1365480215599298.

Bacete, F. J. G., Perrin, G. M., Schneider, B. H., & Blanchard, C. (2014). Effects of school on the well-being of children and adolescents. In A. Ben-Arieh, F. Casas, I. Frønes, & J. E. Korbin (Eds.), *Handbook of child well-being: Theories, methods and policies in global perspective* (pp. 1251–1305). Dordrecht: Springer.

Bahr, N., & Crosswell, L. (2011). Contesting lost ground for the middle years in Australia: Using the case study of Queensland. *Australian Journal of Middle Schooling, 11*(2), 12–19.

Barrett, L., Barrett, P., Davies, F., & Zhang, Y. (2015). The impact of classroom design on pupils' learning: Final results of a holistic, multi-level analysis. *Building and Environment, 89,* 118–133. https://doi.org/10.1016/j.buildenv.2015.02.013.

Benner, A. D. (2011). The transition to high school: Current knowledge, future directions. *Educational Psychology Review, 23*(3), 299–328. https://doi.org/10.1007/s10648-011-9152-0.

Breivik, P. S. (2005). 21st Century learning and information literacy. *Change: The Magazine of Higher Learning, 37*(2), 21–27. https://doi.org/10.3200/chng.37.2.21-27.

Burton, K. D., Lydon, J. E., D'alessandro, D. U. & Koestner, R. (2006). The differential effects of intrinsic and identified motivation on well-being and performance: Prospective, experimental, and implicit approaches to self-determination theory. *Journal of Personality and Social Psychology, 91*(4), 750.

Cannon Hill Anglican College (2018). Retrieved May 18, 2018, from http://www.chac.qld.edu.au.

Chadbourne, R. (2003). What makes middle schools and middle schooling distinctive, if anything. *Queensland Journal of Educational Research, 19*(1), 3–12.

Coffey, A., Berlach, R. G., & O'Neill, M. (2011). Transitioning year seven primary students to secondary settings in Western Australian Catholic schools: A description of the process. *Journal of Catholic School Studies, 83*(2), 6–17.

Cohen, J. (2006). Social, emotional, ethical, and academic education: Creating a climate for learning, participation in democracy, and well-being. *Harvard Educational Review, 76*(2), 201–237.

Daniels, E. (2005). On the minds of middle schoolers. *Educational Leadership, 62*(7), 52–54.

Daniels, E. (2010). Creating motivating learning environments: What we can learn from researchers and students. *The English Journal, 100*(1), 25–29.

Day, C., & Parnell, R. (2003). *Consensus Design: Socially inclusive process.* Oxford: Architectural Press.

Dinham, S., & Rowe, K. (2009). *Teaching and learning in middle schooling: A review of the literature.* Wellington, New Zealand: Ministry of Education.

Dittoe, W. (2006). Seriously cool places: The future of learning-centered built environments. In D. Oblinger (Ed.), *Learning spaces* (pp. 3.1–3.10). Washington, DC: EDUCAUSE. Retrieved May 18, 2018, from https://www.educause.edu/research-and-publications/books/learning-spaces.

Elliott Burns, R. A. (2016). Voices of experience: Opportunities to influence creatively the designing of school libraries. In K. Fisher (Ed.), *The translational design of schools: An evidence-based approach to aligning pedagogy and learning environments in schools* (pp. 195–213). Amsterdam, Netherlands: Sense Publishing.

Flutter, J., & Rudduck, J. (2004). *Consulting pupils: What's in it for schools?*. London: Routledge/Falmer.

Frydenberg, E., Care, E., Freeman, E., & Chan, E. (2009). Interrelationships between coping, school connectedness and wellbeing. *Australian Journal of Education, 53*(3), 261–276. https://doi.org/10.1177/000494410905300305.

Garrison, D. R. (2011). *E-learning in the 21st century: A framework for research and practice* (2nd ed.). New York: Routledge.

Groundwater-Smith, S. (2004). Transforming learning: Transforming places and spaces for learning. *Curriculum Matters, 3*(3), 13–17.

Harris, S. (2010). *The place of virtual, pedagogic and physical space in the 21st Century classroom*. Sydney: Sydney Centre for Innovation in Learning.

Hawkey, K. (2006). Emotional intelligence and mentoring in pre-service teacher education: A literature review. *Mentoring & Tutoring, 14*(2), 137–147.

Khawaja, N. G., Ibrahim, O. & Schweitzer, R. D. (2017). Mental wellbeing of students from refugee and migrant backgrounds: The mediating role of resilience. *School Mental Health, 9*(3), 284–293. https://doi.org/10.1007/s12310-017-9215-6.

Kirby, P., Lanyon, C., Cronin, K. & Sinclair, R. (2003). *Building a culture of participation: Involving children and young people in policy, service planning, delivery and evaluation*. Handbook. London: DfES.

Kuhn, D., Black, J., Keselman, A., & Kaplan, D. (2000). The development of cognitive skills to support inquiry learning. *Cognition and Instruction, 18*(4), 495–523.

Lackney, J. A. (2000). *Thirty-three educational design principles for schools and community learning centers*. Retrieved May 18, 2018, from http://schoolstudio.typepad.com/school_design_studio/33-educational-design-pri.html. Accessed 18 May 2018.

Lampert, J. (2005). Easing the transition to high school. *Educational Leadership, 62*(7), 61–63.

Mander, D. J., Lester, L., & Cross, D. (2015). The social and emotional well-being and mental health implications for adolescents transitioning to secondary boarding school. *International Journal of Child and Adolescent Health, 8*(2), 131.

McGee, C., Ward, R., Gibbons, J., & Harlow, A. (2003). *Transition to secondary school: A literature review*. Hamilton: A Report to the Ministry of Education, The University of Waikato.

McIntyre, D., Pedder, D., & Rudduck, J. (2005). Pupil voice: Comfortable and uncomfortable learnings for teachers. *Research Papers in Education, 20*(2), 149–168. https://doi.org/10.1080/02671520500077970.

McWilliam, E. (2011). From school to café and back again: Responding to the learning demands of the twenty-first century. *International Journal of Leadership in Education, 14*(3), 257–268.

Ministerial Council on Education, Employment, Training and Youth Affairs (MCEETYA). (2008). *Melbourne declaration on educational goals for young Australians*. Canberra: MCEETYA. Retrieved May 18, 2018, from https://eric.ed.gov/?id=ED534449.

Montemayor, R., Adams, G. R., & Gullotta, T. (2000). *Adolescent diversity in ethnic, economic, and cultural contexts* (Vol. 10). Thousand Oaks: Sage.

Nair, P. (2009). Don't just rebuild schools—reinvent them. *Education Week, 28*(28), 24–25.

Oblinger, D. (2005). Leading the transition from classrooms to learning spaces. *EDUCAUSE Quarterly, 28*(1), 14–18.

Osterman, K. F. (2000). Students' need for belonging in the school community. *Review of Educational Research, 70*(3), 323–367.

Pedder, D., & McIntyre, D. (2006). Pupil consultation: The importance of social capital. *Educational Review, 58*(2), 145–157. https://doi.org/10.1080/00131910600584009.

Pendergast, D. (2006). Fast-tracking middle schooling reform: A model for sustainability. *Australian Journal of Middle Schooling, 6*(2), 13–18.

Pink, D. H. (2005). *A whole new mind: Moving from the information age to the conceptual age.* New York: Riverhead Books.

Ruck, M. D., Keating, D. P., Saewyc, E. M., Earls, F., & Ben-Arieh, A. (2016). The United Nations convention on the rights of the child: Its relevance for adolescents. *Journal of Research on Adolescence, 26*(1), 16–29. https://doi.org/10.1111/jora.12172.

Ryan, R. M., & Deci, E. L. (2006). Self-regulation and the problem of human autonomy: Does psychology need choice, self-determination, and will? *Journal of Personality, 74*(6), 1557–1586.

Sabiston, C., Sedgwick, W., Crocker, P., Kowalski, K., & Mack, D. (2007). Social physique anxiety in adolescence: An exploration of influences, coping strategies, and health behaviors. *Journal of Adolescent Research, 22*(1), 78–101.

Salpeter, J. (2003). 21st Century skills: Will our students be prepared? *Technology and Learning, 24*(3), 17–29.

Shussman, Y. M. (2017). Environmental psychology and classroom design as a tool for promoting meaningful learning. *Australian Educational Leader, 39*(1), 48–52.

Silva, E. (2009). Measuring skills for 21st Century learning. *The Phi Delta Kappan, 90*(9), 630–634.

Sinclair, R. (2004). Participation in practice: Making it meaningful, effective and sustainable. *Children and Society, 18*(2), 106–118. https://doi.org/10.1002/chi.817.

Tanner, C. K. (2008). Explaining relationships among student outcomes and the school's physical environment. *Journal of Advanced Academics, 19*(3), 444–471.

Tanner, C. K. (2009). Effects of school design on student outcomes. *Journal of Educational Administration, 47*(3), 381–399.

Thorburn, M. (2015). Theoretical constructs of well-being and their implications for education. *British Educational Research Journal, 41*(4), 650–665. https://doi.org/10.1002/berj.3169.

Thorburn, M., & MacAllister, J. (2013). Dewey, interest, and well-being: Prospects for improving the educational value of physical education. *Quest, 65*(4), 458–468.

United Nations. (1989). *Convention on the rights of the child.* Retrieved May 18, 2018, from http://www.ohchr.org/EN/ProfessionalInterest/Pages/CRC.aspx.

Van den Berghe, L., Vansteenkiste, M., Cardon, G., Kirk, D., & Haerens, L. (2014). Research on self-determination in physical education: Key findings and proposals for future research. *Physical Education and Sport Pedagogy, 19*(1), 97–121. https://doi.org/10.1080/17408989.2012.732563.

van Merriënboer, J. J. G., McKenney, S., Cullinan, D., & Heuer, J. (2017). Aligning pedagogy with physical learning spaces. *European Journal of Education, 52*(3), 253–267. https://doi.org/10.1111/ejed.12225.

Wang, M. T., & Holcombe, R. (2010). Adolescents' perceptions of school environment, engagement, and academic achievement in middle school. *American Educational Research Journal, 47*(3), 633–662.

Waters, S. K., Lester, L., Wenden, E., & Cross, D. (2012). A theoretically grounded exploration of the social and emotional outcomes of transition to secondary school. *Australian Journal of Guidance and Counselling, 22*(2), 190–205. https://doi.org/10.1017/jgc.2012.26.

Wigfield, A., & Eccles, J. S. (2002). Students' motivation during the middle school years. In J. M. Aronson (Ed.), *Improving academic achievement: Impact of psychological factors on education* (pp. 159–184). Boston, MA: Academic Press.

Williamson, R. (2001). Middle level education. In V. Richardson (Ed.), *Handbook of research on teaching* (4th ed., pp. 378–391). Washington, DC: American Educational Research Association.

Woolner, P., & Clark, A. (2015). Developing shared understandings of learning environments: Interactions with students, teachers and other professionals. In P. Woolner (Ed.), *School design together* (pp. 167–183). Abingdon: Routledge.

Woolner, P., Hall, E., Wall, K., & Dennison, D. (2007). Getting together to improve the school environment: User consultation, participatory design and student voice. *Improving Schools, 10*(3), 233–248. https://doi.org/10.1177/1365480207077846.
Žukauskienė, R. (2014). Adolescence and well-being. In A. Ben-Arieh, F. Casas, I. Frønes, & J. E. Korbin (Eds.), *Handbook of child well-being: Theories, methods and policies in global perspective* (pp. 1713–1738). Dordrecht: Springer, Netherlands.

Creating a Sensory Garden for Early Years Learners: Participatory Designing for Student Wellbeing

Adeline Kucks and Hilary Hughes

Abstract Early childhood educators recognise the value of outdoor environments to support students' learning and social wellbeing. However, in schools, outdoor time is often limited to lunch time play and health and physical education, while more attention tends to be paid to the arrangement of indoor classrooms than to outdoor environments that support more informal learning. This chapter presents an approach to designing outdoor spaces that support play-based pedagogy and create opportunities for young learners to engage with the natural environment. It describes a project that incorporated a charrette (collaborative designing process) to create a sensory garden with a group of Prep students (aged 4–6 years) and other members of the school community. This experience illustrates the potential of a participatory designing approach for transforming an underutilised garden into a vibrant space that positively influences teaching practice and student wellbeing.

Introduction

Well-designed outdoor spaces can enhance social engagement and learning, especially in the early years of schooling. As sites for play-based pedagogy, they enable young children to explore the natural world and they play a role as co-educator in fostering empathy, knowledge and wellbeing (Dowdell, Gray, & Malone, 2011). However, this potential is often overlooked in designing early childhood facilities (birth to age 8) as greater attention is generally placed on formal indoor learning environments. Although outdoor education is viewed as a right for young children (Gray & Martin, 2012), external spaces are often envisaged only in terms of lunch time play and physical education. This chapter illustrates how, with a little collaboration and imagination, a modest school playground can be transformed into a vibrant social learning space. It outlines a project to create a sensory learning garden for Preparatory Year (Prep) students at a primary school in Queensland, Australia where Prep is the first year of compulsory schooling.

A. Kucks (✉) · H. Hughes
Queensland University of Technology, Brisbane, Australia
e-mail: akuck3@eq.edu.au

© Springer Nature Singapore Pte Ltd. 2019
H. Hughes et al. (eds.), *School Spaces for Student Wellbeing and Learning*,
https://doi.org/10.1007/978-981-13-6092-3_12

This chapter views participatory designing from the first-hand perspective of an early years educator (Adeline Kucks). After introducing her understanding of wellbeing and presenting an overview of the literature that informs her practice, this educator outlines the design project and participatory designing process that she led with a range of stakeholders who included Prep students, parents, teachers, school administrators and design professionals. To inform similar initiatives in other early years contexts, the chapter concludes by reviewing the potential of participatory designing in a school context and the influence of the resultant learning space on teaching practice and student wellbeing.

Wellbeing—From the Perspective of an Early Years Educator

As I explain in this section, through my professional experience as early years educator, I have come to understand the importance of the school playground as a potential space for wellbeing. I am also aware that to ensure their wellbeing young learners need nurturing in safe, inclusive spaces where they can inquire, take risks and develop literacy and numeracy through exploratory play. However, while the playground offers a canvas of opportunity for playful and social learning, it takes considerable commitment to develop natural and constructed features that are inclusively safe and enticing.

This understanding of the relationship between children's outdoor play environment and their wellbeing emerged through my interest in learning space design and my attention to variations in play spaces and the ways they are used. My enthusiasm for designing better play and learning spaces was piqued by an incident I experienced when teaching in England. Having grown up with wide expanses of grass at my Brisbane school, I was dismayed by the stark concrete school playgrounds in London. I remember blowing my whistle during a school playground duty to halt a game of 'tiggy' because I was concerned about the children's safety when running on the concrete. However, the teacher's aide quickly informed me that as this was the children's designated play space 'running is of course permitted'.

While undertaking the Master of Education at QUT (2015–2016), I made it my mission to research how to engage students, teachers and families in effective age-appropriate pedagogies in the pre-Prep and Prep years. In particular, the unit of study Designing Spaces for Learning gave me the chance to explore research and theory through a project to redesign the Prep play area at my school (Kucks, 2016). The project was an opportunity to continue my exploration of Maria Montessori's philosophy (Feez & Miller, 2011) and the use of differing indoor and outdoor learning experiences to engage young learners and holistically support their social, emotional and ethical development. I came to recognise that this holistic approach to 'educating for life' (Feez & Miller, 2011; Lillard, 2013) promotes student wellbeing.

This understanding is further informed by the Australian Curriculum which recognises a relationship between children's engagement with their world and their wellbeing:

> Children have a strong sense of identity; children are connected with, and contribute to, their world; children have a strong sense of wellbeing; children are confident and involved learners; and children are effective communicators. (ACARA, n.d., p. 9)

While curriculum documents support outdoor learning, there is limited guidance for involving children in the design of outdoor spaces. Therefore, with a view that inclusion contributes to wellbeing, I adopted a participatory designing approach to ensure the voices of all stakeholders are reflected in the new space (Casey, 2007).

Underpinning Concepts

The project was further underpinned by the three interrelated concepts discussed in this section, namely: Early years curriculum, outdoor play and learning, and participatory learning space designing. While curriculum documents provide the policy impetus, participatory design processes such as a charrette (Hughes, 2017) enable key stakeholders including Prep students and teachers to create outdoor spaces that respond to the learning and wellbeing needs of young children. Thus, the project concurs with the view that:

> Garden- based learning should not be viewed as an adjunct to the primary curriculum but rather as an interdisciplinary portal through which places and subjects can be explored and woven together (Green, 2008, p. 15).

Early Years Curriculum

Four Australian curriculum documents relevant to the Prep context informed the project:

- *Australian Curriculum*: a document which sets learning goals for students in all Australian schools from Kindergarten to Year 12 (ACARA, n.d.).
- *Early Years Learning Framework* (EYLF): a document which aligns with the Australian Curriculum and in particular supports children's learning from birth to age 5 years in early learning and care centres, and their transition to school. The EYLF offers a cyclical model for curriculum decision-making which places learning at the centre and integrates principles, holistic pedagogical practice and learning outcomes (DEEWR, 2009).
- *Early Years Curriculum Guidelines* (EYCG): although no longer current policy, the Queensland focus of this document was still informative for this project (QCAA, 2006).

- *National Montessori Curriculum*: approved in 2011 as an alternative curriculum for Australian schools (Feez & Miller, 2011).

In Queensland, Prep constitutes the first year of formal schooling when children are aged 4–6 years. At this stage, the curriculum emphasises the engagement of students in active learning with a focus on real-life situations, investigation and play (QCAA, 2006). This approach is intended to support brain development by enabling children to learn using all five senses. It responds to research showing that neurological networks already exist and active participation creates more and new pathways in a child's brain, as the essence of learning (Rushton, Juola- Rushton, & Larkin, 2010). Similarly, the EYLF promote children's natural curiosity about their world (DEEWR, 2009). Meanwhile, educators assist them to construct new knowledge through age-appropriate pedagogies (DET, 2015).

Play is an essential component of early years learning. For example, EYLF Outcome 2 highlights play as a means for young children to investigate their environment and explore new ideas. However, prescribed curriculum is often at odds with philosophical understandings around play based pedagogy. Much of the Prep level learning experience centres around formal learning activities aligned with Australian Curriculum (ACARA, n.d.) content and assessment standards (Nedovic & Morrissey, 2013). Therefore, it is important to ensure that Prep students' environment is conducive to formal and informal learning.

Early years curriculum requires stimulating, active learning environments that are purposefully designed to engage the minds of young children and so foster brain growth (Rushton et al., 2010). The EYCG specifies purposefully constructed learning environments which are 'flexible, inviting, comfortable, accessible and responsive to children, their families and local community members' in order to provide 'engaging, stimulating and challenging experiences' that aid children's holistic development (QCAA, 2006, p. 34). The EYLF encourages teachers to create welcoming learning environments including outdoor spaces and to foster children's capacity to understand and respect the natural environment and the interdependence between people, plants, animals and the land (DEEWR, 2009, p. 14). However, limited information is offered regarding how children might participate in creating their own learning environments. For example, the EYCG aims to draw children into productive play in the natural environment, although it indicates that the space and props should be constructed by the teaching staff:

> In the outdoor environment, teachers purposefully arrange fixed and moveable items to extend children's learning as they engage in real-life experiences, physical activities and games, construction, investigations, dramatic play, oral language and literacy activities, sand and water play and artistic experiences (QCAA, 2006, p. 34).

Therefore, the participatory designing process outlined in this chapter offers an opportunity for students to create learning environments that directly respond to their wishes and needs.

Playing and Learning Outdoors

There are strong arguments in favour of play based learning in outdoor and natural environments. Gray and Martin (2012) contend that outdoor education is worth valuing and preserving as an educational right for Australian children. It can be beneficial in motivating students holistically by allowing mind, body and spirit to engage on levels that may not be realised inside a classroom (Cooper, 1996).

Outdoor, green environments extend the quality and quantity of opportunities for children to play constructively and engage their imaginations. They also provide a platform for ongoing environmental education (DEEWR, 2009). Outdoor learning environments provide children with opportunity to wonder, and to develop empathy and scientific knowledge and processes in a natural co-operative space. This in turn fosters children's feelings of belonging to the natural world and an understanding of their relationship to life on earth (Cooper, 1996, p. 12).

Links have been drawn between green playgrounds and physical, social and mental stimulation (Dowdell, Gray, & Malone, 2011; Louv, 2008; Nedovic & Morrissey, 2013). School gardens can enhance literacy and learning in an outdoor setting across the curriculum (Green, 2008; Pascoe & Wyatt-Smith, 2013). Direct exposure to nature and wild spaces contribute to physical and emotional development, as natural elements have been shown to improve cognition, creativity and concentration in students (Louv, 2008; Taylor, Wiley, Kuo, & Sullivan, 1998). Immersion in natural environments (Louv, 2008) may also encourage courteous play and children's respect for themselves, others and the environment.

Learning outdoors is a significant feature of early years education, where outdoor activity realises the constructivist understanding that for young children play and work are inextricably linked (Feez & Miller, 2011). Both Montessori and Reggio Emilia early childhood approaches recognise importance of intentionally creating environments that encourage constructivist learning. Thus, Montessori emphasises careful preparation of indoor and outdoor environments, with a garden as an extension of the classroom. Reggio Emilia principles, which encourage free flow between indoor and outdoor learning environments, highlight the influential role that the learning environment can play as a third educator (Strong-Wilson & Ellis, 2007).

Designing Outdoor Learning Spaces

The type of outdoor spaces that are constructed for children can have a direct impact on their cognition, agility, balance and general motor fitness (Cooper, 1996; Nedovic & Morrissey, 2013). A comparative study showed that children with a more natural, uneven school play area with trees, leaves and sticks tested better for balance, agility and motor fitness than children with a flat, mowed play area (Nedovic & Morrissey, 2013). Moreover, in a well-designed outdoor learning environment, it becomes less necessary for adults to actively manage play as children tend to function more productively and purposefully, with decreasing incidents of problematic behaviour (Casey, 2007).

Curriculum documents offer teachers some broad principles for learning environment design. For example, a key point of EYLF *Outcome 2: Children are connected with and contribute to their world* is that children are 'socially responsible and show respect for the environment' (DEEWR, 2009, p. 29). These documents prompt spatial design that enables the development of skills and knowledge through and about the environment, including children's appreciation and care for natural and constructed environments, exploration of relationships between living and nonliving things and awareness of human impacts on environments. In addition, Casey (2007) indicates the following eight criteria to aim for when designing outdoor learning environments:

1. Varied and interesting physical environment
2. Challenge in the physical environment
3. Playing with natural elements
4. Movement
5. Manipulating natural fabrics
6. Stimulation of the 5 senses
7. Experiencing change in the environment
8. Social interaction.

Incorporation of universal design principles contributes to the ongoing usability of learning spaces, by ensuring that they inclusively accommodate all users and can flexibly adapt with changing needs (Rodesiler & McGuire, 2015, p. 25; Story, 2010, p. 7). These principles require the design to:

1. Be equitable and inclusive of children with special needs both physically and cognitively.
2. Be flexible to accommodate a wide range of physicality and mobility.
3. Be readily modifiable to accommodate cross curricula outcomes.
4. Allow simple and Intuitive use so that children can self-regulate their play and peer tutor each other through innovation and discovery.
5. Provide perceptible information so that children are able to use their senses and fully engage with all elements within the space; and educators can manipulate the space to include a variety of materials and resources to stimulate discussion and problem solving.
6. Allow tolerance for error to enable reasonable risk while minimising hazards.
7. Be of a size and spaciousness to allow children to fully use the site and move freely regardless of mobility or co-ordination.

An inclusive designing approach contributes creating welcoming learning environments that invite students to engage in their own ways with a variety of materials (DEEWR, 2009). Therefore, it is important to develop a locally focused design prior to commencing any outdoor play construction project (Fjortoft, 2001). Ideally, this involves a participatory designing approach which includes a range of stakeholders, especially the students and teachers who use the space (Clark, 2011). Both Montessori and Reggio Emilia promote the inclusion of young children in the design of their learning experience and learning environments (Feez & Miller, 2011; Lillard, 2013; Strong-Wilson & Ellis, 2007).

With such diversity of potential stakeholders, participatory designing requires a creative yet supportive process. For example, a charrette is a kind of a collaborative workshop that can involve people of differing ages and backgrounds (Hughes, 2017). In a charrette, participants develop a consensus-based design concept by evaluating a particular space, brainstorming (re)design ideas and creating a visual representation of one or more design options. A charrette encourages low-tech hands-on participation so that everyone involved can have a say. The resultant ideas and drawings may be shared with professional designers as a basis for formal planning.

The Sensory Learning Garden Project

The sensory learning garden project took place at a relatively new primary school in South East Queensland, Australia. The school's student enrolment had grown rapidly to about 1000 students, including six Prep classes. The project aimed to transform the Prep play area into a stimulating outdoor learning space that captivates the inquiring imagination and senses of young children. To ensure the participation of multiple stakeholders, the project incorporated a charrette (Hughes, 2017). This collaborative designing initiative took weeks not days and involved a rolling process of meetings and online interactions depending on participants' availability.

Purpose

At this school, the Prep students' play area is separate from the rest of the school. Before the project, it offered a quite dull space, having fallen into the trap of easy maintenance rather than ongoing development (Dowdell et al., 2011). Play here was generally limited by 'three zones' similar to those identified by Casey (2007) for taught games, adult management and segregation by age. Thus, only Prep children had permission to play there and the games they could play were mainly taught and managed by an adult. As the Prep cohort grew, the play area became crowded and negative impacts became apparent in students' deteriorating behaviour during break times and a rise in 'time out' and other penalties. Seeking to address these behavioural problems, the school principal proposed the development of a vegetable patch as a source of interest and activity for Prep students. While excited by this idea, I saw a wider opportunity to create a sensory learning garden. Therefore, with the principal's support I gained funding to realise this project. In implementing the project, I sought to address the EYLF claim that:

> Children's early learning influences their life chances. Wellbeing and a strong sense of connection, optimism and engagement enable children to develop a positive attitude to learning. (DEEWR, 2009 p. 9)

Therefore, the purpose of the sensory garden was to facilitate quality teaching moments and inquiry based learning across the curriculum while playing a role itself as third educator (Feez & Miller, 2011; Lillard, 2013; Strong-Wilson & Ellis, 2007). I anticipated that the space would facilitate cross-curricular links and holistically support students' physical, social, moral and academic development. It would reflect contemporary policy and research associated with early childhood education, and outdoor learning curriculum and practice, as outlined above. From a practical perspective, the redeveloped play area would accommodate a growing number of Prep students as well as other community groups such as the local kindergarten. In all these ways, the project would contribute to developing tomorrow's citizens to be *creatively confident*, as the school motto states.

Stakeholder Participation

In line with participatory designing principles, the project involved a range of stakeholders from across the school community. This wide involvement ensured the inclusion of multiple perspectives in the redesign process (Green, 2008). It responded to curriculum and administrative imperatives, as well as allowing 'buy in' from the wider professional and parent groups with an interest in Prep education. Of particular importance, the project incorporated the voices of children who are often not consulted in school designing (Casey, 2007).

The following stakeholders participated in various ways at differing times:

- Prep teachers and students as principal users of the intended space
- Special education teachers with an interest in the sensory garden as a space of calm for children
- Support teachers keen to use the garden as an alternative space for numeracy and language support
- Perceptual Motor Program teachers
- Head of Curriculum as adviser on learning and teaching across the school
- The Principal as decision-maker on school budget and strategy
- The Groundskeeper as information source about physical features like underground power and water pipes; and also assistance with practical construction and gardening
- The Parents and Citizens group as a funding source; and also as representatives of Prep parents
- The Head of Student Services as source of administrative information
- Professional organisations such as the Creche and Kindergarten Association, a local childcare centre and a Montessori playgroup.

As project leader, I tracked the planning and implementation of the project and managed communication among participants. I negotiated budget details and resolved problems, in addition to exchanging information via email and phone. I worked closely with the school's workplace health and safety team to ensure legal compliance.

Evaluating the Space

The project charrette commenced with evaluation of the existing Prep play area by myself and other stakeholders. First, I undertook reflective observation of the space, adopting a metaphorical lens to review its design challenges and potential (Burge, 2001). Thus, I came to consider this space as *the paddock,* in the Australian colloquial sense of an expanse of undeveloped roughly grassed land. I identified that the fundamental problem was the sparseness of the existing Prep play area and its lack of features to stimulate children's engagement in productive, imaginative play. As the children had few play props other than balls and a sandpit, they tended to engage in fast, rough and disorganised play that often resulted in injury or disagreements. Moreover, teachers seldom took advantage of this space for constructive outdoor learning. These observations led me to recognise that this *paddock* did not reflect theoretical understandings about the importance of outdoor education or age-appropriate pedagogies with regard to student wellbeing, physical education, cognition, co-operation and self-sustainable play with others and the environment. Extending the metaphor, I envisaged the paddock as a perfect landing ground for hot air balloons that could enable children to take off academically, physically and socially. In this space, the children could transition from frantic, disorganised play to active engagement and learning. A redeveloped paddock could ignite their imagination and help develop their ability to fly high as lifelong learners, problem solvers and negotiators.

In order to gain children's first-hand insights about the space, I engaged approximately 20 Prep students in an informal playground survey which had an inclusive intent and focused on curriculum driven play (Casey, 2007). Table 1 outlines the key aspects surveyed, the child-friendly questions asked and a summary of student responses. The students' responses complemented my observational impressions that the space was too expanisve and sparse to inspire productive informal learning or imaginative play.

Creating the Sensory Garden

Having evaluated the Prep play space, I contacted adult stakeholders to request their participation. To explain the problem and ensure that they all had a common understanding of the project goals and process, I outlined the evaluation findings about the existing Prep play area. Next, I invited the participants to imagine how the current Prep play area could be reinvigorated as a sensory garden. In their imagining, I encouraged the participants to consider who and what is (and will be) valued in this space (Elliott Burns, 2016). I also explained that the redesign needed to suit:

Table 1 Playground survey. Adapted from Casey (2007). *Environments for outdoor play: A practical guide to making space for children* (p. 37). London: *Sage*

Location: Prep playground—at a Queensland public primary school	*Date*: 18th May 2016

Observer: A Prep teacher

Observer's general impressions:
While the space is open and sparse, which is good for kicking and ball sports, it is too big for productive play opportunities. Generally, the space is not utilised to its potential for young children. Staff do not plan for inquiry or use of objects to ignite imagination or assist play

Aspects	*Questions*	*Summary of student responses*
Flexibility	Are there things that you can change and play with in lots of different ways?	We have 1 playground and sandpit but we don't all fit. We only have balls to play with and we can run
Shelter	Is there any shelter here? What's it like?	The obstacle course is under cover, otherwise it is very hot in the sun when you are running
Centres of interest	Are there any really interesting things to play with? What are these?	We can play in the playground, sandpit or on the obstacle course. They're busy
Natural features	Are there natural things to play with like trees, long grass or pebbles?	We don't have anything like this. We are not allowed in the gardens
Atmosphere	What is it like here? Does it feel friendly or not?	I like to play with my friends here sometimes, except when they are running and pulling me. Sometimes the ball hits me
Sensory elements	• Are there things: • To touch? • To smellSmell? • That make a noise? • That are interesting to look at?	We don't have anything to play with in our playground that we can smell or that makes noise. Our home corner is only for girls. We can touch the playground, balls and sand toys. I don't like getting sand in my shoes
Accessibility	Can you get to everything that you want to?	I don't always get a ball to play with. Sometimes my friends play tag because you can't play in the sandpit when it's busy
Risk and challenge	Are there things that are quite exciting and adventurous?	I like the rope on the playground. Sometimes the obstacle course is tricky
Practicalities	Is it easy to get there?	We can play at first and second break, we just walk out of our classroom

Fig. 1 3D conceptual model for an outdoor classroom (Author)

- A Queensland public primary school;
- Growing enrolment of Prep students; and
- Intended heavy daily use of the play area by a variety of groups, including six streams of Prep students, the adjacent creche and kindergarten, and other play groups.

The participants shared with me and each other many ideas for redesigning the Prep play area, verbally and in writing. To visually represent their ideas, some created collages and 3D models of the imagined sensory garden, such as Fig. 1.

The school contracted an educational landscaper and an early years resource consultant to provide the necessary professional expertise for realising the design project. Following participatory practice, these professionals considered all the ideas presented by the adult and young stakeholders. To assist decision-making they assessed the potential of the space and the feasibility of various options, determining what would work best within the allocated budget. The educational landscaper was particularly helpful in relating design suggestions to the educational goals of the Australian Curriculum (n.d.). Once the final sensory garden design was completed, the school gained a government grant which enabled construction to begin.

Fig. 2 The newly constructed sensory garden (Author)

The sensory learning garden was constructed on the paddock in about two months. It included a sustainable vegetable garden with self-watering system and a rockery, as shown in Fig. 2. At each stage of design and construction, we carefully considered how the garden would enable children to play and learn. Practical gardening aspects were also addressed. For example, matting was put under the bark chips and sand to keep weeds away. Aesthetic features included the mud coloured concrete that the rocks were laid in to blend with the ground.

As project leader, I needed to address some problems to ensure the design process could move forward. For example, when filling out the Education Department's workplace health and safety forms for the sensory garden, I became aware that the rockery edging was considered a safety hazard and would not pass final inspection. I had two choices, either to fence the rockery or remove it. As the rockery was integral to the garden design, I proposed building the sensory fence drawn previously by a professional stakeholder. The principal agreed to fund this extra feature as it not only resolved the safety risk but also added further audio and tactile appeal to the learning environment. As shown in Fig. 3, the fence features wooden beams at child-friendly heights to which can be attached to a variety of plastic and metal everyday objects such as drainage pipes and kitchen pans. During learning and play activities children also hang a changing array of found and self-created items on the fence.

Prior to opening the garden, the educational landscaper gave teachers a 90 min training session on how to best utilise the space for ensuring positive impacts and outcomes for student wellbeing while addressing curriculum demands. Before stu-

Fig. 3 The sensory fence (Author)

dents were free to play in the new sensory learning garden, each class participated in a one hour social skills lesson there. Prep teachers provided guidance to the children on different opportunities for play and ways to use their imagination safely and inclusively. On completing the social skills lesson children were issued a play licence.

Although already proving successful, the sensory garden represents only the first of three envisaged stages in redesigning the Prep play area. The stakeholders' ideas for further development include larger constructions such as tunnels, rope swings, climbing hills, a slippery slide, a wet, rockery and an archway. The educational landscaper left us with plans, although it will be necessary to apply for further grants to see the whole design through to completion.

Reflections on the Project Outcomes and Impacts on Student Wellbeing

Reflecting on the sensory garden project, this section reveals a range of wellbeing impacts on the Prep students and the wider school community. It also outlines lessons learned through this participatory project and implications for future practice in designing learning spaces.

Educational and Social and Wellbeing

The sensory garden now supports children's educational and social and wellbeing, as they use it throughout the year for a variety of themed inquiry learning activities and informal play. As an extension of the classroom, the garden offers self-governing learning zones in a sustainable environment that enhances young children's outdoor learning experiences (Hass & Ashman, 2014). It contributes opportunities for cross-curricular learning while drawing benefit from the natural environment as a learning resource for science and social/ physical development. While engaging the senses of young children, the sensory garden provides a sustainable environment to nurture the wellbeing of creative thinkers, problem solvers and engineers of the future. For example, a group of students embarked on a treasure hunt and spent days hiding and finding treasure while designing and making tracks, using self-made maps and in turn cultivating higher order thinking and problem solving skills (Hass & Ashman, 2014).

From a social wellbeing perspective, the new garden appears to have a positive impact on student interactions, as teachers have noticed a decline in behavioural incidents during playtime with children engaging in slower and more focused play in the space. For example, one young boy who often struggled to play with others without being overly physical said, 'Thanks for putting out the logs Mrs K, I was good today and we dug.' Another group of boys who were consistently engaged in frantic and unorganised play said, 'Can we dig in the tyre please? We can make big holes to the middle of the earth.' This comment suggests that the new garden fired imaginative play. Moreover, by engaging the boys over several days, the digging project had a positive impact on their behaviour. It gave them a focus to collaborate together, without the previous need for 'time out'.

Contributing to the health and wellbeing of the wider school community, the Prep children continue to grow vegetables in self-sustaining garden beds which are fertilised by worms provided by older students. The Prep children harvest the produce themselves for use during their cooking lessons. They also take orders, then bag and hand deliver vegetables to school staff. The Prep children take their parents and caregivers to the garden beds to gather vegetables for their evening meal. They even hosted a parents' afternoon tea which they prepared with ingredients they had grown.

Participatory Designing—Strengths and Challenges

The participatory designing process and outcomes of the sensory garden project has contributed to the collective wellbeing of the school community and educators' professional growth. As an early years educator, the project allowed me to explore the participatory designing practices that I learned whilst undertaking a Master of Education. In particular, the charrette (Hughes, 2017) provided the tools, language and design parameters I needed to complete design projects. Working with my colleagues on a variety of levels in this project provided beneficial professional development. As the principal designer, I needed to devise ways to finance the project, which in turn required me to build collaborative relationships with community organisations. I learned how to negotiate with administrators and landscapers, who are senior to me, as well as with my fellow Prep teachers and Prep support teachers. I also had to negotiate the location and excavation of the garden with the school's groundkeeper and business services manager. Balancing the educational outcomes and feasibility of the space stretched my ability to see both sides of a proposal and have all concerned parties work together to achieve the goal of an outdoor learning environment.

The project also provided an inclusive space where all stakeholders, including teachers and students, had a voice that was valued and considered. No stone was left unturned as we continued to have meetings and ensure that financially, spatially and pedagogically all elements of the design project met our needs. The charrette-inspired process also created a constructive thought bubble to explore how to combine pedagogical knowledge and philosophies around early childhood education and student wellbeing with the practicality of better utilising outdoor space (Rodesiler & McGuire, 2015; Story, 2010). This process enabled the participants to consider the space from many perspectives and engage in shared decision-making. For educators, the participatory designing process gave impetus to evaluating our teaching and designing practice and then using these insights to create a space that would become the third educator in our early years precinct (Strong-Wilson & Ellis, 2007). It also allowed us to engage more purposefully with various community groups and professional designers.

Lessons Learned

The project experience also presented various challenges. Working with diverse stakeholders was sometimes stressful for participants and a key learning that emerged was the need for clear guidelines around roles and responsibilities (Gray & Martin, 2012; Hass & Ashman, 2014). Applying for grant applications forced the project team to consider the breadth of our design and what it would cost us financially to achieve our goal. This required making compromises which caused some tension between stakeholders. There were also concerns that the sensory garden would take open space away from the current playground and limit children's ability to 'run off steam'. This suggested the need for further professional development to explore the relative benefits of thoughtful, productive outdoor play experiences and 'free' running or roaming play (Gehris, Gooze & Whitaker, 2015). In addition, we discovered that the new design features resulted in more direct responsibility and a long-term commitment from staff (Rushton et al., 2010). For example, the new sensory garden will need ongoing maintenance with costs negotiated and allocated in the school's annual budget. Teachers will need to reconsider how they currently plan and what they need to change to make use of the garden and scaffold children's activity in this space.

Implications for Designing Practice

The combined experience of this project and my professional application of the Montessori approach demonstrates the importance of engaging young students in varied outdoor learning experiences (Feez & Miller, 2011; Lillard, 2013). Drawing upon this experience, I offer the follow suggestions to peer educators:

- Focus on the values and needs of your learners, e.g.: How old are your learners? What learning goals, social outcomes and curriculum requirements apply in this context?
- Become familiar with contemporary learning environment research and practice, and justify projects with evidence that demonstrates the potential impacts of design changes on students' wellbeing and learning
- Be a visionary who can creatively problem solve barriers within the project.
- Gather stakeholders and key participants along for the journey. Show them the research evidence and potential for students to flourish as a result of the project.
- Be vigilant with costings and budgets, but work towards providing well resourced spaces where students can flourish
- Have a diversity mindset to ensure that the spaces you create inclusively accommodate all students.

Conclusion

This chapter has provided insights about the process and benefits of a participatory design project that created a sensory learning garden to enhance the educational and social wellbeing of young children. It is of potential interest to educators and designers seeking to develop innovative outdoor learning spaces for early years students.

Like a hot air balloon, the sensory garden has lifted off. On the ground hot air balloons look like a disorganised mess, sometimes being dragged by the wind across the ground with the heavy basket leaving holes in the ground. Similarly, the sparse grassy paddock that was the Prep play area lacked lift and vitality. It had no inspiring features, no practical organisation to it. Children were not stopping to rest, or to take in a view or learn something new. This prompted the plan to create a sensory garden where children can rise above the mundane in a safe space, like the balloon basket. In this new space, they are now free to observe and discuss all that they can see, feel, hear, taste and smell. They can plan where to land and listen, as the wind blows around the sounds from nature. The sensory learning garden is sensitive to the needs of our community and children who have a variety of special needs. It invites shared and individual journeys that will challenge students to enjoy discovering and investigating through and in nature.

For all hot air balloon enthusiasts, planning the trip and destination are important parts of the adventure. Just as the balloon to basket ratio must be equal and appropriate, a sensory learning garden must be safe and manageable. Taking care of the balloon and basket is essential for it to be used again next time. Similarly, caring for a garden and planning what flowers and trees to plant ensures that it is sustainable and accessible all year round. Designing this sensory garden has been rewarding. It promises constant adventure in the years to come for children as they float through nooks and crannies, rising up and coming down to explore or rest while learning about themselves, others or the environment.

References

Australian Curriculum Assessment and Reporting Authority (ACARA). (n.d.). *Australian curriculum.* Retrieved from https://australiancurriculum.edu.au/.

Burge, L. (2001). *People development: Reflective practice for educators. Keynote speech for the Networking 2001 Conference.* Brisbane, Australia, October 14–18. Retrieved from http://www.ibrarian.net/navon/paper/People_development__Reflective_practice_for_educa.pdf?paperid=312345.

Casey, T. (2007). *Environments for outdoor play: A practical guide to making space for children.* London: Sage.

Clark, A. (2011). Breaking methodological boundaries? Exploring visual, participatory methods with adults and young children. *European Early Childhood Education Research Journal, 19*(3), 321–330.

Cooper, G. (1996). The role of outdoor education in education for the 21st century. *Australian Journal of Outdoor Education, 1*(3), 10–14.

Department of Education and Training (DET). (2015). *Age appropriate pedagogies for the early years of schooling: Foundation paper.* Brisbane: Queensland Government. Retrieved from https://det.qld.gov.au/earlychildhood/about-us/age-appropriate-pedagogies.

Department of Education, Employment and Workplace Relations (DEEWR). (2009). *Belonging, being and becoming: The early years learning framework for Australia.* Canberra: Commonwealth of Australia. Retrieved from https://docs.education.gov.au/node/2632.

Dowdell, K., Gray, T., & Malone, K. (2011). Nature and its influence on children's outdoor play. *Australian Journal of Outdoor Education, 15*(2), 24–35.

Elliott Burns, R. A. (2016). Voices of experience: Opportunities to influence creatively the designing of school libraries. In K. Fisher (Ed.), *The translational design of schools: An evidence-based approach to aligning pedagogy and learning environments in schools* (pp. 179–197). Rotterdam: Sense.

Feez, S., & Miller, J. (2011). *Montessori national curriculum.* Five Dock, NSW: Montessori Australia.

Fjortoft, I. (2001). The natural environment as a playground for children. *Early Childhood Education Journal, 29*(2), 111–117.

Gehris, J.S., Gooze, R.A., &, Whitaker, R.C. (2015). Teachers' perceptions about children's movement and learning in early childhood education programmes. *Child: Care, health and development, 41*(1), 122–131. doi: https://doi-org.ezp01.library.qut.edu.au/10.1111/cch.12136

Gray, T., & Martin, P. (2012). The role and place of outdoor education in the Australian national curriculum. *Australian Journal of Outdoor Education, 16*(1), 39–50.

Green M. (2008). Learning in place: Pedagogical pathways for place making. In Jeffrey, P. (Ed.), *AARE 2008 International education research conference: Brisbane: papers collection:* [Conference of the Australian Association for Research in Education, 30 November–4 December 2008]. Melbourne: Australian Association for Research in Education. Retrieved from https://www.aare.edu.au/publications-database.php/5652/learning-in-place-pedagogical-pathways-for-place-making.

Hass, C., & Ashman, G. (2014). Kindergarten children's introduction to sustainability through transformative, experiential nature play. *Australasian Journal of Early Childhood, 39*(2), 21–29.

Hughes, H. (2017). Charrette as context and process for academic discourse in contemporary higher education. In T. Miranda & J. Herr (Eds.), *The value of academic discourse: conversations that matter* (pp. 79–102). Lanham, MD: Rowman and Littlefield.

Kucks, A. (2016). *Learning spaces* [blog]. Retrieved from http://addiek81.edublogs.org/.

Lillard, A. (2013). Playful learning and Montessori education. *American Journal of Play, 5*(2), 157–186.

Louv, R. (2008). *Last child in the woods: Saving our children from nature-deficit disorder*. Chapel Hill: Algonquin Books.

Nedovic, S., & Morrissey, A. (2013). Calm active and focused: Children's responses to an organic outdoor learning environments. *Learning Environments Research, 16*(2), 281–295.

Pascoe, J., & Wyatt- Smith, C. (2013). Curriculum literacies and the school garden. *Literacy Learning: The Middle Years, 21*(1), 34–47.

Queensland Curriculum and Assessment Authority. (QCAA). (2006). *Early years curriculum guidelines*. Brisbane: Queensland Government. Retrieved from https://www.qcaa.qld.edu.au/p-10/qld-curriculum/eycg.

Rushton, S., Juola-Rushton, A., & Larkin, E. (2010). Neuroscience, play and early childhood education: Connections, implications and assessment. *Early Childhood Education Journal, 37*(5), 351–361.

Rodesiler, C., & McGuire, J. (2015). Ideas in practice: Professional development to promote universal design for instruction. *Journal of Developmental Education, 38*(2), 24–31.

Story, M. (2010). Maximizing usability: The principles of universal design. *Assistive Technology, 10*(1), 4–12.

Taylor, A., Wiley, A., Kuo, F., & Sullivan, W. (1998). Growing up in the inner city: Green spaces as places to grow. *Environments and Behaviour, 30*(1), 3–27.

Strong-Wilson, T., & Ellis, J. (2007). Children and place: Reggio Emilia's environment as third teacher. *Theory Into Practice, 46*(1), 40–47. https://doi.org/10.1207/s15430421tip4601_6.

Creating the Third Teacher Through Participatory Learning Environment Design: Reggio Emilia Principles Support Student Wellbeing

Vanessa Miller

Abstract Early childhood educators in the municipal schools of Reggio Emilia (Italy) recognise the potential of the learning environment acting as a 'third teacher' to promote student learning and wellbeing. This chapter presents essential understandings and a new practice framework that draws upon the author's participatory action research findings and Reggio Emilia principles. It suggests an evidence-based model for teachers and students to co-create student-friendly spaces that are conducive to contemporary socially engaged learning.

Introduction

Participatory designing offers a holistic approach to promoting student learning and wellbeing. Increasingly, studies have demonstrated the value of seeking teachers' and children's points of view in the school design process (Arnot & Reay, 2007), with reported benefits including increased student wellbeing, engagement and motivation (Rudduck & McIntyre, 2007), improved academic performance (Blackmore, Bateman, Loughlin, O'Mara & Aranda, 2011a), improvement in the design quality of the school (Woolner et al., 2010), increased understanding about the complexity of the role of the teacher (Dudek, 2000), and a shared sense of ownership amongst users of the facility (OECD, 2017). Such studies reflect an increasing acknowledgement of the capability of young people to form and freely express their own views in matters that affect them, as upheld by Article 12 of the United Nations *Convention on the rights of the child* (1989). Therefore, this chapter aims to extend knowledge about the role schools have in promoting the wellbeing of their students (Urbis, 2011), through various co-curricular educational programs designed to cater for different aspects of children's physical and socio-emotional wellbeing (Farrell, 2008; Queensland Government, 2008).

This chapter illustrates the wellbeing-related potential of participatory designing, as revealed through my doctoral research: *Teachers creating the third teacher: An*

V. Miller (✉)
Queensland University of Technology, Brisbane, Australia
e-mail: vanessamiller8@gmail.com

© Springer Nature Singapore Pte Ltd. 2019   239
H. Hughes et al. (eds.), *School Spaces for Student Wellbeing and Learning*,
https://doi.org/10.1007/978-981-13-6092-3_13

action research approach to learning environment design (Miller, 2017). The study was informed conceptually by Reggio Emilia principles, in particular, the notion that the physical learning environment has the capacity to engage students as a *third teacher*. The study's aim was to understand how a participatory designing process may support teachers in creating learning environments conducive to contemporary pedagogical approaches such as inquiry-based learning. Thus, the study explored taken-for-granted processes and practices that may inhibit the potential for educational spaces to support innovative pedagogy. In keeping with the participatory focus of the research, I undertook participatory action research (PAR) with three teachers. To gain insider perspectives on participatory designing, I used the Mosaic designing approach (Clark, 2017) and the VAST evaluative framework (Elliott Burns, 2016) as mediating tools for teacher encounters that involved collaboration, exchanging ideas, gaining insights and learning through the designing process. The findings and my literature review highlight the need for a theoretically informed participatory process to support teachers and their students as learning space designers in the creation of transformative learning environments. As shown, mediated participation and user engagement in all stages of the design and construction process enable the achievement of local needs and individualised design solutions.

In this chapter, I share the story of three primary school teachers' experiences as they enlisted the support of their students as co-designers to enhance the Kindergarten, Year 1 and Year 5 learning environments in which they practice. The first section reviews the literature related to learning environment, participatory design principles and process, and innovative practice. The second section outlines the aim and implementation of the study, which combined participatory action research (PAR), the Mosaic approach and Reggio Emilia principles; and it describes how three teachers engaged in a series of action research cycles with their students to transform an indoor or an outdoor space into an environment conducive to inquiry-based learning. Next, I present the study's key findings before introducing a new practice framework for supporting participatory designing of learning environments for primary school communities. This framework integrates a shared vision of designing, learning and the principles of Reggio Emilia. Thus, it offers an authentic approach to enhancing student wellbeing through teachers and students co-creating spaces conducive to contemporary socially engaged learning.

Literature Review

The study was underpinned by several inter-related concepts, which this literature review discusses, namely, *Participatory pedagogical practice, learning environments, participatory design principles, and participatory design process*. Here, participatory pedagogical practice is associated with the Reggio Emilia approach to designing and using learning environments that embody the concept of *the third teacher*. Participatory design principles inform the creation of learning environments through a participatory design processes. Thus, teachers as designers are at the heart of the participatory designing process.

Participatory Pedagogical Practice: Reggio Emilia

The Reggio Emilia educational project is a cooperative of schools for young children run by a community of parents and teachers in Northern Italy. Its design principles and pedagogical approach arose initially from sustained collaboration in teaching and learning processes between Professor Loris Malaguzzi and the 'teachers, *pedagogistas* (pedagogical coordinators) and *atelieristas* (art studio teachers) in the schools' (Giamminuti, n.d., p. 3). According to Gandini (2012), the Reggio Emilia project is not intended as a model to imitate, but rather as a provocation for thought and change. A complex and symbiotic relationship exists between the learning environment and pedagogy. The environment acts as a 'container' that holds 'educational content' or 'educational messages' (Gandini, 2012, p. 320), which are the 'the ideas, values, attitudes, and cultures of the people who live within it' (p. 339). Concurring with the view, others also consider the ability of the learning environment to communicate underlying pedagogical values and beliefs of the people who inhabit the space (Wall, 2015; Woolner, Thomas & Tiplady, 2018).

Learning Environments

Learning environments include social, cultural, temporal, physical (built and natural) and virtual aspects (Blackmore et al., 2011a). Learning environments are often claimed to influence learning outcomes, although the relationship is complex and the evidence is inconclusive. However, the physical learning environment can shape relationships and create the conditions for physical and mental wellbeing that are conducive to learning (Blackmore et al., 2011a). Further, the physical design, layout, and use of schools play a role in transmitting social and educational values (Wall, 2015).

Reggio Emilia educators have long recognised the importance of simultaneously considering the design and the use of the physical environment to promote learning, and they acknowledge the symbiotic and complex set of relationships that exist between the environment, the student and the teacher (Rinaldi, 2006). The environment as *third teacher* metaphor is a key Reggio Emilia principle (Rinaldi, 2006; Strong-Wilson & Ellis, 2007). Reggio Emilia educators in some municipal preschools (3–6 years) and infant–toddler centres (0–3 years) use this term to describe the potential for communication, encounters, and relationships within aesthetically designed and organised classroom learning environments. Highlighting how the environment communicates meaning, Gandini (2012, p. 326) suggested '…space offers a strong possibility to let people who enter the schools know about the care teachers have for the wellbeing and learning of young children'.

The physical environments of schools designed according to Reggio Emilia principles are highly aesthetic and invitational for children (Fraser, 2006). The aim of the architectural design of the infant–toddler centres is 'to create amiable spaces … that guarantee the wellbeing of children and teachers as they construct learning together' (Fraser, 2006, p. 323). To this end, the spaces are designed to welcome families and 'become reference points for the community' for meetings and other events (Gandini, 2012, p. 323). Suggestive of the complex interaction between learners and their environments, Rinaldi (2006, p. 80) indicated 'architecture is not the assembling of spaces, it involves a philosophy, a way of thinking about education, learning, the teaching/learning relationship, the role of action and doing in the construction of knowledge'.

Participatory Design Principles

Participatory design involves the engagement of key stakeholders with the principles of contemporary learning environment design, reflecting the nuances of the individual learner and knowledge areas. In this study, the term is used to describe a process to support teachers in creating learning environments conducive to inquiry-based learning. This study explored the process of teachers and their students imagining, and also acting on what they imagined, and how it led to a greater sense of agency, that is, their 'ability to exert control over and give direction to one's life' (Biesta & Tedder, 2007, p. 134). Further, the process of exploring and designing new possibilities for physical learning spaces was transformative in creating 'disruption, challenge and change' (Willis, 2016, p. 83).

The educational project of Reggio Emilia exemplifies participatory designing. It offers a set of evidence-based learning and spatial principles that characterise its pedagogical philosophy. These principles are both informed by and inform research and practice of learning environment design and contemporary pedagogical approaches such as inquiry-based learning.

The Reggio Emilia approach regards participation as the 'value and the strategy that defines the way in which the children, the educators, and the parents are stakeholders in the educational project… as participation gives value to and makes use of the hundred languages of children, and is viewed as plurality of points of view and cultures' (Reggio Children, 2010, p. 11). The invitation to democratic participation which is extended to children, parents, teachers and the wider community is 'a central value and integral to the educational experience' (Rinaldi, 2006, p. 11). Through participation, the municipal schools have 'provided new sites for democratic politics, while at the same time extending the scope of politics to new areas' (Rinaldi, 2006, p. 11). Thus, designing school learning spaces is 'a political as well as creative activity' (Willis, 2016, p. 83).

These progressive democratic principles offer inspiration and insight for participatory designing through a socially constructivist approach which encourages teachers to critically examine the pedagogic values and beliefs that inform their practice. In this way, the learning and design principles that underpin the educational project of Reggio Emilia are a 'constant source of provocation' for educators as they engage with others in an 'in-depth dialogue between the pedagogical and architectural languages' (Rinaldi, 2006, p. 80). The Reggio Emilia participatory approach has the potential to be a catalyst for deeper teacher reflection leading to pedagogical change:

> what we are talking about is not the application of some finalised model, universal in scope and definitive in nature, but rather the adoption of a process of questioning, dialogue, reflection and meaning making which leads we know not where and has no obvious end point: it is work continuously in progress. (Dahlberg, Moss, & Pence, 2007, p. 16)

Participatory Design Process

The participatory design process allows people of various backgrounds to have a say in the built environments that are created for their use. Therefore, the participation of teachers and students in all stages of the designing process is most effective for creating innovative school environments (Clark, 2017; Dudek, 2000; Flutter, 2006; Willis, Bland, Hughes & Elliott Burns, 2013). Teachers and their students are well positioned to inform the design of learning environments as 'they notice the physical environment and develop opinions about it which influence their attitudes and views to the learning experience as a whole' (Woolner et al., 2010, p. 2). As Nixon and Comber (2011) suggest, students and teachers can provide significant insights through their experiences of learning environments, which enable their democratic participation as end-users.

There are many approaches to participatory design in schools that involve the users' direct involvement in the design and decision-making process (Arnot & Reay, 2007; Clark, 2017; Flutter, 2006; Woolner et al., 2010). In this study, the Mosaic approach (Clark, 2017) and the VAST heuristic (Elliott Burns, 2011, 2016) enabled me to gain 'insider perspectives' (Clark, 2011, p. 311) of teachers, and facilitated the participatory design process. For example, the Mosaic approach captured teachers' authentic voices, and made visible their knowledge and experiences as learning space designers (Clark, 2011). In this way, participatory methods help by 'facilitating the process of knowledge production as opposed to knowledge 'gathering', as is the case with methods such as individual interviews, surveys and checklists' (Veale, 2005; p. 254).

As highlighted in this study, the participation of key stakeholders in the design and use of learning environments is not without its challenges, especially with regard to consultation (Woolner, McCarter, Wall & Higgins, 2012). Some of these challenges include: investment in lead time for project planning (Bland, Hughes & Willis, 2013); readiness of an institution to research and evaluate the 'values-foundation of the educational organisation' (for example, pedagogy, timetables, policies, professional learning opportunities) and the time taken to understand the values and needs of all key stakeholders (Elliott Burns, 2016, p. 194); and associated tensions between co-participants in the design process. Whilst the benefits of end-user participation in learning space design are well known, students and teachers as key stakeholders are rarely consulted about the learning spaces they inhabit (Rudduck & McIntyre, 2007). As a result, 'student voice is confined to school management matters and opportunities for students to participate in more transformative action such as issues of pedagogy and whole school reform are less common' (Bland & Atweh, 2007, p. 340).

Research Gap

Despite a range of well developed spatial design principles and frameworks for professional designers (for example, Lippman, 2010; Nair, Fielding & Lackney, 2009) there is an apparent lack of practice-based guides for school leaders and teachers about undertaking projects to enhance their school learning environments. In her review of commercial publications designed to support stakeholders in the school planning process, Elliott Burns (2011, p. 109) indicated that few publications 'cite supporting evidence or refer to evaluative studies of their own design recommendations, nor do they explore exemplar cases to discuss the impacts of their recommendations on student learning'.

Research Design

Responding to the research gap identified above, I undertook this participatory action research (PAR) study over a six-month-period in 2015. By limiting the focus to the experiences of three primary school teachers, I was able to capture and render meaning to what they said and did as a product of how they understood the events within their world at a particular time and in a particular context (Lincoln & Guba, 1985). At the same time, I came to understand how their spaces both shape them and are shaped by them (Crotty, 1998).

PAR Approach

The study followed the cyclical PAR process of Plan-Act-Observe-Reflect (Zuber-Skerritt, 2001) and involved a close collaborative relationship between myself as lead researcher and three teachers as co-researchers. Embedded in the study were transformative mini PAR projects by the three participant teachers who worked with their students to design a learning space conducive to inquiry-based learning.

Responding to the need for a variety of visual tools to facilitate the participation of teachers (as well as students) in the design process (Woolner et al., 2012), we used the tools of the Mosaic approach (Clark, 2011, 2017) to mediate our encounters and support data collection and analysis. This involved teachers in evaluative *tours* of their current learning environments; *map making* to represent the findings of their tour as a basis for planning their transformation projects; and *meaning making* to review the outcomes of their projects. The data collection methods included interviews, observations, photography and reflective writing. In this way, the study created opportunities for teachers to make visible their knowledge and experiences as learning space designers.

Co-researchers

In this PAR project, I positioned myself as an integral part of the research process and product, while seeking to maintain the teachers' authentic participation. Following PAR practice, I developed a close collaborative relationship with the teachers, remaining responsive to their needs by assuming multiple roles as lead researcher, *pedagogista*, and co-researcher (Rinaldi, 2006, p. x). As lead researcher, I scaffolded and guided the participatory design process. This included the facilitation and gathering of data through a series of focus groups, classroom observations, and individual meetings with teachers. As co-researcher, I remained a critical, subjective participant who brought skills, experiences and an interest in the change process by discussing changes and offering suggestions throughout focus groups.

My role as *pedagogista* aligned with underlying principles of the educational project of Reggio Emilia by providing pedagogical support and leadership to the participant teachers as they carried out their individual PAR projects. This included providing verbal support during focus groups and individual meetings, and written encouragement through notes and emails. To support their understanding of the PAR process and design principles, I also provided participant teachers with reading resources (for example, education and learning environment design books, architectural magazines, links to websites, and research articles). As a critical friend, I mentored the teachers and provided an outsider's perspective.

Research Implementation: Bringing Learning Spaces to Life

The impetus for the study was the principal's desire for contemporary learning environments, coupled with the participant teachers' desire to explore alternative classroom designs conducive to inquiry-based learning. During my project proposal meetings with school leaders in March 2015, the principal explained that the Kindergarten and Year One teachers had expressed a shared concern about the limited space in their classrooms, wondering 'How can we make the Kindergarten and Year One building a more usable space?' When I probed further about his aspirations, the principal said that he hoped the participatory design project would promote discussion amongst staff about the current use of their learning environments and he posed this provocation: 'How can teachers take the spaces they currently inhabit and bring these to life?'

The school principal's personification of the environment as 'having life' is a view also shared by the educators in Reggio Emilia (Strong-Wilson & Ellis, 2007). Although the school leaders made no reference to the education or design principles of Reggio Emilia during our meeting, the design of the school's new contemporary building reflected many of these principles, including teacher collaboration, dedicated art spaces, student-centred learning, connecting indoor and outdoor learning environments, and collaborative learning.

PAR Enacted

Adopting cyclical PAR process of Plan-Act-Observe-Reflect, the three teachers and I engaged in reflective action to instigate change in learning environments (Zuber-Skerritt, 2001). *Reflection* denoted a key phase in the PAR cycle and also contributed to the co-researchers' practice. Through reflection I remained aware of my contribution to the construction of meanings throughout the research process as the lead researcher and co-participant. To make explicit how my understandings were formed, and what 'pieces of the world' I brought with me, I wrote field notes and a reflective research journal. These assisted me in recording and making sense of the teachers' experiences as designers, as they engaged with their students in the co-designing process. In addition, the teachers wrote reflective journals to record key actions, thoughts and feelings throughout the course of the project. Thus, we were able to holistically observe changes over time, in our cognitive and affective responses and our practice.

The project's four stages all centred around a series of PAR cycles. In the first phase the teachers formulated a general plan to evaluate their current practice and determine their ideal learning environment. They also began planning their own learning environment transformation projects. In the second PAR phase, the teachers carried out their transformation projects with their students. For example, the Year One students undertook a project to research and create a frog pond that would enhance the outdoor environment near their classroom and invigorate their inquiry about life cycles. The completed Frog Hotel represented the student's intention to design a safe habitat for frogs and other animals. In the third PAR phase, the teachers and I evaluated the process and outcomes of the transformation projects. We also reflected on the whole PAR process and identified further research and practice needs. Figure 1 below, shows the iterative PAR model (Zuber-Skerritt, 2001) that directed the project.

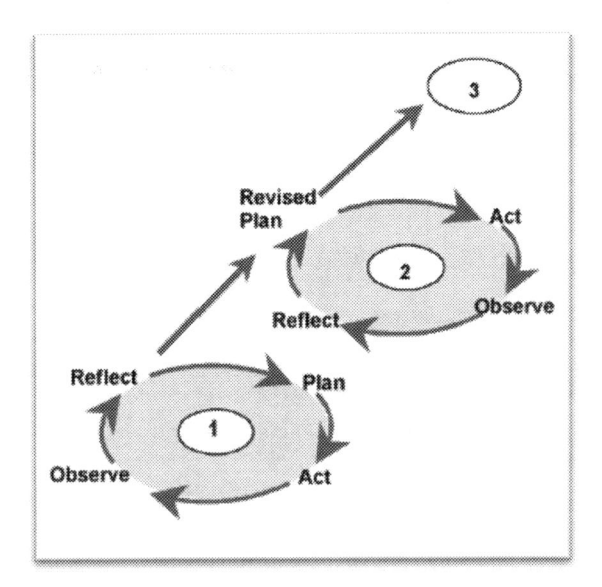

Fig. 1 The spiral of action research cycles From 'Action Learning and Action Research: Paradigm, Praxis and Programs', by O. Zuber-Skerritt, in S. Sankaran, B. Dick, R. Passfield, & P. Swepson, (Eds.), *Effective Change Management Using Action Research and Action Learning: Concepts, Frameworks, Processes and Applications* (p. 15), 2001, Lismore, Australia: Southern Cross University Press. (Reproduced with permission of Ortun Zuber-Skerritt and Bob Dick)

The Mosaic Approach

This study integrated the Mosaic approach which comprises three activities: Tour, map and meaning making (Clark, 2017). The 'multi-method, polyvocal approach' (Clark, 2017, p. 17) was first developed to listen to the views and experiences of young children under five and subsequently adapted to work with adults. This approach provided structural and conceptual support in various ways and at different phases of the project. It allowed me to use a range of participatory methods that included visual methods, such as digital photography and map making, and the more traditional qualitative methods of observation, focus group interviews and reflective journal writing.

Tour

Following the Mosaic approach, the teachers first undertook a tour of their respective learning environments. The teachers documented what was important to them through photographs, sketches and written notes, and they evaluated their learning environments using the VAST heuristic (Elliott Burns, 2016). The VAST heuristic is a self-questioning device that supports an 'interrogative, participative exploratory approach' to learning space evaluation and designing (Elliott Burns, 2011, p. 254). It draws upon the work of Tom Heath (2010). VAST is an acronym that represents four key aspects to be considered when evaluating a built space, namely: Values, Activities, Site/System and Technology. The underpinning thesis is that 'people have Values, in relation to aspects [Activities] of buildings [Site/System] which must be expressed in built form [Technology]' (Elliott Burns, 2016, p. 197). It supports the proposition that designing involves a creative process of problem-solving, evidence gathering and discovery.

Visual Data

In line with the Mosaic approach, digital photography provided an important source of visual data arising from the teachers' tour and my own observation (Clark, 2017). We took photographs of indoor and outdoor learning environments before, during, and after the teachers' individual PAR projects to visually record design changes made throughout the project. I drew a layout of each teacher's classroom during my initial observation and used this to select photo spots for my observations. I deliberately selected vantage points that were unobtrusive and from where I could clearly observe the teacher and students. During the observation period, I maintained a written digital photo-log and noted changes over time in my researcher journal. In this study, taking and viewing photographs enabled the teachers to identify important things, spaces and people. Photographs and sketches were used in this study to explore the perspectives of teachers as they considered their current and future learning environments.

Map Making

Following the tours, the teachers and I met to discuss the spaces they had chosen to photograph. Then, using their tour photos they created individual maps to illustrate the least and most preferred aspects of their learning environments, as shown below in Figs. 2, 3 and 4.

The aim of the map making was twofold for the teachers: to visually document their learning environments; and to provide an opportunity to reflect on their experiences of being in these environments. Thus, like mirrors, the maps reflected the experiences of the teachers and became a form of documentation which made visible the teachers' values and teaching practices.

Meaning Making

Meaning making (Clark, 2017) involved the participants in using their maps to reflect on what was of value to them in their learning environments, and to consider their experience of being in them. The maps became a tool for mediating knowledge as

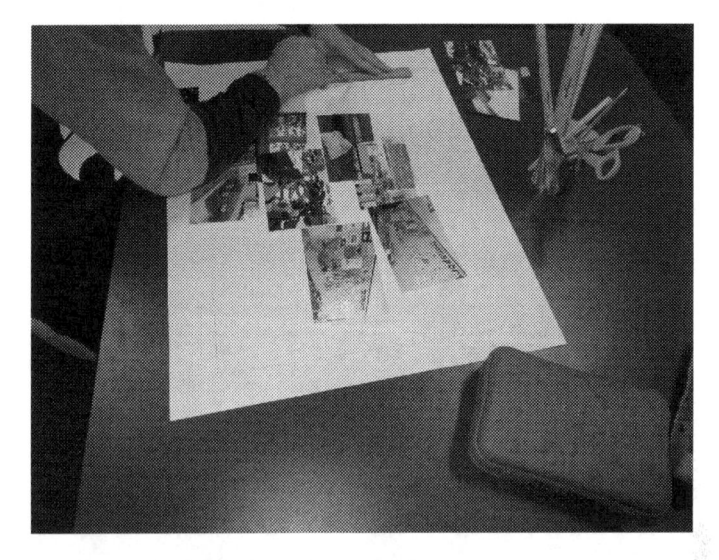

Fig. 2 Teacher's map of their learning environment (1)

Fig. 3 Teacher's map of their learning environment (2)

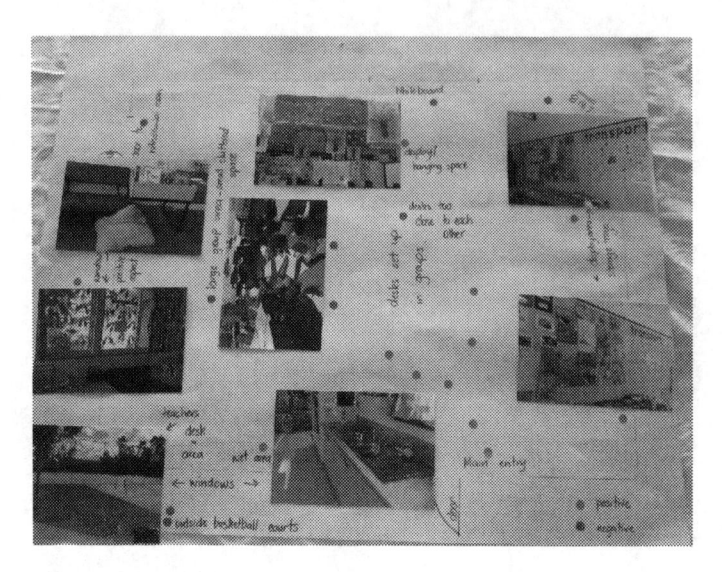

Fig. 4 Teacher's map of their learning environment (3)

teachers discussed their selection process and placement of photos on the maps. In addition, the maps became a tangible focus for meaning making, enabling teachers to co-construct knowledge and develop a set of shared meanings about their preferred and least preferred learning environments. Thus, the meaning making was a participatory, democratic process that led to values-based judgment (Dahlberg et al., 2007). Teachers' findings from the tour, map making and meaning making underpinned their subsequent learning environment design projects with their own students.

Essential Understandings

An account of the whole project and full findings, illustrated with photographs, drawings and participants' reflective comments, can be explored in my thesis (Miller, 2017). The following section discusses four Essential Understandings that emerged through the study and which relate to:

- The complexity of participatory designing for learning environments
- The dynamic nature of the participatory designing process
- The transformative potential of the participatory designing process
- The importance of teachers' professional learning to support the participatory designing process

These understandings show how participatory designing can be a creative problem-solving experience for teachers that build trust and authentic relationships, where opinions can be expressed and views explored (Clark, 2017), while also contributing to student wellbeing.

Essential Understanding 1: The Complexity of Participatory Designing for Learning Environments

As the study's findings indicate, participatory designing is a complex process. This is revealed through the participants' thoughts and feelings about their preferred and less preferred spatial features and imaginings of ideal spaces. It was also evident in the ways they addressed learning environment design challenges and opportunities. These responses are useful because they help to understand the potential challenges experienced by teachers and students in their current learning environments and can serve as a catalyst for future spatial and pedagogical change. Viewed respectively from the participants' perspectives as practicing teachers and learning space designers, the study's findings concur with other research which reveals that designing contemporary learning environments is complex (Blackmore et al., 2011b; Fisher, 2016; Woolner et al., 2018). These findings correspond with those of Cleveland (2011) and others (for example, Flutter, 2006) who found that spatial redesign catalysed a process of re-visioning pedagogical practice which led school leaders to broaden their thinking regarding new education frameworks.

Essential Understanding 2: The Dynamic Nature of the Participatory Designing Process

The study also shows participatory designing to be a dynamic process. By nature this process is disruptive, authentic and theoretically based. The findings illustrate how the teachers' authenticity, trust and collaboration developed through the PAR process and enabled the teachers to question and 'make visible' (Rinaldi, 2006, p. 68) their taken-for-granted practices of teaching and learning that may inhibit the potential for educational spaces to influence student learning. Disruption created by teachers' participation in the learning environment design process was essential for growth and change in thinking and practice. In this way, the physical setting offered a 'visible and tangible focus for reflection on existing practices' (Woolner et al., 2018, p. 237).

By adopting a reflective process, the teachers became aware of the changes that had occurred in their thinking and this flowed onto their awareness of changes that could occur in their spatial practices. The reflective nature of participatory designing enabled the teachers to move beyond 'taken-for-granted' that may be so 'ingrained in practice that they are invisible to those using them' (Woolner et al., 2012, p. 58) and that may inhibit the potential for educational spaces to influence student learning.

Further, the participatory designing process enabled their continuous examination of pedagogic values and beliefs about their image of children, and their role as teachers.

Combined use of PAR, Mosaic and the VAST evaluative tool mediated the teachers' encounters and supported innovation and learning through the designing process. This dynamic process helped the teachers clarify their sense of purpose and led to empowerment. It influenced a shift in the value systems through which the teachers framed their understanding about teaching and learning, as a basis to bring about spatial and pedagogical change.

Essential Understanding 3: The Transformative Potential of the Participatory Designing Process

The study's findings revealed the potential of the participatory designing process to be transformative as teachers modify and adapt their thinking and practice in the new learning environments. The findings also highlight the array of strengths and challenges that teachers experience in this transformative process through engaging in a reflective approach with their students to re-imagine and plan for changes in pedagogy and learning space design. As in similar studies, the participatory designing process enabled the reappraisal of teaching practice and the learning setting (Woolner et al., 2012), and the 'possibility of change, without imposing an ideological viewpoint which is unlikely to influence subsequent behaviours and activities' (Woolner et al., 2012, p. 58). Supporting this understanding, the study provided evidence of teachers' and students' transformative capabilities as vernacular designers and supports the need to involve teachers and students as key stakeholders in the designing process to achieve positive change in the learning environment (Blackmore et al., 2011a; Bland et al., 2013; Rinaldi, 2006; Woolner et al., 2012).

For this study, the VAST heuristic (Elliott Burns, 2016), PAR (Zuber-Skerritt, 2001), and Mosaic approach (Clark, 2017) provided a framework for participant teachers to engage in learning that included challenging traditional assumptions and learning new practices (Willis et al., 2013). In particular, the VAST heuristic (Elliot Burns, 2016) supported the transformative process as a values-based evaluative design framework that has the potential to enable the sharing of beliefs to 'create new norms of action' necessary for pedagogic change to occur (Opfer & Pedder, 2011, p. 392). Use of this framework enabled the transformative process of redesigning the physical learning environment as it 'provoked disequilibrium, but also enabled experimentation' (Willis et al., 2013, p. 5).

Essential Understanding 4: Importance of Teachers' Professional Learning to Support the Participatory Designing Process

This study highlighted the importance of preparing teachers in the design and use of new learning environments through ongoing professional learning, to ensure they can participate at various stages in the design, transition to, and occupation of new learning environments (Blackmore et al., 2011a; Wilks, 2010). It also revealed that the participatory designing process offers teachers a form of contextualised professional learning through critical reflection and sharing their design ideas and experiences. Thus it offers the benefit of 'job-embedded' learning that is 'in-depth, content focused, collaborative, and encouraging of reflective thinking' (Newmann, King & Youngs, 2000).

A Participatory Designing Process to Support Teachers as Designers of Contemporary Learning Environments

The literature and the findings of this study (Miller, 2017) highlight the need for a theoretically informed participatory process for creating learning environments that are conducive to contemporary learning approaches. Teachers (along with their students) are principal stakeholders in learning environments, and need sound yet flexible guidelines to support transformative learning environment designing. Such support is vital as teachers seldom have formal training or experience in design. Therefore, the following conceptual model and practice framework aim to support teachers' understanding of and engagement in the participatory designing process for school learning environments.

Conceptual Model of the Participatory Designing Process for School Learning Environments

Based on the study's findings, the model shown in Fig. 5 illustrates how teachers can bring about transformative outcomes through the participatory designing process. The model represents a process that leads to new ways of learning and teaching, with the arrows indicating the progression from voluntary participation, through end-user involvement, to growth and change.

As shown above, enactment of this process depends upon the *voluntary participation of teachers* and their commitment to *growth*. Through engagement with new concepts, they can develop a designerly *mindset* with which to bring about changes in learning environment and pedagogy. As *end-users* they are key stakeholders in the *participatory designing process,* which requires ongoing *professional learning,*

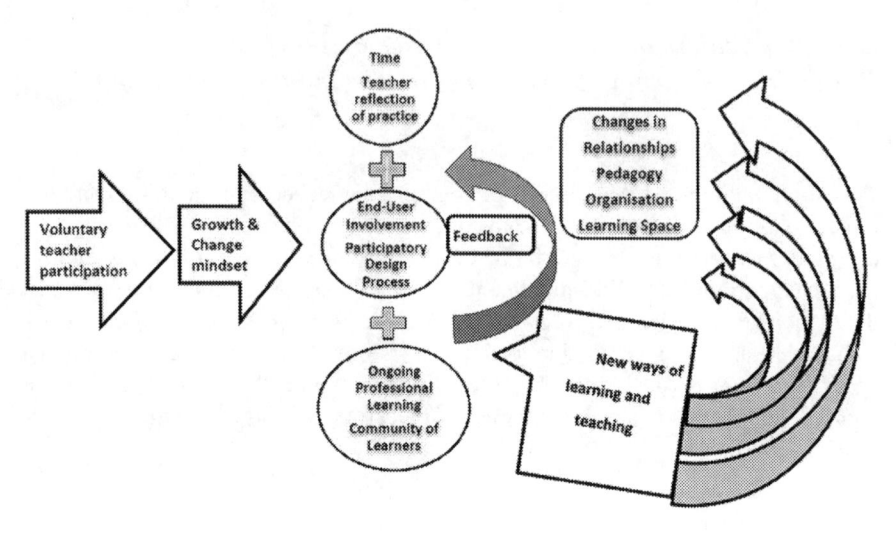

Fig. 5 Evidence-based model for engaging teachers and their students in creating the third teacher learning environment designing projects

including membership in a *professional learning community*, and time for *reflection* on their practice. These conditions support a designing approach that brings about transformation in *learning spaces* and *pedagogy* which are expressed in changes in teachers' *learning and teaching* practices.

Practice Framework Incorporating Reggio Emilia Principles

The above model supports the development of a practice framework to support participatory designing of learning environments that involves teachers and students. While the framework is informed by the study's findings (Miller, 2017), it also incorporates principles of the Reggio Emilia education project which promote student wellbeing through the creation of child-friendly, aesthetically and educationally conducive environments. As demonstrated in my review of the literature and observed during my own professional visits to Reggio Emilia, these principles have the potential to support the design of transformative learning environments. Therefore, this framework adopts the emphasis that educators in Reggio Emilia place on their image of children and their own role as teachers. This 'seamless and symbiotic relationship' (Gardner, 1998, p. xvi) between pedagogic values and teaching practice enables the learning environment to play a significant role as 'third teacher' (Rinaldi, 2006; Strong-Wilson & Ellis, 2007).

Table 1 below introduces the proposed framework, with the new participatory guidelines shown in the right-hand column. It shows how concepts associated with the study's findings (in the left column) align with relevant Reggio Emilia principles

Table 1 Practice framework to support participatory designing of learning environments

Key findings (Miller, 2017)	Reggio Emilia principles	Participatory designing guidelines
Complexity of teacher's role: Strengths and challenges	Child as collaborator Child as communicator	Engage students in the design and use of learner-centred, flexible and dynamic educational environments, adaptable to suit a range of learning and teaching approaches
Disruption	Progettazione Documentation	Undertake ongoing evaluation and (re) designing of learning environment using VAST heuristic and Mosaic tour and mapping
Participation and sharing	Participation Collaboration Hundred languages of children Pedagogy of relationships and learning	Undertake PAR projects to explore the transformed learning environment. Attend to all stakeholder voices including student' voices through Mosaic methods
Learning and design principles	Collaboration Environment as 'third teacher' Pedagogy of relationships and learning Documentation Hundred languages of children	Develop a contextualised learning environment design framework based on agreed set of education and design principles, reflective of the changes over time in the pedagogical function and sustainability of the learning environment
Professional learning needs	Teacher professional learning	Design and support a professional learning approach responsive to the needs of teachers to enable their effective use of the physical instructional space for a pedagogical advantage
Catalytic effect	Environment as 'third teacher' Pedagogy of relationships and learning	Create opportunities for ongoing teacher reflection and collaboration through professional learning communities, sharing new learning within and outside of the school community
PAR, Mosaic and VAST support participatory designing	Participation Collaboration Hundred languages of children Pedagogy of relationships and learning	Engage teachers and students in the co-design of learning environments using PAR, and the tools of the Mosaic and VAST to support the participatory design process

(middle column) and how the findings and principles underpin participatory design guidelines. As indicated, the guidelines also draw upon the PAR process (Zuber-Skerritt, 2001) and Mosaic approach (Clark, 2017) modeled in this study.

Conclusion

The study *Creating the third teacher* (Miller, 2017) provided an opportunity to interrogate and apply a participatory process to learning environment designing in an Australian context. Informed by the principles of the educational project of Reggio Emilia, in particular, the concept of the *third teacher*, it explored the potential of learning environments to support student learning (Rinaldi, 2006; Strong-Wilson & Ellis, 2007). The three teachers' stories of engaging with their students in a participatory designing process, and emergent essential understandings, demonstrate how educators as vernacular designers can contribute to the creation of transformative learning environments. The study's findings provide a foundation for further research and a framework for innovative practice that focuses on the learning environment's role as *third teacher*. They also highlight the catalytic effect of participatory designing on pedagogy through changes to the learning environment which provoke teachers to modify their thinking and practice. Therefore, the process and outcomes of participatory designing underpinned by Reggio Emilia principles in a school context can enhance the wellbeing of students.

Acknowledgements This article draws upon my completed doctoral research. It received ethics clearance from the Queensland University of Technology Ethics Committee (Ethics approval: 1500000390) and written consent from the principal and the three participant teachers at the school.

References

Arnot, M., & Reay, D. (2007). A sociology of pedagogic voice: Power, inequality and pupil consultation. *Discourse: Studies in the Cultural Politics of Education, 28*(3), 311–325. https://doi.org/10.1080/01596300701458814.

Biesta, G., & Tedder, M. (2007). Agency and learning in the lifecourse: Towards an ecological perspective. *Studies in the Education of Adults, 39*(2), 132–149.

Blackmore, J., Bateman, D., Loughlin, J., O'Mara, J., & Aranda, G. (2011a). *Research into the connection between built learning spaces and student outcomes: Literature review.* Melbourne, Vic: Victorian Department of Education and Early Childhood Development.

Blackmore, J., Bateman, D., Cloonan, A., Dixon, M., Loughlin, J., O'Mara, J., & Senior, K. (2011b). *Innovative learning environments research study.* Melbourne, Vic: Deakin University. Retrieved from http://www.learningspaces.edu.au/about.php.

Bland, D., & Atweh, B. (2007). Students as researchers: Engaging students' voices in PAR. *Educational Action Research, 15*(3), 337–349. https://doi.org/10.1080/09650790701514259.

Bland, D., Hughes, H., & Willis, J. (2013). *Reimagining learning spaces: A research report for the Queensland Council for Social Science Innovation.* Queensland University of Technology, Brisbane. Retrieved from http://eprints.qut.edu.au/63000/.

Clark, A. (2011). Breaking methodological boundaries? Exploring visual, participatory methods with adults and young children. *European Early Childhood Education Research Journal, 19*(3), 321–330. https://doi.org/10.1080/1350293X.2011.597964.

Clark, A. (2017). *Listening to Young children: A guide to understanding and using the Mosaic approach* (3rd ed.). London: Jessica Kingsley.

Cleveland, B. W. (2011). *Engaging spaces: Innovative learning environments, pedagogies and student engagement in the middle years of school.* (PhD thesis.) The University of Melbourne. Retrieved from https://pdfs.semanticscholar.org/e602/1e9e1df68311a7374a600c9ec3fb69a9b700.pdf.

Crotty, M. (1998). *The foundations of social research: Meaning and perspective in the research process.* London: Sage.

Dahlberg, G., Moss, P., & Pence, A. (2007). *Beyond quality in early childhood education and care: Languages of evaluation* (2nd ed.). London: Routledge.

Dudek, M. (2000). *Architecture of schools: The new learning environments.* Oxford: Architectural Press.

Elliott Burns, R. A. (2011). *Voices of experience: Opportunities to influence creatively the designing of school libraries.* (Doctoral dissertation). QUT, Brisbane. Retrieved from http://eprints.qut.edu.au/48974/.

Elliott Burns, R, A. (2016). Voices of experience: Opportunities to influence creatively the designing of school libraries. In K. Fisher (Ed.), *The translational design of schools: An evidence-based approach to aligning pedagogy and learning environments in schools* (pp. 195–213). Amsterdam, Netherlands: Sense Publishing.

Farrell, A. F. (2008). Building schoolwide positive behaviour supports. In R. W. Christner & R. B. Mennuti (Eds.), *School-Based Mental Health: A practitioner's guide to comparative practices* (pp. 87–124). London: Taylor & Francis.

Fisher, K. (2016). *The translational design of schools: An evidence-based approach to aligning pedagogy and learning environments.* Rotterdam: Sense Publishers.

Flutter, J. (2006). This place could help you learn: Student participation in creating better school environments. *Educational Review, 58*(2), 183–193. https://doi.org/10.1080/00131910600584116.

Fraser, S. (2006). *Authentic childhood: Experiencing Reggio Emilia in the setting.* Toronto, Canada: Thomson Nelson.

Gandini, L. (2012). Connecting through caring and learning spaces. In C. Edwards, L. Gandini, & G. Forman (Eds.), *The hundred languages of children: The Reggio Emilia experience in transformation* (pp. 317–341). (3rd ed.). Santa Barbara, CA: Praeger.

Gardner, H. (1998). Foreword: Complementary perspectives on Reggio Emilia. In C. Edwards, L. Gandini, & G. Forman (Eds.), *The hundred languages of children: The Reggio approach—Advanced reflections* (p. xvi). Greenwich, CT: Ablex Publishing.

Giamminuti, S. (n.d.). *Documentation as a tool for co-constructing situated communities of learners: A case study of early years educational environments in Reggio Emilia and Western Australia.* (PhD Research Proposal). Retrieved from http://www.web.uwa.edu.au.

Heath, T. (2010). *Learning architecture, teaching architecture: A guide for the perplexed.* Brisbane, Qld.: Denarius Design Books.

Lincoln, Y., & Guba, E. (1985). *Naturalistic inquiry.* Newbury Park, California: Sage.

Lippman, P. C. (2010). *Evidence-based design of elementary and secondary schools: A responsive approach to creating learning environments.* New York: John Wiley.

Miller, V. (2017). *Teachers creating the third teacher: An action research approach to learning environment design.* (Doctoral dissertation). QUT, Brisbane. Retrieved from https://eprints.qut.edu.au/view/person/Miller,_Vanessa.html.

Nair, P., Fielding, R., & Lackney, J. A. (2009). *The language of school design: Design patterns for 21st century schools* (Rev ed.). Minneapolis, Minn: DesignShare.

Newmann, F. M., King, M. B., & Youngs, P. (2000). Professional development that addresses school capacity: Lessons from urban elementary schools. *American Journal of Education, 108*(4), 259–299. https://doi.org/10.1086/444249.

Nixon, H., & Comber, B. (2011). Redesigning school spaces: Creating possibilities for learning. In J. Sefton-Green, P. Thomson, L. Bresler, & K. Jones (Eds.), *The Routledge international handbook of creative learning* (pp. 253–263). London: Taylor & Francis.

OECD. (2017). *The OECD handbook for innovative learning environments*. Paris: OECD.

Opfer, V. D., & Pedder, D. (2011). Conceptualising teacher professional learning. *Review of Educational Research, 81*(3), 376–407. https://doi.org/10.3102/0034654311413609.

Queensland Government. (2008). *Guide to social and emotional learning in Queensland State schools*. http://education.qld.gov.au/studentservices/protection/sel/pdfs/sel_booklet.pdf.

Children, Reggio. (2010). *Indications: Preschools and infant-toddler centres of the municipality of Reggio Emilia*. Reggio Emilia, Italy: Author.

Rinaldi, C. (2006). *In dialogue with Reggio Emilia: Listening, research and learning*. London: Routledge. https://doi.org/10.4324/9780203317730.

Rudduck, J., & McIntyre, D. (2007). *Improving learning through consulting pupils*. Abingdon, UK: Routledge.

Strong-Wilson, T., & Ellis, J. (2007). Children and place: Reggio Emilia's environment as third teacher. *Theory into Practice, 46*(1), 40–47. https://doi.org/10.1207/s15430421tip4601_6.

United Nations. Office of the High Commissioner for Human Rights. (1989). *Convention on the rights of the child*. Retrieved from http://www.ohchr.org/EN/ProfessionalInterest/Pages/CRC.aspx.

Urbis. (2011). *The psychological and emotional wellbeing needs of children and young people: Models of effective practice in educational settings*. Prepared for the Department of Education and Communities. Retrieved from https://www.researchgate.net/publication/308067185_Meeting_the_psychological_and_emotional_needs_of_children_and_young_people_Models_of_effective_practice_in_educational_settings.

Veale, A. (2005). Creative methodologies in participatory research with children. In S. Greene & D. Hogan (Eds.), *Researching children's experience: Approaches and methods* (pp. 253–272). London: Sage.

Wall, K. (2015). The built environment of primary schools: Interactions between the space, learning and pupil needs. In P. Woolner (Ed.), *School design together* (pp. 32–54). Abingdon, UK: Routledge.

Willis, J. (2016). Imagining ourselves as twenty-first century learners. In D. Bland (Ed.), *Imagination for inclusion. Diverse contexts of educational practice* (pp. 83–94). Abingdon, UK: Routledge.

Willis, J., Bland, D., Hughes, H., & Elliott Burns, R. (2013). Reimagining school libraries: Emerging teacher pedagogic practices. In *AARE 2013 International Conference of The Australian Association for Research in Education, 1–5* December 2013, Hilton Adelaide Hotel, Adelaide, South Australia. Retrieved from https://eprints.qut.edu.au/66925/.

Wilks, S. (2010). Building pedagogy. *Teacher, 201*(April), 38–40, 42-43.

Woolner, P., Clark, J., Hall, E., Tiplady, L., Thomas, U., & Wall, K. (2010). Pictures are necessary but not sufficient: Using a range of visual methods to engage users about school design. *Learning Environments Research, 13*(1), 1–22. https://doi.org/10.1007/s10984-009-9067-6.

Woolner, P., McCarter, S., Wall, K., & Higgins, S. (2012). Changed learning through changed space: When can a participatory approach to the learning environment challenge preconceptions and alter practice? *Improving Schools, 15,* 45–60. https://doi.org/10.1177/1365480211434796.

Woolner, P., Thomas, U., & Tiplady, L. (2018). Structural change from physical foundations: The role of the environment in enacting school change. *Journal of Educational Change, 19*(2), 223–242. https://doi.org/10.1007/s10833-018-9317-4.

Zuber-Skerritt, O. (2001). Action learning and action research: Paradigm, praxis and programs. In S. Sankaran, B. Dick, R. Passfield, & P. Swepson. (Eds.). (2001). *Effective change management using action research and action learning: Concepts, frameworks, processes and applications* (pp. 1–20). Lismore, New South Wales: Southern Cross University Press.

Part IV
Reconceptualisation of School Spaces for Wellbeing and Learning

Designing 'Space' for Student Wellbeing as Flourishing

Jill Franz

Abstract This chapter proposes a holistic approach to designing school spaces that envisages student *wellbeing as flourishing*. It focusses on the potential of design and the physical school environment to enhance student capability enabling students to flourish by living a life they have reason to value. The first part discusses a *capabilities approach* to wellbeing and explores the role of the senses, perception and emotions in wellbeing and the existential possibility for flourishing that they afford. Building on this conceptual foundation, the second part presents a new Salutogenic design framework for wellbeing as flourishing which offers a theoretically based holistic design approach for educators as well as designers that responds to the values, interests and needs of the students who experience school spaces.

Introduction

Current approaches to school design tend to adopt understandings of wellbeing that delimit potential for design and the physical school environment to support students in profound and enduring ways. Therefore, this chapter proposes a holistic approach to designing school spaces that envisages student *wellbeing as flourishing*, where wellbeing is understood to align with *capability* and the inspiration and freedom this provides in leading a life of value (Sen, 2009). A new salutogenic design framework for wellbeing as flourishing supports theoretical understanding and practical implementation of the proposed approach.

The chapter begins by exploring the way in which a focus on *capabilities* philosophically and theoretically connects *wellbeing, education* and *design* in the context of schools and their physical spatial and material environment. The potential of the physical school environment to make a contribution to *wellbeing as flourishing* is revealed in the second section through an exploration of the fundamental role played by the senses, perception and emotions, and the existential possibility for flourishing these offer through *affect* and atmospheric sense of place. The chapter concludes

J. Franz (✉)
Queensland University of Technology, Brisbane, Australia
e-mail: j.franz@qut.edu.au

Fig. 1 Capability integrating wellbeing, education and design

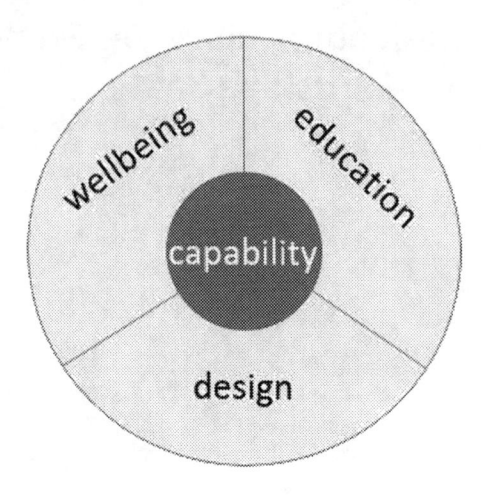

with a framework that provides a pragmatic as well as conceptual basis for designing *space* for student wellbeing as flourishing. In other words, the framework recognises as fundamental a focus on potential and possibility, and, in this respect, it emphasises the role of design and designing as capabilities that *make space for* and *help provide the freedom* for a life of value to be realised.

Capability Integrating Wellbeing, Education and Design

The lack of a coherent framework for the design of school environments for wellbeing invites further attention to wellbeing, education and the physical school environment, and how they might connect conceptually. Therefore, this chapter proposes that *wellbeing as flourishing*, as conceived by Amartya Sen (see Sen, 1985, 2009) and Martha Nussbaum (see Nussbuam, 1993, 1997, 2006, 2011), has the most potential to connect education and design through the underpinning notion of *capability* (Fig. 1).

Fundamental to *wellbeing as flourishing* is the development of capabilities and the potential to *choose* a life that a person has reason to value. Thus, freedom, agency (including moral agency) and autonomy play a central role in this approach. For many proponents of a *capability approach*, including educators such as Wilson-Strydom and Walker (2015) and Spratt (2017), a life of value demands the cultivation of democratic citizenship and a focus on human values such as diversity, equity, and empowerment. Added to this is recognition of the individuality of students and the need to understand what is meaningful for them, what motivates them, and what for them could be barriers in accessing opportunities to be educated; to exercise agency; to engage in learning; and ultimately, to paraphrase Sen, to lead a life they have reason to value. In terms of the capability approach, value is placed on developing *functionings* (Sen, 1985) to do with collaboration, critical thinking, imaginative understanding and the associated ability to empathise as well as be creative (Nussbaum, 2006). In this respect, and with the affective aspect of learning at the fore, nature and the creative arts play vital roles (Nussbaum, 2006; Macmurray, 2012; Spratt, 2017).

In operationalising these values in education there is a tendency to focus almost exclusively on pedagogy and the curriculum, ignoring the organisational and physical environment of the school. In terms of the physical environment, there is emerging research (as featured in Woolner, Thomas, & Tiplady, 2018) that provides examples of how teachers already value design and the capability this affords substantively through the physical environment in terms of its spatiality and materiality. While there is alignment between the values of a capability approach just summarised and particular qualities of the physical school environment in the everyday practice of teaching, there is no framework that brings these together in a theoretically coherent way.

With respect to research undertaken in the design area, a substantial body of work exists to do with wellbeing and how the built environment supports physical, social and emotional wellbeing. However, wellbeing is generally approached in a compartmentalised as opposed to holistic sense, and with negligible attention to the notion of existential wellbeing. Even fewer studies adopt a capability approach, with no research found that situates the capability approach phenomenologically in the context of existential possibility *and* salutogenic design, where the former recognises the embodied and aesthetic nature of wellbeing, and the latter considers the agentic nature of the physical environment. As will be highlighted later in the chapter, capability and salutogenic theory both play a crucial complementary role in informing the design of school environments that actively optimise as well as support wellbeing as flourishing.

One of the few studies in design that brings together design for wellbeing and a capability approach is that by Brey (2015). Acknowledging the original development of a capability approach to wellbeing by Sen (1980) and Nussbaum (2000), Brey describes how wellbeing is dependent on having basic capabilities that allow engagement in activities that promote wellbeing. In the context of product design, Brey provides several examples including how technological products can help protect people from injuries, in the process helping them remain healthy and stay alive (two of the basic capabilities identified by Nussbaum (2000)). Further to this, Oosterlaken (2009) proposes that 'capabilities offer an alternative for human dignity and human rights as the grounds for, or first principle of, design' (p. 91). Designed and engineered products, he reminds us, are not neutral instruments but rather highly value-laden (p. 95), which means that:

> … the *details of design are morally significant*. If technologies are value-laden and design features are relevant, we should—so it has been suggested—design these technologies in such a way that they incorporate our moral values (p. 95).

As noted by Oosterlaken (2009), and previously by Sen and Nussbaum, the capability approach draws attention to human diversity, not only in terms of what is of value to individuals, and associated issues of agency and choice, but also in terms of the personal, social and environmental factors that can influence the conversion of opportunities into capabilities and functionings (p. 98). However, while various researchers such as Brey and Oosterlaken recognise the need and potential for design to enhance wellbeing as flourishing through a capabilities approach, their work is in its infancy and, as noted, restricted to the design of objects disconnected from a setting. To this end, there appears to be no design research that: explicitly situates and seeks to operationalise the capability approach in the spatial and material sense of school settings; explores how the physical school environment can be *designed* to facilitate student development of *functionings* to enhance *capabilities* for engaging with education through schooling; or examines how engagement provides opportunities for learning and developing further *functionings* and the freedoms to achieve wellbeing as flourishing. The following discussion aims to address this situation by focussing on the qualities of *what* is designed and *how* the physical environment of the school can be conceived to facilitate student wellbeing as flourishing.

The Physical School Environment and Wellbeing as Flourishing

As will be highlighted in this section, the potential for the physical school environment to facilitate student *wellbeing as flourishing* becomes more apparent when it is reframed as *wellbeing as existential possibility*. Integral to this is embodiment and aesthetic meaning.

Embodiment and Aesthetic Meaning

A *capability approach* to *wellbeing as flourishing* points to the relevance of design through objects and environments for enhancing capabilities and access to *functionings* that enable doing or being what is considered of value. However, the literature is vague about the nature of the relationship between people, objects and environments and the qualities of each that relationally (rather than discretely) establish the conditions for people to thrive. It might be really obvious but, suffice to say, we are always in and part of an environment, not separate to it. As suggested by Stevens (2010), 'we are not isolated bodies passing through an external environment; actors playing out roles against a painted backdrop' (p. 265), but rather we are embedded in a medium physically, biologically, psychologically and socially (p. 266). Fundamentally, it is our nature as embodied beings that through our senses we are physically connected to our world and it to us. For Stevens, embodiment describes how 'our behaviours, motivations, thoughts and feelings are both generated and constrained by our physical nature…[our] physical body' (p. 266). And further to this, he argues:

> …as embodied beings, we can only understand who we are by being aware of our physical nature; as 'embedded' beings, self-understanding can only come if we are equally aware

of our physical environment" and of our mind as not separate to our body but as integrally connected through embodiment (p. 266).

This is echoed by Johnson (2008) who writes:

We are born into the world as creatures of the flesh, and it is through our bodily perceptions, movements, emotions, and feelings that meaning becomes possible and takes the forms it does (p. ix).

From a design perspective, the notion of embodiment demanding closer attention to sensing, perception and emotion describes an *aesthetic* view of meaning. For Johnson, this visceral understanding of meaning is aesthetic wherein *aesthetics* is described as: '...the study of everything that goes into the human capacity to make and experience meaning' (p. x). The significance of aesthetics to issues of the mind and cognition, he argues (p. xi), has been misconstrued and undervalued due to the misconceptions that:

- The mind is disembodied;
- Thinking transcends feeling;
- Feelings are not part of meaning and knowledge;
- Aesthetics concerns matters of mere subjective taste; and
- The arts are a luxury (rather than being conditions of full human flourishing).

In this chapter, capability (to exist, grow and flourish) is understood to be fundamentally and intrinsically connected to how we sense, perceive and feel. Our senses and perceptual systems immerse us in and allow us to engage at a pre-reflective (primordial) as well as more consciously constructed level with our world, and they do so by working together. Our body is constantly in touch with our surroundings. Thus, in the haptic system [the system which pertains to our sense of touch], 'the hands and other body members are active organs of perception' (Robinson, 2015, p. 145). Our haptic system helps us in various ways, including helping us make sense of others' experiences by activating our own sensory systems. When we perceive the tactile experience of others we can feel through embodied simulation what they feel. As Robinson asks: 'If, in fact, our sense of touch is implicated in our capacity for empathy and, by extension, in social perception, is it not imperative to design for human touch'? (pp. 147–148). However, what tends to happen is that we prioritise sight. A recourse to the dominance of the eye in architecture distances and detaches, alienates—weakens our capacity for empathy, compassion and participation in the world (Pallasmaa, 2012, pp. 24, 25). When sight is emphasised there is a tendency to place us as spectators of the world-denying our embodied and embedded relationship with the world. In contrast, when sight is considered in relation to other senses it can help to reinforce these senses (pp. 28, 29).

Johnson (2008) advocates that another major sense system supporting perception is movement—our bodily motion as well as our interaction with moving objects (p. 19). As he states: 'there is no movement without the space we move in, the things we move, and the qualities of movement... tension, linearity, amplitude, projection' (p. 20). Motion and movement of objects and bodies are also central in our phenomenological experience of time (Johnson, 2008, p. 29).

The discussion thus far highlights the fundamental role of sensing and perceiving in contributing to meaningful engagement and the significant role of the physical environment, its materiality and spatial quality. The significance of environments, and the process of designing and constructing environments, whether exterior environments or buildings and their interiors, is well recognised in phenomenology as fundamental to our very being. In using the term *architecture* in the general sense of the art/science of construction, Robinson (2015) states:

Architecture is not optional - it is not a luxury item – it is and always has been the very fabric of our survival, our potential flourishing, or our possible demise (p. 7).

According to Johnson (2015):

Architecture at its best goes beyond the mere expression of a world to creatively transform the conditions of our human habitation and interaction. This is its moral imperative – to make the world a better place in which to live (p. 48).

At the heart of experiencing meaning from what we sense and perceive are our feelings and emotions, and in terms of the physical environment the spatial and material 'affects' of atmosphere and its relationship to mood. Feelings as qualitative awareness of our sensations and any subsequent emotional responses '…lie at the heart of our capacity to experience meaning' (Johnson, 2008, p. 53); 'emotion and feelings are the means by which we are most primordially in touch with our world, are able to make sense of it, and are able to function within it' (Johnson, 2008, p. 54). When we experience feelings they are feelings of something:

…of qualities [of things, people, situations, and relationships], sensory patterns, movements, changes, and emotional contours. Meaning is not limited only to those bodily engagements, but it always starts with and leads back to them. Meaning depends on our experiencing and assessing the qualities of situations (Johnson, 2008, p. 70).

Emotions are important in helping us to maintain a balance in life; their origin and expression are in situations rather than minds or brains (Dewey cited in Johnson, 2008, p. 67).

Our biology, then, forces us to acknowledge a fundamental connection to our physical world, and correspondingly, our social world. 'In the everyday world our bodies spontaneously express our moods; others directly pick them up and respond to them. Merleau-Ponty calls this phenomenon "intercorporeality"…' (Pérez-Gómez, 2015, p. 228). While *wellbeing as flourishing* presents it as embodied and embedded, a capabilities approach extends it to *wellbeing as existential possibility* which permits, indeed demands, greater attention by designers and educators to the notion of *affect* and design of the physical environment in the atmospheric sense. 'Atmospheric characteristics of spaces, places and settings are grasped before any conscious observation of details is made' (Pallasmaa, 2012, p. 15).

Table 1 Existential possibilities and 'affect' (Adapted from Todres & Galvin, 2010; Galvin & Todres, 2011)

	Existential possibilities		
Existential domains	Existential mobility and affect	Existential dwelling and affect	Existential dwelling-mobility and affect
Spatial	Sense of adventure	Sense of being at home	Sense of abiding expanse
Temporal	Sense of flow and forward movement and orientation	Sense of being grounded in the present moment	Sense of renewal
Intersubjective	Sense of mysterious interpersonal attraction	Sense of kinship and belonging	Sense of mutual complementarity
Mood	Sense of excitement or desire	Sense of peace	Sense of mirror-like multi-dimensional fullness
Personal identity	Sense of "I can"	Sense of 'being at one with the world'	Sense of layered continuity
Embodied	Sense of vitality	Sense of comfort	Sense of grounded vibrancy

Wellbeing as Existential Possibility and 'Affect'

With regard to *existential possibility*, we owe much to the ground-breaking work of Todres and Galvin in the context of health and social care; work which I argue not only philosophically aligns with the discussion thus far but extends it, revealing the potential to inform design for student wellbeing. According to Todres and Galvin (2010), wellbeing is about access to one's existential possibilities through experiences involving the body intimately interconnected with the world. Existential possibility '…is the potential to exercise one's engagement with the world and the future in all the ways that may beckon' (Dahlberg, Todres, & Galvin, 2009, p. 267). However, as Dahlberg et al. maintain, this is a possibility of wellbeing before it is subdivided into different domains of wellbeing, such as social wellbeing. In this sense, *wellbeing* is associated with possibilities of access to *existential dwelling* or *existential mobility* or, the deepest experiential possibility, *dwelling-mobility*. These possibilities can have different domain emphases such as a spatial or temporal emphasis, that affords corresponding wellbeing experiences or *affects* (Table 1).

Adopting a capabilities approach, such experiences may well be regarded as *functionings* that inform and/or articulate capabilities of existential dwelling and mobility and ultimately *wellbeing as flourishing*. To explain this a little more, mobility, for example, describes ways (such as spatially, temporally, through mood, our body, others and personal identity) in which we can have access to the feeling of possibility. This can be experienced, for example, as a sense of adventure or a feeling of capability and freedom. The other side of the coin to mobility is dwelling. In the words of Todres and Galvin (2010):

> By dwelling, we mean a sense of "at homeness" with what has been given. There is a sense of rootedness, of settling into what is there, a 'letting be' and a certain peaceful attunement (n.p.).

In later work by Galvin and Todres (2011) an additional and deepest possibility of wellbeing is expressed as the paradoxical unity of mobility and dwelling, that is, *dwelling-mobility*. As they explain, this is wellbeing in the primary sense with situations of everyday life reflecting various mobility or dwelling emphases.

Existential Possibilities and Affect in School Life

To illustrate the applicability of the concepts presented in Table 1 related to existential possibilities and affect to schooling and school life, one could ask similar questions as do Galvin and Todres (2011) in their paper. For example, in terms of spatial mobility the question could be posed: what adventurous horizons in the physical school environment can be provided or supported concretely or metaphorically? As we know from literature and the experience of everyday teachers, the natural environment offers opportunities for risk-taking and adventure, both real and imagined. For psychologist Edith Cobb, the child's sense of nature is:

> ...basically aesthetic and infused with joy in the power to know and to be. These equal, for the child, a sense of the power to make. ...The child's sense of wonder, displayed as surprise and joy, is aroused as a response to the mystery of stimuli that promises "more to come" or, better still, "more to do" (Cobb in Kellert, 2005, p. 72)

For school students, access to nature can vary considerably, from total immersion as in a natural setting through to urban schools with restricted access to nature. Irrespective, through design there is the potential to broaden access to nature even for these schools and to more fully exploit the agency of the built environment. In addition, spatial mobility can be considered in metaphorical ways such as through imagination and the spatial trajectories afforded through literature; not to mention, technology and its ability to dissolve boundaries and virtually transport students in time and space to, what Galvin and Todres would describe as: 'places of promise' ('adventurous horizons') (2011, n.p.).

Likewise, we can ask the question in relation to spatial dwelling and explore opportunities through the design of the physical school environment where students can feel settled and at home. The significance of this is particularly apparent when students transition from primary school to secondary school, inviting questions about the new environment and how it can be made more familiar by incorporating elements associated with primary school, or providing students with a space that they can design and occupy that promotes a sense of belonging in ways that are meaningful for them and their peers. In terms of spatial mobility-dwelling, a sense of abiding expanse might be facilitated in the school context through the provision of liminal zones or transition spaces that hold in tension a sense of home as well as adventure. In this respect, libraries play a central role (see Bland, Hughes, & Willis, 2013) through the provision of informal safe, neutral spaces as well as formal spaces; for example, through makerspaces that actively engage imagination and playfulness, and quiet spaces furnished with soft seating and low lighting that promote reflection and a sense of peace.

While the spatial dimensions of mobility, dwelling and dwelling-mobility enable relatively straightforward exploration of their implications for the design of the physical school environment, Galvin and Todres (2011) also point to how the other emphases or pathways such as temporal, intersubjective, can also be accommodated through consideration of the physical environment. In addition, the same aspect of a physical environment can foster a range of wellbeing possibilities.

Although this chapter presents a somewhat limited exploration of the work of Galvin and Todres (2011), its implications for school design are clear. Drawing on this research enables me to:

- Expose the existential quality of wellbeing as flourishing;
- Highlight the affective experiential nature of wellbeing as flourishing and associated environmental qualities that facilitate embodied and meaningful engagement;
- Connect a wellbeing theory of possibility with a capability approach and underpinning notions of freedom and choice, and in terms of these aspects; and
- Provide a conceptual bridge to design for student wellbeing as flourishing.

Design for Student Wellbeing as Flourishing

To this point, the discussion has focussed on the role of capability as central to a philosophically and theoretically coherent understanding of the existential interplay of *wellbeing as flourishing*, schooling and the physical school environment. In this section, I draw upon the theory of *salutogenics* to help reveal how one might approach the design of the physical school environment in order to enhance its wellbeing capability. I also reveal the opportunity to consider design in its procedural sense both as pedagogy and as a capability in its own right.

The Wellbeing Capability of Design Through the Physical School Environment

This section explores the relevance of *salutogenics* as an umbrella framework for a capability approach to wellbeing *as flourishing* and the design of the physical school environment. Salutogenics was developed originally by the medical sociologist Aaron Antonovsky (1987; 1996) to shift attention in the medical area to factors that actively promote and support human health and wellbeing (a salutogenic approach) rather than those that cause disease (a pathogenic approach). According to Antonovsky (1996), health and wellbeing are related to a person's ability to cope with the stressors of human existence by seeing the world as *making sense*, cognitively, instrumentally and emotionally. In his words, having a *sense of coherence (SOC)* enables the person to perceive the world on a continuum, as comprehensible, manageable and meaningful (p. 15). Very broadly, comprehensibility is defined as a belief that you can understand events in your life, including challenges. Manageability is the belief that the resources needed to take action are available and that things are manageable and within your control. Meaningfulness is the belief that things in life are interesting, a source of satisfaction and a motiving driving force (Janssen, Könings, & van Mërrienboer, 2017, p. 226). For Antonovsky, then, the strength of one's *sense of coherence* in terms of the attributes just described is 'a significant factor in facilitating the movement to health' (p. 15). Similarly, in this chapter, I propose facilitating the movement to students' *wellbeing as flourishing*, by promoting understanding about what can be done in a school community to strengthen its sense of comprehensibility, manageability and meaningfulness for students (and teachers).

Early work in the area of salutogenics focussed on everyday settings concerned with healthcare facilities and the therapeutic capability of the physical environment to facilitate the healing process. In more recent times, this has expanded to a range of settings including: neighbourhood environments; work environments; correctional centres; schools; and universities. (For a comprehensive overview see Mittelmark, Sagy, Eriksson, Bauer, Pelikan, Lindstrm, & Espnes, 2017). In terms of schools, Janssen et al. (2017) provide an extensive review of the application of salutogenesis. Through the review they found that the salutogenic concepts informing a sense of coherence are rarely used in relation to schooling and school settings, the exception being in Scandinavian countries. In contrast, there is substantially more research in education focussing on associated concepts such as resilience, self-efficacy, empowerment and wellbeing. In this respect, there is a tendency to see *wellbeing* as separate to other concepts such as self-efficacy and even health. In contrast, I propose that *wellbeing*, particularly *wellbeing as flourishing*, is an umbrella concept gathering beneath it concepts such as health. As Todres and Galvin (2010) explain, wellbeing is 'a positive possibility that is independent of health and illness, but is a resource for both. In other words, wellbeing can be found within illness and wellbeing is more than health' (p. 5).

In schools currently, the more comprehensive approaches to health and wellbeing involve: a formal health curriculum; a values approach informing school ethos and promotion through the physical and social environment of the school; and engagement with the community and families, recognising these have significant influence on students (Jensen et al., 2017). In brief, Jensen et al. argue that the need remains for further integration of what they refer to as health promotion with education as the core task of the school, hinting that a salutogenic framework may facilitate such integration. While whole heartedly endorsing this view, I contend that this is only possible if wellbeing—not health—is the meta-concept, which through a capabilities approach to *wellbeing as flourishing*, enables a seamless integration of wellbeing and learning in a physical and social school environment conceived holistically according to salutogenic principles.

From a salutogenic perspective, the spatial and material structures and qualities of the physical environment can be considered as resources (what Antonovsky would term, *resistance resources*). In the school context, these resources can be employed so as to make the physical school environment comprehensible, meaningful and manageable. While there is emerging research and practice that explores the potential for the physical environment to be salutogenic, no examples could be found that explicitly relate to the physical school environment, and very few that deal with environments outside healthcare facilities. Of the research dealing with healthcare facilities, the most cited include Dilani (2006, 2008) and Golembiewski (2010, 2014, 2016, 2017). In terms of other environments, there is research to do with work environments that look promising, including that of Ruohomäki, Lahtinen, and Reijula (2015). An interesting aspect of this work is its recognition of the substantial research already undertaken in environmental psychology in relation to wellbeing and its attempt to situate this within a salutogenic framework. A disappointing aspect of the work, however, is that, rather than using the dimensions of salutogenics to organise their findings, the authors use the usual physical, physiological, social and psychological dimensions of wellbeing. This approach tends to reinforce a compartmentalised view and prioritise dimensions that are traditionally considered in relation to risk and prevention, and as in most research, it disregards the existential dimension. Addressing these limitations, I present a salutogenic framework in the following section for designing physical school environments to promote student *wellbeing as flourishing*.

Salutogenic Design Framework for Wellbeing as Flourishing

The proposed salutogenic design framework for wellbeing as flourishing (Fig. 2) attempts to expand the salutogenic approach by gathering together the ideas raised previously in this chapter as three dynamically interconnected zones.

In contrast to the general compartmentalised understanding of wellbeing that pervades current educational discourse, the new salutogencic framework supports a holistic capability approach to *wellbeing as flourishing*. It offers an opportunity to explore wellbeing as an existential phenomenon, the implications of which reveal more vividly the significant role of the physical school environment in educating students for life. The embedded, embodied, and as such, experiential nature of wellbeing as existential possibility is made more apparent through the work of Todres and Galvin (2010) and Galvin and Todres (2011) with its 'affective' emphases revealing further how we might design environments but in more holistic, authentic and atmospheric ways. Thus if we are interested in exploring how the physical environment of the school could be more meaningful for students we might, for example, look more closely at the mood of the environment (a particular space or the school as a whole) and how it can evoke feelings of excitement or peace or both. Recognising

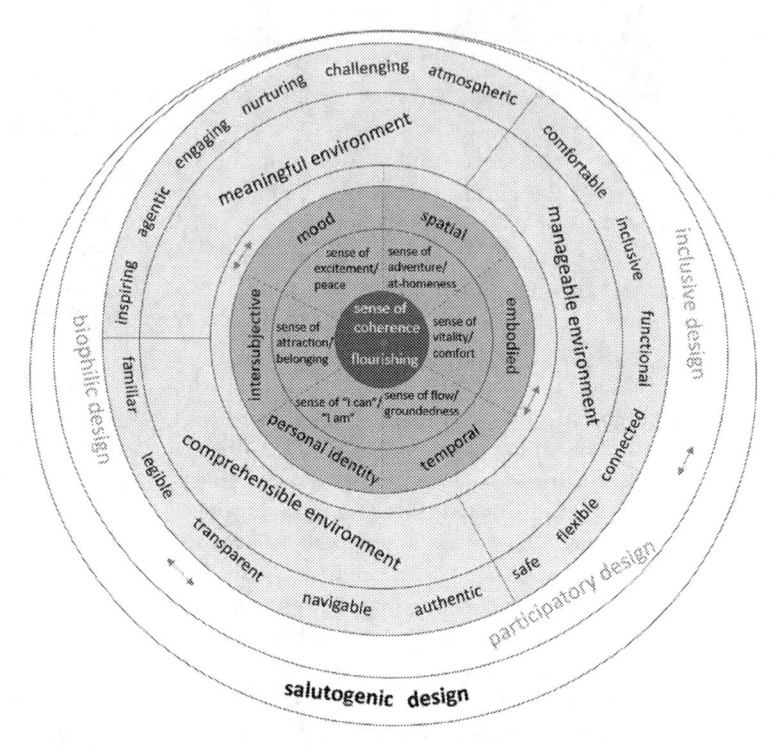

Fig. 2 Salutogenic design framework for wellbeing as flourishing (Informed in part by Antonovsky (1996) and his salutogenic approach to health promotion, and Galvin and Todres (2011) and their theory of existential wellbeing)

how everything is interrelated, we might also consider how a sense of excitement could be reinforced through a sense of adventure, and in addition vitality through active bodily engagement with the physical environment either individually or with others.

The opportunity to do this is further enhanced through a salutogenic approach that invites us to adopt a more proactive and aspirational approach to wellbeing facilitated through a sense of coherence and being able to see and experience the world as meaningful, comprehensible and manageable. To support implementation of this approach, the main elements of the proposed salutogenic design framework for wellbeing as flourishing, as shown in Fig. 2, are explained in turn below.

Meaningful school environments direct the attention of the student to important and sustaining phenomena in life; to motivate the student's desire for a sense of coherence and the capability for existential possibility. Environments that facilitate this are inspiring, agentic, engaging, restorative, challenging, and atmospheric. In many respects, these environments exceed expectations and invite embodied engagement through their appeal to the senses and desire for aesthetic richness. Particularly effective in this regard are natural environments and built environments that engage the senses through material qualities of colour, texture and pattern, and atmospheric qualities of light, temperature and sound.

The potential of nature to meaningfully engage students invites further exploration of *biophilic design*, located in an outer zone of the framework, which accommodates design approaches that can help enrich the value of salutogenic design for student wellbeing as flourishing. Biophilia acknowledges an inherent tendency in human beings to connect with nature; a connection that is emotionally meaningful (Kellert & Calabrese, 2015; Kellert & Wilson, 1993; Kellert, 1997; 2012). Supported by empirical research, Kellert and Calabrese claim that the application of biophilic principles can have several outcomes. With specific relevance to the capabilities approach underpinning this chapter, examples from their work include:

- Expanded sense of relationship and social and environmental responsibility;
- Better coping and mastery skills;
- Increased problem solving and creativity;
- Increased motivation;
- Enhanced attention and concentration;
- Increased comfort and satisfaction; and
- Improved social interaction.

Contact with nature for students does not have to be direct, although this is the most ideal as it offers greater potential for multi-sensory experience. Design can also facilitate indirect experience of nature through natural analogues such as images of nature, natural materials and colours, natural geometries and forms. In addition, certain psychological and physical responses normally associated with immersion in nature can be achieved through different spatial configurations, including those that offer prospect and refuge, and organised complexity (Kellert & Calabrese, 2015, p. 10). Mazuch (2017) citing Salingaros (2015) summarises the key design elements in biophilic design as: '…light, spatial permeability, sensory engagement, liminal spaces, organic shapes and forms, natural processes and patterns such as fractal geometry' (p. 44).

Comprehensible school environments are legible and transparent in helping students make sense of what is occurring or could occur in the environment. These environments orientate and reassure through the use of familiar elements and features that connect to the everyday (for example, the use of domestic seating) and that is easily navigated through environmental features and spatial organisation that provide perceptual cues and control spatial capacity and density (thereby avoiding crowding that can obscure clarity). Comprehensible environments are authentic; they are genuine and honest conveyed through the use of natural materials and construction devoid of superfluous decoration and detailing.

Manageable school environments, as the name suggests, are those that support the student through being well resourced, enhancing their ability to cope, develop further capabilities, and undertake the required/desired activities. While such resources include obvious things such as technology and equipment, the term also refers to environments that allow students to exercise control and support activities by being comfortable, safe, and accessible. In particular, they are responsive to a diverse group of students some of whom may have impairments or conditions such as autism that demand attention to what appear to be conflicting needs, and consider how they can be addressed through design that makes the experience of the environment richer for all. Research in inclusive and universal design provides further support in this regard (see for example, Myerson & Lee, 2010; Imrie, 2012). Also crucial is flexibility and the potential of the environment to respond to change. In this regard, participatory processes play a crucial role, particularly participatory design that involves students in undesigning and redesigning the spaces in ways that respond to their needs and aspirations individually and collectively (Könings, Bovill, & Woolner, 2017).

In addition to what is designed, design as process also has much to offer as a capabilities approach in education for *wellbeing as flourishing*. The benefits of involving students in decisions about their environment that affect them and are meaningful for them are also noted in research on participatory design (Woolner & Clark, 2015; Elliott Burns, 2016). In the main, design provides opportunities for active engagement with diverse people in a process of creative endeavour, and associated opportunities to reveal underlying values, develop communication skills, sense of belonging, and empathy. Ultimately it increases the potential for the physical environment to have greater personal and collective meaning. Further to this, it invites speculation about design's ultimate purpose and potential and its implications pedagogically.

Pedagogy of Design for Wellbeing as Flourishing

While it is most commonly regarded as a process undertaken by design professionals, in reality everyone can and does design. Indeed, as stated by Nelson and Stolterman (2012), '…it is our very ability to design that determines our humanness' (p. 11). However, without also considering desires and aspirations as well as needs, design will remain reactive, focussing on *what is*, without consideration of the ethical and moral imperatives of *what ought* or *could be*; an aesthetics without ethics: 'As humans, we use our desires as a way to understand how we can fulfil our lives and how we can become more human' (Nelson & Stolterman, 2012, p. 111). Specifically, a focus on desire helps initiate a certain kind of design action, capacity or agency linking this human capacity to human achievement in a highly productive way, central to which is imagination. Desire creates energy, and hope, fuelling the generative capacity of humans individually and collectively (Nelson & Stolterman, 2012, p. 117). Not only does a focus on desire help develop 'awareness of future possibility' (Pignatelli, 1998, p. 347) but it also provides the capability to act on this awareness.

Conceptualising design in terms of desire is highly sympathetic with a capabilities approach to *wellbeing as flourishing* based on the notion of potential and possibility for leading a life of value that also extends beyond the individual. Second to this is the point that the wellbeing capability of design is accessible to everyone through the physical environment as well as through it as a basic human activity. Such views have been proposed before in work by Stables (2013) and previous work of my own

(Franz, 2013). We both describe the wellbeing value of developing design capability for individuals and society. Moreover, we both regard it as more than a literacy which is how it traditionally exists in school curricula under an assortment of names including home economics or more currently, design thinking. In both works we develop fundamental arguments that design capability expands the potential for *wellbeing as flourishing*. So beyond how designing is currently considered in schooling, I reiterate the question posed in my previous work (Franz, Lindquist, & Bitner, 2011): *how can designing extend a student's capacity for purposeful and transformational change, and in this respect, what is the role of the teacher?*

For insights that respond to this question, one only has to turn to the work of John Dewey who declared:

> Need and desire – out of which grow purpose and direction of energy – go beyond what exists, and hence beyond knowledge, beyond science. They continually open the way into the unexplored and unattained future" (Dewey cited in Pignatelli, 1998, p. 337).

Desire in particular 'seeds hope' which is 'at the centre of the art and craft of teaching…Creating hope in oneself as a teacher and nourishing or rekindling it in one's students is the central issue educators face today' (Kohl cited in Pignatelli, 1998, p. 337). In response, I argue that desire is central to a capabilities approach to *wellbeing as flourishing* that is mobilised and made coherent through a pedagogy of design, and at the very least recognises the physical school environment and the existential capability it affords.

Practical Implications of the Salutogenic Framework for Wellbeing as Flourishing

Before concluding, it is important to draw attention to the following:

- The framework is just that—a framework. It is not intended to be prescriptive. Indeed its conceptualisation as a resource for informing the development of student *potential* means that it can only ever be regarded in terms of its *generative capacity*.
- The framework is also incomplete. It relies, certainly initially, on developing a co-creational relationship with students.
- At a very pragmatic level, it reminds us to be more attentive to atmosphere and mood and what it is in an environment that first affects us and contributes to our sensory, perceptual and emotional impression. Herein is a thinly veiled reminder to architects, designers and facility managers to not allow their intellectualised viewpoints mask what is meaningful at the level of everyday lived experience. It is also acknowledgement of what many teachers already know implicitly.

Conclusion

This chapter commenced by adopting a *capability approach to wellbeing as flourishing* to conceptually connect wellbeing, education and design. In terms of design this was initially conceptualised in terms of the physical school environment. The potential of the physical school environment to facilitate *wellbeing as flourishing* was revealed by considering *flourishing* in phenomenological terms as existential possibility and the fundamental role played by the senses, perception and emotions. To guide design in a holistic and coherent manner, the chapter concluded with a salutogenic inspired framework which embraces potential and possibility, and, in this respect, the role of design and designing as capabilities that *make space for* and *help provide the freedom* for a life of value to be realised.

References

Antonovsky, A. (1987). *Unravelling the mystery of health*. San Francisco, CA: Jossey-Bass.

Antonovsky, A. (1996). The salutogenic model as a theory to guide health promotion. *Health Promotion International., 11*(1), 11–18.

Bland, D., Hughes, H., & Willis, J. (2013). *Reimagining learning spaces. Final report to the Queensland Centre for Social Science Innovation.* https://eprints.qut.edu.au/63000/.

Brey, P. (2015). Design for the value of human-being. In J. van den Hoven, P. Vermaas, & I. van de Poel (Eds.), *Handbook of ethics, values, and technological design: Sources, theory, values and application domains* (pp. 365–382). Dordrecht: Springer.

Dahlberg, K., Todres, L., & Galvin, K. (2009). Lifeworld-led healthcare is more than patient-led care: An existential view of well-being. *Medical Health Care and Philosophy, 12,* 265–271. https://doi.org/10.1007/s11019-008-9174-7.

Dilani, A. (2006). A new paradigm of design and health in hospital planning. *World Hospitals and Health Services, 41*(4), 17–21.

Dilani, A. (2008). Psychosocially supportive design: A salutogenic approach to the design of the physical environment. *Design and Health Scientific Review, 1*(2), 47–55.

Elliott Burns, R. A. (2016). Voices of experience: Opportunities to influence creatively the designing of school libraries. In K. Fisher (Ed.), *The translational design of schools: An evidence-based approach to aligning pedagogy and learning environments in schools* (pp. 195–213). Amsterdam: Sense Publishing.

Franz, J., Lindquist, M., & Bitner, G. (2011). Educating for change: A case for a pedagogy of desire in design education. *Proceedings of the DesignEd Asia Conference 2011*, Hong Kong Polytechnic University, Hong Kong Convention & Exhibition Centre, Hong Kong, 1–6. https://eprints.qut.edu.au/49909/.

Franz, J. (2013). [Design] learning: A productive force for engaging the radical self. Keynote Presentation for the DRS. In *Cumulus 2013. 2nd International Conference for Design Education Researchers. Oslo, 14–17 May, 2013.* (Unpublished).

Galvin, K., & Todres, L. (2011). Kinds of well-being: A conceptual framework that provides direction for caring. *International Journal of Qualitative Studies on Health and Well-being, 6*(4), n.p. https://doi.org/10.3402/qhw.v6i4.10362.

Golembiewski, J. (2010). Start making sense: Applying a salutogenic model to architectural design for psychiatric care. *Facilities, 28*(3/4), 100–117.

Golembiewski, J. (2014). Mental health facility design: The case for person-centred care. *Australian and New Zealand Journal of Psychiatry, 49*(3), 203–206.

Golembiewski, J. (2016). The designed environment and how it affects brain morphology and mental health. *Health Environments Research & Design Journal, 9*(2), 161–171.

Imrie, R. (2012). Universalism, universal design and equitable access to the built environment. *Disability and Rehabilitation, 34*(10), 873–882. https://doi.org/10.3109/09638288.2011.624250.

Janssen, F., Könings, K., & van Mërrienboer, J. (2017). Participatory educational design: How to improve mutual learning and the quality and usability of the design? *European Journal of Education, 52,* 268–279.

Johnson, M. (2008). *The meaning of the body.* Chicago, IL: University of Chicago Press.

Johnson, M. (2015). The embodied meaning of architecture. In S. Robinson & J. Pallasmaa (Eds.), *Mind in architecture* (pp. 33–50). Cambridge, MA: MIT Press.

Kellert, S., & Wilson, E. O. (Eds.). (1993). *The biophilia hypothesis.* Washington, DC: Island Press.

Kellert, S. (1997). *The value of life: Biological diversity and human society.* Washington, DC: Island Press.

Kellert, S. (2005). *Building for life: Understanding and designing the human-nature connection.* Washington, DC: Island Press.

Kellert, S. (2012). *Birthright: People and nature in the modern world.* New Haven: Yale University Press.

Kellert, S., & Calabrese, E. (2015). *The practice of biophilic design.* www.biophilic-design.com.

Könings, K. D., Bovill, C., & Woolner, P. (2017). Towards an interdisciplinary model of practice for participatory building design in education. *European Journal of Education, 52,* 306–317. https://doi.org/10.1111/ejed.12230.

Macmurray, J. (2012). Learning to be human. *Oxford Review of Education, 38*(6), 661–674. https://doi.org/10.1080/03054985.2012.745958.

Mazuch, R. (2017). Salutogenic and biophilic design as therapeutic approaches to sustainable architecture. *Architectural Design, 87*(2), 42–47. https://doi.org/10.1002/ad.2151.

Mittelmark, M., Sagy, S., Eriksson, M., Bauer, G., Pelikan, J. M., Lindström, B., et al. (Eds.). (2017). *The handbook of salutogenesis.* Cham: Springer. https://doi.org/10.1007/978-3-319-04600-6.

Myerson, J., & Lee, Y. K. (2010). Inclusive design research initiatives at the Royal College of Art. In W. Preiser & K. H. Smith (Eds.), *Universal design handbook* (2nd ed.). New York: McGraw-Hill Professional.

Nelson, H., & Stolterman, E. (2012). *The design way* (2nd ed.). Cambridge, MA: MIT Press.

Nussbuam, M. (1993). Non-relative virtues: An Aristotelian approach. In M. Nussbaum & A. Sen (Eds.), *The quality of life* (pp. 242–269). Oxford: Oxford University Press.

Nussbaum, M. (1997). *Cultivating humanity: A classical defence of reform in liberal education.* Cambridge, MA: Harvard University Press.

Nussbaum, M. (2000). *Women and human development: The Capability Approach.* Cambridge: Cambridge University Press.

Nussbaum, M. (2006). Education and democratic citizenship: Capabilities and quality education. *Journal of Human Development, 7*(3), 385–395. https://doi.org/10.1080/14649880600815974.

Nussbaum, M. (2011). *Creating capabilities. The human development approach.* Cambridge, MA: Harvard University Press.

Oosterlaken, I. (2009). Design for development: A capability approach. *Design Issues, 25*(4), 91–102.

Pallasmaa, J. (2012). *The eyes of the skin: Architecture and the senses* (3rd ed.). Chichester: John Wiley.

Pérez-Gómez, A. (2015). Mood and meaning in architecture. In S. Robinson & J. Pallasmaa (Eds.), *Mind in architecture* (pp. 219–235). Cambridge, MA: MIT Press.

Pignatelli, F. (1998). Education and the subject of desire. *Review of Education/Pedagogy/Cultural Studies, 20,* 337–352.

Ruohomäki, V., Lahtinen, M., & Reijula, K. (2015). Salutogenic and user-centred approach for workplace design. *Intelligent Buildings International, 7*(4), 184–197. https://doi.org/10.1080/17508975.2015.1007911.

Robinson, S. (2015). Nested bodies. In S. Robinson & J. Pallasmaa (Eds.), *Mind in architecture* (pp. 137–159). Cambridge, MA: MIT Press.

Salingaros, N. (2015). *Biophillia & healing: Healthy principles for designing the built world*. New York: Terrapin Bright Green.

Sen, A. (1980). Equity of what? In S. M. McMurrin (Ed.), *The Tanner lectures on human value* (pp. 195–220). Salt Lake City: University of Utah Press.

Sen, A. (1985). Well-being, agency and freedom: The Dewey Lectures 1984. *The Journal of Philosophy, 82*, 169–221.

Sen, A. (2009). *The idea of justice*. Cambridge, MA: Harvard University Press.

Spratt, J. (2017). Wellbeing, equity and education: A critical analysis of policy discourses of wellbeing in schools. Cham: Springer.

Stables, K., (2013). Designerly well-being: Implications for pedagogy that develops design capability. *Paper presented at DRS//CUMULUS 2013. 2nd. International Conference for Design Education Researchers*. Oslo, 14–17 May 2013. http://research.gold.ac.uk/9786/.

Stevens, P. (2010). Embedment in the environment: A new paradigm for well-being? *Perspectives in Public Health, 130*(6), 265–269.

Todres, L., & Galvin, K. (2010). "Dwelling-mobility": An existential theory of well-being. *International Journal of Qualitative Studies on Health and Well-being, 5*(3), 5444 http://www.tandfonline.com/doi/pdf/10.3402/qhw.v5i3.5444.

Wilson-Strydom, M., & Walker, M. (2015). A capabilities-friendly conceptualisation of flourishing in and through education. *Journal of Moral Education*, 44(3), 310–324 https://doi.org/10.1080/03057240.2015.1043878.

Woolner, P., & Clark, A. (2015). Developing shared understandings of learning environments: Interactions with students, teachers and other professionals. In P. Woolner (Ed.), *School design together* (pp. 167–183). Abingdon: Routledge.

Woolner, P., Thomas, U., & Tiplady, L. (2018). Structural change from physical foundations: The role of the environment in enacting school change. *Journal of Educational Change*. https://doi.org/10.1007/s10833-018-9317-4.

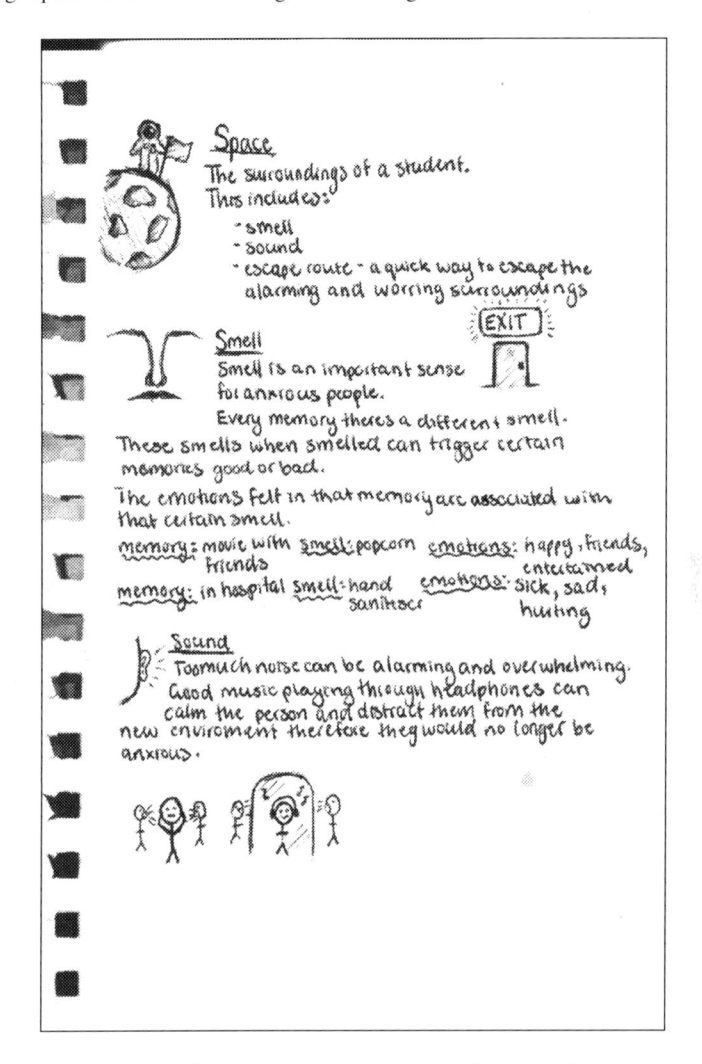

The smells and noises of school spaces (Neve Willis)

Neve is a 16 year old student from Brisbane. She was patiently waiting for a ride home when the research team were discussing the very first ideas for this book. While the adults spoke about the importance of space for student wellbeing, and making sure the book represented student perspectives as well as teacher perspectives, she quietly did this drawing. She wanted the research team to know that spaces in schools are landscapes made up of smells, noises, emotions and memories. Her artwork reminds us that school spaces can be a source of anxiety for some students, and that students are more than inhabitants of a space. As agents who have creative ideas about spaces of wellbeing within schools, their voices are essential to the designing process.

Index